ALTRUISTIC ARMADILLOS, ZENLIKE ZEBRAS

ALTRUISTIC ARMADILLOS, ZENLIKE ZEBRAS

A Menagerie of 100 Favorite Animals

JEFFREY MOUSSAIEFF MASSON

BALLANTINE BOOKS *New York*

Published in the United States by Ballantine Books, an imprint
of The Random House Publishing Group, a division of
Random House, Inc., New York.

BALLANTINE and colophon are registered trademarks of Random House, Inc.

LIBRARY OF CONGRESS CATALOGING-IN-PUBLICATION DATA

Masson, J. Moussaieff (Jeffrey Mousssaieff).
Altruistic armadillos, zenlike zebras: a menagerie of 100 favorite animals.
p. cm
Includes biographical references
ISBN 0-345-47881-9
1. Animals.   I. Title.

QL45.2.M374 2006
590—DC22   200647531

Printed in the United States of America on acid-free paper

www.ballantine books.com

2 4 6 8 9 7 5 3 1

First Edition

Book design by Simon M. Sullivan

Dedicated to my four favorite animals:
LEILA, ILAN, MANU, AND SIMONE

PREFACE

My idea was that if I were to sit down with you for an evening, and we began to talk about animals, and you were to say to me, "What is your favorite animal?" I could honestly answer, "Well, I have at least a hundred favorite animals but we have all night, let's talk about them." I meant this book to be a conversation, or at least the beginning of one. Only one hundred? At a conservative estimate, there are between five and ten million different kinds of animals on our planet, most of them unclassified. If I had written two pages for each animal *already* classified, you would hold in your hands a book of four million pages.

If somebody were now to ask me what my single favorite animal is, I would find the question impossible to answer. As I began to research each creature here, I found myself increasingly absorbed in the life of *that* particular animal. I was especially happy when I discovered a remarkable monograph that I did not know about before. Reading a good book by somebody in love with the animal he or she is writing about has been one of the great pleasures of my life. Books on ducks, on whales, on butterflies and beetles, and on many other animals have kept me up into the night, pondering the treasures in them.

In working on this book I discovered that there is no single animal, whether a beetle, or a hummingbird, or a lion, for which there is not a good case to be made for spending a lifetime doing the research. Indeed, many have. I am afraid that try as I might, I can find no better word than *love* to describe the feelings that came over me as I read in greater and greater depth about any given animal. Especially when I was learning from someone else who felt love for this animal, it was almost impossible not to feel this love transferred.

I have come away from writing this book with a new determination to forcefully reject the idea of privileged species, species that somebody considers more intelligent, more beautiful, or more useful than some other. All animals are as intelligent as they need to be to survive in the ecological niche they occupy; all animals are beautiful, certainly to the opposite sex; and no animals, including the human animal, should have to justify their existence in terms of how useful others find them. A kind of sublime humility overcame me as I was doing my research. Paul Johnsgard, writing about migration in ducks, geese, and swans, put it as well as anyone: "Waterfowl were doubtlessly traversing the boundaries of North America and Eurasia, and probably transmitting the details of their migrations from one generation to the next, at a time when our knowledge of the world's geography was limited to the view provided from a nearby tree or hilltop, and our communication consisted of babbling gibberish."

"What?" somebody said to me the other day. "You dare to present yourself as an expert on lobsters, when I have spent my whole life studying them and still would not pretend to understand even a fraction of their behavior?" No, no, I protest, not an expert at all, far from it; merely an amateur in every sense of the word. Somebody fascinated by them, who reads what I can find on them, ponders them, talks to people who know far more than I about them, and then writes up what I feel. But experts, I have observed, are reluctant in the extreme to say anything about the animals that cannot be backed up by facts. I know that I make a habit of going out on a limb, but often the best view is from precisely there.

As the reader will quickly notice, I have not shied away from speculation, personal remarks, personal enthusiasms, and pet peeves. And while I have attempted to showcase the best, most interesting material about each animal from various recent sources, I would have felt foolish simply repeating this information with nothing to indicate how each animal is special—from the hummingbird, that amazing jewel, to the gentle giraffe, to the long-finned eel, a heroic creature that reminds us of our own tenacity to live. I wanted to say at least *something* about each animal that you will not find in the standard encyclopedias, even the good ones. Their authors, too, I am sure, have their personal opinions, but they feel, perhaps correctly, that it is their job to impart information to the reader, not feelings. In line with my own personal publishing history, which has been primarily about the feelings of animals, I felt it only fitting that I should acquaint the reader with *my* feelings about animals for a change.

Almost everybody I spoke to about writing this book urged me to give particular attention to endangered animals, such as the golden lion tamarin in the coastal rain forests of Brazil, of whom there are only 150 left. Or the babirusa of Sulawesi, an odd-looking pig whose population in the wild is down to a few thousand. This is absolutely heartbreaking: There are at least five thousand endangered animal species. It was a tempting proposal, but I was not sure how I could go about it. Would I have chosen the hundred most threatened, or only those whose loss seemed inconceivable? Today only six thousand blue whales remain in the world. It is conceivable that my grandchildren will know about them only from books. When I try to imagine a world without blue whales in it, I become unutterably sad. What cheers me up is the recognition that people like you, who read books like this, care deeply—as much as or more than I do—and our numbers are increasing. We *can* take equality seriously, and apply it to an increasing number of lives every bit as important, as fascinating, and as precious as our own. My one wish is that this book does just a little bit to push us ever so slightly closer to that goal.

CONTENTS

Contents

ALTRUISTIC ARMADILLOS, ZENLIKE ZEBRAS

ARMADILLOS

Family Dasypodidae

RMADILLO IS A SPANISH WORD referring to the armorlike shell protecting this remarkable animal. This defense system led early zoologists to classify them with turtles—and allowed this animal to survive for fifty-five million years. I recently saw a photo of an armadillo on the Web that totally captured me: It was rising vertically in the air. The caption explained that when armadillos are surprised, they often jump straight up! Travelers in America's Gulf States often see them by day scattered along the roadside after they've been killed during the night by cars and trucks. But being hit by the wheel isn't what kills them. Rather, it is their unusual jump reflex: When a car roars over them, they bound off the road almost vertically, hitting a car's underside. I am not sure how this startle response evolved: Did it unnerve their predators? And then of course there are species of armadillos constructed so that they can curl up in a ball, completely safe from any predation.

Armadillos are distant cousins of anteaters and sloths, who originally come from South America. There are at least twenty species, ranging from the fairy armadillo, only five inches long and weighing in at three ounces, to the giant armadillo, who is almost four feet long and weighs 130 pounds. The best known is the nine-banded armadillo—*Dasypus novemcinctus* (so called because of the nine movable bands on the armor-like skin). Perhaps the term *best known* glosses over the fact that almost nothing is known about the other living armadillos, even less about the extinct ones. The nine-banded armadillo existed in the United States several million years ago and then vanished five to ten thousand years ago for unknown reasons, only to reemerge in Texas in 1854. (Today they are found from Argentina to Colorado.)

We tend to associate the nine-banded armadillo with the Lone Star State, primarily because Texans have taken to armadillos. Just this one species of armadillo lives in Texas. And a good reason they are welcome is that, like their cousins, they are inordinately fond of ants, especially fire ants, the scourge of the state. For some reason, armadillo races are popular with humans in Texas, though there is no evidence that armadillos share the enthusiasm.

Scientists are fond of armadillos for a number of reasons. One is that a reproducing female armadillo can delay implantation for several months, and gestation can last up to twenty months—as long as an elephant. The *Oxford Encyclopedia of Mammals*, page 799, reports a case where a female gave birth three years after the last date at which she could possibly have been inseminated! That's not all: After this long gestation, she gives birth to identical quadruplets, all coming from a single egg. The embryo divides in two, and those two embryos divide into two more. These are the only mammals who routinely give birth to genetically identical quadruplets. Derived from a single fertilized ovum, all the babies are of the same sex and all contain identical sets of genes, a treasure trove for geneticists.

Also of scientific interest is that the nine-banded armadillo is one of the few animals susceptible to infection with the leprosy bacillus. Although the bacillus was isolated more than a century ago, no scientist has yet succeeded in growing it from a culture (all of it derives from human patients). The World Health Organization (WHO) has reported an estimated ten to twelve million cases of leprosy worldwide. The search for a vaccine has become more urgent because the drugs used to treat leprosy are showing signs of losing their effectiveness as the disease becomes more immune to them.

For many years, WHO kept a colony of armadillos as a source. The idea was to create another antileprosy vaccine, but I do not believe that a more successful one has been created so far, though many are in trial. However, the placid, agreeable armadillo is nonetheless reluctant to breed in captivity. Keeping a colony thriving is difficult if not impossible without bringing in animals caught in the wild.

The scientist who discovered that leprosy occurs naturally in wild armadillos, Dr. Eleanor E. Storrs, said that her discovery signaled the end of the stigma associated with the disease: "Before then, many believed that leprosy was a unique punishment inflicted by God on humans for their sins. Now it must be looked upon as a bacterial infection devoid of religious significance."

There are so many reasons to be interested in these fascinating animals. They are nocturnal, sleeping during the day in burrows they excavate. They dig these holes—sometimes as long as twenty-five feet—at an astonishing speed, hardly stopping to breathe. Indeed, armadillos can go without breathing for up to fifteen minutes by storing air in the trachea. And a single armadillo can have up to twenty burrows in a home range of ten acres. These burrows have several openings, for emergency exits.

Such emergencies are rare, however, and here is what I like most about these animals: Generous by nature, they seem to willingly share their burrows with a whole collection of other creatures. Perhaps if you are one of four identical quadruplet armadillos, you learn to share, at least with your clone. If you look at a photo of a perfectly formed newborn armadillo (page 798 of the *Oxford Encyclopedia*), you would want to help, too. Looking in an armadillo burrow, you might find opossums, striped skunks, cotton rats, and burrowing owls. One man found a four-foot-long rattlesnake and a half-grown cottontail in side chambers "in the den of this armadillo."

Hunters are known to have died hunting armadillos: They pulled on what they thought was the armadillo's tail sticking out of a burrow, only to be mortally bitten by a rattlesnake. Why would anyone hunt this gentle animal? Roy Bedichek, who loved them, noted that "the curious little beast was slaughtered mercilessly" because it had a reputation for destroying the nests of ground-dwelling birds. Research showed this was completely false.

Unfortunately, tourists in Texas have bought a huge number of baskets made from armadillo shells. As late as 1982, one dealer advertised that he wanted twenty thousand dead animals. Instead of hunting them for sport, or forcing them into silly races, or consuming them (as they still do happily in Latin America), wouldn't an alternative moneymaking scheme be preferable: Allowing curious tourists to simply observe this delightful creature in the wild?

AUSTRALIAN MAGPIE

Gymnorhina tibicen

P ROFESSOR GISELA KAPLAN from Australia's Centre for Neuro-science and Animal Behaviour at the University of New England, Armidale, New South Wales, describes the Australian magpie using adjectives such as *gentle* and *tender*. What a pleasure to hear a scientist speak this way! And having spent more than ten thousand hours observing these wonderful birds, she should know. Professor Kaplan tells of one hand-raised juvenile looking at her with an expression of "great tenderness" and an almost audible purr!

Although the birds are not native to New Zealand (where I live), next door to us is a magpie. These birds were introduced here (and in Fiji) in the nineteenth century. In Fiji, for unknown reasons, they have just about died out. In New Zealand, they are thriving. But here is a mystery: Here they only live to about six, whereas in Australia they live twenty to thirty years. Why this is, nobody knows.

The magpie who lives next door was found as a baby, probably having fallen out of a tree, by our neighbor, Joan Chapple, a plastic surgeon with a great love of birds. She hand-raised "Fuzzbucket," who became a sociable little bird. He especially liked to wander over to our house and play with our dog. We often looked out the window and enjoyed seeing them chasing each other on the lawn down to the beach and back. Gradually, however, Joan realized that Fuzzbucket's fearless friendliness could well be his undoing. He might walk up to a strange dog and be met with something other than kindness. So she has reluc-tantly put him into a large aviary. I get to hear him every morning around five. As soon as it is light, Fuzzbucket breaks forth in loud, melodious song.

We all know that some wild birds, perhaps even most, if hand-raised as babies, will bond with humans and can make delightful companions for us, but I am not certain they are equally delighted. This is true of parrots, ravens, crows, magpies, and many other species of birds who live in socially complex groups. Though I have always thought this wonderful, I have lately become less certain. I long ago decided that buying birds and keeping them in a cage was not something I wanted to do. But when we have no choice, as when the bird would otherwise per-ish, this is a different story. Still, can birds ever have the same quality of life in captivity that they would have in the wild? The answer must be no. If the bird can be eventually released, that is the ideal. Sadly, it appears that many birds (Fuzzbucket among them) are simply no longer equipped to survive on their own; they expect handouts, they can no longer distinguish friend from foe, and they are far too optimistic about life in general. Alas, they must remain as diminished prisoners in an alien world. This doesn't mean they can't be happy, but it will never be the exquisite happiness they'd experience under natural conditions.

Most people in Australia know and love the sounds and mimicry of the magpie. We have made the correct anthropomorphic assumption that such a rich variety of sounds is used to convey meaning. Long gone are the days when we thought of nonhuman sounds as mere twaddle. We sometimes forget, though, how much is communicated by gestures, though most are well aware of this when it comes to dogs. Who is not familiar with the play-bow, where one dog solicits play with another by bending low on forepaws and raising the back part of the body, wagging the tail? It is common to see dog play escalate into something rougher, and just when we assume the worst, one dog rolls over and exposes the belly. We recognize submission when we see it, even in dogs.

Magpies also play-fight with human friends (and one another), acting as if angry when they are merely pretending. They also make the same gesture of submission. Professor Kaplan describes how they roll over and expose their bellies during play. And when a juvenile has done something wrong and is being chased by an adult magpie, the bird will often resort to this same appeasement gesture: *Forgive me, I'm sorry.* It works.

Professor Kaplan writes me: "I have hand-raised about thirty kook-aburras by now—some from age two days post hatching and not one has ever bonded to me. They will take the food from me very readily and express a vast variety of behaviour that I have observed them displaying to their parents in the wild but as soon as they are fully fledged and an adult group of kookaburras nearby has indicated that they are willing to adopt, the hand-raised bird will follow their call and abandon me without looking back."

Since magpies are a sedentary species defending relatively large territories it is important that they be able to convey information to other magpies, other birds, and even mammalian intruders. Professor Kaplan believes that magpies may well have a specific alarm call for eagles and another for monitor lizards. She tested this by playing back the calls and watching the reaction: Playback of the eagle call almost invariably is followed by the magpies scanning the sky for an aerial predator.

In a paper published in the February 2005 issue of *Nature Neuroscience Reviews*, the Avian Brain Nomenclature Consortium declared:

In the light of new evidence about the function of the vertebrate brain, the international consortium of neuroscientists has reconsidered the traditional, 100-year-old terminology that is used to describe the avian cerebrum. Our current understanding of the avian brain—in particular the neocortex-like cognitive functions of the avian pallium—requires a new terminology that better re-

flects these functions and the homologies between avian and mammalian brains.

In short, birds are not the birdbrains everyone thought.

According to Professor Kaplan, magpies engage in the melodious
singing for which they are famous as a form of leisure activity. They do
it simply to pass the time by engaging in something that is pleasurable
and harmonious. Of course they don't do it to give other species pleasure as well, but it happens that at least one species *does* take pleasure
in the songs of magpies.

Along with the lyrebird, the magpie is probably the best mimic
among birds in bird-rich Australia, and also among the best in the
world. Magpies mimic cats, dogs, horses, humans, other birds, and even
potential predators such as the barking owl. Professor Kaplan offers
some fascinating theories as to what this mimicry signifies, having to do
with constructing a vocal map of their territory. She suggests they become used to the presence of certain other animals (including humans)
and the sounds these animals make. If I understand her correctly, by imitating these sounds, the magpies construct a kind of inventory of their
territory. But is this inventory intended for the other species or for
themselves? Is it like counting: *Here is what belongs to my home*? Or is it
more like a simple murmuring under one's breath? What is certain is
that magpies *only* mimic species who share residency. It is hardly random and must have a purpose.

Still, I remain uncertain as to what mimicking achieves. When magpies are captive, or for that matter when any bird is, they imitate human
words. The psychology of that cross-species gesture is still obscure.
Alex, the famous African grey parrot of Irene Pepperberg, uses his
speech to communicate much as a human would. But he has been taught
to do this, and I do not think that wild birds imitating human sounds
are communicating in the same way. This is a young field of inquiry, and
there will be many astonishing surprises in the years ahead.

BADGERS

I LOVE THE IDEA of a whole country taking a leap in consciousness about a particular animal because of a single person's passion. This happened with badgers, and the person who brought them to life, as it were, is Ernest Neal (1911–1998), an English schoolmaster from Somerset. His 1948 book *The Badger* contained on its frontispiece the first color photograph of a wild badger to be taken at night. Part of the reason that this common animal, found from Ireland to China and Japan, was unloved was that it is entirely nocturnal. Few people had ever even seen one, let alone knew about its habits. That changed in 1948 because of Neal's book and a series of TV documentaries that showed films of badger life in the sett (the badger burrow). Setts are remarkable feats of fossorial life: Neal visited one that covered an area of about sixteen hundred square yards, with more than eighty entrances. Some of these setts have been in use for centuries!

Partly because people thought they preyed upon lambs, a cruel fantasy with no truth whatsoever, they engaged in the horrible "sport" of digging for badgers. That involves sending fox terriers down the sett, flushing them out, and then killing them by smashing in their sensitive noses. However, increasingly more people nowadays choose instead to sit by the sett and watch for them, or photograph them in the dark. As Sir David Attenborough put it in his foreword to Neal's *The Natural History of Badgers*: "Soon, naturalists in woods all over the country were holding badger-watching parties. It was almost as though a new species of mammal had suddenly been added to the countryside. And at last the badger acquired the hold on the public's affections that it had always deserved."

Neal also had the humility to defer to people who got to know badgers as individuals. Not that these badger-watchers tamed them, but the animals grew habituated to their presence, allowing them to see aspects of their badger nature that a normal scientist, even one as sympathetic as Neal, would not know about. For example, Chris Ferris got to know badgers in Kent, and they became used to her presence. When a female cub injured her paw, she allowed Ferris to examine the wound. Ferris treated the wound with hydrogen peroxide and antibiotics, and a month later the cub completely recovered. From that time on she was not only totally trusting, but would greet Ferris when she appeared. Neal is also prepared to drop his own prejudices when information is available that he considers reliable. In speaking of the "wary armed neutrality" that exists between foxes and badgers, he writes: "Sometimes, however, all the rules are broken and Wijngaarden and Peppel (1964) cite a case of a sow badger adopting the cubs of a couple of foxes which had been shot and providing them with food."

Unlike most other members of their family, Eurasian badgers live in groups called clans, a little bit like the clans of early human societies. The American badger, though, while similar in every other respect to the Eurasian badger, is a loner. There is nothing about badgers that makes them intrinsically fascinating to humans; nor does the study of biology, ecology, or the natural behavior of the badger throw any particular light on the equivalent human activity. So it is good—in fact, it is more than good—that the public takes such interest in them. It speaks to something decent in the British character that Ernest Neal could single-handedly achieve this without the usual hype that would be required in America.

What is the purpose of the handsome black-and-white stripes on the head of the badger? It could not be camouflage, since this is an entirely nocturnal animal, so much so that badgers dislike moonlit nights, where they can be distinctly seen. Neal suggests that the coloration is due to the fact that they are fearless—or rather, they have little to fear from any predator (except, as per usual, us). Just as skunks use their anal glands for protection and are rarely attacked by any other animal, adult badgers have no natural enemy, for their bite is formidable. It would even appear that where they have no experience with humans, they show no fear of us, either.

Is it possible that the badger is the only other animal, besides humans and elephants, to have a sort of ritual around death and burial? Neal believes it not entirely impossible. He repeats a touching scene recounted by Brian Vesey-FitzGerald of how a sow who lost her mate made a mournful sound, which brought out from another sett a male. (Badgers appear to be one of the few monogamous mammals.) Together the male and female dragged the dead body to a warren, interred it, and then separated. Neal asks: "One wonders if all badgers are buried in this way or whether these rites are characteristic only of such special occasions as when a sow loses her mate." I could find no further information on this, but it strikes me as plausible. In his later book, though, Neal pronounces himself more skeptical: "All that can be said at present about badger funerals is that if they do occur, they are very rare events. But badgers are remarkable creatures and it is well to keep an open mind about the possibility. I'm still hoping that one day I shall see a badger funeral myself."

BALD EAGLE

Haliaeetus leucocephalus

I HAVE JUST FINISHED reading Brenda Cox's *Conversations with an Eagle*, and one thing I know: I will never attempt to train an eagle in the ancient art of falconry, as she did. Her description of this particular eagle as vibrant, cantankerous, regal, and dangerous is certainly true, but surely it makes more sense to observe these qualities from a distance, in a free-flying bird? On the other hand, she met Ichabod at a wildlife sanctuary in British Columbia, where the bird had been consigned because she had been found as a nestling on the ground. She was what the author and others call an imprint—she had imprinted on humans. In the case of harmless birds, this is usually harmless. But in birds of prey, it means they lose their fear of humans and are especially aggressive. An animal the size of a bald eagle, with a thousand pounds of pressure in each talon, is a dangerous adversary indeed. I find it remarkable that Brenda Cox did not suffer more injuries than she did.

"Thrilling" I can understand, but when practically the last words of the book describe a late encounter that ends with Brenda Cox's foot bloodied, being stared at "with an expression that, in a human, could only be called malignant," well, I conclude that raptors and humans do not belong together.

Cox speaks of the "single-mindedness of a predator." Ichabod had no need for human companionship and was in no way prepared for it. ("If I tripped I knew Ichabod would attack me.") Her interest was in prey: "Her predatory nature was evident in her every action and look." How can we provide anything equivalent for such an animal; indeed, why should we try?

This raises important questions, ones being asked as if for the first time: Do humans have *any* place with *any* animal? Heretical thoughts, I know, coming from a man who wrote *Dogs Never Lie About Love* and *The Nine Emotional Lives of Cats* as well as *The Pig Who Sang to the Moon*, but it seems to me, now, that we must ask ourselves what we can bring to the lives of animals to increase their happiness. I don't see anything we can give a free-living animal that could possibly replace the life evolution designed. For some reason, this strikes me with even greater force when it comes to birds: How can birds, with the entire sky as their home, ever be happy in confinement? We must seem alien to them, the cages we confine them to very much like, well, a cage.

And what kind of cage are we going to put a bald eagle into, in any event? Consider the Northern California nest of a bald eagle. True, it was a record, but just think about it for a moment: 150 feet above the ground, 12 feet long, 20 feet deep, lined at the bottom with soft moss and feathers where the two to three eggs—fratricide is common—were laid in a nest cup and the nestlings could stay for thirteen weeks. This nest weighed an incredible six thousand pounds. What can an eagle see from a cage? In the wild, it is speculated they can see a group of other eagles fourteen miles away. And what opportunities can we give them to fly, when they can drop on prey at a speed of two hundred miles an hour?

As for the notion of "cooperative hunting," that is mere semantic spin. This is how some falconers refer to the "sport" of taking a masked bird into the country on your fist, thrashing a hedge to force rabbits to flee, then releasing the birds to kill the rabbits. The birds are not cooperating—they have no choice—and the training invariably involves food rewards.

Why are such apex predators so antagonistic to humans? Or is it that they are antagonistic to all animals except their mates and young? (They mate for life.) They hiss like snakes, and even after eight years of constant contact this hand-raised eagle was barely civil to Brenda Cox. I can think of only one thing: They are still hunted (though killing an American bald eagle is prohibited). From as many as half a million birds when European settlers arrived, by the 1960s the number was down to a mere five hundred. Now, fortunately, the numbers are back up, but there is always a risk.

Ted Hughes, in his well-known poem "Eagle," wrote how "the Wolf-Cub weeps to be chosen" as prey. But I have yet to hear of any eagle attacking a wolf cub. With adult wolves around, it would be suicide, and eagles are notoriously cautious, much preferring to steal their food than to hunt it. A bald eagle is much more likely to seek out spawning salmon, a favorite food, and sometimes as many as three thousand of them gather in the winter at the Chilkat River near Haines, Alaska, to fish. But while they enjoy fishing, it would seem that they enjoy just hanging out even more. Bald eagles love to idle, and will spend up to 90 percent of their time simply perching. They may occasionally glance at their favorite fishing hole, but they also have that inscrutable stare into the distance, giving the impression that they are contemplating deeper pleasures than merely a sated stomach. From the beginning of time, this look has never failed to impress humans. It's not hard to understand why.

BATS

Order Chiroptera

THERE IS NO ANIMAL, no insect, no life-form, without value. Upon examination, none fails to instruct and delight. Consider bats and their poor reputation. As recently as 1973 *National Geographic* published an article titled "Bats Aren't All Bad." More recently, thanks primarily to Merlin Tuttle and Bat Conservation International, this negative attitude has evolved.

Part of the problem was the way people saw bats, literally. Explains Tuttle:

In about 1978, the National Geographic Society asked me to write a chapter in their book *Wild Animals in North America*. I went to Washington to help their photo editors go over bat pictures. I was horrified. All the pictures they were going to put with my chapter were close-ups of tormented, snarling bats. In those days no one knew how to photograph bats. They'd just grab one, the bat would close his eyes and hunker down, thinking he was going to die, then they'd torment him until he snarled, then they'd take a picture. Then they'd blow the picture up to page size. No wonder everybody feared bats.

Across the globe, the Persians and the Chinese saw the bat as a sym-bol of longevity and happiness in traditional stories and legends. How-ever, in the West, the animal was held in low esteem. Remember the potion the three witches in *Macbeth* brewed? It contained "wool of bat." Vampires took the form of bats in Bram Stoker's *Dracula*, and in general the Western church took a dim view of them. The common bad-hair-day myth about bats—that they get themselves trapped and tan-gled in human hair—seems to have stemmed from the Christian notion that women's hair attracts demons, the same idiotic idea that made Saint Paul order women to cover their heads in church. In medieval Eu-rope the devil is often depicted with bat wings.

Humans have always feared animals who roam in the dark, and espe-cially an animal who can do so with such speed and accuracy. It strikes us as uncanny and unnatural. Of course, in bygone years, people did not know that bats were mammals! Only in the last twenty years or so has serious research into bat biology and ecology turned these extraordi-nary mammals into heroes of the animal world.

And rightly so. Bats have a wider distribution of any group of terres-trial mammals other than the human race. They can be found every-where except the polar regions and some oceanic islands. Every fourth mammal on earth is a bat. (This is nearly literally true: There are about 4,000 mammal species, and 925 or so distinct types of bats.) And for such small mammals, they are remarkably long-lived, up to thirty years. Best of all, bats are the only mammal able to fly!

They vary greatly in size, too, from the minuscule hog-nosed or bumble-bee bat from the bamboo forests of western Thailand that weighs less than a penny, to Lyle's flying fox with a wingspan of nearly four feet. One fruit-eating flying fox (*Pteropus vampyrus*) has a wingspan of six feet! Then there is their remarkable echolocation, dis-covered by Harvard undergraduate Donald Griffin in 1938, when he lis-tened to bats with a microphone that could detect ultrasound. He found that bats emit high-frequency sounds (far beyond the human range) that rebound to their ears, enabling them to detect objects as fine as a human hair in pitch-dark. At least a third of all bats are insectivores and hunt at night, using echolocation to find and dispatch insect prey. The hearing of almost all species of bats is exceptional. Some can hear an insect walking on a leaf.

No other mammal—in fact, no other animal—forms such huge colonies. Bracken Cave in central Texas Hill Country is home to more than twenty million Brazilian free-tailed bats! (Arizona's Eagle Creek Cave once had fifty million individuals living inside.) Every evening these tiny (half an ounce) bats emerge in huge columns. In a single night they can catch half a million pounds of pest-insects. Actually, these Texas free-tailed bats can eat up to a thousand *tons* each night of corn earworm moths, the major agricultural pest in the United States. They fly as high as twenty-five hundred feet to catch them with echolocation. They may even fly as high as ten thousand feet. Their cave homes offer protection from most predators as well as allowing bats to conserve energy, since the temperature is more or less constant.

How wonderful that there is a network now of at least ninety groups in the world working to promote bat conservation. Still, as Professor Theodore H. Fleming reminds us: "Eleven species of bats have gone extinct, and sixty-two species are currently listed as endangered by the International Union for the Conservation of Nature and Natural Resources."

Of course the most damaging myth about bats is that they all wish to suck our blood. In fact, there are just three bloodsucking species of vampire bats in Central and South America. Their usual prey are other animals, especially cattle. They approach them when sleeping, cut a small piece of skin off the surface of their hide, then lap up the blood—which does not coagulate thanks to anticoagulant chemicals in the saliva of these bats. (The anticoagulant from these bats' saliva has been synthesized and is now used in medications for human heart patients.) They will also, sometimes, "attack" humans, drinking a small amount of blood, no more than two tablespoons. The wound is hardly serious or painful. The problem is that they are known to transmit paralytic rabies, though the number of people who develop it is small. However, the largest urban bat populations consist almost exclusively of colonial species, not vampire bats, and there is no evidence linking them to increased transmission of rabies to humans.

It may surprise many to learn that the common vampire bat (*Desmodus rotundus*) is one of our planet's most altruistic animals. Since a vampire bat can go only three days without food before it starves to death, when a well-fed bat returns to the common roost, he or she might regurgitate blood to a companion who has been unsuccessful and is in dire need of nourishment. Given that bats are as susceptible to paralytic rabies as humans and sharing blood from the mouth is a perfect way to transmit the virus, this unselfish act is even more astounding. Why would bats risk infection to help a companion, one who might not even be related? Only, it would seem, as insurance against winding up on the opposite side of the fence one day. There is also a great deal of mutual grooming that goes on in these colonies, some of which serves to alert one bat to the weakened state of a companion. And vampire bats adopt orphaned infants. It seems, in fact, a lot like human altruism, which probably originated the same way and for the same reasons.

Bats are among the animal world's best mothers. They birth pups weighing as much as 40 percent of the mother's body weight and nurse them for more than six months—a long time for such a small mammal. Mothers also nurse unrelated pups. It was thought for some time that they could not tell who their own babies were, but they know perfectly well. It is presumed that they do this so their own babies benefit from similar benevolence on the part of a different but equally unrelated mother. Some females have been seen helping to groom baby bats not their own, and sometimes even helping to maneuver them into the proper suckling position! Young vampire bats show no aggressive behavior, even when they play and wrestle with other juveniles. In the roost juveniles perform a gesture of appeasement where one folded wing is lifted and the body is bent to one side. It is indeed, as the *Oxford New Encyclopedia of Mammals* exclaims, "an amazing reciprocal-exchange system." If it is so useful and logical, I wonder why more animals have not developed it.

Bats are enormously useful to a whole world of plants. One bat-pollinated vine in the Neotropics directs bats to its nectar with a petal that reflects the energy of the echolocation call directly back at the bat. *Come and get me fast* is the message. There are fruits that rely primarily on bats either for pollination or seed dispersal such as wild bananas, lychees, mangoes, avocados, and 160 others.

Moths, of course, are chiropterophobic. Along with many insects that are bats' prey, they evolved bat-detecting ears, and often pay attention only to these sounds. Others evolved a special click, the emission of which lets the bats know that they are inedible. Truth in advertising works so well that a bat need only hear this click to wheel away in search of tastier prey. Some moths fly low to the ground in the hope that ground echoes will protect them from bats. This acoustic crypsis is part of the arms race between predator (bat) and prey (moths). It has been wonderfully speculated that some moths "learned," millions of years ago, to turn into sunshine-loving butterflies simply as a means of avoiding hungry, nocturnal flying bats.

I DID NOT APPRECIATE BEETLES. God does, of course. So much so that He has made every fifth living species on earth a beetle. But I've seen the light. It came about, like most good things for me, through a book. You know the game: If you could take just ten books to a desert island, what would they be? I have a candidate for you: Arthur V. Evans's and Charles L. Bellamy's *An Inordinate Fondness for Beetles* turned me into a true believer—in beetles, that is.

Of course, the ancient Egyptians appreciated the beauty of these animals long ago. They looked at scarab beetles, and especially *Scarabaeus sacer*, as sacred symbols of the divine. They observed the lamellicorn dung beetle (or scarab) rolling a tiny ball of dung with his hind legs to bury it. It reminded the Egyptians of their sun god, Ra, rolling the ball of the sun across the sky. The sun sets, but is reborn, just as small beetles later emerged from the ground. The Egyptians saw rebirth and immortality. For thirty centuries, the scarab was venerated—hence its name *Scarabaeus sacer*, the sacred scarab. French entomologist Yves Cambefort even suggests that the pyramids were built and mummification practiced as a direct result of observing dung beetles.

How we humans differ! Consider how these very same beetles were regarded throughout the Middle Ages, with people basing their knowledge of natural history on the ancient Greek text the *Physiologus:* "the dung beetles are the heretics, defiled with the stench of heresy . . . the balls of dung . . . which they roll back and forth on the ground are evil thoughts and heresies, created out of wickedness and foulness."

In France during the Middle Ages, stag beetles were believed responsible for setting houses on fire, for it was thought they carried burning embers in their jaws. Perhaps people saw bioluminescent beetles (fireflies) and made the imaginary connection with fire. In fourteenth-century Avignon, they actually had an ecclesiastical proceeding against a beetle. Two priests dressed in their finest formal attire visited affected land and announced publicly that any beetle who did not attend the trial would be excommunicated forthwith! One must wonder whether they had a sense of humor.

We are still nowhere near knowing all about beetles, nor even knowing how many there are in the world. Humans have identified 350,000 species in 166 families, but even in the beetle-drawers of tiny museums around the world, there are probably thousands of unknown species yet to be recognized. Scientists estimate that there could be as many as eight million.

No other living being I have ever seen so closely imitates the color and glitter of gemstones as the miniature beetles commonly known as jewel beetles or flying jewels. In Costa Rica the ruteline scarabs of the genus *Chrysina* are golden, or silver, or two-toned, with golden thorax and silver elytra (the thickened wing covers that protect the delicate, veined membranous hind wings beneath). They are becoming increasingly rare as collectors spend thousands of dollars to obtain these prizes, forgetting that they are *living* beings who have as much right to their existence as we have to ours. Though these and other beetles are threatened primarily by habitat loss, not collectors, the combination of threatened habitat and commercial demand is worrisome to conservationists.

At fifteen I accompanied my father on a gem-buying trip to Ceylon, as it was then known. Some of the gem merchants wore a jewel buprestid as a brooch, while their children kept these same beetles on tiny leashes as pets. I wanted one. Today I consider it cruel. There is still a fad in Japan for pet stag beetles, as popular there as dogs and cats in the West. Especially large ones fetch thousands of dollars. One good thing that has come out of this practice, though, is that *Dorcus curvidens*, for example, is no longer endangered, since many Japanese children breed them. I hope some can be induced to return them to their natural home.

I should not be so uppity about this passion for beetle collecting, though, considering that it was this habit that provided young Charles Darwin with his first scientific interest: In his *Autobiography* he recounts how at Cambridge he found beetles more interesting than his classes:

> I will give a proof of my zeal: one day, on tearing off some old bark, I saw two rare beetles, and seized one in each hand; then I saw a third and new kind, which I could not bear to lose, so that I popped the one which I held in my right hand into my mouth. Alas! It ejected some intensely acrid fluid, which burnt my tongue so that I was forced to spit the beetle out, which was lost, as was the third one.

Was it their appearance that fascinated Darwin, the chitinous exoskeleton that shines like metal? Or did Darwin already have some vague internal stirrings that beetles might well provide the clues he would one day seek about evolution? Perhaps he was fascinated by the fact that some beetles are parthenogenetic. Females give birth on their own to other females. Or he may have known that the larvae of some beetles can take up to thirty-five years to emerge as adults.

Evans and Bellamy present a detailed, fascinating account of the different kinds of beautifully colored mimicry in beetles. Some of their brilliant colors and distinct patterns act as a warning. Are they meant to imitate the colors and patterns of other insects so unpalatable that their predators learned to avoid eating them? In the Namib Desert there are two closely related species of dung scarabs—one with black elytra, the other with orange. The beetle with orange elytra is a remarkably fast flier, and can hardly be caught on the wing. Perhaps, it has been suggested, the orange coloration is an advertisement to that effect: *No use chasing me; once you see the orange, I am gone.* Two other flightless relatives of this beetle, who are black elsewhere, in this desert develop orange elytra as well! They lie to predators: *I can fly, and fast, so don't waste your energy.*

Some beetles use crypsis and resemble tree bark or leaves or lichens, but others stand out gloriously. You would think that the extraordinarily bright colors of so many beetles would call attention to them. But consider the beautiful beetle who, upon lifting its elytra, suddenly shows a bright metallic blue-green abdomen with bright yellow "eyes." No doubt this sudden appearance confuses any predator.

There is another form of mimicry in which some beetles come to resemble a certain kind of ant, and then are able to successfully solicit food from the ants. These beetles live with ants, even eat their eggs, without the ants being in the least bit disturbed. Another species (the European *Lomechusa strumosa*, a staphylinid beetle) does not resemble its host ant (*Formica sanguinea*), but secretes appeasement chemicals that are consumed by the ants, quelling their aggressive tendencies. Is there some as-yet-undiscovered symbiosis whereby the ants get something in return that we simply cannot as yet see? Or are the ants simply fooled? These beetles, by the way, have the wonderful designation of myrmecophilous, ant-loving.

If anyone were ever to say to me that studying beetles is no way to spend a life and that trying to protect the endangered subspecies of elderberry beetle, the *Desmocerus californicus*, officially on the list of endangered species by the U.S. Fish and Wildlife Services, is a waste of valuable time, I will be delighted to refer him to a quote by E. O. Wilson: "Biodiversity is our most valuable but least appreciated resource . . . a rare beetle sitting on an orchid in a remote valley of the Andes might secrete a substance that cures pancreatic cancer."

BENGAL TIGER

Panthera tigris tigris

I LIVED IN INDIA for several years and once stayed in the hill station of Mahabaleshwar, near Poone, not far from Bombay. I was in a shop on the main street of the little town when a man dressed as a tiger walked in. The shopkeeper dropped everything and rushed over to put money into the hands of the man-tiger. The man then left without a word, moving on to the next shop, where the same thing happened. I asked what that was all about. The shopkeeper explained: "Man come in dressed as tiger, so I gave him money and he left." "I *know* that," I said in frustration. "I saw that. I want to know *why* he is dressed as a tiger and why you gave him money." But the man would say nothing further. All I know is that it had something to do with Indian tiger cults and the concept of a *tuindak*, a tiger who turns himself into a man. (The opposite—a man who turns into a tiger—is also a popular staple of folktales). Whatever the villagers thought this man was, they hastened to ensure his goodwill. Tigers are much feared and much respected in India, and have been for thousands of years.

The tiger has been described as the perfect killing machine. Indeed, when you read the rather large literature on tigers, what is immediately apparent is how much time is devoted to killing, to exactly how and who they kill as well as anything having to do with their lethal capacities. This is a bit odd when you consider that tigers are only successful one out of every twenty tries, hardly different from any other animal, and this is an animal who can jump a full thirty feet! Perhaps the difference is that the tiger often takes down extremely large animals; indeed, some are seven times the predator's weight, such as water buffalo or gaur—formidable animals who can weigh more than two thousand pounds and who often kill their predator.

Will there be any tigers at all for my young son Manu to see when he is an adult? We take their land and their skins as trophies. Worse, there is a growing demand for tiger bones for use in medical delusions: to cure fright, and against devil possession. Tiger fat is used as an aphrodisiac. (There is no such thing, by the way, beyond the human brain.) Their collarbones are used as charms against evil; their hearts are eaten to acquire strength, courage, and cunning. And their brains are mixed with oil and rubbed on the body to cure laziness! Such are the beliefs of the "superior species." In Russia two pounds of crushed tiger bone are worth more than three hundred dollars (a small tiger can yield fifteen pounds of bone), and a tiger skeleton is worth more than ten years' salary. There is as yet no tiger cure for human greed.

Although tigers in a cage look conspicuous and obvious, their coat pattern is an almost perfect camouflage for their environment. The black stripes against a dark gold background breaks up the body outline, and the cat almost fades from view. White tigers are not albinos with pink eyes, but are descendants from a single white male cub, Mohan, captured in the forests of Rewa in Madhya Pradesh, India, in 1951.

Recently it has become clear how sophisticated the communication system of tigers is, leading researchers to classify them as solitary but not asocial, since the marks they make with their claws on trees exist to be read by other animals. Not only do they use their claws, but they can also spray a target with "marking fluid," an odorous, musky liquid. It seems that only the animal who holds territory sprays, as a sign of ownership. But the marking fluid also contains information about the individual: identity, sex, reproductive condition, and the time the marking was made. A tiger returns every three weeks to freshen the scent, since it fades after about that long. This is not the only way tigers recognize one another. Facial markings may play a role, since the stripes and marks on a tiger's face and body are unique to each. We recognize a tiger this way, so there seems to be no reason not to assume that other tigers have the same ability, though this has never been proven.

When a tigress is in estrus, she scent-marks more frequently, letting the male know it is time for him to show up. And even when a female accepts a male, mating is still a delicate, perhaps even dangerous, affair. She always appears ambivalent. She makes a special sound, similar to the reassuring sound that has been named prusten: a friendly, fluttering exhalation made through closed lips, and also what is called poking, which resembles the call of a sambar (hence some have suggested it is a decoy call to lure a deer to doom). She rolls on the ground in front of the male, just as house cats do. But then she suddenly leaps up and spits at the male, striking out with her claws.

Arjan Singh has a persuasive hypothesis about solitary versus gregarious animals. He argues that the environment is the deciding factor: Animals who live out in the open, such as swamp deer and chital, are gregarious. Those who live in a closed habitat, such as the sambar and barking deer, are withdrawn and shy. The tiger and the leopard are solitary because of the terrain they live in, whereas the more social lions inhabit open plains.

Do tigers prey on humans? They certainly kill them. In the Sundarbans of Bangladesh, 100 to 150 people are killed every year by tigers. Why would tigers kill humans more regularly than do lions, leopards, or pumas? It seems to have something to do with tradition. But the comment by Jim Corbett, who was once a lion and tiger hunter, still stands many years later: "A man-eating tiger is a tiger that has been compelled, through stress of circumstances beyond its control, to adopt a diet that is alien to it. The stress of circumstances is, in nine cases out of ten, wounds and in the tenth, old age."

Man-eating tigers almost always carry old wounds. These wounds are often the result of being shot by hunters. Isn't it logical to think the tigers knew they had human enemies, and fought back? Killing humans was more or less unknown in Myanmar, Thailand, Malaysia, and Sumatra. In most places on the Indian subcontinent, tigers do not kill humans. While we may never entirely understand the reason for the high number of humans killed in the Sundarbans, a successful and remarkably inventive method has been discovered to end the killings: Since it is known that tigers attack from behind, not face-to-face, in 1987 the area's eight thousand honey collectors were outfitted with rubber face masks to wear on the back of the head. In that year not one person wearing the masks was killed, but twenty-nine people who temporarily removed the masks were.

BILBY

Macrotis lagotis

ACCORDING TO THE AUSTRALIAN NATIONAL DICTIONARY Centre, the word *bilby* comes from Yuwaalaraay, an Aboriginal language of northern New South Wales.

The graceful little bilby is a bandicoot. This is not a line from a Lewis Carroll poem, but the truth. A bandicoot is a smallish marsupial from Australia and New Guinea. (The word itself is borrowed from the south Indian Telugu language's word for a pig-rat, a rat in India and Sri Lanka the size of a rabbit, called a pandikokku. A friend tells me that the word is contained in one of the most famous tongue twisters in Telugu: *Gadi lona kandipappu gadi kinda pandikokku.* Try saying it to yourself and you will see how nice it sounds!) There are nine species of bandicoots. One, the pig-footed bandicoot (*Chaeropus ecaudatus*), was last seen alive in 1907 and was the only specimen to have been captured (read: *killed*) in the twentieth century. It is almost certainly extinct, as is the desert bandicoot and the lesser bilby.

There are two species of bilby, the lesser and the greater (referring to their size). The last lesser bilby (*Macrotis leucura*) seen alive was reported in 1931 from Cooncherie in northeastern South Australia. A skull was found in a wedge-tailed eagle's nest in 1967 in the desert near

Alice Springs (of Ayer's Rock fame), but it was impossible to say how old it was. As recently as 1990, some scientists still hoped to find another lesser, but it is now increasingly doubtful that any will be found. The species appears, alas, to be extinct.

But the greater bilby is becoming an iconic animal for many Australians. This is due partly to the fact that they are so lovely to look at, with their long, silky blue-gray fur, white feet, and black claws. Their extra-long ears give them acute hearing, keep these animals cool in the hot summer, and perhaps allow them to communicate using high-frequency sounds beyond the human range. The bilby's long black tail, with a white tip and a prominent tuft, is evidently used for communication.

These animals look a bit like rabbits (they are about the same size, and hop like them, too), and there is a movement in Australia to replace introduced rabbits with this native species. No doubt rabbits compete with bilbies for food and perhaps even burrows, since bilbies dig burrows as deep as six feet. They use them only for resting during the day, since they are strictly nocturnal animals. When they are inside, they block the entrance with soil to keep out predators or possibly other bilbies. They are basically a solitary species. Like other bandicoots, they have a short gestation period. (The shortest recorded in a mammal is the long-nosed bandicoot—just twelve days from conception to birth!) The diminutive newborns enter the mother's pouch, but remain attached to her placenta via a long, elastic umbilical cord for almost three months. By the time they emerge, they are nearly sexually mature and ready to reproduce. But even with these remarkable arrangements for rapid reproduction, a bilby mother can probably only successfully raise about eight young in her lifetime of about eight years. (Only about 10 percent of offspring survive.)

Bilbies once occupied more than 70 percent of mainland Australia, but there may well be *only a few thousand* wild bilbies left. With extinction looming on the horizon, Australians are taking notice. This beautiful, graceful little animal should not be permitted to disappear. Nobody knows for certain why it is so rapidly vanishing, but introduced species

are undoubtedly the culprits: foxes, cattle, feral cats, and—most noxious of all—humans! It is not certain that a single bilby will be left in
ten years' time. Captive breeding colonies do seem to make sense in this
emergency, and several of them are operating in Australia. The Arid
Recovery Project, which is a partnership between BHP Billiton, the
University of Adelaide, the SA Department of Environment and Heritage, and Friends of Arid Recovery, is fencing a fifty-three-square-mile
reserve in the South Australian outback, and removing all feral cats,
foxes, and rabbits. (See the website www.aridrecovery.org.au.) Researchers have so far successfully introduced the greater stick-nest rat,
the burrowing bettong, the greater bilby, and the western barred
bandicoot, and have conducted a trial release of numbats in 2005. After
that, they intend to bring in Woma pythons.

The Commonwealth of Australia Endangered Species Program
chose the bilby as a mascot representing all endangered species, and
there are several flourishing programs for reintroduction. Perhaps the
most unusual is in the nearly half-million-acre Astrebla Downs National
Park in Queensland's remote southwest desert, where temperatures
regularly reach 131 degrees Fahrenheit, hotter than Death Valley in the
United States. The park is home to the world's most venomous reptile,
the western taipan. Peter McRae, a Queensland National Parks and
Wildlife Service senior zoologist, along with Frank Manthey, a former
kangaroo shooter, is building a fence and shooting feral cats to protect
the 350 or so local bilbies (a third of the population of Queensland bilbies). He's also breeding and reintroducing others. How can even the
bilbies survive in those temperatures? By staying all day in their cool
burrows, where the temperature remains a constant and comfortable
seventy-seven degrees. How the humans survive has not been explained. There are some excellent articles about this recovery plan that
I list on my website: www.jeffreymasson.com.

BISON CAME TO NORTH AMERICA during the Pleistocene epoch via the Bering land bridge. Eventually they ranged from Canada's Great Slave Lake to Mexico and from eastern Oregon almost to the Atlantic. They especially thrived on the Great Plains, where they formed the biggest mass of large mammals ever to tread the globe.

The one "fact" that most people seem to know about buffalo is that at one point there were sixty million of them in the United States. It turns out that this figure is a pure invention. The real number is closer to thirty million, as we know from the fascinating book *American Bison: A Natural History* by Professor Dale Lott, the preeminent expert on buffalo, who died recently. Strangely, the erroneous figure of sixty million is even repeated in the recent *New Oxford Encyclopedia of Mammals*.

What is not fantasy, and what is also pretty well-known by the general public, is that the number of buffalo still alive at the beginning of the twentieth century was down to a few hundred scattered survivors. What happened? In William Hornaday's 1889 book *The Extermination of the American Bison*, the author, a father of modern conservationism, blamed pitiless mass killing by Native Americans, for whom he had absolutely no affection. However, these same Native peoples had been coexisting with bison in more or less the same way for hundreds of years. Or as Lott put it: "Native Americans hunted bison in North America on foot for at least ninety-eight centuries."

Greedy market hunters seemed to tip the balance. These hunters not only relished the work and the profit, but seemed driven by a curious hatred. It is best expressed by the historian Francis Parkan, who traveled on the Great Plains in the 1840s: "The world may be searched in vain to find anything of a more ugly and ferocious aspect. At the first sight of him [the buffalo] every feeling of sympathy vanishes; no man who had not experienced it, can understand with what keen relish one inflicts his death wound, with what profound contentment he beholds his fall."

Still, the picture became crystal clear when I read Valerius Geist's *Buffalo Nation: History and Legend of the North American Bison*. Said Columbus Delano, U.S. secretary of the interior, in 1873: "The civilization of the Indian is impossible while the buffalo remains upon the plains." In other words, it was U.S. government policy to exterminate the bison in order to civilize (that is, destroy) the Indian. Whether they knew it or not, the hide hunters were simply the instruments of this official, if unspoken, determination. European settlers wanted to take the land that the Indians and the buffalo occupied, and this is what was meant by *civilization*. It was, said the white settlers, "Manifest Destiny." One of the men chosen by this destiny was none other than William "Buffalo Bill" Cody: "During my engagement as hunter for the Kansas Pacific Railroad—a period of less than eighteen months—I killed 4,280 buffaloes." Hence his nickname. When he died in 1917, twenty-five thousand people filed past his casket, and President Theodore Roosevelt eulogized him as "one of those men, steel-thewed

and iron-nerved, whose daring progress opened the great West to settlement and civilization."

This "progress" was seen somewhat differently by Native people:
"A cold wind blew across the prairie when the last buffalo fell . . . a
death-wind for my people," said Hunkpapa Sioux chief Sitting Bull.
The buffalo meant life for the Indians; in this at least, the U.S. government was prescient. Oglala Sioux holy man Black Elk explained that
"the buffalo represents the people and the universe, and should always
be treated with respect, for was he not here before the two-legged peoples, and is he not generous in that he gives us our homes and our food?
The buffalo is wise in many things, and, thus, we should learn from him
and should always be as a relative with him."

As a species we seem to have an inordinate need to be liked, and not
simply tolerated. Surely this is at least one component in our need to
tame, and to take taming a step further into domestication. So when in
recent years the buffalo has made something of a comeback, and people
raise them on private ranches, they also want to demonstrate that these
great animals return our affection. They rarely do. Part of the problem
might lie in their size. A large male can be six feet tall at the shoulders
and weigh two thousand pounds. They are accustomed to a certain respect. Lott described several instances in which a "pet" buffalo turned
around and drove his or her horns deep into the belly of the naïve
"owner." Idaho rancher Dick Clark raised a bull from a calf. Even when
he was full grown, he let Clark pet him and climb onto his back. He
seemed friendly until the day he killed Clark. They were not friends
after all. As Lott persuasively argued: "A relationship with a buffalo is
a dangerous liaison. Bison are immune to our charm, sincerity, personal
integrity, and peaceful intentions. We have to learn to value them without believing that they value us." After all, as wild animals, he explained, bison were not selected to interact with us. We need, he
pleaded, to appreciate what they really are, rather than what we want
them to be. I suspect he would have been entirely opposed to domestication. The hardest thing for us humans to do, but perhaps the most
valuable, is to *leave other species alone.*

Perhaps as we find it increasingly rare in our own species, we seem to have a deep sentimental need to find nobility in other species. I know that I am personally uncomfortable if I fail to find some trait in an animal that calls forth admiration at a moral level. I may think of aggression in buffalo as far less deadly than human aggression, but it's probably not true. In most years 5 or 6 percent of the mature bulls in any population die of their wounds in confrontations with one another over breeding rights. While many human males kill each other every year, the numbers hardly reach 5 or 6 percent.

What I do know is that when bulls threaten each other, the fight is over when one animal submits. Even if one bull is in mid-attack, he stops as soon as the other bull makes a sign of submission, usually by turning away. The loser is now vulnerable. The winner could kill him with a single lunge with his horns, but almost never does. Nobility? Alas, no, at least not according to Dale Lott, whose arguments are convincing. Moral scruples do not enter the calculation at all; it is simply too costly in terms of energy:

> In the final analysis, the winner does not spare his defeated rivals, he spares himself. The prolonged forewarnings, the reluctance to fight, and the generosity to losers are neither the last noble vestiges of chivalry in our time nor nature's way of exhorting humans to live on a higher ethical plane. Rather, they are carefully balanced behavioral adjustments to the social and ecological circumstances in which the competition between bulls evolved.

We (myself very much included) need to stop searching nature for lessons and simply be content with observation. It's narcissistic emotional cannibalism to do otherwise.

BLACK-TAILED PRAIRIE DOG

Cynomys ludovicianus

THE PRAIRIE DOG, of course, is not a dog as its name suggests, but a large burrowing ground squirrel whose name derives from the barkinglike sound made when one detects a ground predator such as a bobcat or coyote or an aerial predator such as a hawk or eagle. The black-tailed prairie dog from the Black Hills of South Dakota is a member of the order Rodentia, and is considered the most social of all rodents.

For many years our knowledge of these remarkable animals came from a 1955 PhD dissertation by John A. King of the University of Michigan. These plump, tawny rodents, weighing about two pounds and measuring fourteen to seventeen inches, make their own towns, which contain more than one thousand individuals and cover as much as seventy-five acres, sometimes even square miles. Their burrow entrances are surrounded by mounds one to two feet high and five to six feet across. On top of these mounds sit sentries, scanning the skies and the surrounding countryside, on the lookout for enemies. Prairie dogs have evolved eyes set high on their foreheads so that when they emerge from their burrows they can immediately see a hawk or eagle overhead.

When they do see one, they emit a sharp bark, warning the community. The call is then taken up by other prairie dogs. King claims that when the danger has passed, there is a special sound (indicating "all clear") that the prairie dog makes by throwing himself into an upright posture—a kind of defiant, joyous *Yes!*

Recently, a scholar from Arizona, Con Slobodchikoff, discovered that prairie dog calls are even more sophisticated than previously thought. Not only do they have distinct calls for different enemies, but they also have a special sound made only for human beings approaching their territory, and yet another different sound for a human male armed with a gun. Moreover, if the same man returns months later without his gun, the prairie dogs remember that he once came by with a gun, and give the warning sound for *man carrying gun*. Such complexity was never imagined possible, and even now there are many scientific skeptics who find the idea of such sophisticated communication unsettling.

In the nineteenth century prairie dog towns were commonplace, and people imagined that they had elaborate social systems. Washington Irving wrote in 1832 that the animal "is, in fact, one of the curiosities of the Far West, about which travelers delight to tell marvelous tales, endowing him at times with something of the politics and social habits of a rational being, and giving him systems of civil government and domestic economy." Early travelers spoke of towns stretching many miles across the prairies; in Texas one such group was said to cover an area of twenty-five thousand square miles and to house four hundred million animals. At one point there must have been billions of them in the United States. This is little exaggeration, for David Costello says that he saw, in the late 1930s, a town of nearly one thousand acres in eastern Colorado. This led, needless to say, to a more or less successful campaign to completely eradicate this wonderful creature from the West. Farmers considered them nothing other than pests, and poisoned them in huge numbers.

Today the Utah prairie dog is in danger of extinction. In fact, there are probably fewer than four thousand left, and it is still *legal* to shoot them or destroy their burrows on private land. A wonderful group, Forest Guardians, is attempting, so far without success, to stop this idiocy (see its website: www.fguardians.org/library/paper.asp?nMode= 1&nLibraryID=150).

Nor are black-tailed prairie dogs completely safe. Here is what Forest Guardians says about them: "In most states across its historic range of 11 states, southern Canada, and northern Mexico, prairie dogs remain entirely unprotected from multiple threats, including shooting, poisoning, habitat destruction, and isolation and fragmentation of their remaining acreage." The group further warns: "With the decline of prairie dogs, a suite of closely associated species has also declined. These include the Endangered black-footed ferret, mountain plover (proposed for listing as Threatened), swift fox (recently removed from the Ecological Society of America candidate list), ferruginous hawk, and burrowing owl. Scientists warn of an impending wave of secondary extinctions of this suite of species and possibly others, if prairie dog decline is not reversed." (Thanks to Professor Con Slobodchikoff for bringing this site to my attention.)

The prairie dog town is divided into wards. Within wards, there is an even more significant division invisible to the naked eye: a coterie, the territory of a clan. This consists of an adult male, several adult females, and their offspring. We cannot call these male harems, since sometimes there is more than one adult male. One coterie that King observed consisted of only two old males and a barren female!

When two individuals from the same coterie meet in a prairie town, they turn their heads toward each other, open their mouths, and kiss. Even if racing back to their burrows to escape danger, they still hurriedly give each other a kiss. At other times, though, the kiss is prolonged. King tells us that "two animals will meet and kiss; then one will roll over on its back, still maintaining oral contact. Often the kiss ends with both animals rapturously stretched out side by side." It appears that this kiss is a means of identification, much the way dogs smell each other, to find out who they are, how well they know each other, and what their past relationship has been. But the kiss, King tells us, is only a preliminary. What is really aimed at is the grooming experience, engaged in by all the animals of a coterie, especially the pups, who chase adults in order to crawl under them and encourage them to groom. They nibble and paw and lick and expose their whole body to the ministrations of their grooming partner.

The odd part of prairie dog life is that this friendly state exists only among the members of each coterie, and does not extend *between* coteries. *Clans* is therefore a well-chosen designation. Prairie dogs love their own coterie but not the coterie of a neighbor. However, aggressive encounters between coteries seem to have, much like wolf aggression, a ritualized aspect (involving exposure of the anal glands under the tail). Real damage is rare. But, like wolves, prairie dogs do not have an entirely peaceful nature, as we will see.

Curiously, the grooming obsession of the pups seems to play an important role in emigration. Pups never seem to cease their desire for adult attention. Prairie dog etiquette does not permit the adults to rebuff the pups, and sometimes to escape their continuous and tireless pursuit, the adults pull up stakes and emigrate. King thinks this forbearance accounts for the extremely low morbidity rate among the young. He observed only one pup out of fifty-eight who died during the time of his observation. The pup is king in prairie dog town:

After leaving his birthplace the emergent pup meets his father and other members of the coterie and enters a pup paradise. He plays with his siblings and the other young. All the adults kiss and groom him as his mother does, and he responds to them as he does to her. He readily accepts foster mothers and may spend the night with their broods. He attempts to suckle adults indiscriminately—males as well as females. A female will submit quietly; the male gently thwarts him and grooms him instead, rolling him over on his back and running his teeth through the pup's belly fur. The pup's demands for this treatment increase as he grows. He follows the adults about, climbs on them, crawling under them, doing everything he can to entice an adult into a grooming session. Sometimes, if he fails to win attention, he may playfully jump at them, and they may enter into the game. Only on the rarest of occasions is he rebuffed by an importuned adult; seldom is he kicked or bitten or drubbed.

Which one of us would not like to be the object of such warm affection for much of the day?

But it seems that the more we learn, the more some of our ideals, or, in any event, fantasies, about the harmonious life of animals are toppled. Today the world's leading expert on the black-tailed prairie dog is Dr. John Hoogland, at the University of Maryland Appalachian Laboratory. He is the author of *The Black-Tailed Prairie Dogs: Social Life of a Burrowing Animal*. Dr. Hoogland has discovered that like other animals in their family (ground squirrels and marmots), prairie dogs are infanticidal, both males and females. The infanticidal males, however, are almost always yearlings, and males never kill their own juvenile offspring. Whereas Dr. King, years earlier, had not seen a single baby harmed, Dr. Hoogland's recent research shows that about 10 percent of all babies are killed by an adult prairie dog. However, in his investigation of another prairie dog species, the Gunnison, he did not find a single case of infanticide after watching them for seven years (which is still not proof, of course, that it never happens). How are we to account for such differences between almost identical species?

I was curious about what Dr. Hoogland considered the most important thing he had learned about prairie dogs, assuming it would have to do with infanticide. Instead, when I called him, he told me, "One of the most important things that prairie dogs have taught me is that individuals vary tremendously." So, yes, prairie dogs can kill helpless infants. But not all do. Is it a matter of choice? I am sure no biologist would agree that it is, but I wonder.

We will probably never have a complete understanding of prairie dogs or of any other animal, including the individual human animal. Had you asked somebody, even a zoologist, fifty years ago about prairie dog fathers he would have looked at you blankly. But because of people like Dr. King and Dr. Hoogland this is now a valid field of study. The future will bring many treasures, I am sure.

BONOBO

Pan paniscus

THIS EXTRAORDINARY PRIMATE, known previously as a pygmy chimp, was only "discovered" in 1929. A German anatomist was looking at a skull in the colonial Belgian Tervuren Museum and realized that it was the skull of an adult, but much smaller than was customary. He named it *Pan paniscus*. The term *bonobo* was applied because somebody along the way thought this was the Zairian word for "chimp." It is not. In any event, the name stuck, and is now the preferred term.

The difference between the "common" chimpanzee and the bonobo was recognized by two German researchers, Eduard Tratz and Heinz Heck, from observations they made at the Hellabrunn Zoo. As they put

it, memorably, "The bonobo is an extraordinarily sensitive, gentle creature, far removed from the demoniacal *Urkraft* [primitive force] of the
adult chimpanzee."

Bonobos are physically different from chimps: They have relatively
small heads, delicate hands, pink lips, small ears, and wide nostrils. With
their narrow shoulders, thin necks, and slim upper bodies, they resemble human intellectuals in college.* The females have visible breasts.
Both sexes have long black hair, parted in the middle. They easily walk
upright on their long legs.

Bonobos are restricted to the swampy equatorial forests of the left
bank of the Congo River in a small region of central Zaire now known
as the Democratic Republic of the Congo. Bounded by the Zaire and
Kasai rivers, in the Cuvette Central region of the province of Equateur,
here is the second largest stretch of rain forest in the world, representing half of all remaining African rain forests, an area about the size of
Great Britain. In the past decade more than half of the bonobos have disappeared, hunted for bush meat or because of deforestation. Two recent
wars have worsened the situation, and it is not clear that bonobos will
survive at all.

The bonobo is a prince among apes. The distinguished primatologist
Frans de Waal, director of the Yerkes Regional Primate Research Center in Atlanta, has contributed most to their newfound fame and popularity, both among the general public and among animal scientists. Who
could not love this animal?

Even though they are smaller than the more muscular males, the females are dominant—meaning they have first access to food; males put
their hands out to beg from them. The males also have sharp canine
teeth missing in the females, but they display little aggression, either to
other males or among their community, and certainly not to their

---

* Humans, it has been speculated, are a neotenic species—that is, we preserve many features into adulthood that belong to childhood. For example, many human adults are extraordinarily playful. We have this in common with bonobos. Their adult voices are
shrill, like those of juveniles, and they keep their white tail tufts, which chimpanzees
lose after they are weaned. All in all, adult bonobos strike us as childlike.

young. In fact, bonobo life is centered on the little ones. They are not punished, and they are refused nothing.

What has perhaps most captured the human imagination is the sex life of bonobos. Perhaps no other animal displays such overt, carefree, joyous sexuality. Whenever things get tense, sex is called into play. Not counting humans, I don't believe any other animal besides the bonobo engages in tongue kissing. Bonobos peer into the faces of their partners with great intensity, gauging the degree of their pleasure and involvement. Sexual relations are as frequent between two females (known quaintly by primatologists as "GG rubbing"—genito-genital) as between the sexes. In zoos, bonobos initiate sex once every one and a half hours—more frequently than any other animal, I believe.

All this sexuality solves two major problems: aggression and the premature death of children. Whereas infanticide by males could well account for nearly 40 percent of infant deaths among chimpanzees, there has never been recorded a *single instance* of infanticide among bonobos. Why? Probably because when sex is so freely offered and engaged in, no male can ever be certain who his children are, and it would not be in his genetic interest to kill a child for fear it could be his own. Moreover, whenever aggression risks raising its ugly head, sex replaces anger, and aggression vanishes. It's brilliant!

In all the years that bonobos have been observed in Wamba and Lomako, no example of murder has ever been seen, even though large groups—sometimes as many as a hundred individuals—provide the perfect soil for internecine struggle. Freely offered, copious sexuality is one reason. Another is the gentle upbringing. And yet another is the female dominance over males, via coalitions. I suggest a fourth reason. The person who has done the most research on bonobos, Takayoshi Kano, has noted that when he was observing food gathering, he saw that the animals were spending an inordinate amount of time digging up earthworms in the swamps. They did this for hours, with meager results, often no more than a single earthworm every half hour. Could it be, wondered Kano, in a piece of inspired anthropomorphism, that they were engaging in a leisure activity—simply digging for the sheer amusement of it? Like people on vacation, it seemed a purely recreational activity.

I also wonder whether the largely frugivorous diet of the bonobos contributes to their peacefulness. While they are not strictly vegetarian, animal foods make up only about 1 percent of bonobos' diets. The more warlike chimpanzee eats a great deal more meat. Chimpanzees form hunting teams to kill monkeys and even other chimpanzees. So far as is known, such an activity is absent in bonobo society.

When chimpanzees meet other troops on their border, it mostly results in the equivalent of war. Not so bonobos. On the contrary, after a suitable *getting-to-know-you* period the bonobos begin grooming one another, and then have sex. And whereas chimpanzees make a nest and sleep alone, bonobos congregate and work together on the communal nests.

Sympathy and sensitivity to the suffering of others have also been noticed in bonobos. One of the most striking examples comes from a bonobo named Kuni at England's Twycross Zoo. When a starling in the cage hit the glass of her enclosure and lay stunned, Kuni picked up the bird with one hand and climbed into the highest tree, carefully unfolded the wings, spread them wide open, then flung the bird into the air and freedom.

For years, there was a taboo against killing bonobos, based on an old belief that they were human ancestors. But in the 1980s that lifesaving taboo disappeared. Today there are probably no more than between ten thousand and twenty-five thousand bonobos in all Zaire. There are about one hundred in zoos around the world.

I cannot do better than end with a quote from the preeminent researcher Frans de Waal:

Who could have imagined a close relative of ours in which female alliances intimidate males, sexual behavior is as rich as ours, different groups do not fight but mingle, mothers take on a central role, and the greatest intellectual achievement is not tool use but sensitivity to others? Any scientist proposing such a list of traits as even remotely likely in a member of our immediate lineage would have been laughed out of the halls of academe in the 1960s! Today, more people may be prepared to accept this description—all the more so since we are not talking about a mere supposition but about actual observations. Nonetheless, it will undoubtedly take an entire generation of students of human evolution for the implications to fully sink in.

BOTTLENOSE DOLPHIN

Tursiops truncatus

I ONCE PARTICIPATED IN several swim-with-dolphin programs in Florida, which I now regret. It became apparent to me that the dolphins did not want to swim with us. It was a job for them, they were paid in food, and they were indifferent. And it could not possibly be healthy for them. Although we were told they were free to come and go, that was simply untrue. What on earth would induce them to do this work if they were not forced to?

In the Florida Keys I visited the pioneer of dolphin-assisted therapy, Betsy Smith. What I saw was impressive, but no more so than any other pet-oriented child psychotherapy. I was glad to learn that in 1992 she stopped all dolphin-assisted therapy research, saying, "Perhaps it is time for us to leave the dolphins alone."

There are also dangers to humans in these programs. It is not that dolphins are vicious, but they are wild animals. They have never been domesticated and are unpredictable. They often give fair warning, but not everyone is familiar with their system of so doing. Humans who ignore several warnings can be severely injured. These are powerful animals, after all, who can easily dispose of a large shark. We have the myth that they are always happy. In fact, they are not; it is simply part of their physiognomy that they appear to us to always be smiling.

Some juveniles and a few older dolphins do sometimes seem to want to be around humans, but the better their acquaintance with large numbers of humans, the less they seem to desire our company. In New Zealand the bottlenose dolphins in the Bay of Islands are avoiding swimmers more and interacting with them less. There are too many people out there wanting a piece of the action. On the other hand, several researchers (see Christina Lockyer and Monica Muller in *Between Species*) have noted that dolphins seem to like playing with dogs as much as humans do, and are fascinated by them.

It is not always easy to tell male dolphins from the females, since they are mostly the same size, the genitalia are ventral and internal, and the mammary slits are often hard to see. Females may live for more than fifty years, and males more than forty. The young will attempt to nurse up to five years of age, and some lactating females have been accompanied by calves of seven to nine years. In one interesting case an anemic eleven-year-old male, the size of a four-year-old, was observed nursing. Obviously, he needed the extra nutrition. Despite the good care, nearly half of all calves die before weaning. The main predators are sharks.

But dolphins are no angels, either. They are one of the few mammals known to direct lethal, nonpredatory aggression at another mammalian species, in this case the harbor porpoise. What purpose this serves is not clear. They do not eat porpoises—is it that they are competing for food? Or is there some ancient enmity we do not know about? Another fairly recent discovery that is somewhat disillusioning is that male dolphins form coalitions in order to coerce females into mating when it is clear that the females do not want to copulate. Sometimes the female escapes, and sometimes she swims away with no objection from the males. Dolphin researcher Kathleen Dudzinski tells of a fascinating episode ("Letting Dolphins Speak: Are We Listening?" in *Between Species*) when two adult male dolphins were attacking a subadult female. She was bleeding, and whistling repeatedly. In the water at the time were two researchers and two people who wanted to swim with the dolphins. To the re-searchers, it sounded like she was calling for help. Suddenly, she swam directly into the circle formed by the humans, and the males kept their distance. For the moment she was safe. Had the male dolphins pursued her, the humans could have been severely hurt. The swimmers thought it was all fun and games, but the two researchers recognized what was happening. Although they didn't use the word *rape*, I think this is what was about to happen.

It is not the only time that dolphins have come to humans for assis-tance: Rachel Smolker tells about Wilf Mason, who "described an in-cident where a strange adult dolphin who was clearly in trouble came into the shallow at Monkey Mia and approached him. She had a large fishing hook lodged in her mouth. This dolphin, unaccustomed to human contact, permitted Wilf to remove the hook with a pair of pliers."

When I went to visit the dean of dolphin researchers, Dr. Ken Nor-ris, at the University of California–Santa Cruz, I was appalled to see the animals he was studying kept in small holding tanks. This was in the 1980s. Had there been no progress? While Norris's research holds up, the ethical issues still jumped out at me. We had a tense conversation. For all his real intelligence, Norris could not see what any grade school child sees today: that there is something just plain wrong with putting sensitive fellow animals in prison for research purposes. People who work with animals in laboratories are simply not prepared to recognize the extent to which the environment is artificial and limited—and how everything they learn can be questioned as being due to the artifice of the confinement.

Moreover, as we now realize, capturing a dolphin or a whale is hardly a simple, straightforward procedure with few consequences. A recent study found that the risk of mortality for dolphins increases six-fold in the month or so immediately following capture. Dolphins in cap-tivity die at the same rate that they do in the wild, and this *despite* food, protection from predators, veterinary care, and other so-called advan-tages. You would expect them to live much longer, yet they don't—

something that those in favor of holding captive dolphins have never ex-plained or addressed. Clearly captivity, both the process and the state, is not good for the health of dolphins. Naomi Rose, in her hard-hitting article "Sea Change," points out that no captive orca has ever lived past about thirty-five. To be imprisoned in a barren concrete box is clearly harmful. These quarters are the equivalent of human slums, especially if you consider that these same animals had the entire ocean as their play-ground.

It is not that I believe we have learned nothing from laboratory ex-periments. That would be a ridiculous position. Everyone by now knows the famous experiments of Karen Pryor, who trained dolphins to do "something new." At first flexible-minded rough-tooth dolphins did what she asked only by chance, but soon they got the idea and under-stood that if they wanted a reward, they would have to do something that had not been previously rewarded. But to be very churlish, what does knowing of this ability achieve either for us or for the dolphins? It is like "discovering" America—excuse me, it was already inhabited. The dolphins knew they could do this. We behave with them like eter-nal tourists: "Wow, that's amazing!" Since my special interest is the emotions of animals, I have often had to ask what we can possibly learn about an animal who is taken out of the natural environment that would not be in some sense artificial. Joanna McIntyre Varawa (of *Mind in the Waters* fame) put it well: "Learning from captive animals is much like learning about humanity by watching men in the exercise yard at San Quentin."

It has been estimated that the sensitivity of a dolphin's echolocation capacity is ten times greater than that of the most highly advanced elec-tronic sonar equipment available today. We have long believed that dol-phins use this sophisticated apparatus to study us, much as we use what we have available to study them. This suits our narcissism: "They are as curious about us as we are about them." True, once in a while, a wild dolphin seems driven to understand more about these curious creatures on the surface of the ocean, but most of the time dolphins are going about the business of their lives without much concern for us. They are not waiting to warn us about catastrophes we have created for us and for them. We have to be our own early-warning system. Perhaps, though, when (and if) we can avert the disasters looming over humanity, we can establish some different kind of bond with these deeply intelligent creatures that have lived peacefully for millions of years in the waters of our shared earth.

BOWERBIRDS

THE AUSTRALIAN AND NEW GUINEAN bowerbirds construct such intricate and elaborately decorated bowers that many people find it hard to believe a bird has built them. In fact, the first European naturalist to find a bower, Odoardo Beccari, believed it of human rather than avian origin. The bower of the bowerbird is not a nest, but rather a site for courtship displays. There are two types of bowers, avenue bowers (with parallel rows of vertical twigs) and maypole bowers, in which the twigs crisscross and interlock around a small sapling. The male bird dances around this maypole, and as he dances he raises and fans out a brilliant orange circular crest on his head. Some maypole builders, such as the gardener bowerbird (*Ambylornis* spp.), build a bower by neatly interweaving sticks against a sapling on the floor of a mountain rain forest. Around the tower he places a kind of saucer made of moss. The towers are large, with roofs and internal chambers. The courtyards are made of moss and are decorated with blue beetle wings, fruits, spider silk, and fresh flowers—changed daily for months on end.

The striped gardener bowerbird (*Ambylornis subalaris*) builds a circular hut of twigs with a dome roof. He leaves a large opening at one side, the "forecourt," which he decorates with colorful fruits and fresh flowers that are also changed daily. Colors play an important role for many bowerbirds. The male satin bowerbird (*Ptilonrhynchus violaceus*) selects shiny blue objects that resemble the lilac-blue color of his eyes and the sheen of his glossy blue-black plumage. Gerald Borgia, one of the leading researchers of bowerbirds, has pointed out that "the male prunes the leaves above the platform, apparently to allow sunlight to illuminate the platform. The display of shiny blue objects, which are relatively uncommon, and their placement on a yellow background suggests an attempt to give an unambiguous and highly visible signal." A brown gardener bowerbird, when replacing flowers in his bower with fresh ones, carefully inspects each blossom as he puts it in place, shifting its position if not satisfied. Many observers have commented on the birds' aesthetic sense as similar to our own.

Avenue builders actually *paint* their bowers: The male—taking a bit of fruit pulp, bark, chewed green vegetable material, or charcoal in his bill—stimulates the flow of saliva and applies the secretion with his beak to the inner walls of the avenue, staining them a different color. Some birds (satin bowerbirds) use a chewed dried hoop pine needle. Nobody knows what the function of bower painting is. Could it possibly be a substitute for courtship feeding, or perhaps identification of the individual male owning the bower, since the females taste the paint? It seems to me the bowerbirds must derive some aesthetic pleasure from the bright colors. Darwin thought so, too: In *The Descent of Man* he wrote, "If female birds had been incapable of appreciating the beautiful colours, the ornaments, and voices of their male partners, all the labour and anxiety exhibited by them in displaying their charms before the females would have been thrown away; and this it is impossible to admit."

In bowerbirds there seems an inverse relationship between the complexity of the bower and the colorfulness of the male bird, as if it would require simply too much energy to excel at both. The bowerbirds who make the most elaborate bowers are exceedingly plain looking! Species with sexual dichromatism (colorful males, drab females) build relatively simple bowers, while the males of the plain-colored species, in which the sexes are colored alike, build larger, more elaborate, and highly decorated bowers. The greatest painters, the most aesthetically sensitive, the birds who collect the most beautiful shells and build the most elaborate towers and tend the finest gardens, are the dullest-colored bowerbirds.

No doubt this was noticed for years without anyone thinking about it in depth, until E. Thomas Gilliard, the late curator of birds at the American Museum of Natural History, made a series of trips between 1948 and 1964 to New Guinea. An astute observer and fine ornithologist, he noticed something extraordinarily simple, but profound: "These objects have in effect become externalized bundles of secondary sexual characteristics that are psychologically but not physically connected with the males. The transfer also has an important morphological effect: once colorful plumage is rendered unimportant, natural selection operates in the direction of protective coloration and the male tends more and more to resemble the female." Gilliard went on to suggest that the bower building has embedded in it many aspects of nest building. The wall of sticks, the lining of grass, even the way the male places egg-sized berries or pebbles near the center of the basketlike structure resemble what happens when a bird builds a nest. (But Dr. Borgia tells me, "Most avenue building species do not place egglike objects in the bower avenue. The only one I have seen with really large objects is the yellow-breasted bowerbird, which uses aqua-colored fruit.")

Natural jewelry replaces brilliant feathers. The bower replaces the nest. The bird becomes the lonely eccentric artist, not expected to participate in daily household activities: He does not build a true nest; he does not take care of the kids. He is an artist, lost in his own world. He has more direct benefits, too: He need not call attention to himself with his brilliant feathers, thereby avoiding making himself the target of predators. He is inconspicuous except when he is painting in his courtyard (though Borgia points out there are some brightly plumed bowerbirds who live alongside dull ones).

How did these remarkable behaviors evolve? The males and females live apart most of the year. The males, during the breeding season, spend all their time at their bowers, in their courts (called arenas), where they await the females. These birds have no true pair-bond, and the males play no part whatever in building or defending the actual nest or in rearing the young. But they do court. Arena behavior is found in any number of birds around the world. The courtship behavior, however, is in sharp contrast with the behavior of the other 99 percent of the world's birds.

BUTTERFLIES

W E LIKE THEM BECAUSE they are beautiful. We are intrigued by the metamorphosis they undergo, from a caterpillar into a butterfly, from a creature bound to the earth to one who sprouts wings. It lends itself, of course, to metaphors, for there is nobody alive who has not (literally) dreamed of gaining the ability to fly. I think, too, the fact that their lives are so ephemeral fascinates us. Some species of butterflies live a very short time. One species studied in Costa Rica, for example, can expect to live for about two days. No adult butterfly lives for more than a year. Monarchs, with their long migrations to Mexico, during which they can travel nearly two thousand miles, live six months. On average, butterflies live two weeks as an adult.

The stages in the life of a butterfly never cease to intrigue humans. Think of it: An adult butterfly leaves an egg on the ground near a favored plant, or attaches it to the plant. The tiny egg of some species (they come in all shapes) has a yolk not unlike a chicken egg. It contains a small larva who eats his or her way out of the egg (hatches) after what can be as long as several months, but is usually about ten days. Out crawls a caterpillar (also called a larva). The caterpillar lives off the leaves of the tree, and often will eat only from that one tree. Life is precarious, which is the reason you see brightly colored caterpillars such as the monarch. This is a warning to other animals: *I am poisonous*. They are cyanogenetic, too: They eat leaves from a host tree that contains the same toxins. They protect themselves in other fascinating ways as well. The best known is camouflage. They can be as green as their host plant, and barely visible. Or, like the tiger swallowtail, they may resemble bird droppings that nobody wants to eat. Best of all are the fascinating eyespots on the caterpillars (even more noticeable on the wings of the adult butterfly), which serve to startle predators, or give the impression that they are being watched. If caterpillars survive their many enemies, the most they can expect to live is generally two weeks to a month. They will grow to thirty thousand times their weight before they pupate. If a nine-pound human baby grew at this rate, by adulthood he or she would weigh 240,000 pounds.

When caterpillars have reached their final stage of growth, they make a chrysalis, which they suspend with a silk thread. This is a kind of hardened case, an integument inside of which the metamorphosis takes place. The integument is often sculptured and brightly colored, as with the monarch butterfly, whose chrysalis is soft green with gold spots. The caterpillar *becomes* the chrysalis, or pupa. *Pupation* refers to the stage during which the insect is transformed into the adult butterfly. The metabolic changes taking place inside the chrysalis are nothing less than extraordinary. What emerges is the imago, or adult form, the butterfly herself!

Now begins the process of finding a mate. (Some butterflies dispense with this stage altogether: Species of *Heliconius* butterflies mate while still in the chrysalis. The female emits a pheromone, and the male is with her before she emerges!) How are mates chosen? Color surely plays a role. Kendra Robertson at the University of Buffalo has also found that females are attracted to the "sparkle" created by the ultraviolet reflectivity of the pupils, the white circles at the center of eyespots. The actual mating can be fleeting, or it can last a whole day. The latest research by Japanese scientists shows that males have light receptors at the end of their abdomens connected to their sexual organs. When the photo receptors are darkened, it signals the time to transfer sperm to the female. What he gives, during copulation, is his spermatophore, a packet of nutrients, salts, and sperm. It is a gift, a big one, for it can weigh as much as half his weight.

I love the idea that certain butterflies suffer from myrmecophily, an excessive love of ants. Actually, it isn't excessive. The larvae of some butterflies—many of the bright blue ones, for example—have a honey gland that ants milk, much as they do aphids. So they tend the larvae, protect them, drink from them, and then let them go. It seems to do no harm to the larvae. The ants even protect the larvae from their natural predators (mostly birds), often carrying them into their nests and providing them a safe place to pupate. They don't do it because they like them or find them beautiful, of course, but because they are an energy bar for them.

This raises another interesting question: Do butterflies find butterflies beautiful? Well, that's how they find mates. But do they, then, respond to the brilliant colors? The question of color vision in other animals is not yet fully developed; much remains to be discovered. Many animals definitely see color, and some see more colors than we do—brightly colored parrots, for example, or hummingbirds. Butterflies, it would appear, have the widest visual range of any animal. Like many birds, they see into the ultraviolet spectrum. Since younger female butterflies have less ultraviolet than older individuals, males often prefer them. Because butterflies often lay most of their eggs in the first quarter of their short life, choosing a younger female butterfly is a male's strategy to ensure his genetic immortality. You would think, though, that he need do nothing more than stand by the chrysalis, since females can mate on the day they emerge!

Every butterfly enthusiast has favorites. A recent convert, let me offer a few of mine: The lilac tree nymph (*Sallya amulia*) is noted for her shimmering upper sides. In *The Butterflies of South Africa*, D. A. Swanepoel described a migration of thousands of these butterflies as looking "for all the world like a snowstorm of silvery blue flakes." The krishna peacock (*Papilio krishna*), which I saw on the Himalayan steppes of Nepal, is one of the world's most beautiful swallowtail butterflies. The orange-red eyespots on the hind wings of this large butterfly look like those on a peacock. Then there are the strange luna moths (*Actias luna*), with their delicate antennae and similar-looking eyespots and long flowing tails on their hind wings. These huge green-and-yellow animals live only a week. When the night-flying male finds the female who has released her airborne pheromone he remains mated to her until the next evening. The female lays her eggs the next day. Finally, there is the spectacular reddish brown *Rothschildia cincta* moth (also called the girdled silk moth) from Arizona and Mexico, whose cocoons were used as rattles and traded as currency by several Native American tribes, including the Yaqui and Tarahuamara. (For more information, see www.insects.org/ced4/peigler.html.) The adults take no food at all. For Native Americans, these animals symbolize birth, death, and the soul. Even looking at photographs of them, it is easy to see why.

I am completely opposed to collecting. The main scientific organization, the Lepidopterists' Society (www.lepsoc.org), however, is not. Officially, this group describes the collection of Lepidoptera as "a means of introducing children and adults to awareness and study of their natural environment." Isn't there a better way to celebrate nature than killing spectacular creatures? How about taking your kids for a walk through the woods instead?

CAMELS

Camelus dromedarius and *C. bactrianus*

I N EGYPT I ONCE TOOK A CAMEL RIDE into the desert. It was not easy
for me to sit, and I was certain I would fall off at any moment. You
are much higher up than on a horse, and the camel seems supremely
indifferent to you in ways that horses do not. But I suppose this was
simply my lack of familiarity with the animal. When most people think
of camels, they think of smelly animals who spit. In Egypt the smell was
there, and I learned that it comes from a sticky substance on the back of
the neck exuded by male camels at certain times of the year. As for the
spitting, that's real, too, and seems to have evolved as a defense mechanism: Camels spit a foul-smelling substance that comes from their stomachs when they are harassed or in other ways annoyed. It is an effective
strategy.

Most people do not realize that the African and Asian camels, the
one-humped dromedary (also called the Arabian camel) and the two-
humped Bactrian camel (a small remnant of the wild Bactrian camel is
still found wild, it appears, in the Mongolian steppes), are part of
the same family as the two South American domesticated camelids, the
llama and the alpaca, as well as the wild and endangered vicuña and

the wild guanaco. Like the horse, the camel evolved originally in North America (including Alaska) some forty million years ago, and migrated to Asia (as well as South America) across the Bering Strait, when there was dry land linking the two continents in the late Pliocene or early glaciation times, only two to three million years ago. The earliest known ancestral camel was no larger than a hare.

Of the fourteen million camels in the world today, some 90 percent are dromedaries, with 63 percent of all camels living in Africa. The Bactrian camel which formerly had a vast range, is now confined to parts of Afghanistan, Iran, Turkey, Russia, China, and Mongolia. With its habitat in the unique, fragile desert ecosystems in the Gobi and Gashun Gobi deserts in northwest China and southwest Mongolia, the wild Bactrian camel (*Camelus bactrianus ferus*) is critically endangered. There may be no more than six hundred existing in the wild, making it even rarer than the giant panda. (See www.wildcamels.com for more information.)

Domestication of the two species of Old World camels does not seem to have led to any significant modification. Camels lead a life that has been little modified from their wild state, for they are neither stabled nor penned. This being so, it is odd that there are so few wild camels. The claim that there are wild Bactrian camels on the Mongolian side of the Altai Mountains is based primarily on a single photograph, seen in F. E. Zeuner's book *A History of Domesticated Animals* (page 339), where a herd of camels is racing away. You can discern in the photo the two humps in rudimentary form, so that at least this physical modification has taken place under domestication. It is generally conceded that wild dromedaries have not existed for the last two thousand years, probably because they are so valuable to the people where they are indigenous that they are never left alone.

According to Zeuner, "their low intelligence renders impossible any training comparable with that given to the horse." Possibly there is another explanation. After all, every single horse who eventually is used for riding has to be "broken"—not true for camels. Moreover, it is much easier for a camel to go feral and survive in the wild than it is for a horse, a relative rarity.

The bad temper of many camels is legendary, though this does not make it true. It is claimed that males, when rutting, even if castrated, will sometimes fight to the death. But Hilde Gauthier-Pilters, who observed camels for years in the western Sahara among the Reguibat, the only remaining pure nomads, saw but a single serious fight between two males, and neither was killed. She did not see any fights between female camels or between males and females. Then again, what have camels to be good-tempered about? After all, often their reward for taking an entire family across an otherwise impassable desert is to be slaughtered upon arrival, long before their normal life span of forty years. None is ever allowed to live that long.

It must also be remembered that camels would never have been domesticated in the first place (think of zebras, whose bad temper kept them wild) except that they are remarkably placid. No doubt this comes from the fact that in their native state they had virtually no predators, and were therefore unaware of the slavery they were about to be subjected to when introduced to humans.

It has been claimed that camels can go up to ten months without water if they are not working. This may sound impossible, but I have checked with several sources, and it is indeed true. The legendary physiologist Knut Schmidt-Nielsen found that in the Sahara grazing camels are not given water at all during winter, and that some who "had not drunk for as much as two months refused water when we offered it to them." When they do drink, they can drink up to thirty gallons in a short time, even though they are simply rehydrating and not storing water.

They are well adapted to the desert. They eat thorn trees avoided by all other animals. Their nostrils can be closed to keep out blowing sand, while long lashes protect their sensitive eyes. Their humps store fat so they can go for long periods without eating. It had long been thought that camels stored water in their humps; how else, it was wondered, could they go so long without water? The hump seemed the logical place for the vast reservoir needed for long desert treks. However, the hump only stores fat, not water. The reason camels can go without water for so long, discovered only fairly recently, is that they sweat very little, even in the hottest temperature, and have the ability to reuse nitrogenous waste by returning urea to the stomach via the blood-stream and liver. In other words, they pee little and infrequently.

When camels are lost they will head instinctively to the nearest well, which they can sense long before a human can. An Arab proverb says that a foal knows the well where her mother came to drink before she gave birth to her. It is not clear how they can find their own home range again over vast stretches of trackless desert, but they do. Nomads will not provide water to the camels who arrive, because if they were given water they would wander away again. Gauthier-Pilters comments on how distressing she found it to watch these thirsty camels waiting next to a well for days without being allowed to drink. Left unguarded for a few weeks, camels seem to forget their former association with humans, and are difficult to approach.

A word should be said about the camel in Australia, for Australia contains the second-largest expanse of arid and semiarid lands in the world, a place most suitable for camels. And indeed, camels have been there as long as the first European settlement on the continent in the early nineteenth century. Moreover, while feral dromedaries are almost unknown anywhere else, they are common in Australia. Officially clas-sified as "vermin," they are shot on sight. As geographer Tom McKnight puts it, the presence of the camel in Australia "is acknowledged almost universally by no other form of recognition than a soft-nosed bullet." Considering how much humans owe camels, and what gentle, forbear-ing animals they are, this breaks my heart.

CHEETAH

Acinonyx jubatus

C HEETAHS ARE KNOWN TO MOST because they are the world's fastest land mammal, reaching speeds of nearly seventy miles an hour for short periods. From a standing start, the cheetah reaches a speed of fifty-five miles an hour in two seconds. Among those who know them, adjectives often used to describe cheetahs include *elegant*, *lithe*, even *friendly*. Cheetahs have never posed any kind of threat to humans; I haven't heard of a single case of a cheetah attacking a person.

So unwarlike is their behavior that cheetahs are prey for lions, leopards, and even hyenas. They lack powerful jaws or fanglike canines. Only their speed protects them. Female cheetahs with cubs, who stay with their mother for at least a year, are particularly vulnerable. (A female generally has up to six cubs, but while other large cats have only four or six teats, cheetahs have twelve—perhaps in recognition of the mortality rate for the cubs, which can be as high as 90 percent over the first two years.) Perhaps the reason zoologists speak of their "retiring" nature is that even in a hunt, prey who stand their ground or remain motionless are unlikely to be attacked. Careful of their physical integrity, cheetahs do not like taking chances. And when attacked by a larger animal, they "moan" much the way we do, as if calling for help from their mother.

Female cheetahs are excellent mothers. For their first two weeks, her helpless newborns remain hidden in one spot with the mother. After that, as a protective measure, she moves them to a new den every few days. When her litter is large, the mother often returns to a former nesting spot to make certain she has not left anyone behind. One mother whose cubs were killed in a forest fire stayed at the nest site for four long days, either hoping in vain her babies would return or mourning their loss. But danger is everywhere and, on average over their lifetime, females in the Serengeti manage to rear only 1.7 cubs to independence. The greatest threat is from lions, who regularly seek out and kill cheetahs' cubs. The lions rarely eat them (though the mother later may), and I'm at a loss to understand the rationale behind these killings. Perhaps the lions are simply trying to lessen the competition for food later on.

In general, these beautiful animals are timid, retiring, secretive, and shy, quite difficult to approach. Nevertheless, their association with humans goes back thousands of years. A silver ornament found in a Scythian burial site dated between 700 and 300 BCE in the Caucasus depicts a cheetah wearing a collar. And during the Mogul occupation of India (between the thirteenth and sixteenth centuries) emperors used them for hunting. Akbar the Great kept at least a thousand cheetahs in his stables for hunting at any given time (nine thousand altogether over his forty-nine-year reign). Cheetahs were evidently plentiful in India back then. Today they are extinct there, as they are just about everywhere they once lived but Africa. There are a mere two hundred cheetahs still in Iran. The last cheetah in Israel was seen in 1956. Emperor Leopold I of Hungary hunted deer with the big cats in the Vienna Woods. The last emperor of Ethiopia, Haile Selassie, also had cheetahs roaming his palace grounds.

To what extent were these hunting companions tame? Certainly cheetahs did not choose to hunt with humans the way that some dolphins in the Amazon are known to have. These cats were captured as adults and kept in pens with a hood over their eyes, which must be extremely disorienting to an animal so dependent on sight. I would think, too, that it completely broke the spirit of these free-living animals. Starved, they eventually accepted food to sustain life and became somewhat habituated to human contact. Taken out to hunt, the hood was only removed when prey was sighted. Why the big cats did not then run away remains puzzling.

Certainly cheetahs were never good candidates for domestication. These cats have been prized by the aristocracy as hunting "companions" (I use the word very loosely here), rather than "pets" (yet another loose word!). Yet Joy Adamson (of *Born Free* fame) claims in her book about Pippa the cheetah—whom she lived with for years (*The Spotted Sphinx*)—that "cheetahs are the easiest of all wild cats to tame," and she should know something about this topic. (On the other hand, she also believed Pippa was telepathic.)

As far as is known, until 1956, not a single cheetah in captivity gave birth to viable young. (Akbar's son, Emperor Jahangir of India, claimed that once a litter of cubs was born in his palace, though he also said they did not survive.) It's unclear why it has proven so difficult to induce male cheetahs to mate. Perhaps the problem lies with the females, who might not look kindly on having their choices narrowed this way. For both males and females there seems to be a psychological block operating: "This is not the way we do things at home." Although there have been sporadic breeding successes, by and large the population in zoos is not self-sustaining. Most cheetahs in zoos are caught in the wild, a practice morally abhorrent by any standards, even those of the zoo community. This way lays extinction. (Might it even be possible that Akbar's huge captured cheetah menagerie was ultimately responsible for the disappearance of the cheetah from India?) There have been notable successes: South Africa's De Wildt Cheetah Breeding Centre claims to have bred 750 cheetahs over the years. Some are destined to be returned to the wild, but the website (www.dewildt.org.za) suggests that many are exported to game parks and zoos.

There are probably no more than nine to twelve thousand cheetahs alive in the world. The largest single population (twenty-five hundred, less than half of what it was ten years ago) is to be found in Namibia, in extreme southwestern Africa. In 1991 Laurie Marker co-founded the Cheetah Conservation Fund (CCF) with her husband, Daniel Kraus, to protect the cats. Namibia is apparently the only country in the world to include protection of the environment *and* native wildlife in its constitution. CCF has tried to find imaginative ways to keep farmers happy by reducing conflicts with cheetahs, for example, providing them with livestock-guarding dogs—a great success in keeping cheetahs away from vulnerable lambs, goats, and calves. Imagine a world where such splendid animals lived with us in peace, perhaps even in tolerant friendship. If we are to save this planet's endangered animals, what's needed are original thinking and creative strategies like those of the Cheetah Conservation Fund.

I once played with a three-legged adolescent male cheetah at the animal refuge of Tippi Hedren (the actress who starred in *The Birds*). This gregarious big cat astonished me by rubbing against my leg much like a tame house cat. He *was* tame, and acted as an excellent goodwill ambassador to visitors. Imagine my surprise when I heard the cheetah purring so loudly it sounded like a sports-car engine revving up. If you visit my website, www.jeffreymasson.com, you can see a photograph of me with this sociable cheetah. It is indeed a remarkable experience to play with an animal this size!

CHICKEN

Gallus gallus domesticus

W ITH US FROM ALMOST THE VERY BEGINNING of domestication, chickens are among the few domestic animals that can
be found worldwide. Yet while humans have shared their
lives with these marvelous birds for thousands of years, most have a
poor understanding of them. Why should these animals have become
subject to that all-purpose insult—*birdbrain*? It's true that, unlike mammals, birds do not have a neocortex, the region of the brain believed to
be the seat of higher mental processing. But different need not mean
less, and we should be cautious when comparing the intelligence of different species. Biologists Page Smith and Charles Daniel have said that
the brain of a chicken "represents to even the most capable and san-
guine neurophysiologist a structure of almost unimaginable complexity." As to their behavior, the more I observe the seemingly lowly
chicken, the more fascinated and intrigued I become.

To this day nobody is certain why the rooster crows at dawn—as
well as three times during the night. The evening crowing seems to be
an attempt to call the flock together to roost in safety in trees. As for
crowing early in the morning (at least forty-five minutes before what we
consider to be dawn), it must be said that, with his superior vision, a

rooster perceives the light long before a human can. Many species of birds, including chickens, can see well into the infrared spectrum, something that allows them to detect polarized light, and therefore direction, with greater sensitivity than humans. They see into the ultraviolet spectrum as well. Many birds are also able to hear and discriminate low-frequency sounds, far below the human range of detection. It is now thought that this may be how migrating birds are able to find their direction, perhaps using the sounds of ocean surf or wind passing around and through mountain ranges.

Karen Davis, in her excellent book *Prisoned Chickens Poisoned Eggs*, points out that each rooster can recognize the crow of at least thirty other roosters:

> If a rooster spots danger, he sends up a shrill cry. The other roosters echo the cry. Thereupon, the whole flock will often start up a loud, incessant, drum-beating chorus with all members facing the direction of the first alarm, or scattering for cover in the opposite direction. When it looks safe again, an "all clear?" query goes out from the rooster, first one, followed by the others, in their various new places. Eventually the bird who first raised the alarm sends up the "all clear" crow, and a series of locator crows confirms where every other rooster and his sub-flock are at this point.

F. E. Zeuner, the great historian of domestication, points out that—unlike mammals—we know little about the domestication of birds in general: "Being capable of flight, and on the whole extremely cautious, contacts or overlaps of their environments with those of man are few." Could it have come about through imprinting? The chicken is part of the same family as the wild jungle fowl. If, long ago, one of these wild birds were to abandon her eggs in the vicinity of human habitation, the chicks emerging from the eggs might easily see a human and be genetically programmed to believe they had found their mother. Konrad Lorenz, who won the Nobel Prize and is considered the founder of ethology, is usually credited with discovering imprinting. In fact, he

simply named it. The phenomenon was certainly known to our Neo-
lithic ancestors.

The Dutch ethologist J. P. Kruijt stated in his monograph about the
wild Burmese red jungle fowl, "no great differences exist in the Behaviour of domesticated and wild *Gallus gallus*." Their calls are almost
identical to those of their wild ancestors, conveying, according to Val-
erie Porter, an expert on domestic fowl, "food discoveries, alarms,
territorial claims, concern, fear, pleasure, frustration, dominance, appeasement and so on." The wild cock and the domestic rooster both
crow at dawn, but also toward the end of the day. And when he finds
something delicious to eat, he calls his favorite hen, crooning to her in a
special voice reserved for just such an occasion. The female in turn does
the same to draw the attention of her chicks to a particular food item.
You can see a rooster picking up a choice morsel, then putting it down
again, and repeating this until the hen, duly called, takes it from him.

People who live with chickens (such as Karen Davis, one of the foremost authorities on the lives of chickens and founder of United Poultry
Concerns, an organization in the United States dedicated to promoting
knowledge about them) say that they are naturally sociable; they will
gather around a human companion and stand there serenely preening
themselves or sit quietly on the ground beside someone they trust. It
may be surprising to think of a chicken showing trust, but it is a decision
that must be made on any given day, whether or not to trust a specific
person or other animal. Instinct does not help here, for the chicken's instinct is not to trust anyone who could be considered a predator.

Wild jungle fowl are notoriously shy and so nervous, it is difficult to
even see them. Nicholas and Elsie Collias, who were among the first ornithologists to study them, report, "Direct observation of predation on
jungle fowl by various animals is exceedingly rare, even by persons with
a lifetime of experience in the forest." They add, "It was our impression
that the red jungle fowl in nature is one of the wariest species of birds
in the world." To unlearn this antisocial behavior requires a great deal
of thought, based on experience.

Many writers about animals have noted that chickens form unusual
friendships. Maurice Burton, in his book *Just Like an Animal*, tells of an

aged hen, Aggie, who was almost totally blind and had become a pet, wandering as she wished about the garden. Her owners could not pluck up the courage to put her down. She was protected by a bantam (a bird from a breed of miniature chickens) and they became inseparable companions, sunbathing and dust bathing together. At night, the bantam led Aggie to her roost. And when she died, the bantam went into a depression and also died within a week. Burton asks: "Can anyone doubt that this was a real friendship, one that was not based on any kind of need, but simply of taking pleasure in one another's company?"

It is strange to think that a chicken is a *bird*. This is because, with few exceptions (penguins, for example), we tend to think of birds as flying creatures. People do not think of chickens as having the ability to fly. Chickens rarely fly. Having seen their wild ancestor the Burmese fowl, or northern red jungle fowl, all over India and Bali, I can confirm that these birds do fly, and quite well. Their evolutionary cousin, the eider duck, is one of the fastest flying of all birds. People who free chickens from incarceration in small cages invariably report that within days the hens take to roosting in trees. They retain an ancestral memory of what has given them pleasure (not to mention safety) over millions of years of evolution in much the same way that we seek out shade on a hot sunny day.

When the late professor David Wood-Gush and his colleagues released chickens on an uninhabited island off the coast of Scotland in the spring of 1975, they were surprised at what they found. While previous research on domestic chickens indicated that they were highly territorial birds, Wood-Gush found that "while the hens foraged no evidence was seen of any territoriality." Not only that, but the hens were perfectly at ease when the chicks of another hen entered their territory and became, however fleetingly, members of the family.

In the wild both hen and cock elude their enemies, form intense friendships, protect their brood, and greet the golden dawn with a burst of song. This is how chickens and roosters were meant to live. We, I believe, were meant to protect this life, and to take delight in knowing about it and from time to time catching a glimpse of the joy of pure wildness.

COCHINEAL

Dactylopius coccus

I N MY ARIZONA CHILDHOOD, I loved prickly pear, or cactus pear, fruits from a cactus called nopal (*Opuntia* spp.). I often saw a white fuzzy-looking piece of fluff on them. What I did not know was that this tentlike, silklike piece of fluff was a camouflage, a wax-based material produced by a female insect, a scale insect called cochineal. I also did not know that if you squeezed this silver insect, which is about a quarter inch long, her body fluids squirted out as a deep maroon pigment, the world's most precious dyestuff and the most potent natural red dye in the world. This bitter, astringent chemical is called carminic acid. The cochineal produces it to repel potential predators, such as ants.

The Aztecs in southern Mexico in effect domesticated the insect. On cold nights the Aztecs built fires to keep them warm, and shelters to keep them safe from heavy rains. Until, that is, they killed them by scraping them off the plant with sticks or brushes, then placing them in ovens and drying their tiny bodies in the sun. To get the best grade—called plateada, referring to a silverlike surface—the insects were left in the sun for several weeks, where they died a slow death. Wild cochineal continued to thrive on their own, but they never produced the same bright red, which turned out to be their salvation.

When the Spaniards arrived in Mexico, they were fascinated by the intense red color of the cochineal dye, brighter than anything they knew in Spain. It was the closest anyone had ever seen to Perfect Red. Next to gold, nothing that came from the New World was as valuable as these insects. Oddly enough, it was not until the early 1600s that the Spaniards learned the true source of the dye. They had thought it came from a plant. Odd, when you think that the Indians producing it knew, but the Spaniards, for whom it was produced, did not. Did the Indians make a point of not telling them? Did they, in any way, consider the insects sacred? I have not been able to find anything about this interesting topic in the literature. Be that as it may, thousands of tons of the dried insects, representing trillions of actual bodies, were exported to Spain. So valuable was the commodity that nobody but officials of the Spanish crown was allowed to visit the cochineal nopalries (where the insects lived on the nopal cactus plants) of New Spain under penalty of death. These were high stakes indeed, and the crown depended on Spanish merchants on both sides of the Atlantic, since the last thing they wanted was for any "foreigner" to discover the secret of cochineal.

Forbidden to visit Mexico, English, French, and Dutch naturalists were able to obtain the actual dried insects, but their microscopes were simply not powerful enough to discern what the substance really was. Robert Tomson, a merchant championed by the great geographer Richard Hakluyt, visited Mexico in search of the source of cochineal. He wrote that it was "a berrie that groweth upon certain bushes in the wilde fielde, which is gathered in time of the yeere, when it is ripe."

The poet John Donne, as a young sailor, was sailing with a pirate, the earl of Essex, when in 1597 he captured a Spanish ship from Havana that had fallen behind the rest of the Spanish fleet. To the jubilation of Queen Elizabeth, in the hold were twenty-seven tons of the dried insects, the largest cochineal prize of the century, valued at more than eighty thousand pounds and worth several hundred million dollars in today's currency. (At the time, a person could live comfortably in England for one year on eighty pounds.)

Sir Walter Raleigh was one of the first to promise that he would find a substitute but ultimately failed. Attention then turned to breeding the insects in Europe. By 1600 opuntia, the cactus, grew wild in Spain and in botanical gardens in Italy, Germany, the Netherlands, and England, but even Carolus Linnaeus could not obtain a live cochineal. The scientist on Captain Cook's *Endeavour*, as well as the director of the Royal Botanic Gardens at Kews and president of the Royal Society, Joseph Banks, was convinced that the insect could be raised in India and that it would enormously benefit the East India Company. After years of attempts, however, his plan failed.

Emperor Napoleon was no more successful. The Dutch introduced nopal into Java in the middle of the nineteenth century. They did not thrive there, however, primarily because of the rain. There were also problems because of the level of exploitation of the workers.

Spain's Canary Islands, with their mild sunny climate, proved a better home, as did Guatemala. In both places the nopalries survived, as did the cochineal insects living on the cacti. Between 1830 and 1845 Guatemala increased its exports twentyfold. In 1851 the country exported two million pounds.

As far as I know, in the elaborate history of cochineal, there was not a single person to have raised the question of whether it was in the best interest of the insects themselves to be burned to death and crushed into powder. It simply never occurred to anyone until vegans began asking uncomfortable questions about the animals involved. Most people do not give this much thought. Indeed, we are more or less completely ignorant of what goes into products we use on a daily basis. Our word *crimson* comes from the kermes, a wingless insect living on certain species of European live oaks, another source of dye. Imperial or true purple comes from two species of shellfish. Who knew? The people involved, of course, but they didn't care. They counted on the fact that the public at large probably did not care, either. But that is changing.

What do you do, though, when an entire economy and the livelihood of thousands of people depend on what we now regard as a cruel practice? There are no easy answers. Long after cochineal ceased to be a profitable industry, the Canary Islands were still producing immense amounts every year (as many as five or six million pounds—three times the output of the rest of the world put together), presumably because they did not know how to do anything else. It took a good long time before they were able to switch to growing bananas.

What caused the decline? Mostly the invention of synthetic dyes, though these were not without their problems as well. In any event, even though carminic acid could be synthesized in the laboratory, the process is so complex that it is not done commercially. Thus cochineal is still in use: It is found today as a coloring in yogurt, fruit juices, cheese, lipstick, rouge, eye shadow, even applesauce. Most of the cochineal used today comes from Peru. The reasons are not reassuring, however: The wages there are extraordinarily low by world standards. Amy Butler Greenfield points out that "earnings from the dyestuff are believed to support as many as 40,000 rural families, who collect the insects in the Peruvian mountains." I would not want to confront them about the cruelty involved when they can barely make ends meet. Cruelty meets cruelty.

COCONUT CRAB

Birgus latro

OCONUT, OR ROBBER, CRABS are the world's largest arthropods (a phylum that includes spiders, insects, and crustaceans). They are also the world's largest hermit crabs. (They are sometimes called "crazy crabs.") I think the biggest on record was nearly three feet long. He weighed in at thirty pounds, and could lift up to sixty-four pounds with his claws. Unlike other hermit crabs, *Birgus* does not need a gastropod shell for protection. When you are that big, you don't have many enemies (other than humans, that is).

Recently our family visited the island of Efate, in Vanuatu. Vanuatu consists of eighty-three islands and used to be called New Hebrides, a name Captain Cook gave them in 1774. I was eager to see Vanuatu's famed coconut crabs. Alas, while these once flourished there with a population in the millions, it was now impossible to find a single one in the wild. While I wandered through the colorful fruit market in the capital of Port Vila, I did see a single *Birgus*, cruelly secured with coconut rope. His colors were magnificent: bright blue, with flakes of orange, red, and purple. This beautiful creature looked so miserable, I wanted to buy him simply to release him, but he was clearly too far gone to survive. When I touched him, he made a feeble movement with his large claws, *hello* or *help* or *get me out of here*, perhaps simply *I'm still here*—though not for long, as he was meant for a meal.

Even though every guidebook tells you coconut crab is these islands' most delicious dish, I *was* pleased to see that not a single restaurant offered it. The reason? It is illegal. With the species nearly extinct, it is a serious crime to catch *Birgus* or eat one. It may be too late in the day, however. Nobody knows how many still exist, perhaps not enough for a viable population.

These amazing-looking crabs are also found on Christmas Island (named for the day of its discovery), a little island close to Java with a human population of four hundred. I don't think anybody has yet taken a census of the coconut crab inhabitants.

These fascinating crabs are coenobitids, or terrestrial hermit crabs. Their large gill chambers, surrounded by spongy tissue, must be kept moist. These act as a kind of lung, allowing them to live on land. To reproduce, however, the females must release their eggs in the sea. We don't know why all the female crabs release their eggs the same night. These eggs then hatch as planktonic pelagic larvae, called zoeas, which swim for twenty-eight days in the sea. Next, they settle as small juveniles for twenty-eight days, finding a tiny gastropod shell and moving offshore. Adolescent crabs use the discarded broken half of a coconut shell to protect their sensitive abdomen. Sometimes they're found as far as four miles inland. These giant crabs have a highly developed sense of smell, but their red stalk eyes provide poor eyesight. It has been posited that they may live thirty to sixty years, though no one knows for certain. They mature at eight years, which, as far as I know, is the longest maturation of any known arthropod. These crabs cannot swim, and if put in water they will drown in a matter of minutes. They can, however, drink salt water.

How did they come to be identified as coconut crabs? Most islanders believe the crabs deliberately climb coconut trees, cut down a coconut, then return to the ground and slowly peel the outer layer. When they reach the three eyes on the coconut, they insert a pincer into the soft one, bore a hole, and use their claws to remove the meat inside. While scientists have acknowledged this impressive feat, until recently they still questioned the crabs' "intent." Do the crabs "intend" the result— that is, do they know what they're doing? The scientific doubt stemmed from an experiment where a coconut crab was left surrounded by coconuts for weeks. The crab slowly starved to death, proving to them that the animal didn't recognize the coconut as food or didn't know how to penetrate the coconut's hard layer. It seemed not to have occurred to the experimenters that they had set up an artificial situation and that the crab may have deliberately committed suicide, or simply may have been too disoriented by captivity to know how to survive. Finally in the 1980s German biologist Holger Rumpf witnessed a coconut crab in the wild climb a coconut tree and cut down a coconut. One would think that settled the matter. But even Rumpf thought the crab cut down the coconut by accident and then—again, by accident!— found the coconut lying on the ground after it descended. To me, it makes considerably more sense to believe the act was deliberate.

When I lived in Berkeley in the 1970s and 1980s, I gave in to my daughter Simone's strong desire to have hermit crabs as pets. All the other children had them. They could be bought then in any pet store (where they have been available since the 1950s). The animals' price depended on their size. The bigger they were, the more expensive. Some reached the size of a fist.

At the pet store, Simone told the owner that she wanted to breed hermit crabs. He laughed. "So would I," he said, somewhat mysteriously. He claimed that just one person knew the secret of successful breeding and that this breeder had a lock on the market. However, I have since learned that nobody has yet succeeded in breeding hermit crabs. No one's even seen one mate! They are "harvested" in the wild, mostly by one distributor, and sold directly to pet stores. And that's how Petunia the crab came to join our household.

Children are fascinated by hermit crabs because they are colorful and interesting to observe. Also, they may eventually become habituated to one person, and will even come out of their shell when called. Their diet of mostly fruit can be fed from the palm of the child's hand, a great thrill. Nonaggressive and clean, they tolerate one another easily. Keeping them requires some knowledge, easily obtained from any of the many books about them in pet stores, but they are low-maintenance animals.

Seeing Petunia molt was a fascinating experience: She emerged from her shell, and her exoskeleton gradually fell off. She then buried herself in the sand, which we had to keep moist. Petunia emerged a month later with a new carapace. It was also fascinating to watch her lock herself into her shell by using her large thumb claw as a stop. This would effectively keep her in a safe, moist, and sterilized environment for as long as she chose to stay in there. Once Petunia kept herself in there for a whole week. I thought she was hibernating; Simone thought she was sulking. We had recently purchased a large companion for her, and she may have been frightened of his size. Alas, I could find no expert to ask. *The Secret Life of the Coconut Crab* is begging to be written.

ATTLE ARE BASICALLY HERD ANIMALS. When they calve, cows withdraw from the herd and isolate themselves as much as possible. The calf is then hidden, or "lies out" from the herd, only able to join when the "king" bull approves. Cattle expert Marthe Kiley-Worthington believes there have been few changes in the social organization, communication systems, and behavior from this animal's wild ancestry up to its modern domesticity. Nobody knows how long cows would live in natural conditions, but in domestication just one in a hundred thousand reaches her nineteenth birthday.

The eye of the cow is very large, allowing in a great deal of light. The image entering a cow's eye is about three times brighter than what a human sees. The cow's eyes are positioned on the side of the head to provide a wide field of vision, good for predator awareness and nocturnal vision. (Our visual field is little more than half that of a cow, though, as Valerius Geist tells me, we have acute daylight and color vision thanks to our treetop legacy.) Mothers often recognize their calf by coat color. It's clear that certain bright colors, ranging from yellow to

red, sometimes cause bulls considerable irritation. It has also been suggested that red is known to the bull as the color of blood. Moreover, the
retina of a bull is normally attuned to the green of green pastures, so
when he lifts up his head and is provoked by a red cape, it could prove
confusing and lead to aggression. In hider species—meaning that they
hide their young—calves are said to have practically no odor for the
first few days of life to reduce the risk of attracting predators. (Valerius
Geist warns me that I am a primate ruminating about a ruminant's
vision!)

Little is known about cow calls, but there are at least six and probably many more. Observing semiwild cattle in France's Camargue,
Robert Schloeth noticed something that had been overlooked by everyone else: Calves have signals to let other calves know that they are
about to commence play, and that everything that happens after this
signal should be so interpreted. What would otherwise be aggressive or
sexual is then to be meant only as play. They use a special call, and a special run. He said: "They curl their wooly tails and wave them on one
side only, which makes them readily visible as a signal." Dogs, as we
know, do something remarkably similar.

Domestic cattle (except those found in Southeast Asia) are all descended from a single wild species, *Bos primigenius*, otherwise called
the aurochs, the last of which was killed in a Polish park in 1627. The
bulls were large, up to six and a half feet at the shoulder, and often
equipped with very long horns. This was a formidable animal, swift,
strong, courageous, and with no affinity for humans.

These ancestors of our domestic cattle have actually been "reconstituted" by Lutz and Heinz Heck, two brothers, the second of whom was
the director of the Munich Zoo. On the theory that the various characteristics of the aurochsen are still to be found in different contemporary
breeds, the brothers crossed Hungarian steppe cattle with Scottish
Highland cattle, Alpine breeds, Corsicans, and others. Their scheme
worked (though Geist, who lived close to these cattle, told me that the
cattle who did not breed true or did not conform were butchered). By
1951, forty of these reconstituted aurochsen were allowed to run wild

in Bialowieza in Poland. They almost exactly match pictures of the French cave paintings in Lascaux, and the four hundred even older paintings in the Ardèche, in the Paleolithic cave known as Chauvet. (These have been carbon-dated to 31,000 BCE.)

Today there are approximately 1.2 billion cattle worldwide. Most authorities estimate that they were domesticated about eight thousand years ago in the Middle East. Nobody knows for certain why cattle were first domesticated. It was certainly not for milk: Most of the world is lactose-intolerant (especially central Africa and eastern Asia, where there is no tradition of milking). When such Roman writers as Columella and Varro discuss agriculture, they do not mention cattle except as draft or sacrificial animals. The Romans did not drink milk, and, as Juliet Clutton-Brock points out, "this is reflected in the physiology of their descendants today." The advantages are clear for dogs in choosing domestication, or in permitting the transaction, but one cannot think of any good reason why wild cattle would want to be in the presence of humans. What advantages could they derive from giving up their freedom? We did not need to protect them from enemies, since there was hardly a need to protect an animal as powerful as the wild ox. No animal could kill an adult, and the young were protected by circling.

The earliest account we have of cattle in English is by William Youatt, who begins his book about cattle by saying that "cattle are like most other animals, the creatures of education and circumstances." Later he says that "he has become the slave of man, without acquiring the privilege of being his friend." But cattle can be "warmed with a degree of human affection." The most affecting passage in the book is at the beginning, an account of a traveler in Colombia:

I was suddenly aroused by a most terrific noise, a mixture of loud roaring and deep moans, which had the most appalling effect at so late an hour. I immediately went out, attended by the Indians, when I found close to the ranch, a large herd of bullocks collected from the surrounding country; they had encompassed the spot where a bullock had been killed [butchered] in the morning, and they appeared to be in the greatest state of grief and rage: they roared, they moaned, they tore the ground with their feet, and bellowed the most hideous chorus that can be imagined, and it was with the greatest difficulty they could be driven away by men and dogs. Since then, I have observed the same scene by daylight, and seen large tears rolling down their cheeks. Is it instinct merely, or does something nearer to reason tell them by the blood, that one of their companions has been butchered? I certainly never again wish to view so painful a sight: —they actually appeared to be reproaching us.

In Indian classical literature, as you might expect, cows are treated well. The heavenly cow Surabhi, the mother of all cows, wept and lamented when just two (out of billions!) of her children were exhausted and beaten by a plowman. And elsewhere in the epic, the Ramayana, Kausalya is said to have cried out "like a cow seeing her calf bound and dragged away." M. K. Gandhi once said, "Cow protection to me is one of the most wonderful phenomena in human evolution. It takes the human being beyond his species. The cow to me means the entire sub-human world. Man through the cow is enjoined to realize his identity with all that lives." Considering the date at which this was written, we must recognize that Gandhi, in this as in other matters, was before his time.

The photo accompanying this essay shows a cow who looks happy. It is always dangerous to infer emotional states of other animals (or other people) from their appearance, but surely this particular cow, free to enjoy the grass she would normally eat, in the sun, gazing out to the sea and the islands beyond, is enjoying the life she was evolved to live. Her happiness is contagious: people stop when they see her and remark on how content she looks. She gives us more pleasure that way than any other I can think of. Long may she live.

COYOTE
Canis latrans

NUMEROUS LEGENDS EXIST in almost all Native American traditions about the coyote's cunning ways, his shape-shifting, and most of all his much-admired ability to survive against all odds. In Maricopa legends coyotes have curative powers. There are accounts of coyotes lying next to a sick or injured person they find in the desert and licking the wound, which they do for their own wounds and those of their companions.

This respect and appreciation was not passed on to the white settlers who took over their land. On the contrary, we have had a long history of hating the coyote. In Nebraska in 1861 Mark Twain saw his first coyote, which he described in *Roughing It* using shocking adjectives: the animal was "sick and sorry-looking," "scrawny," "furtive." He had an "evil eye" as he "slinked away," "poor, out of luck, and friendless." Twain had no doubt this coyote was a thief and a coward, a view that unfortunately came to be widely shared. In François Leydet's *The Coyote: Defiant*

Songdog of the West, he points out that the same derogatory adjectives are used in Twain's account to describe the Gosiutes, Native American relations of the Utes and Paiutes. In Twain's jaundiced eye they were "the wretchedest type of mankind I have ever seen . . . small, lean, scrawny creatures . . . a silent, sneaking, treacherous-looking race." What a pity this writer's considerable talents were put to use to disseminate ignorance and prejudice.

If instead of devising ever-newer methods to exterminate coyotes, biologists had spent even a fraction of this time learning about their actual lives, we would know a great deal more today about coyote behavior than we do. It is only now becoming clear that male coyotes, like male wolves (but unlike male dogs), are patient, amicable mates who help the female provide for the pups.

The hatred is supposedly caused by the belief that coyotes killed innumerable young cattle. Indeed, such incidents occur, but in much smaller numbers than is commonly thought. And coyotes are thought to be cruel. But, like every other animal, coyotes kill to eat, and there is no sadistic emotion involved in their pursuit of food. Naturalist George Schaller said about African lions that "prey is captured unemotionally, silent, and with bland features, whereas bared teeth and ferocious snarls accompany fights." Coyote kills could be similarly described, as those who have witnessed them can testify.

Humans have found a hundred cruel ways to exterminate this "enemy." Denning is one, a brutal practice in which a coyote is trailed to a den where there are cubs. Then gasoline is poured into the den and lit with a match. Trapping is another, perhaps the oldest, method. Death comes slowly. Trapped coyotes may last three days in summer before the heat kills them. In winter they drink snow, lasting until they starve to death. The trap cuts to the bone, shutting off circulation. It is not unusual to find a coyote who has chewed off his own foot to escape.

But the most common extermination method, even today, is using compound 1080, a white, odorless, powdery, essentially tasteless substance that is highly soluble in water. Six to eight hours after ingesting this powerful poison with no known antidote, the coyote shrieks in

pain, vomits, and is racked by painful convulsions before finally suc-
cumbing. And since 1080 does not break down in the body, any animals
or birds who feed on the carcass of a victim may be poisoned, their bodies yet more lethal baits. The gigantic numbers of casualties that result
from this bit of human cruelty staggers the imagination.

At one time, and for many years, an estimated one million coyotes
were killed annually in "sport hunting." But coyotes are amazingly flexible and adaptive. They are able to respond accordingly: Litter sizes increase immediately after such a "cull" (*attempted genocide* would be a
better term). Yearlings start breeding, something they normally do not
do. I cannot imagine what mechanism tells them to do this. But it has
been widely and reliably reported. It seems to resemble a decision rather
than to be a hardwired instinctive response.

The irony is, as study after study has convincingly demonstrated,
that there is no evidence that coyotes are killing significant numbers of
sheep. As for cattle, in great areas of the West cattle and coyotes live together with absolutely no predation whatever. In the entire history of
the United States there is only a solitary case of a fatal human attack by
a coyote: In 1981 a three-year-old girl was killed as she sat on the curb
outside her Glendale, California, home.

The futile attempts to eradicate coyotes because of their perceived
threat to lambs are especially upsetting, since there is a simple, proven,
and relatively inexpensive way to completely stop coyote predation:
Raymond and Lorna Coppinger at Hampshire College in Amherst,
Massachusetts, have raised Great Pyrenees and Anatolian shepherds
alongside sheep. The large guard dogs completely identify with the
sheep and challenge any animal who may harm them. Coyotes *never*
challenge these big dogs. The mere sight of them is enough to keep them
away. Only a minority of sheepmen, however, is able to overcome these
ancient and deep-rooted prejudices and use these dogs, the perfect solution.

Why do coyotes, when they discover a trap, dig it up, turn it over,
and urinate or defecate on it? Is this contempt? Does it show a sense of
humor? It must be something like that, for while coyotes, like dogs and

wolves, mark their territory with urine, traps could hardly be considered territory. In fact, they do have a highly evolved sense of humor. Everyone who has observed coyotes remains awed at their flexible intelligence. It is hard to compare intelligence across species, even from the same family, but people who study dogs, wolves, and coyotes seem agreed that coyotes show a particularly acute intelligence when it comes to humans. For example, a widely held belief, which I am prepared to accept, is that coyotes know whether a person is armed or not. It is true that antelope will often remain indifferent to a lion passing close by because they can read the signs of whether the lion is in hunting mode or not, and modify their behavior accordingly. But this "intelligence" has evolved over hundreds of thousands of years of cohabitation. Coyotes have achieved the same sense over a much shorter period. This is yet another instance of their extraordinary capacity to adapt to altered circumstances. There have been newspaper photographs of coyotes attempting to enter an elevator in downtown Seattle, for example. No wolf would live in such close proximity to humans.

There are even reports of wild coyotes forming a kind of friendship with an individual person. One man reports that he was working for a livestock company in Seligman, Arizona, and "made friends with an old coyote. It took almost two years for me to gain his confidence but finally he came to consider me as being more of a friend than a foe. I would save up my table scraps and when I had enough to make a meal for him, I would whistle and pretty soon I would hear him answer. He would bark a few little short barks, then after a little while he would show up."

My friend Mark Bekoff of the University of Colorado–Boulder has been studying coyotes for more than twenty-five years. He points out that almost any generalization about them is wrong. In some areas they live alone, in others they live with a mate, and still in others, they live in what resembles a wolf pack with "aunts" and "uncles" who help to raise the young. Sometimes coyotes are territorial and sometimes they don't seem to bother. But one thing you can be sure of is that they are remarkably intelligent "protean predators" who seem to change form at will. This may explain why it has proven all but impossible to get the better of them. Better, says Mark, to simply love them and let them be. And how can one not love an animal for whom play seems the very essence of his life?

The primary senses of the coyote are extraordinarily acute, as has been so well noted by an old Indian saying: "A feather fell from the sky. The eagle saw it, the deer heard it, the bear smelled it; the coyote did all three."

DOG

Canis familiaris

OGS CONTINUE TO ASTONISH US with their abilities. I believe these incredible animals have certain emotions and capabilities beyond what humans are at present capable of. However, I'm not speaking of the ability of dogs to do things on a physical plane that continue to astonish us. (For example, *The New York Times* recently reported on their ability to sniff out lung cancer with greater accuracy than any other known method, including MRI scans.)

No other animal lives with us on such terms of intimacy. The usual explanation is that wolves (the direct ancestors of dogs) are hypersociable, and—being pack animals—are used to hierarchy and looking up to an alpha leader. We have become that alpha leader for dogs. I have read a great deal about wolf packs, and while they display a great deal of solidarity, play, joy in meeting, and so on, there remains something unique in the bond fashioned between a dog and her human.

The pleasure stems, I believe, from the dog's hyperemotionality. They *feel* more than we do. Indeed, from my limited experience, I would say that dogs feel more than any other living thing on the planet. I know, I know: How would I know? How could this ever be tested? I can hear the many objections, but I nevertheless believe it's true. Watch a dog being told "Yes, we *are* going for a walk." That crazy dance of joy! The unparalleled enthusiasm! Dogs are *the* champions of the high five. *Yes!* is their favorite word. And when dogs put their heads in our laps, looking up at us with adoration, something beyond our comprehension passes from them to us. Nobody, as far as I know, has ever lived with a wild wolf pack on terms of intimacy, so we don't really know if such gestures, such loving looks are to be found among members of that pack, but I have a feeling they are not.

Now I venture out onto thin ice indeed, because my belief is that the depth and intensity of this remarkable bond comes from the very fact that it *is* interspecies love. Do dogs exhibit such focused adoration for their own? I haven't witnessed it. And this astonished joy travels both directions. We've all known people whose love of their dog was beyond anything imaginable.

How could evolution have ever prepared us for this? Even more amazing is how it prepared *dogs* for this. Humans have an extraordinary capacity for self-deception. Dogs do not. So I can imagine a psychoanalyst (after all, I was one myself, once upon a time) arguing that the love we *think* we feel for our dog is simply a transference, a replacement, taking the love we *ought* to feel for a human and placing it where it *ought not* to belong, on an animal. Uh-uh. I don't think so. No. That's one reason I'm no longer a psychoanalyst: They are so damned obtuse, especially when it comes to emotions. Especially when it comes to the emotions between dogs and humans.

I believe dogs have the capacity to express enthusiasm to a degree unseen in any other animal. The same for fidelity. And then of course for love, always undisguised in dogs. Then there's the wonderfully pure joie de vivre. Disappointment, too, seems to me beyond a doubt stronger in dogs than in any other creature. Observe your dog when you have to say,

"No, no walk now. Maybe later." She cocks her head to make certain she heard the correct words. Disbelief slowly comes over her face. She sighs, then flops to the floor in a kind of physical despair. Now, I know that I am making invidious comparisons here, and it would be easy for many to take me to task. But those infected with dog love know of what I speak. What we feel for a dog is extraordinary, as is what we get back from the dog. That's why when I read the literature on "pet mourning," a growing field, the most poignant tales are almost always about the loss of a dog. For many, it is more devastating than the loss of another person.

I don't pretend to understand this deep, mysterious connection, but my belief in this unique, magnificent interspecies bond is shared by many people.

DOMESTIC CAT

Felis silvestris catus

THE EGYPTIANS USED THE SOUND of cats for their name: *mau*. As did the Chinese, *mao*. The English word *cat* comes from the Nubian *kadiz*, which also gave rise to *chat*, *katze*, *gato*, and the lovely Russian word *koshka*.

I live on New Zealand's North Island, fifteen minutes from the country's largest city, Auckland. Our eco-house is on a small beach called Karaka Bay (where the Treaty of Waitangi was signed; this country's equivalent of the United States' Declaration of Independence). I met my German wife Leila eleven years ago when she was a resident in Pediatrics at the University of California at San Francisco, and we have two sons, ten-year-old Ilan ("tree" in Hebrew), who was born in California, and four-year-old Manu ("bird" in Maori), born here in New Zealand a year after we arrived. Also living with us are our three beloved cats, Moko, Megala, and Tamaiti. Every evening, the seven of us walk the beach down to the seven-hundred-year-old Pohutukawa tree where the cats and the kids play until dark sends us home.

We live in greater intimacy with cats than with any other animal except dogs. I believe this has given cats access to emotions they would never have had occasion to feel in their wild state: pleasure in the company of a member of a different species, for example. We are like catnip to cats, a drug, and the addiction works both ways. People rarely merely *like* cats; they are indifferent, hate them, or adore them. For those of us who love them, the reward is great, for with no other animal is it easier and more enchanting to cross the species barrier, an almost universal desire throughout human history, than with cats.

It is now pretty much universally accepted that the domestic cat is descended from the African wildcat *Felis silvestris lybica* and not the European wildcat, *F. s. silvestris*. The reason seems to be that the African wildcat is easily tamed, whereas the European wildcat can almost never be tamed. The African wildcat is so secretive that according to the most authoritative book on the topic (*Wild Cats of the World*), nobody knows for certain whether it even exists in Georgia, Azerbaijan, and Armenia, though it is *thought* to be there! Why there should be such variability in species that in almost all other respects are nearly identical I find puzzling. However, in an important article in the *Biological Journal of the Linnean Society*, it has been pointed out that many small cats are inherently friendly or easily tamed, but only one has been domesticated. This would suggest that it is *not* the preadaptational qualities of the cat that were of decisive importance in leading to domestication, but accidental factors, in this case having to do with ancient Egypt.

Even though the ancient Egyptians considered cats godlike, there is no concrete evidence of affectionate interactions between people and cats at the time. Cats were admired for aesthetic reasons but rarely, it seems, fondled, petted, and made much of. Purring is not referred to in ancient texts. There is no ancient Greek or Latin word for "purr," which suggests that it went unobserved even by the great Greek naturalists. Or were the cats never given a reason to purr? I am convinced that purring, like tail wagging in dogs, is exclusively communicative: Cats purr to convey a message, usually of contentment. They also purr as a form of self-medication when in distress. It's a voluntary act, not a reflex. It cannot be faked, unlike the human smile. It could be that each cat's purr is slightly distinctive, hence a signature purr, indicating individuality.

Subordination and dominance play little role in the lives of wildcats for the obvious reasons that they arrange it so that they rarely meet one another. In a feral cat colony, however, meetings are not only obligatory, but seem to give pleasure. Is this because feral cats carry the memory of domestication? There is some debate as to whether domestic cats demonstrate a hierarchy. By and large, I think they do not. Still, in one large colony of feral cats in Fitzroy Square in central London, members showed a peculiar deference to one small white cat, even though many others were bigger, younger, and stronger. She was the matriarch—mother, grandmother, or aunt of most of the other cats.

Another difference between a wildcat and our domestic tabbies is that solitary wildcats have never been observed to play. Still wild in so many ways, the domestic cat is often playful into old age. Almost every young animal plays, but no solitary wild animal does so throughout his or her life. What I have noticed is how often what begins as play in two adult cats often ends in what appears to be a ferocious fight. This may be because cats lack the ability (so noted in dogs) to apologize: *Sorry, I didn't mean to hurt you.* Since they are well equipped to harm, they may do so when they don't intend to, and afterward they refuse to acknowledge the mistake. The reason they lack the canine ability to apologize is almost certainly that their wild ancestors, being largely solitary, have no use for this ability.

On the other hand, there is little doubt in my mind that cats recognize the pleasure that can come from play with a member of another species. My three cats wait every evening for me to announce "Walk on the beach," and then they materialize from somewhere in the house, make their way to the front door, and from there head to the seashore for our long, complicated walk. They wouldn't miss it for anything. The mystery remains: Why wait for us? Why could they not organize such a walk on their own? They wait for it, they love it, and yet *we* have to initiate it.

There's no doubt that cats derive from a solitary animal, and many cats retain this heritage. However, many do not. There is nothing in their evolutionary history or in their biology to prepare them for living with an alien species, yet they do. And they do it well. They even enjoy it. They have been transformed. I believe the cat is the only animal whose nature has completely altered in this way. Dogs descend from sociable wolves, so they are used to submission and friendly relations with others. Adaptation for them is not nearly as extreme as it is for cats.

It is odd that an animal from such a lineage is now the most popular domestic pet in the United States. In 2005 there were an estimated ninety million pet cats in the United States, compared with seventy million dogs. Our love for the cat has a long history. Ancient Egyptians took their devotion of cats so far that if people saw a sick or injured cat in the street, they fled for fear of being held responsible for the creature's demise. The penalty for killing a cat in ancient Egypt was death.

However, the Middle Ages marked the beginning of three centuries of persecution of the cat. Most had to do with delusions and superstitions. "Witches" were even known (obviously under torture) to confess to having an unnatural nipple with which they suckled their cats. The first official trial for witchcraft in England, in 1566, involved a cat: At the trial, witnesses said Agnes Waterhouse and her daughter Joan "had a whyte spotted catte" and that they "feed the sayde cat with breade and milkye . . . and call it by the name of Sathan." They were executed as witches. For the next three centuries in England (and throughout Europe) vicious acts toward cats were encouraged. Perhaps we haven't gotten over this stage in our own evolution, for despite the number of cats in the United States, surveys show that there are nearly seven times as many cat haters as there are dog haters.

The milk of domestic cats contains eight times more protein than human milk and three times as much fat, so kittens grow quickly. By the second or third day of birth, each kitten has established teat ownership and suckles exclusively from his or her own nipple. This avoids fights and makes sure that each kitten has a functioning nipple. Within days the kittens develop the milk tread, wherein they knead their mother's belly with their front feet. Most cats retain this behavior throughout their life, and use it on us, which is evidence, I believe, that we act in loco parentis for cats. We are their mother. No wonder they like us. It is an extreme example of neoteny, retaining the features of infancy into adulthood, and gives cats their gentle, friendly, and charming character-istics. This is why, I believe, we love them so—and why they love us, too.

How much, though, is friendliness simply inherited? It has been claimed, recently, that the gene for friendliness in cats is inherited from the father. I think it may have more to do with the critical period in the kitten's life. Unfortunately that period is from three to seven weeks. A kitten never touched during this time will most likely turn out to be far less tolerant of humans than kittens who are gently touched and held briefly from three to seven weeks. The problem is that weaning is rarely complete until about eight weeks, and most people only adopt their kit-tens at that time. If they have not been touched during that early pe-riod, it will be difficult, though not impossible, to make friends with them in later life. The miracle is that so many cats turn out to be the closest friend that many humans will make.

Family Anatidae

THE TERM WATERFOWL (in America) or *wildfowl* (in Britain) is applied to some 160 species of ducks, geese, and swans. They all belong to a single family, the Anatidae (a word derived from the Latin verb *anas*, to swim). With webbed feet, short legs, long necks, and beaks with plates that act as filters when they eat, their bodies are designed for aquatic life. All can swim and dive, and have thick, waterproof plumage with a dense coat of insulating down underneath. (Down is not hair, but a rudimentary feather.)

Ducks and geese are not only family-oriented but enjoy being in large congregations (bevies of ducks, gaggles of geese) as well—as do many other species of birds. They show pronounced gregariousness. This is so concentrated in some species that it has proved possible to photograph the total inhabitants of a continent in a single aerial shot. Such, for example, was a photograph of Pacific black brant geese showing 173,740 birds and another showing most of the forty-two thousand greater snow geese. There is safety in numbers: The likelihood of being selected by a predator is vastly decreased if you are one of several hundred thou-sand rather than flying on your own. And there are many eyes to alert others to danger, too. However, it also seems the birds are exuberant and enjoy one another's company for the sheer pleasure of it.

Like many animals who flock, ducks seem to have an altruistic streak. Catching sight of a fox on a pond's bank, they mass together, then swim parallel to the fox as he trots along the shore. It's an unmistakable visual signal to the pond's other inhabitants: *Look out, a fox is here!* Scientists find this behavior troubling and puzzling: How could a duck wish to warn other animals about a dangerous fox? What's in it for the sentinel duck? Is it just a warning, or are the ducks mocking their enemy, secure in their knowledge that he cannot attack them? (No fox can swim as fast as a duck.) Is it a means of letting him know that he has been seen and there is no point in staying around, for tonight he will not have duck for dinner? These are among the secrets ducks keep.

Ducks, when seized alive by a fox in his mouth, will pretend they're dead. They do it in such a convincing manner that the fox will drop the duck, who can then fly away. Many people happen upon a duck when she is with her ducklings, only to notice something strange: The duck suddenly seems injured. Her ducklings scatter, and the duck begins what looks like a crazy dance, fascinating to us and evidently to other predators (of which we are just a larger version for a duck). We cannot help but follow the "injured" duck, forgetting her young. When we are lured far enough away from the ducklings, suddenly she is miraculously cured and flies off, emitting the equivalent of a sigh of relief. We have just witnessed the distraction display, or injury feigning: a bird acting as though her wings and back were broken. For anybody who sees this amazing trick, it's hard to believe that the mother bird is not conscious of what she is doing.

While some ducks eat fish, others, and as far as I know just about all geese, are vegetarian. That is why tame geese are so easy to feed. Their diet is mostly grass, so there is little competition for a scarce resource, meat. Maybe this is why ducks and geese appear so peaceful. Aggression is always greater in carnivores than in vegetarian species, since hunters need weapons and a willingness to use them. Strangely, though, geese can be more aggressive with humans than are ducks. Ducks are not terribly aggressive with any other animal, especially one familiar to them. Darwin in *The Descent of Man* mentions ducks lying down and basking in the sun next to a cat and dog they know, but running from ones they do not know.

One reason we love ducks is that their calls are readily understandable. For example, the desertion whistle of a duckling is easily translated: *I am lost, find me.* I find it fascinating that the affection-indicating slow quacks between adult ducks derive from these infantile sounds. No doubt the slowness suggests that it's a comfort sound rather than a desertion sound. A desertion sound is difficult to misunderstand; the nonstop peeping is clearly from a bird in distress. I wonder if females' decrescendo call during fall and winter might not indicate that individuals are trying to locate one another at the end of the season. If this is true, it may be that old pair-bonds are renewed more commonly than has been generally supposed for ducks (unlike for geese, where it is common).

Perhaps the answer to why ducks fascinate children lies in the fact that ducks live in such close families: You see the mother swimming, her half-dozen ducklings right behind. If she moves left, they move left. She dives, they dive. They look so happy, so carefree, so safe. It is every child's fantasy to be part of a completely reliable world, protected by somebody who loves without boundaries and will do everything in her power to see to it that her child is safe.

Geese are so wary of danger that "enemies" rarely get close. When feeding, at least one goose is always on the watch and warns the feeding flock of danger. Geese tend to remain paired for life. Do geese mourn the loss of a partner? Nobel Prize–winning Konrad Lorenz had no doubt of this, nor should we, though scientists cite the fact that the surviving partner seeks out another mate as proof that this cannot be the case. It's strange that a stricter definition is used for geese than for humans.

There is a sound of great significance to geese that Lorenz called the sound of the triumph ceremony. This is heard whenever a gander drives off an intruder. At such a time, he invariably utters a triumph call, and equally invariably the female repeats the note and stretches out her head and neck close to the ground. The young, including even down-covered goslings, show their appreciation by performing in the same approving way. *Look what I did!* is the unmistakable meaning of this ceremony. A version of this triumph ceremony can be seen when two geese mate. The gander swims in a particularly proud way, his wings slightly raised, his tail cocked, and his neck curved. He dips, a kind of bow, to the female. Then they raise their wings together, extend their heads straight into the air, and give a honk of joy or celebration or achievement to announce that the deed has been done.

Unfortunately, until recently it was not considered necessary to think about the minds or the inner lives of these animals. Part of the problem is that we were getting information only from "experts," animal behaviorists trained in a certain tradition where thinking about the emotional lives of any animal was more or less verboten. We would have been better off, I believe, to enlist the aid of amateurs and animal lovers, people who watch ducks and live with ducks or geese because they love them. This seems to have been the case long ago, in a book such as *Life Histories of North American Wild Fowl,* by Arthur Cleveland Bent, originally written in 1923, and again more recently, as in Bob Tarte's amusing 2003 book, *Enslaved by Ducks: How One Man Went from Head of the Household to Bottom of the Pecking Order.*

A word about hunting. Recently I have come across an argument that hunters are the ones preserving wetlands and other habitats that ducks and geese need, and they would not do so if they did not get the pleasure of shooting them. G. V. T. Matthews makes a familiar argument: "A shooter has more of a vested and practical interest in the survival of his quarry species, and of the countryside in general, than has a city-bound 'anti-blood-sport' protagonist."

Just because somebody has a vested interest in something does *not* mean that person will do more or better than somebody without that particular vested interest. However, noted biologist Bernd Heinrich, professor of biology at the University of Vermont and the author of many prizewinning books about wildlife, writes that it is hunters and former hunters who *have*, in fact, done more to protect swamps and wetlands. I'm not sure I'm prepared to accept on faith that this *is* a fact, but for the moment, let's assume it is. The hunters, according to this argument, want to make certain that birds have places to go so they can kill them there. Isn't it a little bit strange that we are willing to ignore motivation, as long as the result pleases us? If somebody were to employ this reasoning with regard to humans we would reject it as heartless, insensitive, and insulting.

Surely we can be concerned with the preservation of wetlands for their own sake, as well as for the sake of the animals, trees, and other life that thrives there, because *everything* deserves to live, and not simply because we want the freedom to go there to slaughter whatever species takes our fancy. Surely this is the more evolved moral position.

ECHIDNA

Tachyglossus aculeatus

FOUND ONLY IN AUSTRALASIA, echidnas are also called spiny anteaters because of their habit of eating ants and termites. There are two species: one, critically endangered, lives in the highlands of New Guinea; the other, the short-beaked echidna, in Australia. But for their long narrow tubelike snouts and tiny little mouths with no teeth, they look just like hedgehogs or small porcupines.

Echidnas are monotremes. The only other member of that family is the platypus. Monotremes are mammals, but are the only mammals who lay eggs rather than give birth to live young. They arose 120 million years ago, and are considered closely linked to reptiles. Because of this, their brains are of particular interest to scientists. All mammals dream, except, it would appear, the echidna. Alone among mammals, echidnas lack the part of the limbic brain that enables them to dream during sleep. Odd.

Even odder, though, is the size of the echidna's neocortex, the site in the brain of higher cognition. That's why, we've been told, mammals have them and birds lack them. (True, though it turns out that birds have something similar; their brains are different, but not necessarily inferior.) Echidnas, although considered primitive in the sense that they branched off from the mammalian family tree so long ago that they are the oldest of the twenty-six surviving mammalian orders, have enormous neocortexes, occupying about half of their brain volume. What on earth do they use them for?

Possibly to avoid capture. There is no census of these animals in Australia, because of the extreme difficulty in trapping them. They are wary, preternaturally quiet, and small enough to be overlooked. Even food does not lure them. That's pretty smart. Also, they live everywhere in Australia. They are the most widely spread Australian mammal: They live in the rain forests, the deep deserts of the Australian outback, the swamps, and the mountains, and along the seashore. So these clever creatures must have figured out how to adapt to circumstances that would stump other animals. For example, in the snow of the Australian Alps, they lower their body temperature to a few degrees above freezing as they go into a form of hibernation. If you finally spot an echidna, before you actually approach him, he may well be gone. He's the only mammal who can dig straight down with his powerful short legs and rear claws. What resembled a small dark shrub disappears into the earth in seconds.

Captive echidnas have been known to stack drinking containers in a corner to climb out of an escape-proof cage. Australians call them "porkies," but unlike porcupine quills, the spines on their backs do not detach from their bodies. They use these quills (actually modified hairs rather than quills) to climb rock crevices. And echidnas are unusually gentle: They have never been known to fight. When attacked, they curl into a ball and hope you go away.

Even their mating ceremony is highly distinctive. Almost all other male mammals compete aggressively. The echidna males may compete, but the competition appears to lack aggression: They form a long mating train with a single female in front and up to a dozen males queued up nose-to-tail in a noncompetitive competition that can last for a month or even longer. The female eventually clings to a tree trunk while the males dig a trench around the tree. Then they push each other, but softly. The losers walk away with no evident rancor. (How the winner and losers were determined remains a mystery.) The winner mates. Three weeks later, the female sits down and lays a single soft leathery egg the size of a dime directly into a pouch on her abdomen. Ten days later the "puggle" (the name of a baby echidna) hatches, about the size of a small jelly bean. He stays in the pouch to nurse. If this sounds like what happens to a kangaroo, it is. But the mother has no nipples. The puggle, really just an embryo, must suck up the milk secreted from pores directly onto milk patches in her fur. Within two weeks, the puggle weighs one hundred times its birth weight. At eight weeks he is evicted and placed in a nursery burrow, where his mother will visit every five or six days.

At seven months he's on his own. For a long time. These animals move slowly. They hardly seem to age. Is it that they never fight? Or that they never defend a territory? Or that they take long afternoon naps? Or that they are almost completely solitary? It's uncertain how long they live, but it is conjectured to be as long as elephants. One echidna at the Philadelphia Zoo lived in captivity for forty-nine years.

Like his cousin the platypus, the male echidna has a spur on the ankle of his hind leg, but in keeping with the completely benign character of this remarkable animal, the spur contains no venom. Australian echidnas are not endangered. Is their success a result of their mild and inoffensive nature? Who could be an enemy of this gentle creature? If he does not like what he sees, he simply goes under like a sinking ship, leaving hardly a trace.

ELEPHANTS
Family Elephantidae

W HAT REMAINS TO BE LEARNED about and from the animal kingdom dwarfs what we already know. In recent years scientists have come to recognize that we understand little of most species. While Indian texts at least two thousand years old mention the taming of the majestic elephant, for instance, we still know little of its true life.

In the past our relationship with elephants has been either one of hunting them, or one of dominating and enslaving them—perhaps explaining our ignorance. Out of the hundreds of books written by hunters about elephants, little can be gleaned about their real behavior. So ignorant were hunters that they did not even realize that elephants live in matriarchies. Using human standards of the nineteenth century, they assumed that the almost-always-solitary great bull elephants were "head" of the household. Little was learned, either, from the early, constant attempts to use elephants for human purposes—whether that meant performing silly circus tricks or hauling large trunks in the Burmese forest. Even the Indian Mahouts who lived with elephants in intimate circumstances did not reveal much to the public about the true lives of these animals. Perhaps they, too, did not think about elephants apart from what they wanted from them.

This situation has changed only in the last twenty years, since women like Cynthia Poole and Kathy Payne took to observing elephants under natural conditions in the wild. They have learned that elephants, despite their hulking appearance, are in an astonishing number of ways much like humans. For example, they live from 60 to 80 years, just as we do—not 150, as some early authors thought. Not fully grown until they reach twenty years, they are not really mature until they reach their forties, as is true of humans.

The brains of elephants are large, richly folded, and convoluted, as are human brains. No doubt this complexity has to do with the elaborate social relations they engage in with one another, like us.

At night, they often sleep on bush-pillows. They snore and dream, as we do. One important but as yet unexplained difference: Elephants are very restless at night, and sleep just two to three hours. (Perhaps this is due to fear of harm to their young?) They like a midday siesta, too. Nightmares plague the sleep of young elephants who have seen their mothers killed: They often wake at night screaming, as if reliving the terror. (Their deep grieving can last for months. See Daphne Sheldrick's website, www.africanwebsites.net/sheldrick.html.)

They have a special relationship to their dead, as yet unexplained and not completely explored, which is seen in a death ceremony involving a sort of burial service. Deep mourning takes place over the death of another elephant. Acknowledged by all experts now is the strange behavior elephants exhibit over the bones of deceased relatives. They sniff the bones, handle them, stare at them, and evidently even sigh over them. Tusks they shatter, as if they know their brothers are so often killed for them. Their memories are long and durable, as are ours, especially for trauma.

Most of all, elephants resemble people in the depth of their feelings for their family. (Perhaps the strength of their feelings even surpasses our own.) Ancient Indian texts show humans oddly exploiting these feelings: There are descriptions of elephants acting as babysitters for baby humans. Parents drew a circle, then left a grown elephant tied to a stake in the middle of the circle with their infant child with instructions not to allow the toddler to move outside the circle. Then, if the babe strayed, the elephant would gently pull the child back into the circle with her trunk. Whether elephants extended their familial love to human families is uncertain, but it is beyond question that they exhibit great love for their own children. An entire herd will defy any danger when a small elephant cub is threatened in any way. I learned this the hard way when I approached a large matriarch with her cub in the Indian forest, forgetting she was a wild elephant. Of course, I meant no harm, but how could she know this? When, in my nearly fatal ignorance, I approached too closely, she charged. I barely escaped death. Only a panicked wild run managed to save me from her (understandable) wrath. Moreover, she had provided me with ample warning by flapping her ears, which I mistook for a greeting!

Even given all we have learned in the last few years, so many mysteries remain. You may have seen reports of elephants taking up brushes and painting beautiful art. Do they do anything similar in the wild for the sheer fun of it, or do they do this only in captivity, perhaps as a means of relieving their boredom? Do they have musical ability, as several elephant keepers claim? And why, recently, have elephants killed so many of their keepers that now most zoos around the world are using what is called PC, protected contact, where the elephant cannot actually touch the keeper? Have they simply had enough captivity?

And have we finally understood why adult male elephants periodically enter the state called *musth* (Hindi for "madness")? If it is indeed tied into testosterone and sexuality in males, then why do female African elephants sometimes exhibit it? *Musth* is linked to sexual arousal or establishing dominance, but this relationship is far from clear. At adolescence, males are chased from the herd because of their growing aggression. What emotions do these solitary bulls then feel, after having been cast out of a loving, close family? The Prousts of today have yet to write the great elephant saga.

EMPEROR PENGUIN
Aptenodytes forsteri

T HE EMPEROR PENGUIN (*Aptenodytes* means "wingless diver") was named for the two German naturalists, G. and J. R. Forster, father and son, who accompanied James Cook on his second voyage around the world in 1772–75.

Interestingly enough, the Antarctic was only later discovered because explorers were looking for the breeding colony of this amazing bird, whose hold on the world's imagination has never slackened. (Witness the immensely popular 2005 film *March of the Penguins*, the second-largest-grossing documentary in history.) Robert Falcon Scott set out to the Antarctic seas in 1901 aboard the SS *Discovery* to find the eggs of the emperor penguin. Zoologist Edward A. Wilson was also along, an artist and a surgeon. In 1911 this intrepid investigator set out in late June from Scott's base at Cape Evans for a thirty-six-day round trip. With him were two explorers, Henry Robertson Bowers and Apsley Cherry-Garrard, who later wrote an account of the passage that has been called the greatest travel book of all time, *The Worst Journey in the World*. Wilson and Bowers never made it back to England. After their winter expedition, they joined Scott on the summer race for the South Pole and died with him of exposure and starvation on that tragic journey—but not before Wilson published a significant, long article on his findings about the emperor penguin. Cherry-Garrard finishes his great work with these words: "There are many reasons which send men to the Poles, and the Intellectual Force uses them all. But the desire for knowledge for its own sake is the one which really counts . . . If you march your Winter Journeys you will have your reward, so long as all you want is a penguin's egg."

The truly remarkable thing about the emperor penguin, though, is something Wilson and his colleagues completely missed: not that here is a primitive creature, but that, on the contrary, here is a highly evolved bird with extraordinary paternal behavior. The story he missed is that male penguins are unique, committed fathers, staying with their eggs through the all-but-unbearable winter, fasting, balancing the precious eggs on their feet, barely moving, hardly sleeping until their mate returns from her time at sea.

A reason so many of us are fascinated by penguins is that they resemble us. They walk upright, as we do, and like us they are notoriously curious. They are not even all that much smaller than we are: They can be three feet tall and weigh up to ninety pounds, the size of a large dog. Penguins in the wild walk right up to people, touch them, and look as if they are preparing to study them. Because penguins live only south of the equator, they have no experience of land predators from northern icy climes such as the polar bear. The fact that they have no natural enemies on land helps explain their seeming fearlessness. In this way they are like the birds and mammals of the Galápagos Islands, who were without fear before humans came. Penguins are also more or less without aggression. They have enormous power in their pectoral muscles, but they use it only for movement, whether in the water or on land, and have never developed it for fighting or even defensive purposes.

Early authors thought the feeding at crèches, penguin nurseries consisting exclusively of chicks, was communal or random: Any adult penguin fed any penguin chick. This turns out not to be true. What happens instead is that the parents join up and together approach each crèche in turn and sing. This song may cause no reaction at all until one of the chicks approaches, and gives an answering song. There are some-

times five thousand chicks to be examined. Biologist Bernard Stone-
house describes penguin chicks in their winter crèches when their parents return from the sea to feed them: "The parent stands at the edge of
the crèche, which may contain two or three thousand tightly packed,
sleeping chicks, and gives its own distinctive call. Immediately one little head shoots up from the mass, one piercing whistle sounds a frenetic
reply, and the chick begins to fight its way through apathetic companions to meet its parent for breakfast." Mysteriously, it has been noted
that most birds, including skuas, sworn enemies of penguins, will not attack crèches, even though the babies could do nothing to defend themselves and there are usually no adults nearby to protect them. It is not
clear why this should be so.

Penguins fascinated one of America's great paleontologists, the late
George Gaylord Simpson. At the end of a book he wrote about them in
1976, *Penguins Past and Present,* he said:

> Finally, the question may be asked, "what good are penguins?" It
> may be crass to ask what good a wild animal is, but I think the
> question may also be legitimate. That depends on what you mean
> by good. If you mean "good to eat," you are perhaps being stupid.
> If you mean "good to hunt," you are surely being vicious. If you
> mean "good as it is good in itself to be a living creature enjoying
> life," you are not being crass, stupid or vicious. I agree with you
> and I am your brother as well as the penguin's.

We can go even further, and say that it is good to watch the emperor
penguin, to learn from the emperor penguin, to lionize the emperor penguin as he proudly embraces the tiny ball of fluff on his feet.

FLAMINGOS

Family Phoenicopteridae

EVEN IN A ZOO, pink flamingos are impressive to look at: three to six feet tall, these pink and red orange-eyed birds with black flight feathers, a long sinuous neck, and equally long bright red legs terminating in yellow webbed feet look like giant colorful ducks. But a zoo is no place for these extraordinary birds.

They need space, to be in huge flocks. They need the strange landscape in which they evolved. In nature they congregate in the millions, and the spectacle is enough to take your breath away. The first European man to discover the mystery of flamingos put it like this: "No words I know can convey the spectacle of colour and motion, the sound of their voices, or the remote feeling of being a primitive man making a discovery in some archaic period of time. To ornithologists all I can say is—go and see it for yourself." I can't help wondering whether other animals who first see them are also awestruck at the sight.

This extravagance of color, this eruption of deep pink in the heart of

Africa, is to be found in Africa's Great Rift Valley, which spreads southward from Ethiopia. The birds, both the greater flamingo and the lesser flamingo, are mysteriously drawn to the series of lakes running down the center of the Rift Valley, strange inhospitable places with crystalline salt masses and temperatures that can reach a scalding 140 degrees Fahrenheit. (There are six flamingo species worldwide, including the Caribbean flamingo and two species from South America.) These Rift Valley lakes are known as soda lakes, bodies of water so full of sodium carbonate that they burn almost anything that tries to enter. No other animals want to go near them, and this is what draws the flamingos to them in huge numbers. There could be no safer place for birds who are otherwise completely without any form of defense. They swim in this brackish water with the same ease with which they fly enormous distances.

Their beaks are more similar to the snout of a baleen whale than to the beak of any other known bird. In fact, it is not just the appearance; this unique beak does exactly what baleen plates do for the baleen whales. The lower jaw is large and troughlike, while the upper jaw is much smaller and acts like a tight-fitting lid. Flamingos lower their necks into brackish water, holding their beaks upside down and pointed backward. The lower mandible has a honeycomb of air-filled spores, and floats effortlessly in the water. The tongue acts as a pump, allowing flamingos to siphon up and filter as many as twenty beakfuls of water a second. Minute hairs strain the water out of the food, for otherwise the salty water would kill them. The food is mostly microscopic blue-green algae, that is, spirulina. Despite its color, the carotenes in spirulina provide the red pigment for the feathers of the flamingos.

But when the lakes recede, carotenes become more dangerous. The fresh water the birds need to wash away the salt becomes increasingly hard to find. And if the salt dries and crystallizes on their wings, they could easily die. Moreover, various predators, such as jackals, are now able to walk on the mudflats and threaten the flamingos. This is time to move on. As if at a given signal, the whole flock suddenly takes off.

They migrate in the millions, soaring hundreds of miles every day. Nobody knew where they went for breeding until British ornithologist Leslie Brown discovered Lake Natron, one of the soda lakes, in 1954. This has been called "the most caustic body of water in the world," filled as it is with sulfur, chlorine, phosphorus, and sodium carbonate. The lake is completely caked with salt on the shore, not to mention geothermal pools and boiling mud. Poor Brown had no idea where he was, and on his first attempt to reach a bird colony in the lake the sodium carbonate entered his boots, cutting and burning his feet so badly that both of them nearly had to be amputated. After many skin grafts, he recovered, wondering how those birds' skinny pipelike legs could be immune. At Lake Natron, three million pair of flamingos—three-quarters of the entire world population—assemble miles from shore on mudflats that no enemy could possibly reach. The surface temperature is often 149 degrees Fahrenheit. So far from any human habitation are these mudflats that the Masai who live around the lake thought that since nobody had ever seen an egg, the birds must spring half grown from the center of the lake.

But it is here that they build nests of mud and lay a single egg. Both parents sit on the nest, and both male and female birds care for the chick who emerges. They both must ensure that the chick not fall into the water, for the baby would be scalded to death. (It is a mystery to me how adult birds can stand in water with temperatures approaching 158 degrees and only show mild discomfort by dancing from foot to foot.) The birds do not necessarily breed every year, so the chicks are especially dear. It is important that they be able to produce two surviving offspring in their lifetime—not as easy as it may sound. As for food, both parents produce crop milk, just as pigeons do, only flamingos' milk is bright red!

Like many birds, flamingo chicks make sounds while still in the egg. Later, they will be left in gigantic crèches, with thousands of other chicks. Some crèches reach the size of three hundred thousand youngsters. I don't think there are subtle differences in appearance that only a parent can note, yet when parents arrive for mealtime, they know to feed only their own chick. Since all the chicks are calling at once, they must recognize the distinctive sound of their own offspring.

The chicks stay with their parents for what is a long time for birds, for there is much to learn for the long life ahead. (Some have been recorded to reach beyond fifty years.) *Stick together* is the primary lesson. Only by staying in huge, compact flocks can they avoid predation. Even when an enemy finally comes, they have only a small chance of being individually selected. Mathematically, their chances are better in a flock than solitary.

Here is the saddest thing: One of the soda lakes, Lake Nakuru, was declared a national park in 1968 because of its importance to the millions of flamingos who settle on its waters. But the town that grew up around the lake developed two noxious industries, a battery factory and a tannery, which spewed highly toxic waste with no effective sewage treatment into the waters of the lake. The birds have left. It is very much like the wonderful, radical Dr. Seuss book about environmentalism, *The Lorax*. How can we bring these beautiful birds back to Lake Nakuru? As yet, there's no answer.

BELIEVE IT OR NOT, not everyone everywhere loves frogs. In fact, Swedish scientist Carolus Linnaeus, who gave them the name of Amphibia for his new system of nomenclature, called them "foul and loathsome" creatures. "These animals," he intoned, "are abhorrent because of their cold body, pale color, cartilaginous skeleton, filthy skin, fierce aspect, calculating eye, offensive smell, harsh voice, squalid habitation, and terrible venom; and so their Creator has not exerted his powers to make many of them." Wrong on *all* counts. After all, who could resist the red-eyed tree frog, poster child for the rain forest? And at last count there are 3,975 different species of frogs and toads. Every year another one or two dozen are discovered.

Growing up, I was fascinated by frogs. The small ones I saw around my home in Hollywood, California, were colored a bright emerald green. They were interesting to look at, harmless, and best of all, in real time I watched them turn into froglets from tadpoles (we called them pollywogs). Their tails would get smaller and smaller, and soon they could hop right out of the little ponds in the streams in Ferndale Park in the foothills of the Hollywood Hills where we found them. I remember bringing some home and making an artificial pond for them, but they disappeared within a few days. Now I wish an adult would have convinced me how much better for them it would have been to leave them in their original home.

In the 1980s I was back in California and took to hiking in the mountains again. Much to my surprise, I failed to see frogs. It was not that I was looking for them, but I certainly noticed. They weren't there.

My experience dovetailed with those of much more expert observers. Biologists in Oregon, Colorado, and California noted that certain frogs were disappearing. Yosemite toads, Cascade frogs, leopard frogs, and western toads had dropped in numbers in the early 1980s and were failing to recover. Something dire was happening to frogs across America. Then scientists reported the same disappearances in frogs that were once found in abundance in Peru, Ecuador, Puerto Rico, and Costa Rica. Frogs and toads were on the decline. (Toads are types of frogs, so all toads are frogs. Herpetologists use the word *frog* to refer to both.) It was not just simple habitat destruction. Obviously, if you paved over a bog, you lost the frogs who used to frequent it. But when the charismatic golden toad, only discovered in 1967 in Costa Rica's pristine Monteverde tropical cloud forest, disappeared just a few years after its discovery, there was a sense that something had gone terribly wrong— not only with frogs, but with our planet.

Because frogs must breathe through their sensitive, permeable skin, they act as good biological indicators of the environment's general health. William Souder of *The Washington Post* is of the opinion that we are responsible for causing some major change in the order of life, one that frogs have first sensed. "The frog is telling us something. Will we listen?" he asks.

Sadly, I must now show frogs to my two small boys in books rather than outdoors. I am not sure what it means to say that I love frogs, but I surely do.

Long before I knew of frogs' special qualities, I loved them. I have since learned more about these astonishing creatures, including African bullfrogs. (Bullfrogs are heavy-bodied frogs.) When heat begins to dry up the small ponds where they live, the tadpoles begin calling. The male bullfrog pays close attention. So his offspring can swim to safety, he immediately sets to work, digging a small trench through the mud from the closest pond that still has water. He decides how deep to dig the trench and where it can most easily be accessed by his children. Clearly, this is a thinking frog, a thoughtful one even.

Very little was known about the biology or behavior of frogs until fairly recently. Even the fact that frogs hibernate in winter by burying themselves in mud was not known. (Aristotle proposed that frogs were procreated from the mud.) For example, right into the nineteenth century it was believed that frogs could survive for centuries in stone or in the trunks of trees. It's true that gray tree frogs can withstand temperatures as low as minus twenty degrees Fahrenheit by manufacturing glycerol, an antifreeze ingredient, in their blood. When found frozen in blocks of ice, they thaw out and survive.

Of course it's dangerous to handle dart-poison frogs from Central and South America (so called because Colombian Indians dip their arrows in the poisonous secretions that exude from their skin when harassed). Most species of frogs and toads harbor at least a trace of poison in their glands. Skin rashes from handling frogs are not uncommon, although it's untrue that frogs cause warts. I've no doubt, too, that the frog's place as the victim par excellence in high school dissection classes has contributed to some people's ambivalence toward this exquisite amphibian.

For most frogs, breeding takes place in water. They migrate to their ancestral breeding ponds using an incompletely understood navigation method. To attract females to their breeding sites, males croak during the night. When many male frogs group together to chorus, is it that they derive the benefit of easier mating, or because they lower their risk of being attacked by a predator? Some smaller frogs, less adept at calling, hang out in these groups hoping to intercept some unsuspecting female. When a female arrives, she usually seeks out the loudest male. He mounts her, head-to-head, his thumbs swelling into what are called "nuptial pads," the better to grasp her slippery body. The clasping lasts anywhere from a few hours to weeks or even months—no doubt the longest mating act in the entire world. Why it should take so long is not clear. Since male frogs lack a penis, fertilization is external: When the female frog extrudes eggs from her genital cavity at the end of her intestinal canal, the male releases sperm from his cloaca, covering and thereby fertilizing the eggs. What happens next depends on the type of frog.

In many frog species, the female has finished her maternal task, whereas the male has just begun his. Darwin was fascinated by the unique role of the male in the reproductive process of a tiny frog he discovered in southern Chile (named the Darwin frog, *Rhinoderma darwini*). Just two South American frogs brood their young internally. When the female of these species lays her twenty or thirty eggs, the male guards them for a few weeks. He then picks them up with his tongue and seems to ingest them. But really he has only taken them into his large vocal sac, where they develop. In his mouth, they hatch into tadpoles and grow, taking nourishment from their father's mouth. Eventually they metamorphose into tiny froglets, ready to jump out of the paternal buccal cavity.

People express concern over the evident decrease in frogs around the world because it tells us what's in store for humans as well. But I agree with a comment by naturalist Edward Hoagland, author of *Tigers and Ice*, in which he reminds us that we should be worried for the sake of the animal itself—not just for what it tells us about our own species. The centers in our brain in which our emotions originate are remarkably old and primitive, not unlike those of the "lowly" frog. The term that biologists use to describe instances of identical behavior evolving in different species is *convergence*. However, I think it is not mere coincidence that humans and other animals love their children beyond everything else. I find it comforting, as well as humbling, to see that I have this in common with Darwin frogs.

GANNET

Morus bassanus bassanus

ALSO KNOWN AS THE SOLAND GOOSE, the gannet is a large, impressive seabird. Its rich cultural history goes back thousands of years, much of it having to do with it being the heavyweight of plunge-diving seabirds.

Three miles out to sea from the Scottish seaside town of North Berwick is the largest single-island gannet colony in the world. With at least forty thousand pairs of North Atlantic gannets returning each year, the Bass Rock is regarded by David Attenborough as "one of the twelve wildlife wonders of the World." A precipitous basalt island 350 feet high and almost a mile in circumference, the rock was mentioned in literature as a large colony (called a gannetry) as early as the sixth century. It is now one of the world's most famous bird islands. Dr. Bryan Nelson, the world's leading authority on gannets, lived on the Bass Rock in the 1960s to study their behavior. At that time there were only a few thousand birds, but their numbers have recovered, thanks to a cessation of persecution.

I often drive to a colony of these beautiful birds on an oceanic rock in

Muriwai Beach, an hour's drive from Auckland. These Australasian gannets are slightly smaller than their North Atlantic counterparts. There is another colony on a small island just a few feet away, but I have been told that the birds from one colony keep their distance from the birds of the other. (However, Bryan Nelson assures me this is unlikely.)

Every time I visit, there are always many other human visitors, each eager to impart information. I learned that the birds lay a single egg, which hatches after approximately forty-four days. The squab—sorry, that's what he is called—who emerges is tended by both father and mother. The chicks actually weigh one and a half times their parents' weight! Unusual for birds, the adolescents themselves decide when it is time to sever the tie with their devoted parents, usually at about thir-teen weeks. Now comes the moment that attracts so many human spec-tators: The black-feathered juvenile, too heavy with fat to fly, leaps off the cliff face and glides down to the sea. He cannot rise from the water, and so swims away, heading to warmer southern waters. Our New Zealand birds have to cover, by swimming and paddling, distances of al-most two thousand miles to warmer southern and eastern Australian waters, in a week or so! Two or three years later, still immature birds, they will return to home waters, usually to their natal colony, but maybe to a different part of it, playing for one or two years before begin-ning the serious work of seeking a mate.

When the male is about four years old, he establishes a site at the edge of the colony and begins advertising for a mate. When a female likes what she sees, they become a couple and breed the next season. If they live that long, which few do, they will stay together thirty years or longer, both faithful to each other and their original nest (if fate does not intervene, which it often does in the form of human interference, such as fishing nets).

These glistening white adults, with their black-tipped wings and yellow crowns, are wonderful birds to watch, gliding through the air with six-foot wingspans. Scanning the ocean from above, when a gan-net spots a hapless fish, he suddenly plunges like an attacking airplane. (British World War II antisubmarine high-performing aircraft were called "gannets.") Hitting the water at nearly eighty miles an hour, the bird chases its quarry under the water, almost invariably successfully.

Watching the gannets over several hours, I was surprised at how noisy they were. Most of the noise comes from mates greeting each other and from birds displaying in defense of their territories. The nests were carefully spaced, with just a foot or so between each. I suppose the arguments were about one bird stepping onto the territory of another, but who knows? Perhaps they had weightier topics to dispute. The males are aggressive, even with their mates, making what certainly looked like menacing lunges and even biting the female's neck. To what can we attribute what looks like constant temper tantrums? The seeming aggression between mates stems from the fact that the two sexes look alike, and, unsure whether they are dealing with a rival, elicit site-defense. No less an authority than Bryan Nelson, who has been observing gannets for more than fifty years, says that if he were asked to give a snap judgment "on what impressed me about gannets, my mind would leap not to their plunge diving but to their fights." It has to do with site competition, which is closely linked to breeding success. This matter is far from trivial, involving as it does genetic immortality.

New to gannet behavior, when I first saw a male bow, in my anthropomorphic naïveté I was sure that he was performing a gesture of gallantry toward his mate. If you watch any gannet colony, you'll see this bowing behavior many times in an hour. However, there can be no doubt, after the careful observations of Bryan Nelson, that bowing is motivated by aggression. It means: *I own this site, and I am prepared to fight for it. Stay away!* The noise that is conspicuous in a gannetry is coming from the hundreds of birds bowing and noisily insisting on their right to be right where they are. But we must keep in mind that peaceful gestures and the external signals of peaceful intentions are probably more subtle and harder to discern. I would not be surprised if there were barely visible movements indicating altruistic surrender that we will only understand years from now. Even in birds, it is easier to study and understand aggression than peace.

Some gestures are easier to understand, and anthropomorphism serves us well. For example, when one bird points a beak up to the sky, it clearly means: *I am taking off, leaving you in charge.* Then off this spectacular fisher goes to more plunging and diving, leaving all who watch in awe.

GECKOS

Family Gekkonidae

In the rural areas throughout Latin America, these geckos (subfamily Gekkoninae) and their allies, including Coleonyx (family Eublepharidae), are thought to be highly poisonous. They are reputed to sting or inject venom with their tails, and people believe that even touching one of them will lead to an unpleasant and rapid death. Actually these delicate creatures are neither venomous nor poisonous and are totally harmless.

—JAY M. SAVAGE,
The Amphibians and Reptiles of Costa Rica:
A Herpetofauna Between Two Continents, Between Two Seas

THE INTRIGUING FACTS THAT THESE LIZARDS have mysterious nocturnal habits, large eyes, and astonishing climbing abilities (racing upside down on ceilings) have apparently made geckos uncanny to some people. French writer La Rochefoucauld said what we do not understand we do not admire, so these animals have been deemed by many as "evil." In fact, *all* geckos are completely harmless.

Lizards have always enthralled me, ever since I bonded with one when I was ten. "Tiny" was a tiny lizard who emerged from a small crack in a wall in our backyard. He was, I am now sure, newly hatched, and completely without fear of humans. He stepped lightly onto my outstretched palm and stayed there basking in the sun. That night I took him with me to see a strange movie, *The Boy with Green Hair* (I have never heard about it since, but it moved me at the time). He dozed in my hand the entire time. When I returned, my parents wisely prevailed upon me to put Tiny back into the crevice from which he came. I reluctantly complied, but the next morning when I went to visit his home, he waited for me and eagerly (so it seemed) jumped into my familiar hand. We spent three days like this, and now I have to wonder if lizards have anything like imprinting. Could I have been the first living being he saw, a giant mother lizard? After the third day, he never returned and I mourned our friendship, wondering if he had a parent less understanding than my own or perhaps one not in favor of interspecies friendships. Eric Pianka says it probably fell prey to a predator.

In 1955, when I was fourteen, our family went to live in Kailua on the windward side of the island of Oahu, in Hawaii. The walls were teeming with small, translucent geckos. They had flattened bodies, large heads, and big eyes with no eyelids. I presume, now, that they were house geckos (*Hemidactylus frenatus*). They were an absolute delight to watch, though I must admit that my many attempts to cross the species barrier went completely unreciprocated. These were not friendly. Although they lived next to us, it was as if we were invisible to them. They showed not the slightest interest in us. They did not appear frightened or alarmed by our presence—we were just part of the furniture.

I never tired of watching them and, even better, *listening* to them, for they made a large number of noises. As scientists say of them today, "they have complex multiple click vocalizations." Once in the middle of the night our whole family jumped out of bed because we thought we heard a baby screaming or loudly crying. But it was one gecko saying something indecipherable to another gecko. Talk, geckos do. Female geckos are known to make a single chirp when they have been taken prisoner by a predator. The meaning of this click is crystal clear: *Help!* She is calling other geckos to her aid, though I'm not sure why, since I cannot imagine what another gecko could do to help her once a cat or a rat has caught her in his clutches. It is instinctive, I suppose, as it would be with us in moments of mortal terror. Eric Pianka informs me that sometimes the call could startle a predator, causing it to release the gecko. I was fascinated by the many different sounds they made, which were clearly purposeful: *Here I am! Don't come any closer! How dare you!* They even have a warning growl, and a sound to indicate *But I love you!* The word *gecko* itself is probably a reflection of one of these calls— and it makes sense that these nocturnal creatures should have so many sounds, for they have excellent ears and sleep during the day, needing to find each other only at night.

Bell geckos (*Ptenopus* spp.) of southern Africa attract females by call- ing them from their burrow entrances, which serve as resonating cham- bers to amplify the sounds. Like many frogs, they will also call in choruses, and presumably the female is attracted to the best or the loud- est or the sweetest singer.

Our brightly illuminated living room overlooked the Pacific Ocean, the whole family was in the room, and the geckos were busy devouring the various insects that came in from the balmy Hawaiian nights, at- tracted to our lights. We were happy to see them eat mosquitoes. I sup- pose geckos have always been welcome guests in tropical homes, probably why they show no fear. After all, who would object to their presence? Moreover, you could see how many insects they ate because their stomachs were transparent. Inside were the small black bodies of their prey. I could watch them for hours. I loved to see a small tongue emerge, though not so small that it could not reach their own eyes and lick clean the transparent covering.

Another pleasure I took was finding the tiny little white eggs the fe- males deposited on the ceiling. Not infrequently, I'd be staring at them when suddenly I'd spot activity within. A few minutes later out popped a miniature, fully formed baby gecko. No child could witness this without complete absorption. And then this little baby would scurry away, fast, and upside down on the ceiling!

Each of their four feet has specialized toe pads. On each of the twenty toes there are overlapping rows of scales. Each scale is made up of 150,000 or more projections, hairlike bristles, or setae (attached to nerve cells relaying information to the gecko's brain). Each seta is in turn divided into many hundreds of filaments, like suction cups, visible under a scanning electron microscope, which terminate in endplates or spatulas. Professor Aaron Bauer informs me the molecules of the gecko's toes actually form weak temporary bonds with the molecules of the surfaces they walk on.

Parthenogenesis is not uncommon in geckos. For example, there are no males in the mourning gecko species (*Lepidodactylus lugubris*), which reproduces by parthenogenesis, producing exclusively females. This evolved from the hybridization of two bisexual parental species.

While most geckos are not brightly colored, there are some exceptions, such as the Indian golden gecko (*Calodactylodes aureus*). In this case only the largest male is brightly colored. If he dies or is killed or leaves, lo and behold, the next largest male takes on his coloration and becomes king. (Expert Eric Pianka, however, is skeptical of this.)

Another awful thing I did as a child was to catch lizards. I became quite expert at it, because when we visited the desert in Palm Springs, California, my father would give me a quarter for each lizard I caught. I would release them soon enough, but I sometimes observed that in order to escape my predation they lost their tail. (Autotomy is an ability shared by eleven out of the sixteen families of lizards—the tails have fracture planes in one or more of the vertebrae.) This strategy evolved as a last-ditch lifesaving device: The severed tail wiggled and twisted and jumped, and the fascinated predator lost concentration while the prey escaped. I assumed then that it was cost-free to the escapee. Not so: Australian marbled geckos, for example, are known to live longer when they retain the tail. Eric Pianka informs me that tails regenerate and some can become almost indistinguishable from the original—so that they can use anatomy to escape yet again if the situation demands it.

GIANT PANDA

Ailuropoda melanoleuca

IANT PANDAS ARE the most endangered bears in the world. They may have once lived in Tibet, but today there are fewer than two thousand pandas scattered across five mountain ranges in southwest China.

There is a charming example of how the animal was regarded by the ancient Chinese. In the West Jin dynasty seventeen hundred years ago, the giant panda was called *Zhouyu*. Because it eats only bamboo and does not hurt other animals, the panda was seen as an "animal of justice," a symbol of peace and friendliness. So when two forces met in a fierce battle, if one party showed a flag marked ZHOUYU, the battle halted, for this flag meant peace and friendship.

In the 1920s the giant panda was thought to be extinct. Then the Chicago Field Museum of Natural History sponsored the expedition of brothers Kermit Roosevelt and Theodore Roosevelt Jr., sons of the American president Theodore Roosevelt. In April 1928 they "discovered" an old male giant panda quaking with fear in a hollow pine tree, and shot him dead. This was a much-celebrated event, a fact that gives me hope for the notion of moral progress. "Pandamania" took hold of the West and other expeditions were outfitted, which contributed to the threat of extinction. A new book by Vicki Croke tells the gripping story of Ruth Harkness, a New York socialite who brought the first giant panda to America in 1936, then experienced a change of heart and devoted her life to returning them to the wild.

From the beginning there was uncertainty as to what family this animal belonged to: bear, raccoon, or its very own. If red pandas are bears, they are the world's smallest. They weigh only about eleven pounds, whereas giant pandas regularly weigh more than two hundred. All other bears are carnivores, so it was thought that if pandas were carnivores (they are), they are carnivores who eat no meat. Every day, pandas eat a huge amount, nearly half their weight, eighty-four or more pounds. They spend fourteen hours a day eating. Bamboo is at least 99 percent of their diet. However, there aren't many nutrients in bamboo, which is why they must eat such enormous quantities. The effort is exhausting, and when they finish they lie back and take a nap. Like cats, pandas often just lie around, conserving energy.

In any event, their monotonous diet does not seem to have affected their intelligence. Alas, their intellectual ability has been taken advantage of to amuse zoogoers: Pandas at the Fuzhou Zoo in China have been taught more than twenty stunts, including riding a bicycle and eating with a knife and fork.

It has been noted that the giant panda never hibernates. But then only three of the other eight species of bears do so, and none is an obligate hibernator. Pandas also do not roar like other bears. They bleat. On the other hand, like other bears, pandas are pretty solitary. But unlike other bears, pandas seem to have a thumb. This is really part of the wrist bone. Called panda's thumb, it allows pandas to hold bamboo much as we would. Instead of the usual round eye of other bears, the pupils of the panda are vertical slits like those of a cat, perhaps why the Chinese often called the panda a cat bear. And as noted, like cats, pandas like nothing better than simply lying around.

Not only is the giant panda a bear, but—based on the absence of tauroursodeoxycholic acid in giant panda bile—the latest research makes the panda the oldest extant bear. They are most closely related to South America's spectacled bear (*Tremarctos ornatus*). The giant panda is also distantly related to the red panda (*Ailurus fulgens*), called the lesser panda.

Another peculiarity of the giant panda is how small the babies are. When born, they are pink, toothless, naked, blind, and helpless. They are less than six inches long and weigh three and a half to seven ounces. The female gives birth mostly to twins, but since she can only raise one successfully, she abandons one at birth. The abandoned twin, of course, cannot survive. I wonder if abandonment has always been practiced. There is only one case in captivity where a mother successfully raised twins without human assistance. But obviously this happens at least sometimes in the wild, since naturalist George Schaller and others have seen twins outside a den. Why would a mother have twins only to routinely abandon one? Other bears also sometimes abandon their young; sloth bears are forced to abandon a third cub who cannot fit on the mother's back. In the past, pandas may have been able to successfully raise twins, but their habitat is now so restricted that they may no longer have the needed natural resources. Baby pandas are almost unbearably attractive to humans. Those lucky enough to have touched one say the cub is as soft as a kitten. The surviving twin is irresistible to its mother bear as well: She keeps the babe cradled in her forepaws almost continuously for his first three weeks of life. She sits up and holds her baby to her breast as would a human mother nursing her child. Like many mothers, she nurses for about a year. When she carries the baby in her mouth, she keeps a paw under her chin as a safety net should the cub fall. When she is out foraging, she places her cub in a tree for many hours, and even for periods of more than two days.

China began lending pandas to foreign zoos in the 1970s as a political move. People in the West could not get enough viewing of the giant panda. In the 1980s China lent pandas to American zoos for ten-year periods. The loan fee was a million dollars per year, and any cubs born would belong to China. Lately the fee has gone up; the San Diego Zoo spent ten million dollars for its last panda from China. There are probably some 1,600 giant pandas in the wild, and 160 in zoos worldwide.

Pandas are notorious for reproducing only with great difficulty in captivity. So far only two captive-born males have successfully mated. It could be diet, for they can never be fed the exact same bamboo they would get in the wild. Or it could be that captivity reduces sexual drive: Why propagate if your children will be born into slavery? Perhaps it's depression. Or the matter of choice: We know little about how pandas find each other, but it is not haphazard, and the female must exercise choice, impossible in captivity. The record is definitely improving, however. Part of the problem is simply that we do not know enough about the life of a wild panda. Since 1997 the Chinese government has banned the use of radio collars for studying wild pandas, though nobody knows why. The latest scientific research concludes, "We do not believe that conservation of the giant panda can be assured, nor can its scientific study go forward, without recourse to radiotelemetry."

For a long time the Chinese government imposed the death penalty on poachers of giant pandas. Now it is twenty years in prison. However, harsh penalties have not entirely stopped poaching, considering how much money a panda skin will fetch—in the tens of thousands of dollars. Still, by far the panda's greatest problem is habitat loss. So when the Chinese government decreed a ten-year ban on logging in areas occupied by the giant panda, it was a great victory for the bears. And the fact that the giant panda is the only bear not valued in Chinese medicine has been a great blessing for this entirely charismatic, much-loved animal.

GIANT SQUID

Architeuthis dux

W HO COULD REMAIN UNEXCITED at hearing of a giant mollusk with giant unblinking eyes, a parrotlike beak, eight arms, and two feeding tentacles with suckers containing tooth-like talons? Furthermore, what if I were to tell you that such a creature can grow up to fifty-five feet long, and almost no one has ever seen one alive? The deep sea has many mysteries.

For many, there's a fascination in imagining titanic clashes, and for hundreds of years sailors have trumpeted battles between a giant sea monster—the mysterious giant squid—and huge sperm whales, the creature gifted with the largest brain of any animal ever. However, while the sperm whale tries to ingest, the giant squid is only attempting escape. Still, it is not a one-sided struggle: Not only are giant squid more agile and faster swimmers, but they have a major advantage over their mammalian enemy as well in that they need not surface to breathe, while a whale does. Quite a feat for the whale, though, when you think about it: to hold your breath, dive a mile down into pitch-dark waters, and find a fast-moving giant mollusk for dinner. That said, sperm whales are the world's best divers: Able to descend to ten thousand feet, they can hold their breath for an hour and a half. Still, when you get down below three hundred or so feet, neither squid nor whale sees the other. Toothed whales hunt giant squid by emitting focused sound beams of such intensity that they can stun or even kill giant squid. They are a full-grown giant squid's only natural enemy, simply because these mollusks are too large to be eaten by any other animal.

How many squid does a sperm whale need to eat every day? The figure provided by British whale scientist Malcolm Clarke takes us further into the realm of the unimaginable: As paraphrased by Ellis, "the weight of squids eaten every year by sperm whales is greater than the weight of the entire human race." What this says about the number of giant squid who exist on our planet is mind-blowing. Also astounding to consider is the fact that the only other animal who knows the habits of the giant squid is the sperm whale. Now it's our turn to hold our breath, while waiting for that largest of brains to reveal the mysteries of the deep!

The northeastern coast of New Zealand's South Island, deep in the Kaikoura Canyon, is considered the prime habitat of the giant squid, as well as the year-round home of sperm whales. Nobody has ever spent time with giant squid in their own deep-sea home, but a number of their dead bodies have washed ashore on the nearby coast. The longest was fifty feet and weighed about a ton. Bernard Heuvelmans is a famed cryptozoologist. (He invented this term for somebody who searches for hidden or unknown animals.) Heuvelmans believes a legendary squid is somewhere out there: "There are good reasons to believe that there may even exist specimens . . . around 64 tons." Nonsense, say most teuthologists. Not a single one has been found longer than fifty-five feet. However, many concede that there may well be hundred-footers out there, as science-fiction writer Arthur C. Clarke believes, along with scientist Fred Aldrich. The ocean at its deepest is more than thirty-five thousand feet, or seven miles, farther down than Mount Everest is high. Who knows what creatures live in these benthic depths? We are only at the beginning of knowledge.

We cannot know much about the nature of an animal rarely seen in the wild, even one whose dead body we're able to examine. How it reproduces, with whom, how often, when, and where are all matters of speculation. How big is the newborn? Tiny, it turns out, about the size of a quarter. Is there parental care? Unlikely. The giant squid is a solitary hunter, but how solitary? Is there a period of courtship? Does it involve any feelings? And if she starts out so small at birth, at least part of her life she must be more hunted than a hunter. How many are born at one time, and what percentage grows to become adults? We know none of this.

Do they actively seek out their prey or passively wait for them? Are they gentle giants or lethal killers? Do they come to the surface at times other than when they are sick or dying? Would healthy giant squid spend all their time in the darkest depths of the ocean, thousands of feet down? If so, how would they actually find their food, when there is no light there? Teuthologists endlessly speculate on these matters.

Why have these animals eluded scientists for so long? Sad to think that one of the great researchers, Fred Aldrich, although he descended in a submersible to a depth of eight hundred feet in 1990, died without having seen a living giant squid. And now, at last, an image of the living animal has been captured: In September 2004, Japanese scientists took the first ever photographs of a live giant squid in the wild. The animal was roughly twenty-five feet long and was photographed at three thousand feet beneath the North Pacific Ocean, off the Ogasawara Islands. Japanese scientists attracted the squid toward cameras attached to a baited fishing line, a primitive way to go about capturing images of an animal if there was no intention to harm. The scientists took five hundred images of the massive cephalopod, but when the squid approached the baited line, a tentacle became caught on one of the hooks. It was severed. Could this have been deliberate on the squid's part, a form of autotomy as practiced by many lizards?

It seems illogical that a creature of such massive size could remain invisible for so long when so many dedicated researchers would give their scientific lives to find this fascinating sea animal. However, given what we know about the planet's many creatures who have more interaction with the human world, perhaps the squid's elusive quality is the ulti-mate sign of a vital intelligence.

LTHOUGH FOR YEARS scientists thought they belonged to a separate species, the siamang is actually a gibbon, merely twice the size of other gibbons. The appeal of these nimble swingers is universal. It's impossible to see one of these elegant animals gamboling through the trees with enormous ease without having a sense of awe.

People who live near the evergreen rain forests of the extreme east of India, southern China, Myanmar, the Malay Peninsula, and other parts of Southeast Asia feel a special affinity with the gibbon: Haunting the local poetry are these animals' loud, clear, mysterious, and beautiful duet calls, which can last for almost an hour. Then there is the gibbons' resemblance to humans: no tail, an upright posture, an intelligent expression, and, most touching of all, the close family bonds that tie gibbons together. These creatures are monogamous, unusual for a primate, and the fathers are very involved in raising the single child, especially in the case of the siamang.

They are beautiful to look at as well, with faces resembling a worried or preoccupied human. For some reason, in the north of their range gibbons are sexually dichromatic—that is, the males are all black, and the females are all gray. Some people have mistaken them for two separate species. Not being aggressive, in fact completely *un*aggressive, males and females exhibit no difference in size. Males rarely fight, and surely one of the functions of the calls is to keep distinct groups separate from one another. But then what is the purpose of what has been called the "great call" made only by the females, which has been described as "probably the finest music made by any wild land mammal"?

There are eleven species of gibbons in the world. In 1975 there were estimated to be about four million gibbons. Nobody knows for certain how many are left, but estimates are distressing. Some of the crested gibbons are close to extinction, and the moloch gibbon has declined from about twenty thousand to fewer than one thousand. Two other gibbon species are near extinction as well.

For more than two thousand years gibbons have played an important role in Chinese painting and poetry. The great Dutch sinologist R. H. van Gulik (the creator of the internationally acclaimed Judge Dee detective stories) has written an extraordinary book about this: *The Gibbon in China: An Essay in Chinese Animal Lore*—now rare, but a true treasure. A former diplomat, van Gulik had many of the animals himself when he was in the Dutch embassy in China, and he writes about them with enormous affection and knowledge. For example, he lets us know that gibbons cannot bear to be reprimanded, and must make amends: "Gibbons have a most engaging way of showing remorse, laying their hand on one's arm and making soft, propitiating noises." He realizes that these animals should not be kept by individuals, even though the practice was once common. For one thing, in order to capture a baby, the mother has to be killed. For another, as soon as the infant is sexually mature, he becomes unreliable and miserable. They are wild animals and were never meant to be taken away from their natural habitat. We should remember this for *all* wild species.

But the real treat found in van Gulik's book are the details about gibbons it provides from classical Chinese literature. Who could not be affected by the following story by the eleventh-century writer P'eng Ch'eng, which van Gulik translated for the first time? "The Buddhist monk Wu-k'ung once saw on the other side of the Yangtze River a gibbon with her child sitting on the branch of a tree. An archer spied her out and shot her, hitting her in her belly. She called her mate, and together with her child they began to cry pitifully. Then she pulled the arrow and fell onto the ground dead. The archer broke his arrows and threw his bow away, and swore he would never use them again."

But by far the most extraordinary passage that van Gulik translates comes from one of China's great classical painters and writers: Wen T'ung, who lived from 1019 to 1079. When one of his gibbons died, he wrote this remarkable poem, a lament that is, in van Gulik's opinion (and my own), one of the great laments of history. That is why I reproduce it here in its entirety. It bears reading many times:

Last year a Buddhist monk of Hua-p'ing, in the Min mountains,
Obtained a gibbon for me and had it delivered from afar.
On arrival he was already tame and accustomed to captivity,
And his swift and nimble movements were a delight to watch.
He would come and go as told, as if he understood my speech.
And seemed to have lost all desire to return to his mountains.
Put on a leash he was not interesting to watch,
So I set him free and let him romp about as much as he liked.
On a moonlit night he would sing, swinging from a branch,
On hot days he would sit by the flowers and doze facing the sun.
When my children were around or my guests showed their
    interest,
He would hang upside down or jump about showing his tricks.
I had told a man to look after all his needs,
So that he never even once lacked his seasonal food and drink.
Yet the other day his keeper suddenly told me the gibbon was ill.
He stood on my steps, the gibbon in his arms, and I went to look,

Offered him persimmons and chestnuts, but he didn't glance at
    them.
Legs drawn up, head between his knees, hunched up with folded
    arms,
His fur ruffled and dull, all at once his body seemed to have
    shrunk,
And I realized that this time he was really in great distress.
Formerly you were also subject to occasional slight indispositions,
But then after I had fed you a few spiders as a remedy,
After having swallowed them you would recover at once.
Why did the medicine fail now, though given several times?
This morning when a frosty wind was chilling me to the bone,
Very early I sent someone to inquire, and he reported you had died.
Although in this world it is hard to avoid grief and sadness,
I was tormented by repentance and bitter self-reproach.
You could be happy only when near your towering mountains.
You had been yearning for far plains and dense forests.
You must have suffered deeply being kept on leash or chain,
And that was why your allotted span of life was cut short.
I had his body wrapped up well and buried deep in a secluded
    corner,
So that at least the insects would leave his remains in peace.
Mr. Tzu-p'ing, my western neighbor, a man of very wide interests,
When he heard about this, slapped his thigh sighing without end.
He came to inquire several times, in deep sorrow over my loss,
Then, back home, he wrote a long poem of over a hundred words.
Reading those lines my lonely heart was filled with sadness,
Well had he expressed the grief caused by my gibbon's death!
He also tried to console me by referring to life's natural course,
That meetings result in partings, all subject to the whims of fate.
I took his poem out into the garden, read and re-read it—
Then, looking up at the bare branches, I burst out in tears.

GIRAFFE
Giraffa camelopardalis

L ITTLE IS KNOWN ABOUT GIRAFFES, their behavior, their family life, their inner life, even the scope of their intelligence. Our knowledge about giraffes lags far behind our long love affair with this remarkable animal. The history of giraffes and humans is therefore one of much wonder but little knowledge.

Obviously, the wonder stems from their appearance. Whether seeing them in the wild or in a zoo, nobody can keep from feeling astonishment at their sheer height, at the elegance of their fur, at their remarkable gait. Above all, however, they convey great gentleness. In reading about giraffes this word, and others like it, crop up continuously: Giraffes are gentle, they have forbearance, they are harmless, they are inoffensive, and so on. In this case, as is rarely so, appearances are not deceiving, and there is general agreement on the fact that giraffes are remarkable for their ability to get on with a large variety of other creatures. They almost never fight, either among themselves or with other species, and in any outdoor enclosure you are likely to see giraffes with zebras, wildebeest, ostriches, elands, and various other animals living amicably together and getting on without any signs of friction. The reason, perhaps, for the astonishment at such gentleness lies in the animal's size: Male giraffes can grow up to eighteen feet in height, weighing more than four thousand pounds. Given their size and the strength of their feet, people are amazed that they seem totally lacking in aggression, except when defending their calves. (Make no mistake: If necessary, a giraffe can decapitate a lion with a single swipe—after all, their hooves are the size of dinner plates.) There are no records of a giraffe harming *any* animal except in self-defense. They never kick each other. The only form of combat is primarily a ritualized one of "necking," where two males wrap their necks around each other in an attempt to determine mating priority, but this has almost never been seen to eventuate in harm.

Giraffes are strict vegetarians and complete pacifists. Perhaps their ability to browse where other animals cannot go allows them freedom from any sense of territoriality; its accompanying sense of "mine" seems absent in giraffe society. They have a natural curiosity and are friendly even with their single greatest enemy, humans. Blair Pollock tells of a strange encounter in a tent, where a giraffe seemed to display an odd sense of humor. One does not know whether to laugh or weep for the degradation imposed on this royal animal:

All that was in the tent was a giraffe in a roped off ring surrounded by hundreds of highly amused fairgoers. This particular giraffe played a game with the humans in which he craned his massive head and neck out over the audience until he spotted a man wearing a hat and then leaned over the man and knocked his hat off. The tent rocked with laughter. Then he'd crane some more, find a woman he liked and rest his massive head briefly on her shoulder. Following this, he'd repeat the hat-knocking behavior, but only with men, and canoodle again, but only with adult, two-legged females.

Their inoffensiveness has not spared giraffes from senseless slaughter. There are fewer than a hundred thousand in the world. Even today, with their numbers still not recovered from the nineteenth-century hunters' desire to own trophies, some African nations (South Africa, Zimbabwe, Botswana, Namibia, and Tanzania) sell licenses to shoot giraffes.

Giraffes are reluctant to lie down. They even give birth standing up. Their babies must withstand a nearly six-foot fall to the ground. Strangely, they sleep only about half an hour a day—standing up, of course. And even that short sleep is in the form of five-minute catnaps. They sleep in a circle formation, with all the adults facing a different direction, obviously a means of detecting any potential predator. Since adult giraffes have no predators except humans, this is likely done exclusively for the sake of the young in the herd. Why lie down when getting up is such a complex and lengthy procedure? Evidently such a large frame is also not designed for swimming, and nobody has ever seen a giraffe voluntarily take a bath.

Giraffe calves are born nearly six feet tall, weighing 150 pounds. They are among the most precocial of all young, and are walking and following their mother within fifteen minutes of birth. In the herd these babies are completely protected and need fear no predator. After the first few weeks living exclusively with their mothers, the young calves join a crèche with about nine other young giraffes their own age, where they are nursed by female relatives, groups of cows that stay in the nursery while the mother browses, sometimes at great distances, to make certain they come to no harm. Presumably this is the reason they are not a solitary species, and females are rarely out of sight of another female, even one unrelated.

In 1781 the artist George-Louis Buffon articulated the most famous comment made about giraffes: "The giraffe . . . without being noxious, is at the same time extremely useless." This strange opinion was then often repeated by nineteenth-century naturalists, of which the following comment is typical: "A creature so strangely shaped . . . was certainly designed by the Creator for some other use than browsing upon the leaves of mimosa trees; but that use, man has not yet discovered."

One vocalization giraffes make has been described as being like the sound of a flute, but there is no understanding of when or how it is used. It is unclear to me why so little is known about giraffes. I was intrigued, for example, by nineteenth-century accounts of hunters who shot them at close range, and claimed they shed tears as they were dying. Wrote Captain William Cornwallis Harris in 1840: "I sat in my saddle, loading and firing . . . Mute, dignified, and majestic stood the unfortunate victim, occasionally stooping his elastic neck towards his persecutor; the tears trickling from the lashes of his dark humid, as broadside after broadside was poured into his brawny front." But although I found at least three such accounts, I've been unable to confirm this in any scientific account. I suspect it is a piece of understandable anthropomorphism. After all, they have such long-lashed limpid eyes.

Much like us, young giraffes seem to get joy from spending long periods of time simply gazing out at the countryside. And these majestic animals have none of the hierarchy we associate with herds or packs. They come together for the sheer pleasure of company. Perhaps if we learned the secrets of these gentle giants, we might also follow their example of tolerance, friendliness, and harmlessness.

GLOWWORM

Arachnocampa luminosa

THE MOST FAMOUS FLY IN NEW ZEALAND is the glowworm—not really a worm at all, but a bioluminescent larva. This is not the firefly with which people are familiar in the United States. Every tourist to New Zealand is likely to visit the Waitomo Caves near Auckland, floating quietly in a boat while above it appears that a sky filled with thousands of stars has been imported into the cavern. What you are seeing are bioluminescent larvae (worms), pupae, and large mosquito-like flies. If you shine a light (which you should not), you will also see a sentinel spider, who protects the glowworm from the many larger insects, moths, and beetles who would normally be attracted by the light and consume the source of the spider's bounty. The cohabitation is good for both. I will refrain from asking whether they like each other!

Immediately upon hatching—often in a dark, moist cave—the larva known as the glowworm emits a bright light. Using mucus and silk, the tiny worm constructs a nest, which it suspends from the ceiling of the grotto on silk strands. It then lets down up to seventy vertical fishing lines with small nodules of mucus at regular intervals. Small insects in the streams below are attracted to the light (the hungrier the larva, the brighter it glows) and rise up the silken threads, only to get caught on one of the nodules. The worm, sensing the movement, then pulls up the line and eats the hapless bugs.

After what is a rather long life for a worm, from six months up to nearly a year, the fully grown glowworm prepares for pupation. It uses its fishing lines as a kind of protective barrier into which it hangs and suspends vertically. The transparent worm turns opaque, shrinks in size, and in about twelve days becomes the glowworm fly. The luminous organs still function; this time their purpose is apparently to attract males even as the worm is pupating. As soon she comes out, there's a male fly waiting, attracted by the low-intensity glowing signal sent by the female in her pupal casing. They even mate as she emerges from the cocoon. The flies have no mouths and cannot eat. They don't need to, since their only "purpose" is to produce eggs. The female lives only one or two days, and once she lays her eggs—130 of them—she no longer glows. The male lives longer, up to five days, presumably because he might need all that time to find another mate.

Amazingly, the luminous organ of the larva (worm), the pupa, and the imago (fly) can be switched off and on at will, especially when disturbed by sound and light. If you shine a flashlight at the worms, they immediately shut down (probably thinking it is day).

The Maori called glowworms *titiwai* and had a saying the equivalent of which is to be found in nearly every culture: "The darkness cannot be dispelled by the light of the *titiwai*."

Gerard Hutching reports how an ecology student, Adam Broadley, in 1995 used a time-lapse videorecorder to study glowworms at Waitomo. He captured footage of a female fly emerging with her light shining brightly. A male was attracted to the light and the pair copulated for twenty-six hours, more or less her entire life.

GOATS

Capra aegagrus (wild goat) and
C. hircus (domestic goat)

G OATS AND HUMANS HAVE MUCH IN COMMON. Goats look you in the eye. And they have a sense of humor. They'll butt you for a joke. While cows and sheep are cautious of human contact and actively avoid unfamiliar people, goats seek us out and for some mysterious reason do not perceive humans as a threat. Perhaps this is why they're becoming increasingly popular as companion animals. They are never dull, and seem to have an opinion about everything. Some baby goats are irresistible, and I warn you not to take your young children to a goat farm, especially one that specializes in unusual breeds, such as the gentle Nigerian dwarf or the thirty-five-pound African pygmy goat, or you will wind up with one of these charming friends in your own backyard.

There are about seven hundred million goats in the world. They thrive in almost as wide a range of temperatures as humans. Other reasons for their long-standing popularity include the facts that they are easily managed (even by children), their milk is easy to digest (especially for children), and they provide (alas) meat and fiber for clothing and housing, as well as skins for clothing and lightweight, watertight containers—important in arid desertlike conditions.

There are eight species of goats, but within the family of the domestic goat there are four hundred recognized breeds and varieties. There are more than six hundred million domestic goats throughout the world, kept for milk, meat, and wool. Few seem aware that mohair and cashmere come from goats.

The male goat has a chin beard and a caudal scent gland that makes him disagreeably smelly to humans, though not of course to she-goats. We call the she-goat a doe or nanny goat, the he-goat a billy or buck. A billy's smell is intensified by his habit of bending his head between his forelegs to catch his urinary spray at the time of rutting, for two months of the year, usually November and December, when hormones in the bloodstream activate the scent. All goats have erect tails. The horns of a goat are slender and rise vertically from the top of the head.

Play is important in the life of all young goats. The young of goats are called kids—the origin of our word for human children, probably because of these baby animals' playfulness—"no kidding"! Kids gallop in circles. They make high, arching jumps and little dances. They engage in social play, with the whole herd taking part. They slide, leap onto their mothers' backs, toss their heads, whirl on their own axes, spring vertically, and play-fight one another for hours.

Until recently, it was thought the domestic goat directly descended from wild goats, or bezoars, distinguished by their scimitar-shaped horns. But Valerius Geist tells me the origin of domestic goats is from an island in the Mediterranean where goats feature the odd horn mutation typical of domestic goats. After the dog, the goat was the second animal to be domesticated. Between 7000 and 8000 BCE people in the Middle East took bezoars into captivity, choosing them over other animals because of their eating habits, still notorious today—as depicted in cartoons of goats eating the laundry. Given a choice, goats, like every other animal, choose the food best suited to them, but they seem far less picky than many other animals. And they can, as others cannot, digest high-fiber and high-lignon-content diets. Since herds of goats would eat everything in the vicinity of their nomadic masters, tribes would move without bothering to replant any of the trees or other vegetation destroyed by their goats. It is believed that goats created the deserts of the Middle East and the Sahara in this way. Certainly goats are known for their ability to live in arid lands, which support only xerophytic vege- tation (such as cactus) that would defeat just about any other mammal.

Maybe the reason goats do not fear humans is that goats fear few an- imals. In India goats have been seen to kill leopards. They can revert to the wild and quickly go feral, especially on islands where there are not likely to be many predators, such as Hawaii, New Zealand, the Galápa- gos, and Crete.

There are numerous breeds of goats raised for pure pleasure, valued for their aesthetic look or even in some cases as companions, rather than for their meat or milk. From an early time, some goats developed lop ears and even came in dwarf versions. One breed of dwarfs from Khartoum in the Sudan dates from 3300 BCE. Why ears that flop down is invariably a sign of domestication, I don't quite understand, but it certainly is. In the wild, all animals (with the single exception of elephants) have ears that stand straight up. Is it just that domestic animals no longer need to keep their hearing so sharp as before now that they are not surrounded by enemies the detection of whom is lifesaving?

The often joyous acceptance of goats today is something new. It has not always been so. There have been many negative associations with goats. Even the common term *scapegoat* refers to a bizarre ritual in which one goat is sacrificed and another, "the scapegoat," is allowed to escape, carrying with him the sins of the people. Who can forget Goya's *Sabbath, or the Gathering of Sorcerers*, where the he-goat monster dom- inates the center of the canvas, and an old witch is offering him the sac- rifice of a child? Indeed, at the Last Judgment, goats are on the left, whereas the sheep on the right are headed for salvation, for they have heard and answered to the voice of the shepherd (the origin, probably, of the expression "sorting the sheep from the goats"). What this ac- knowledges is the amazing independence of goats, who are unpre- dictable and, in human judgment, self-centered.

Goats are flamboyant and extroverted, and have playful minds, many people who live with them tell us. For many, goats are reminiscent of

other humans: curious, greedy, and proud. Perhaps it is because we recognize so many human features in goats that, by and large, our myths
about them are generally less negative and aggressive than for just
about any other domesticated farm animal. (The major exception to this
would be the myth of the goat's relation to the devil.) Some of our prejudices are not even far wrong, for no animal is as sexually precocious as
the goat. Kids have been mated at three months by billies of under a year
old and produced young. One male can easily mate with ten to fifteen
females in a single day. "You old goat" is no idle insult (or compliment).

W HEN HE FIRST ENCOUNTERED a large silverback male gorilla in Parc National des Volcans in Rwanda in 1959, the great naturalist George Schaller was immediately struck by this animal's dignity and restrained power. Schaller also felt certain the gorilla was aware of his own majesty. Never before had Schaller, an experienced zoologist, felt a desire to communicate with an animal as he did at this moment. What Schaller wanted the gorilla to know was that he intended him no harm. He felt awe when he looked directly into the gorilla's eyes. And in the eyes of one old female, he saw kindness, tolerance, and a bemused, faraway expression. Schaller felt a sudden recognition of kinship.

Dian Fossey followed in his footsteps and felt the same way. Both managed to convey these feelings to the rest of us, and gorillas have since become an iconic species, demanding from us recognition of their deep and close relationship to humans.

Gorillas are mostly vegetarian. Even when they are presented with animal products in the wild, such as bird eggs, they avoid them. The only exception is ants and termites, which they evidently do eat, though Schaller never saw them do so. And while there are accounts of chimpanzees attacking young African children as a source of food, this has never been recorded for a gorilla.

I am always a bit puzzled by the human fascination with intelligence. How intelligent is that animal, we always seem to want to know. We are especially interested in comparisons: Scientists ask whether the gorilla is less mentally advanced than the chimpanzee, noting that gorillas do not use tools in the wild, whereas chimpanzees do (using twigs, for example, to fish for termites, or rocks to break open nuts). And when animals such as gorillas fail to recognize themselves in a mirror, we are convinced we have found their intellectual Achilles' heel. But what if this is merely a human contrivance with no bearing on the lives of the animals involved? Perhaps gorillas don't need tools, or don't like them, or don't care. Perhaps mirror recognition is an artificial device invented by humans, with no relevance to the lives of the animals tested.

But we wonder, even when we vow not to. George Schaller asked himself why gorillas, who seem to abhor rain, never made efforts to get out of it. The rain comes, the shelter of a large tree beckons, and gorillas stay where they are, miserable with stoic faces and bad tempers. Once he even saw them leave a warm, dry, snug spot under a tree to build their nests in the open rain! Go figure. One day, no doubt, we will understand the reasons behind this puzzling behavior. Best not to attribute it to stupidity, however.

Many people have noted that among animals, only humans seem able to convey information about the day before yesterday. The retort has always been that other animals have no need to do so. I suppose if I woke up tomorrow as a gorilla, I could adjust, but I'd miss reading *The New York Times*. And yet, just fifty years ago, to wake up as a gorilla would be to have been saved from the slaughter of the Second World War. Comparing species has an odious aspect, agreed, but I'm not certain that we have such an advantage, everything else taken into consideration. True, we can convey far more information, but it's possible that gorillas experience far more contentment. Certainly Schaller experienced the enlargement of his own capacity for contentment simply by being in their presence day after day.

Speaking of gentleness, isn't it necessary to give a nod, at least, to the extraordinary spectacle that took place on August 16, 1996, in Chicago's Brookfield Zoo in the primate exhibit? A three-year-old boy fell nearly twenty feet into the gorilla enclosure. While onlookers gasped in horror, Binti Jua, an eight-year-old western lowland gorilla, approached the inert boy, gently picked him up, and carried him to safety. She then sat down on a log in a stream and cradled the boy in her lap, giving him a gentle pat on the back before going to the door of her enclosure. *Time* editors named her one of the "best people" of 1996, and who can blame them? However, there are those who feel it necessary to go to great lengths to explain simple compassion. Some biologists claimed she was "confused" and thought the boy a gorilla. This is absurd, as Frans de Waal, a primate expert, confirmed when he noted, "it is highly unlikely that she, with her own seventeen-month-old infant riding on her back, was 'maternally confused.' "

On the other hand, perhaps we have gone too far in giving gorillas a reputation for gentleness. Some biologists believe Dian Fossey was led to her views by a fantasy almost equally as unrealistic as the earlier one of viciousness and danger to humans posed by gorillas. There has been a backlash, as we can see from Jared Diamond's popular 1992 book *The Third Chimpanzee: The Evolution and Future of the Human Animal:* "Among gorillas males fight each other for ownership of harems of females, and the victor may kill the loser's infant as well as the loser himself. Such fighting is a major cause of death for infant and adult male gorillas. The typical gorilla mother loses at least one infant to infanticidal males in the course of her life. Conversely, 38 percent of infant gorilla deaths are due to infanticide." While Diamond gives no reference for the statement, I found a similar figure of 40 percent from Kelly Stewart, a professor of biology at UC Davis, who has been studying gorillas for thirty years. However, she later says, "In mountain gorillas, infanticide is a relatively rare event." So which is it?

Stewart also says in *Gorillas: Natural History and Conservation:* "As for many other wild animals, infancy is the most dangerous time of life for gorillas, especially early infancy. In mountain gorillas, nearly two out of every five infants (40 percent) die, most during their first year. Unrelated silverbacks kill some of these infants, but *for most deaths, we don't know the cause* [emphasis mine]. One day the baby is in its mother's arms, and the next day it's gone."

These statements seem contradictory, indicating to me that infanticide is difficult to understand, whether in animals or in humans. Recent, authoritative research has highlighted the extraordinary care that the large male silverbacks take of orphaned infants. These small gorillas do not turn to females, but to the silverback, "becoming his little shadow during the day and sharing his nest at night." The large males show a great deal of patience, tolerance, and obvious affection, not to mention protection, for the little tykes.

Schaller often saw a large silverback surrounded by infants and juveniles playing with him or wrestling with one another on top of his body. He was always tolerant, and Schaller never observed the silverback or a female hit a young gorilla in anger. He often observed hugging in affection, much the way we do. (He also saw infants smile, giggle, and laugh.) Schaller never observed any serious fight within a group, and never saw a gorilla harm another member of the troop. He was the first to put forward what has become the predominant, gentle view of gorillas, for he never observed fighting even between individuals of different groups. He also repeatedly makes the point that each gorilla is an individual with his or her own temperament. The large male silverback he called Big Daddy was "the epitome of the tolerant and gentle gorilla," permissive even toward strange male gorillas. This was just a nice guy.

One must always consider, too, contingent causes: Is it not at least possible that something unusual happened to cause the recorded cases of infanticide? After all, the year that Schaller was at the same site, only one infant gorilla disappeared, probably taken by a leopard.

What about aggression toward humans? This, after all, is the image we have carried in our psyches ever since the gorilla was first "discovered" by Western humans a few hundred years ago, one of an implacable enemy intent on harming or destroying humans. Nothing could be further from the truth. Schaller wrote that in all the time "I spent with gorillas, none attacked me." (He was the first person to study them without carrying any sort of weapon, feeling that merely possessing a firearm gave a certain unconscious aggressiveness to a person's actions that could be detected by the gorillas.) Dian Fossey, too, felt that she was never in danger in their presence.

Moreover, as Schaller noted, gorillas were remarkably "amiable" in tolerating his presence. There was curiosity, mixed with fear and apprehension that seemed to morph slowly into a kind of indifference. It is, of course, impossible to know what they thought of him, but it was clear that they accepted his presence as unremarkable and unthreatening. They did nothing to drive him away or to seek to avoid his presence in any way. This is actually a remarkable achievement, and it was one to be repeated by almost all researchers who were later to observe the gorillas in their native habitat. Bill Weber and Amy Vedder, who came as graduate students to work with Fossey, for example, had the freckles on their arms checked out at close range: One bold six-year-old gorilla, Tuck, tried on several occasions to remove them with his fingernails and lips!

GREAT HORNED OWL

Bubo virginianus

I HAVE BEEN CALLED ANTHROPOMORPHIC so often that I am now prepared to believe there must be some truth to the accusation. I confess that it is easier for me to love a peaceful, easygoing, friendly, playful animal than a person who seems intent on causing grievous bodily harm to other animals. Like most people, though, I make exceptions when it comes to cats—devoted carnivores who nonetheless deeply engage me.

The great American horned owl was therefore something of a challenge. These raptors are top predators (hunting mostly, though, by stealth). They will take a skunk or tomcat as readily as a mouse. It appears they will eat just about any animal smaller than they are, but they themselves have almost no enemies (though only half of the young survive their first years, primarily due to starvation).

In a well-known poem, Ann Turner speaks of how the owl vacuums the wood, and leaves evidence of the shrews and moles she has eaten in the form of bones rolled in her own coughed-up fur. The owls themselves look pained when they produce their pellets, some as large as four inches (from the great horned owl). This compact regurgitated detritus, including the fur and skulls of their victims, has proven to be a scientific gold mine, allowing researchers to carbon-date the pellets, and thus determine the age of Neanderthal and Cro-Magnon bones (thanks to these preserved tight little packets, we now know that these two species lived at the same time).

Owls practice siblicide because they eat whatever is in their nest. If there is no other food at the moment, a larger brother will ingest a smaller sister who happens to be there. These are unattractive traits to humans, or at least to this human, and so I determined that I would read at least one book about owls in which a good scientist gets up close and personal with a single owl. Even the best scientists begin to wax anthropomorphic when they live on a day-to-day basis with an animal usually only studied in the wild or in a laboratory. I turned to University of Vermont zoology professor Bernd Heinrich's book *One Man's Owl* and was not disappointed. I highly recommend it. Also good is biologist Max Terman's *Message from an Owl*, which contains a charming anecdote about how a great horned owl raised by Terman rescued him when he was lost in the forest at night.

Heinrich found a baby great American horned owl at the base of a tree, shivering in the snow, close to the point of death. He had no choice but to take it home and try to revive it and hand-raise it. Her, I mean. Him, I mean. Actually, Heinrich never discovered the sex of this bird.

You will have to read the book for yourself to discover all its joys. I must say, however, that I would never, having read the book, consider keeping a predator. Heinrich constantly, in the early days, and even from time to time after that, had to kill, cut up, and deliver animals to his "pet." I do the same for a cat, only I am more squeamish, and so deliver animals straight from the supermarket. The intermediation is my cowardice. I don't think, though, that I will acquire cats again for this very reason.

Heinrich was not in it for the pleasure. His purpose was to observe and decipher mobbing behavior against owls, the fascinating behavior where smaller birds harass a larger predator bird and usually force him to desist his attack. He believes it is a form of parent care, similar to a distraction display, which makes good sense, as well as urging the dangerous bird to get a move on and leave the area where there are young. But pleasure he got. "It gives me a thrill to see the big bird come flying gracefully over the birches, wheeling down into the clearing, and landing beside me when I call him." Who would not be thrilled? I wish Heinrich, with his erudition enlivened by his curiosity, had set his mind to figure out precisely *why* this is so thrilling, and what it says about us as a species. The question that never fails to arouse my curiosity is this: Do other animals ever feel the same thrill? That is, do they ever get the same pleasure from our company that we take in theirs? Or rather: Do they find it equally astonishing?

At one point Heinrich does approach this question, somewhat obliquely. Owls, he notes, "are the quintessential birds of solitude." And yet, he is beginning to believe that Bubo, "his" owl, seeks him out not for food, but for companionship. If this is true, it is extraordinary. Yes, cats are solitary, and yes, they seek us out for companionship, but they have been domesticated. This owl was entirely wild! Seeking us out for food, for shelter, for various forms of help—that we understand. But for a wild animal to seek out a human merely for the pleasure of being in his or her company—that speaks to a complexity of inner life that most scientists are not prepared to accord animals, especially birds. Hence I entirely agree with Heinrich's parting phrase: "Birds may be much more sophisticated than we assume."

Owls, as I emphasized, are primarily solitary (one of the many reasons owls are called "cats with wings"). However, some owls—for example, long-eared and barn owls—sometimes congregate in roosts. Maybe it is that once they are no longer hunting in their own individual fashion, owls are more sociable than we supposed, and need to communicate. It is also possible, some have argued, that social roosting allows the owls to find out about the density of their own local population. They could then adjust reproduction rates. It is not clear that this happens, but there can be no doubt that some owls adjust family size according to the amount of food available.

While I have reservations about befriending a raptor, most people haven't any such hesitation. Owls are right up there next to teddy bears as cuddly toys for children. (Think of "The owl and the pussycat went to sea.") Part of the reason is no doubt due to their appearance: They have soft billowing plumage, and we rarely notice the powerful talons they use for killing, hidden beneath leg feathers just as the beak pokes out between the face feathers. They look a bit like us, with their vertical posture and flat face. We are especially drawn to the enormous eyes (a masterpiece of evolution, designed of course for darkness and acuity of vision, not for cuteness). This is of course pure projection: other animals seeing these large eyes are terrified, with good reason. So effective are they that there is even a moth (*Caligula*) with large eye-spots on its wings to resemble an owl—an effective protective camouflage.

Owls are primarily monogamous (or at least this is true for the barn owl, the great horned, and the screech owl). However, getting to the point of romance is rather delicate for an owl since they are built more for destruction than tender romance, as noted in Jonathan Evan Maslow's *The Owl Papers*. Since male and female plumage are more or less identical, there is always the fear that a "couple" will mistake each other for rivals and engage in combat rather than seduction. This could explain why female owls are much larger and heavier than the males, precisely to prevent any such mistakes and to keep the male intimidated long enough to take his mind off rivalry and on to courtship.

For the ancient Hindus, Native Americans, and twentieth-century English, too, the hoot of the owl foretold death. The ancient Chinese heard in it the sounds of a ghost. For the Western Bible (Leviticus 11: 13–17), the owl, and raptors generally, was considered "an abomination," so it is unsurprising that their odd sounds presaged bad luck. For those of us fortunate enough to hear owls at night, there is something haunting and slightly melancholy about it. Most nights, at our house on the beach here in Auckland, we get to hear the morepork, a New Zealand owl so named because it sounds as if he were saying "more pork," but I hear something else entirely, and it never fails to suggest to me pure enchantment.

GREAT WHITE SHARK

Carcharodon carcharias

S HARKS BELONG TO A LARGE GROUP of fish that include sharks, skates (rays without venomous spines), and rays with venomous spines that all arose during the Silurian period some 450 million years ago, long before the first vertebrates invaded the land. Modern sharks, however, go back less than a million years. Some sharks lay eggs; others give birth live. The eggs are enclosed in a tough horny case called (for reasons I haven't discovered) a mermaid's purse. Hatching can take up to fifteen months. In the grey nurse shark the strongest embryos actually hunt one another in the uterus, leading to the birth of a single surviving pup. Sharks vary greatly in size, from the eight-inch dwarf lantern shark (*Etmopterus perryi*) who weighs half an ounce, to the gigantic fifty-foot whale shark (*Rhincodon typus*) who tips the scales at almost twenty-seven thousand pounds!

The great white is only one of 375 species of shark, most of them harmless. However, no animal works on the human imagination with quite the same malign power as the great white shark—this, despite the chances of anyone being attacked by this apex predator being so remote as to approach zero. According to the respected International Shark Attack File, which has been operating since 1958, in the year 2003 there were fifty-five cases of verified unprovoked shark attacks around the world, with four fatalities. Only thirty species of sharks have ever been known to attack people, and most of those attacks are by just three specific kinds: the great white shark, the bull shark, and the tiger shark. To put things into perspective, consider that from 1959 through 2003 there were 1,857 fatalities in the United States due to lightning, 22 due to sharks, and an annual average of 18 due to dog bites.

The fear is unlikely to have evolutionary roots, for encounters with sharks must have been extremely rare in human evolutionary history. Some of it no doubt goes back only to the release of the late Peter Benchley's phenomenally successful *Jaws*. The book and film created a kind of panic about swimming in the ocean similar in its effects to Orson Welles's 1938 radio broadcast of H. G. Wells's *The War of the Worlds*.

In 1991, in a great surprise, the South African government declared the great white shark a protected species. Louis Pienaar, the minister for environmental affairs, in making the announcement, said that, encouraged by the film *Jaws*, trophy hunters were targeting great whites in South African waters, convinced the great white was a ruthless man-eater to be eliminated. This would no longer be tolerated. It was an enlightened view at the time, and is now pretty commonly accepted as true.

Acknowledging that his information was erroneous, Benchley tried to make amends. He acknowledged that "it is widely accepted that sharks in general, and great whites in particular, do not target human beings. When a great white attacks a person, it is almost always an accident, a case of mistaken identity." He went further in a remarkable mea culpa, admitting, "I couldn't possibly write *Jaws* today . . . the notion of demonizing a fish strikes me as insane." In another publication, he commented, "Shark attacks on human beings generate a tremendous amount of media coverage, partly because they occur so rarely, but most, I think, because people are, and always have been, simultaneously intrigued and terrified by sharks. Sharks come from a wing of the dark castle where our nightmares live—deep water beyond our sight and un-derstanding—and so they stimulate our fears and fantasies and imagina-tions."

Sadly, shark fins have become enormously commercially valuable, selling for up to three hundred dollars a pound. A single shark tooth can sell for $150 and a set of jaws for more than $3,000. Powdered shark car-tilage sells for a hundred dollars a bottle, probably because it is consid-ered to protect against cancer. It does seem true that sharks are intriguingly resistant to cancer. Also, serious wounds heal within twenty-four hours, obviously without veterinary treatment. Lacerated corneas heal rapidly. Clearly, sharks have some remarkable healing properties, but whether there is anything to be learned is in question.

It is not beyond the realm of possibility that the complete extinction of the great white could occur in the lifetime of our children. Unlike other fish, these huge long-lived animals reproduce more like mammals. They may not attain sexual maturity until fifteen, and often produce only one or two pups as infrequently as every three years. Ellis has made the important point that we should all be concerned with the ex-tinction of one of the most powerful and graceful predators on our planet for no other reason than that there should never have to be a rea-son to eliminate an entire class of animals. Whether humans discover a cure for cancer because of sharks is irrelevant. They have as much right to their lives as we do to ours.

My son Ilan wants to know who is "tougher": a great white shark or a killer whale. No contest, I tell him: The largest great white can be up to twenty-one feet in length and might weigh up to three thousand pounds, but a full-grown orca is thirty feet, and tips the scales at ten thousand pounds. And he has a huge, calculating brain! No animal in the ocean messes with him. "Cool," said Ilan, identifying himself with an orca. Smart and dangerous, that's what he likes.

Maybe something else about sharks makes them occupy such a prominent place in our psyches. They are the only wild predator that cannot be tamed. People have lived with lions, wolves, tigers, boa constrictors, leopards, rhinos, orcas, wild boars, dolphins, and just about any other animal you can think of, but nobody, as far as I know, has ever lived on intimate terms with a great white. Stingrays may nestle in the palm of your hand like a butterfly and delicately eat from your fingers, but I don't think anyone has tried anything similar with a great white. Perhaps it's simply obvious that you do not attempt to tame an animal with three thousand razor-sharp teeth. Or you could take a more philosophical approach, the one that Don Reed, a diver at Marine World/Africa USA, took when his "friendship" with an eight-foot sevengill shark came to an abrupt end. After years of being together without incident, she took his head in her massive jaws. Said Reed, "if Sevengill was absolutely no monster, neither was she on this earth to be my pet."

In his wonderful *The Empty Ocean*, Richard Ellis acknowledges that "perhaps the greatest misconception about sharks is that they are particularly dangerous to people. The truth is closer to the opposite." If we learn nothing else about sharks, surely this important countervailing truth is enough.

It has been commonly assumed that sharks, being fish, cannot have any feelings, or much of a brain. This view is outdated. Writing in the journal *Fish and Fisheries*, biologists Calum Brown, Kevin Laland, and Jens Krause made the following comment:

> Gone (or at least obsolete) is the image of fish as drudging and dim-witted pea brains, driven largely by "instinct," with what little behavioral flexibility they possess being severely hampered by an infamous "three-second memory." . . . Now, fish are regarded as steeped in social intelligence, pursuing Machiavellian strategies of manipulation, punishment and reconciliation, exhibiting stable cultural traditions, and co-operating to inspect predators and catch food.

We now realize that some fish recognize individual "shoal mates," use tools, build complex nests, and are capable of retaining memories over a long period of time. So much for the "primitiveness" of fish.

GRIZZLY BEAR

Ursus arctos horribilis

THE GRIZZLY IS A BROWN BEAR, usually classified as *Ursus arctos horribilis*, for reasons one can surmise. The most widely distributed species of bear in the world, it is found in Japan, India, and Tibet, called, of course, by different names (including horse bear and red bear). Before humans came along, the dominance of this large, dangerous bear went unchallenged.

The danger consists in the fact that a large male (usually twice as large as the female) may weigh thirteen hundred pounds and can, at forty-one miles per hour, outrun the fastest man on earth. But bears, even grizzlies with their extraordinary physical power, are not interested in pushing humans around. Their usual response to humans is one of fear, or at most curiosity. According to Andy Russell, who has spent years in bear country, bears somehow know if a person is armed, and this knowledge gets passed on "culturally" from mother to cub. They also know that they are safe from firearms in national parks. Problems arise when bears, driven by hunger, are fed or discover how easy it is to raid the food cache of a careless camper, then lose their natural fear of humans. They are now dangerous animals.

Just how dangerous are grizzlies? Very. You have only to watch the mesmerizing Werner Herzog film *Grizzly Man* about Timothy Treadwell to realize how dangerous idealistic, even compassionate, attitudes toward these animals can become. Treadwell spent twelve years with the grizzlies in Alaska, shooting one hundred hours of extraordinary footage, at close range. His own website (www.grizzlypeople.com) warns against getting closer than a hundred yards to a bear, yet he was often right up in their face, even touching their noses with his finger. Bad idea. In 2003, just minutes after filming, he and his girlfriend were attacked by a male grizzly with whom he was not familiar. Both were killed. Nick Jans, in his excellent book on this case, makes the point that the bears "couldn't care less about human trust or physical affection. They're too busy being themselves and are at best indifferent to our existence unless we insinuate ourselves into their lives." In trying to reconstruct the last hours of Treadwell's life, Jans met a bear whom he says "didn't need anything from us. He wasn't our friend. He had no name. All he wanted was to be left alone." That's a hard lesson for all of us to learn.

The explanation for much of bear behavior, including temperament, has to do with the fact that over an average lifetime, a female bear is likely to raise to adulthood only two or three children, much like a human mother. She comes into heat only every three or four years, for a few weeks. That is the only time she tolerates the presence of a male bear—and even then, just barely. Bears are truly solitary animals (except for the females and her cubs). Male bears are rarely tolerant of anyone else in their territory. And that territory can be enormous. One male on record roamed an area of twenty-two hundred square miles.

Like us, bears have a low rate of reproduction because they have so few enemies. Over their evolutionary history, their enemies have mostly been from within. Bears are what are known in ecology as a *K*-selected species: long-lived animals with low reproductive rates, able to maximize learning, and to occupy stable habitat at a level near its carrying capacity, or *K*. But despite this, as many as two-thirds of cubs die in their first year, mostly due to marauding males. The puzzle of male aggression in both bears *and* humans awaits explanation.

After an hour's copulation, the female and the male separate. But the female will not come into estrus for perhaps another four years. Now pregnant, she develops something quite spectacular: delayed implantation. The fertilized egg floats in her womb for several months. If she does not succeed in eating herself into a stupor (gaining forty pounds a week) during late summer and early fall, she loses the egg. If she is successful, the fertilized egg settles into her uterine wall and continues to develop.

As soon as the snows arrive, she undergoes a metabolic transformation. She stops eating, becoming more lethargic every day. She devotes what little energy she has to preparing a winter den. She is about to go into hibernation, for up to seven months. Her heart rate drops from between forty and seventy beats per minute to only eight to twelve. While hibernating, she will neither urinate nor defecate. Any other animal (including humans) would die of urea poisoning within a week. Bears, though, have developed a unique process of recycling the urea into usable proteins. During hibernation, she gives birth and feeds her cubs (she may have two to four) while losing 40 percent of her body weight. She will probably not emerge from her den until May, by which time the cubs will be able to come out with her under their own steam. For another two months she will be in a state of semidormancy. So three-quarters of her life has been spent asleep (without taking into account her daily sleep during the summer).

There is a situation facing bears that is every bit as dangerous as our unchecked appetite for appropriation of nature. It is one that is entirely artificial, driven by ignorance, greed, and cruelty. Even though China probably has fewer than twenty thousand wild Asiatic black bears, in 1998 there were 247 bear farms in China, many owned by the Chinese government. On a daily basis these farms extract bile from seven thousand bear gallbladders for the Chinese traditional medicine market in China, Korea, Japan, and other countries.

One kilo (2.2 pounds) of bear bile costs more than five thousand U.S. dollars. Between 1988 and 1990, 1,051 kilos (2,317 pounds) of bear bile were exported from China to Japan. In California alone the illegal trade in bear parts was estimated to be worth a hundred million dollars a year. The surgical operation to implant the metal catheters in these bears is dangerous. More than half the bears ("harvested" from the wild) die from complications and infections. They are the lucky ones. The ones who live are kept in coffinlike cages, with barely enough room to lie down. They moan when the bile is taken out and live an existence straight out of Dante's *Inferno*.

At the Stockholm environmental conference in 1972 the Chinese delegation stated, "Man is the most precious of all things." Does that explain the callous disregard for the feelings and the lives of all other beings on this planet? No wonder Treadwell preferred living with bears.

HIPPOPOTAMUS

Hippopotamus amphibius

THE HIPPO HAS BEEN ASSUMED to belong in the same general family as pigs and peccaries (a piglike animal from America), but recent studies of mitochondrial DNA provide strong evidence of a closer relationship with whales. Unlike whales, however, hippos have been little studied, and little is known of them.

An odd myth about hippos is that they sweat blood. Actually hippos, like pigs, cannot sweat, but they secrete a viscous red fluid that dries like lacquer and serves to protect the thin epidermis against sunburn; it probably has antibacterial qualities as well. (It is most copious in fighting males and in females about to give birth.) It has also been suggested that because hippos carry so many wounds from intraspecies fights, the secretion might act as a healing agent. Evidently even severe wounds seem to heal cleanly and quickly. The sunscreen secretion is colorless, but upon exposure to air, it turns reddish brown.

Children's books about hippos make them appear to be comical and friendly. When we see massive, we see cute, but these books for young people fail to mention that hippos can open their jaws so widely (150 degrees) that they can, and do, snap a ten-foot crocodile in two. Hippos have enormous and very sharp canines. When people observe hippos yawning, it's in fact a threat display: *See the size of my teeth?* Hippos often capsize boats, and not by mistake. In one notorious recent case, the man inside was hunting and just about to aim his rifle when the hippo turned the boat over and snapped off the man's head.

I was, however, unprepared for the list of unpleasant characteristics of the hippo that I read about in the most reliable of sources. Among these were that a male forces a female into prostrate submission when he wants to copulate. Her head is forced underwater, and when she raises it to breathe the bull may snap at her. Also, males attack and often kill large numbers of pups for no apparent reason (though there may be one we do not understand). And there's the claim by some that hippos cause more human deaths than any other wild creature in Africa, including lions and elephants.

Filmmakers Alan and Joan Root reared a female hippo named Sally at their home at the peaceful freshwater Lake Naivasha in Kenya, East Africa. But when Sally grew larger and destroyed a car, her "foster parents" decided to part from their "adopted" hippo, transferring her to Kenya's Bamburi Nature Park. As far as I know, this is the only case of a wild hippo who was bottle-fed and raised to adulthood by humans. But I could find no details about Sally beyond what I have just written.

One important bit of hippopotamus information came to me fortuitously. At a watering hole in Kruger National Park in South Africa, a female impala was guarding a group of newborn calves. One small calf had wandered away from the herd and was eating by herself on the grassland. A pack of African hunting dogs suddenly ran into the clearing next to the watering hole. The little impala had strayed too far to get back to her herd. She called out in panic, then ran from the wild dogs. When she reached the river she had no choice but to leap in. A seven-foot Nile crocodile swam swiftly over to the impala, grabbed her in his jaws, and dove under the water to drown the small calf. Suddenly a female hippo, resting in the water nearby, noticed the crocodile with the impala in his jaws and moved away from her group in his direction.

She charged. The crocodile quickly let go of the impala and swam some distance away, then stopped to see what would happen. The hippo gently pushed the wounded impala toward the river's edge, then helped her climb onto the steep bank. The impala limped away, then collapsed on the grass. The hippo climbed out of the river and walked over to the small impala lying on the ground. She opened her enormous jaws and breathed warm, moist air on the impala. Apparently vivified by her newfound protector, the impala struggled to her feet and tried to walk. After a few steps, she collapsed again. The hippo approached and again attempted to breathe life and courage into her. Again the impala got up and tried to walk, but fell to the ground. Five times the hippo persisted in trying to use her own breath to revive the small calf. Sadly, at last the impala died and the crocodile climbed the bank to claim his prey.

Does this sound like a fantasy? Fortunately, there exists a video, sent to me by Sheila Siddle, the director of the Chimfunshi Wildlife Orphanage Trust in Chingola, Zambia. Nobody who viewed the video had ever seen or heard of anything similar by a hippo. Was this the single Saint Francis of Hippos, or are such incidents simply rarely observed by humans? After all, the greatest authority on hippos, René Verheyen, as early as 1954 described seeing a large, full-sized male entirely free from scars. His secret? He refused to fight, even if the challenge came from a smaller animal. Now that I finally managed to find a copy of his rare French book, I see, too, that he describes the great enmity that exists between hippos and crocodiles, since the latter often attack young hippos. Females, especially, then, will chase any crocodile they see. Perhaps this heroic female had bad memories of having lost one of her own young, something that sometimes happens to even the most attentive female hippo.

HONEYBEES

Apis spp.

A T SEVENTEEN WHEN I was living with my family in Uruguay, my parents thought I was too wrapped up in reading and not sufficiently in touch with the "real world." They encouraged an interest I had in beekeeping. I became friendly with the professor of the science of apiculture at the University of Montevideo, and we agreed to start a beekeeping business together on land my parents owned in Punta del Este. The professor came to our apartment to teach me to make beehives out of wood and wax. When my father returned from a trip and saw our living room cluttered with nails, wood, and wax, my mother hushed his incipient criticisms by saying: "Shhh, he's learning to use his hands."

Our business enterprise was a complete failure—from seventy hives, we took only a pound of honey—but the professor was a veritable gold mine of information on bees. Like many beekeepers, he loved the little guys as well as talking about them. He claimed that bees were happy to share their honey with us. In return, we gave them a comfortable house to live in. At the time, and even more so now, it seemed faulty logic.

Bees hardly need artificial hives, especially those constructed not for their comfort, but for ease in extracting honey. And if they were so happy to share their honey, why, before we visited them, did I need to suit up with elaborate gloves and netting to protect myself against their stings? The professor taught me to distinguish between the contented hum the bees made when they were happy with a good day's work in foraging, and the angry hum of having their hive disturbed. There was no mistaking their anger when we intruded to examine their progress. I didn't feel right about it then, and even less so today.

One thing I learned from the professor was how much there was yet to learn about bees. Great scientists have devoted their lives to their study. The International Bee Research Association in Wales has a library of four thousand books, sixty thousand papers, and 130 journals—all devoted to bees. The writer Hattie Ellis claims that bees are the most studied creatures on the planet, after humans.

The Mayans of the Yucatán Peninsula in Mexico kept stingless bees as pollinators and for a small amount of honey. The keepers had a series of rituals in which they spoke to their bees, and believed the bees communicated back. Appalled, the Spaniards considered it witchcraft. The tradition has nearly died out, partly because the present-day descendants of the Mayans understandably refuse to use harmful pesticides. Stephen Buchmann has visited several times and is attempting to revive the tradition before it is too late.

The queen bee can actively determine the gender of her offspring. When she releases spermatozoa, the fertilized eggs become sterile female workers, while unfertilized eggs become male drones with no fathers, only mothers. Generally, there are a few hundred drones in a colony, thirty thousand or more female workers, and of course just a single queen—a division of gender and role remarkably consistent from nest to nest. The poor males are in winter evicted from the nest by their more closely related sisters and left to die out in the cold. Whenever, in fact, things get tough in the hive—any kind of stress at all—the female worker bees simply stop feeding the males. Their only function in life is to accompany the queen on her "virgin flight" and attempt to mate with her. If they succeed, they instantly die. Failing, they return to their lowly position.

Nor does the queen have an easy time of it. Though tended to and fed, her life consists of laying a single brilliant white egg into a cell fifteen hundred times a day, every day of her life, which lasts from two to seven years. The egg hatches in only three days. Nurses (young female bees) feed each egg royal jelly for three days (a hive produces only about a quarter of an ounce). After that, all bees except the queen are fed on a mixture of pollen and nectar called bee bread. On the ninth day of their lives, they spin silk cocoons and enter the pupal stage. They stay there from day eleven to day twenty. When the female emerges during spring or summer, she lives only four to six weeks.

A quarter of the colony consists of mature female workers who gather the raw materials necessary for the colony's survival. They fly, four to eight times a day, up to nine miles from their nests in search of pollen and nectar. They seek out one particular flower (showing flower fidelity over the entire day), putting the pollen they collect in the corbicula, or pollen baskets, on their hind legs. As for the nectar, what they don't use as fuel, they place in a honey sac, a pear-shaped bag on their abdomen.

A typical sixteen-ounce jar of honey represents the efforts of tens of thousands of bees flying a total of 112,000 miles to forage nectar from about 4.5 million flowers! A single female forager bee may have collected enough nectar to make just a quarter ounce of honey, less than half a teaspoonful.

When they return to the hive, they are greeted by another female worker bee, who takes the load of pollen and nectar. The pollen is stored, while the nectar is fanned (a bee can beat her wings two hundred times per second) and regurgitated as many as two hundred times. When it's fully ripened to the correct consistency, a worker caps the storage cells with fresh wax to ensure that the colony will have food over winter.

Austrian biologist Karl von Frisch won the Nobel Prize in 1973 for his study of bees. Von Frisch was certain bees could see colors. What else would be the point of an expensive instrument such as the five compound eyes made up of sixty-nine hundred hexagonal plates that bees possess? Their sight, it turns out, is acute toward the yellow, green, blue end of the light spectrum. He also thought they must be able to smell their beloved sweet flowers. Obviously, these flowers (and their wonderfully appealing smell) evolved to appeal to the bees and other insects upon whom they depend to propagate.

In a series of experiments, he demonstrated that what he called the "waggle dance" of the bee, which had been noticed for centuries (including by Aristotle), was not aimless enthusiasm, but a coded message telling hive mates who had gathered to "listen" exactly where the source of the nectar was to be found. Moreover, the length of the waggle line turned out to indicate the distance of the nectar from the hive (even taking into account factors such as crosswinds and obstacles). Moreover, the sweeter the nectar source, the more vigorous the dance. In all, von Frisch discovered that this dance could indicate nectar source, direction, distance, quality, and quantity. He also showed that, contrary to standard scientific opinion, bees had a good sense of smell, more or less equivalent to our own. It took a great deal of persuasion to convince a skeptical scientific world that a mere insect was capable of the most sophisticated communication outside humans. I highly recommend von Frisch's great book *The Dance Language and Orientation of Bees*.

But even before the world learned of von Frisch's work, there was a justified fascination with bees, and from many different angles. For example, bees seem to have had a profound influence on many architects, including Antoni Gaudí, Mies van der Rohe, Frank Lloyd Wright, and Le Corbusier. The world's greatest mountain climber, Sir Edmund Hillary, was a beekeeper, and when I met him recently and spent an afternoon with him, he told me that the first thing he did when he returned to New Zealand from Nepal was to pick up his beekeeping where he had left off. The American poet Sylvia Plath wrote many poems about bees (collected in *Ariel*). Her father, who died when she was eight, had been a beekeeper, and she, too, tried it with her husband, Ted Hughes. Just before she died, she wrote a letter referring to her plans to resume her beekeeping. Sadly, it was delivered after her suicide.

When I suggested once, in an article, that bees might dream, an evo-lutionary biologist came down hard on me. Pure nonsense, he said. But is it really so nonsensical to believe that a bee brain, small as it is, might be capable of thinking about the past? And if it thinks of the past while asleep, well, that could produce a dream. I have to take my chances with the poets here, in particular George Eliot, who in *The Spanish Gypsy* wrote:

> *But, for the point of wisdom, I would choose*
> *To know the mind that stirs between the wings*
> *Of bees . . .*

HUMMINGBIRDS

Family Trochilidae

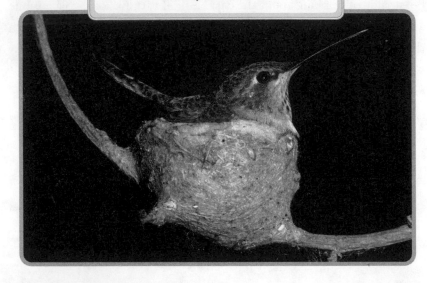

I HAVE FOUND ONE SOURCE of my loneliness here in New Zealand: I will never see a hummingbird here. They live only in the Northern Hemisphere, in South, Central, and North America.

When I lived on a ranch on the California coast south of San Francisco, hummingbirds visited all the time. I was sure that the same birds were coming back again and again, and I persuaded myself that some of them began to be friendly with me. This was not mere anthropomorphism: Hummingbirds are easily habituated to humans, and Robert Burton, a leading authority on these amazing jewels, tells the story of a man who was befriended by a rufous hummingbird (the word refers to the tinge of red in the wings) who flew alongside him on his walks and eventually became so accustomed to him that he would perch on his shoulder for the walks. The man once had to leave his home for a month, and when he returned, the bird was there to greet him!

Ornithologists have explained the apparent affinity of hummingbirds to humans by their curiosity about anything colored red, in case it might contain nectar: Humans wearing red sweaters, or women with red lipstick are often visited by these birds. I still prefer to think they simply like us.

Hummingbirds have fascinated humans for a long time. They are the only bird who can behave like a helicopter: backing up, rising, hovering in one place, all seemingly without effort. They do this by moving their wings at incredible speed: fifty-two beats *per second*. Also, they are so tiny: The Cuban bee hummingbird is the world's smallest bird and weighs less than a penny. But these feats are not achieved without cost: Hummers (another word commonly used for these birds, because of the sound of their wings) may consume more than twice their weight in nectar every day. The energy expenditure is enormous. It has been calculated that if a man used energy at the hummer's rate, he would have to eat forty ten-pound sacks of potatoes every day. In proportion to body size, the hummingbird's heart is larger than that of any other warm-blooded animal. It beats very fast—from five hundred to more than twelve hundred times per minute.

These tiny birds are fast, too. They have been clocked chasing each other at speeds of forty miles an hour, and in a dive can go considerably faster. Energy is also needed for their relatively large brains, densely packed with nerve cells used for learning and for their prodigious memories. Hummingbirds may return to a yard expecting to find the same feeder in the same location, though they have been several thousand miles away for the entire winter.

How can they possibly live so close to the limits of their energy reserves? By going into torpor, a form of nightly hibernation: Their body temperature falls and their heart rate drops dramatically, even stopping for minutes at a time. They need to conserve energy not just for their daily requirements, but also because they are migrating birds. Some rufous hummingbirds migrate more than two thousand miles every year. From their winter homes in Mexico, in early spring they travel to California, following favored hummingbird flowers northward and breeding, sometimes journeying as far north as southern Alaska.

They have keen eyesight, and can see into the ultraviolet spectrum, seeing colors we do not know exist. On their travels, they seek out red and orange flowers. This is a useful tool as they migrate: They can immediately spot the flowers they need for food from a great distance, much the way we notice our favorite restaurants by their logos as we drive along a highway. Biologists have extensively studied the coevolution of flowers and hummingbirds—how flowers modify themselves to fit the long, curved beak of the hummingbird. This was something noticed by Charles Darwin, who pointed out that the "beaks of hummingbirds are specially adapted to the various kinds of flowers they visit." Both the plant and the bird benefit: The hummer drinks copious amounts of nectar, and the flower's pollen is carried directly to another scarlet betony (for instance). Since hummingbirds do this far more effectively than can honeybees, the flowers make it easier for the hummers to enter than for the bees. However, undeterred bees may chew through the blossoms near the base, getting the honey without having to pay anything in return. In Costa Rica cheating bees fly out of passionflowers and zigzag in front of the hummers to drive them away. Hummingbirds have another advantage appreciated by flowers: Being larger than insects allows them to travel farther and thus to visit more widely spaced flowers.

The males are spectacularly colored (to us and to a female—it's only a trick of the light, like oil on water, and has nothing to do with intrinsic pigmentation). However, they are poor fathers. All in all, hummers are pretty solitary creatures. The only time adult hummingbirds touch one another (except when they fight) is for the few-second act of copulation.

A group of males congregates before and during breeding season, competing with other males for the attention of females who visit the traditional sites called leks. Males in the breeding season come together in one or two communal spots shaped like a bowl, with tracks from one bowl to the other. Here they display themselves to passing females, check out the competition, and regally permit young males to visit the bowls and sit quietly, learning what to do themselves later in life. These same sites can be used year after year, and sometimes contain up to a hundred lekking males, each strutting about, hoping to be noticed by a female, and using his puny (and to us unmusical) voice to convince her of his paternal qualities. The little hermit of Trinidad spends eight months of every year in his lek, singing his monotonous song for two-thirds or more of each day.

The female must then build her nest by herself—a perfect tiny cup-like nest bound with spiderwebs and lined with plant material, feathers, and hair, camouflaged by moss and lichen—a jewel much like the birds themselves. She lays her two (always two) half-inch tiny white eggs and incubates them alone for two weeks. She is a good mother: covering the young like an umbrella in the rain and shading them from the hot sun. Within a month of hatching, they can fly themselves. Hummers have few predators because they are so hard to catch. For such small crea-tures, they live surprisingly long lives, some for more than a decade.

Alexander Skutch, America's greatest ornithologist (who recently died at the age of one hundred), stressed that every hummingbird is an individual with his or her own personality. He told me that he never dared to speak his mind on this topic until toward the end of his life, in his fascinating book *The Mind of Birds*, which I recommend to every-body interested in birds of any kind.

HUMPBACK WHALE

Megaptera novaeangliae

THE HUMPBACK IS A MODERATELY LARGE baleen whale, growing up to about fifty feet long. (The average weight of a male's right testis is more than two thousand pounds!) As with most baleen whales, females are larger than males. Humpback are slow swimmers who breed in inshore waters, and thus were at the mercy of commercial whalers. They are perhaps the most highly hunted of all whales, and since the 1920s, when whaling became more high-tech, their numbers have been seriously reduced. In some areas whole populations have been extinguished. There can be no doubt that whaling has had a devastating effect on populations of humpback whales worldwide: Whereas once there were as many as 250,000 humpback whales, there may be no more than 15,000 left. Japan killed 910 whales in 2005 alone under the widely discredited guise of "scientific research." If this country succeeds, through bribery and intimidation, in controlling the International Whaling Commission so that the twenty-year moratorium against the slaughter of whales is overturned, the species may become extinct in our lifetime.

Known to many members of the public because of their highly complex song, these whales are baleen whales, known as mysticetes—they eat their food by straining seawater through comblike structures called baleens that act as filters, catching plankton and small oceanic organisms such as krill and copepods.

Unlike the killer whale, humpback whales do not appear to form long-term associations, but rather exist in small unstable groups that mainly come together on feeding grounds. Mating and calving take place in winter, near offshore reef systems in the tropics. No feeding at all occurs during this time. No birth has ever been observed in this species. Calves are precocious, though, and may begin the migration to the mother's feeding grounds when only a few weeks old. They must learn the migratory routes that in future years take them to the feeding grounds. Here they'll return each spring. A mother is extremely solicitous of the safety of her calf and will place herself between the calf and an approaching boat, steering the calf away.

It is extraordinary that after a long fast, the female is still capable of lactating. While she migrates, the pregnant female does not eat. She gives birth in the tropics, then suckles her calf on her energy reserves for six months until she returns to the feeding area the next summer. The calf grows rapidly thanks to the rich (but expensive in terms of energy for the mother) milk of his mother, further depleting her. She can lose 30 percent of her weight during this time. No other animal can do this. The calves migrate with their mother only once, but they return to the same feeding grounds every year for the rest of their life, even though it is thousands of miles away.

Because so much scientific information about humpbacks was gathered by the whaling industry, it is unsurprising that questions were limited to such technical matters as ecology, feeding behavior, seasonal migration, and the seasonality of breeding behavior. In other words, the whalers were interested in learning how best to exploit the whales, and were rarely or never interested in them for their own sake.

Although it has been widely asserted that killer whales attack humpbacks, nobody has witnessed this in two decades of almost daily observations in the Gulf of Maine (a feeding ground). Almost all humpbacks,
though, have teeth marks on their flukes. The hypothesis now is that
such attacks occur exclusively on newborn calves. What percentage is
successful and results in mortality is unknown.

Roger Payne, the elder statesman of whale research, conceded that
whales are remarkably gentle in the presence of humans. And when a
female accepts a partner, "it is quite tenderly done, each hugging the
other with its flippers." With their calves, he described what they did
as hugging and patting. He described areas that are clearly nurseries for
the young calves.

Several researchers have noted that males can become antagonistic
and aggressive toward other males at breeding times. While many
whales have superficial wounds, serious injuries have not been recorded. The males seem to be "escorting" a female in whom they are
sexually interested, and these violent encounters are presumed to be a
means of preventing any other whale from mating with her. Two males
will sometimes form a coalition to supplant an escorting male. If successful, the female then presumably chooses one of the males as her new es-
cort and mate. His companion receives nothing for his trouble, but
presumably can request payback at some later time.

One of the great remaining puzzles is why humpback whales migrate
from the cold, productive waters in high latitudes to warm tropical environments largely devoid of appropriate prey. It has been assumed that
this gives some advantage to the calves born in these mild climates. And
why would nonpregnant females and males also make the same journey?
What's in it for them? Is it simply tradition?

Humpback whales are best known for two things: their spectacular
aerial displays and their complex and—to our ears—eerie songs. The
aerial displays include breaching, where the whale leaps headfirst from
the water; slapping the surface of the water with the tail; spyhopping
with the head lifted out of the water; and tail breaching.

Roger Payne and Scott McVay noted that whales may sing continuously for many hours. The singers are always male, and almost always alone. All whales within a breeding population sing the same song. Humpback whales from different oceans sing different songs. At least one of the functions of the songs is to attract potential mates. Of course it could also be a means of establishing dominance, or a threat display. The songs could even have a spacing function. It could be all these things at once. Is there an aesthetic quality to these songs appreciated by the whales themselves? Humans find them appealing, as attested to by the fact that the recording by Roger and Katie Payne, *Songs of the Humpback Whale*, is perhaps the best-selling animal music record of all time. What we have learned more recently is that there are no common sounds in songs recorded a decade apart. It is now clear that the whales do not inherit their songs, but learn the detailed acoustic structures. Humpback songs are a form of culture.

Payne described the sounds as lowing, moaning, wild shrieking, and wailing. At the time he wrote he had no idea why the humpbacks sing, and more than thirty years after the discovery we are still not certain. But what we do know is "according to our calculations, if a humpback were at optimum depth, prior to the intrusion of ships' noises, the maximum range of its call would be between 4,000 and 13,000 miles. A circle with a 4,000-mile radius covers about 50,000,000 square miles—some 18,000,000 more than the area of the Atlantic Ocean!"

I N John Steinbeck's introduction to Edward F. Ricketts's and Jack Calvin's *Between Pacific Tides*, he writes: "there are answers to the world's questions which every man must ask, in the little animals of tidepools, in their relations one to another, in their color phases, their reproducing methods. Finally, one can live in a prefabricated world, smugly and without question, or one can indulge perhaps the greatest human excitement: that of observation to speculation to hypothesis."

It was in this book that I found enlightenment about jellyfish (which are not fish at all) by reading about the delicately beautiful plume hydroids. They look like exquisite feathery plants (hence the name *sea ferns*), but in fact are intertidal animals. What looks like a bud at the end of each sessile stalk is actually an animal called a hydranth. If you touch them (you should not), you feel that they have an exoskeleton (outer skeleton). They are branched living colonies, not seaweed. Moreover, they can be dangerous, often containing the stinger tentacles we associate with floating jellyfish. This is what allows them to form a symbiotic relationship with hermit crabs. They defend the crabs from predators, and in return some species get a shell upon which to anchor. There are more than three thousand different species of jellyfish. In reading Ricketts's and Calvin's book, I found this extraordinary information:

> In their alternation of generation, hydroids have a rather startling life history. It is a grotesque business, as bewildering to the average man as if he were asked to believe that rosebushes give birth to hummingbirds, and that the hummingbirds' progeny become rosebushes again. The plant-like hydroid which the shore collector sees gives rise by budding to male and female jellyfish, whose united sexual products develop into free-swimming larvae, the planulae, which attach and become hydroids, like their grandparents. The life cycle, then, is hydroid-jellyfish-larva-hydroid.

So jellyfish are more like butterflies and caterpillars than I would have expected, going through two completely different stages of life: They alternate between a free-swimming medusa (the bell-like shape of most jellyfish, but used for the second form of the jellyfish—that is, when it is not a polyp) and a polyp attached to a stem. The polyp reproduces asexually, by branching and budding, releasing tiny medusae, often in huge numbers, who in their turn reproduce by sexual intercourse.

Later in the book we learn how easy it is to find a group of ivory-white polyps each about half an inch long attached to rocks in tide pools along the Northern California coast. If you touch them, they respond by contracting to half their size. But small as they are, they are the parents of the giant pelagic scypho-medusa. Many people mistakenly assume that jellyfish are hermaphroditic, as some fish are. However, when these ocean-swimming jellyfish release eggs fertilized by a male's sperm, these planulae drift inshore and settle down to become polyps, which resemble tiny sea anemones. These polyps then reproduce asexually, by budding. They produce ephyra, immature jellies. (This is the name scientists prefer to *jellyfish*, on the grounds that jellyfish are not fish at all.)

A few years ago, my family and I were visiting a park in northern

Australia. We were enchanted with the clear waters, the white sand, and the complete lack of bathers. We saw a sign warning of box jellyfish, and a small first-aid station containing vinegar. I assumed that the box jellyfish was similar to the more familiar Portuguese man-of-war, whose sting, while painful, is not so severe that anyone would forgo a beautiful swim. Reader, we all dove into those azure seas, to share the ocean with the box jellyfish. After swimming for a short time, a tough-looking ranger wearing what for all the world looked like nylon pantyhose over his arms and legs, approached and asked us what we knew about the box jellyfish. "Nothing," we admitted.

"Did you, for example, know that the sting is so painful that extremely tough Ossie males will scream uncontrollably, begging to be put out of their misery, and some begin to vomit, have trouble breathing, and go into anaphylactic shock? There have in fact been deaths, more than from sharks and crocodiles combined. At least seventy since records have been kept. One large box jellyfish can contain enough venom to kill seven hundred people."

We scrambled out, grateful to be alive. The vinegar was only there for immediate relief. For unknown reasons, acetic acid, found in vinegar, disables the box jellyfish's nematocysts, or stinging cells, which otherwise would continue to pump tiny poisoned darts into the exposed part of the body. Moreover, anyone trying to take the tentacles off will herself be stung with equal potency. Medical emergency care must be sought immediately. The ranger's bizarre suit was the best-known protection against the stinger, which is triggered by chemicals in flesh.

From above, cubozoans, or box jellyfish, look like a square or rectangular box. They are also called sea wasps, and are really quite extraordinary creatures. There are about twenty species worldwide, but the largest of them, *Chironex fleckeri*, may be the single deadliest animal on the planet. They can grow to the size of a basketball with sixty long tentacles and five billion stinging cells! But their size is not the reason they are so deadly. After all, the *Irukandji* is the second most venomous box jellyfish, and it is less than an inch across. Most people stung by the

Irukandji do not even realize it until later, when the agony suddenly becomes almost unbearable. If this happens when you are diving or swimming far from shore, you are in serious trouble.

When you are that dangerous, you needn't be aggressive. But why would any animal need to be this deadly? These jellyfish feed on shrimp, and a struggling shrimp could destroy the jelly's delicate tentacles. So evolution has seen to it that there is no struggle. Death is instantaneous.

But even more astonishing to me than the might of their venom was what I learned from a 2005 article in *Nature* that showed, for the first time, this animal's highly sophisticated optical system. This surprised marine scientists, since without a brain (though they appear to have four primitive brainlike organs), how would the information from the eye be processed or conveyed? But conveyed from six sets of four eyes it is, providing the box jellyfish with almost perfect vision!

Once again, we learn slowly and reluctantly that we share the planet with most extraordinary creatures. The more we know, the less anthropocentric we become. That's a good thing.

KAKAPO
Strigops habraptilus

THE KAKAPO IS THE WORLD'S RAREST PARROT: There are only eighty-six of them in all of New Zealand. Besides being rare, weighing up to nine pounds, the kakapo is also the world's heaviest parrot. They are the only flightless parrot in the world and are distinguished by their unique scent: a fermented musty smell produced by bacteria in their feathers. Not unusual enough? This bird also growls like a dog!

Nobody is certain how long kakapos live, because from the time people began observing them for purposes other than cooking them (the aim of the early settlers to New Zealand), none has died of natural causes. Presumably they can live almost as long as most humans.

How did a parrot become flightless? By evolving in New Zealand, the mildest of all countries. So benign is New Zealand that even birds had virtually no enemies. Why use up energy flying when nobody is after you? At night these strictly vegan birds walk through the forests on their sturdy legs, often for several miles, using their powerful claws to climb the rimu tree in search of their favorite food: its seeds.

We tend to think of parrots as gregarious birds, flying in vast flocks and hanging out together. Not so the kakapo, who is, as far as I can tell, the only completely solitary parrot. The only time kakapos get together with other kakapos is during the mating season. And even this only takes place for a single night, every two to four years! It's not much so-cial contact, even less than cats.

Kakapos stake a claim for being the only parrots (as well as the only bird in New Zealand) who visit the traditional sites called leks (dis-cussed earlier in the hummingbird essay). In the breeding season, males compete by puffing up air sacs on their chests and emitting a deep, low booming sound that can be heard in the forest for up to almost five miles. As well as booming, males also make a high metallic call, known as chinging. Either because of the competition, or because of female scarcity, males boom continuously throughout the night for up to three months. It has been calculated that in a single night a male will boom and ching as many as twenty-four thousand times!

Drawn to the far-reaching sound, a female arrives and watches the males dance: They strut before her, showing off iridescent green mot-tled feathers (the perfect camouflage for the New Zealand forest), then patiently waiting to be chosen or rejected. After mating, she wanders off to lay her eggs in a primitive nest. She gets no help in brooding, or feeding, or taking care of the young from the male. His job is done.

It's not certain how often mating takes place. It is not every year, and perhaps as rarely as once in four years. It depends on the sense the birds get of the abundance of food. Their decision seems to be based upon whether there will be enough food to feed their young. An early conservationist, Richard Henry, noted more than a hundred years ago that the male boomed only in years when the tussock seeded well. He expected expert ornithologists to mock him, and mock they did. But re-cent research has proved him right. The bird's behavior depends on whether he feels he can predict the weather and hence the abundance of seeds three months further on, when the chicks would be born. Whether this knowledge is innate, acquired, or even deduced is not known.

By 1840 there were hardly any kakapos to be found on New

Zealand's North Island. First the Maori wanted their feathers, then settlers ate them. Predators such as *Felis catus* and stoats—neither of whom kakapos recognized as a threat (for these were introduced species)—nearly finished them off in the early part of the nineteenth century. Few humans noticed or cared. By the time people took note, in the late 1950s, there were only a few parrots remaining, most in Fiord-land, in the valleys near Milford Sound. The trouble was, when patient and courageous researchers reached those almost inaccessible valleys (where sheer mountain walls on all sides had kept out most predators, including humans) and finally were able to see a living kakapo in 1974, the three birds sighted were attempting to breed, all right, but they were all males! By 1987 the existence of just five more male kakapos re-maining in Fiordland was verified using helicopters. The only hope was to transfer all birds to a predator-free island.

From 1987 through 1997 only three kakapo chicks were raised to ma-turity, and only one female, but a recovery plan in this animal's natural habitat is ongoing at Codfish Island, at the bottom of the South Island. There are no possums or cats here, only a small number of stoats—and they, too, will eventually be killed off, leaving the kakapo to wander at will. The latest news is very good. Nine nests have been found so far, and at least twenty-one eggs have been laid.

· · ·

I am grateful to Paul Jansen, the National Kakapo Team leader and a conserva-tion manager, who for the last twenty-six years has focused on developing strate-gies to recover New Zealand's endemic birds, especially those most at risk, including the kiwi and kokako (a rare and endangered wattle bird), as well as the kakapo, for reading this entry and correcting it.

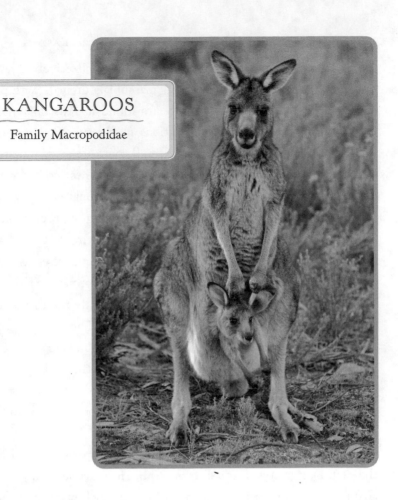

KANGAROOS

Family Macropodidae

K ANGAROO WAS ONE OF THE FIRST Aboriginal words introduced into English. Captain Cook's ship *Endeavour* was nearly wrecked on the Great Barrier Reef in the far north of Queensland in 1770. When its sailors came ashore, they saw their first kangaroos, called by the Aborigines *gangaru*. (I have also heard that this word was a response to the question "What is this animal called?" *Gangaru* meant: "I don't understand the question." However, this sounds apocryphal!) Joseph Banks, the naturalist onboard, remarked: "To compare it to any European animal would be impossible as it has not the least resemblance of any one I have seen." In 1788 surgeon Arthur Bowes Smyth commented that kangaroos were so extremely shy,' " 'tis no easy matter to get near enough to them even to shoot them." How silly of them.

Kangaroos, wallabies, and wallaroos are collectively known as macropods, the world's largest living marsupials, animals with pouches like the Americas' opossums. They are found in Australia and New Guinea, and there are feral populations in Hawaii, England's Penine Hills, Germany, and New Zealand. In all there are sixty-nine separate species, including bettongs, potoroos (one of the best noses for truffles in the world), pademelons, tree-kangaroos, and quokkas.

In general usage, *kangaroo* refers to the six largest species, including the well-known red kangaroo, already described in 1863 as "the most beautiful member of the family," and two sibling species, the eastern grey and the western grey. The two other large species are the common wallaroo (or euro) and the black wallaroo, and finally the antilopine kangaroo, so called because it resembles an antelope. The smaller species are commonly known as wallabies. There are large numbers of the red (8.4 million) and eastern grey (9 million), although nothing like the number in Australia before Europeans arrived—on the order of one or two hundred million. Sometimes these numbers call forth the absurd term *plague*.

Of course, in their natural world kangaroos experience predation. In the past their greatest fear was from a quite formidable enemy, the giant goanna, *Megalania prisca*, a monitor lizard, which had twice the body length of the world's largest living lizard, the Komodo dragon. Once these died out, though, only eagles presented serious problems—until, that is, the arrival of humans between forty and sixty thousand years ago. But the Aboriginal Australians had a modicum of respect for kangaroos, and not a single species went extinct because of their hunting. Once the dingo was introduced about four thousand years ago, the story changed, though the introduced European fox presented a much greater problem—but still nothing to match the most merciless, least logical of predators: humans, in the form of European settlers. Within the two hundred years of European occupation, Australia has seen the extinction of more mammal species than any other continent on earth.

Kangaroo birth is an extraordinary phenomenon. The embryonic-looking newborn macropods are about one-fifth of an inch, the size of a bean, but their forearms are strong enough to enable them to crawl up the mother's fur into her pouch, where they clamp onto a teat and re-main for half a year. (Eastern grey joeys do not push their furry heads out of the pouch for 186 days.) When able to stand, they emerge from the pouch for only brief periods—the first day, no more than a single minute before they go straight back in. As they grow stronger and big-ger, they spend more time outside than inside the pouch. When the next baby is born, they are not allowed back in, but they still stick their heads inside to nurse. The weaning time is often given as exactly 365 days, but it varies. Amazingly, each mammary gland is under separate hormonal control, and the mother provides two completely different kinds of milk: one for the young-afoot, and the other for the newborn. She also has a dormant embryo. Perhaps this unique arrangement ex-plains why when a dingo is chasing a female, tradition has it that she ex-pels her young from the pouch, either to distract the dog or to increase her speed.

There is also the intriguing question of gender preference. It appears, from research at Fowlers Gap Research Station under the direction of David Croft, that rearing a male is far more expensive than rearing a fe-male, and mothers who successfully rear a male baby suffer a physical decline such that they are not always successful in raising subsequent young. Also, males associate with their mothers for only six or seven months after they leave her pouch, whereas daughters will often remain for three or more years. When times are tough (usually associated with drought), mothers raise a higher proportion of females, and it has been suggested that the males are disposed of at an early age, perhaps within the first couple of weeks. I am not sure I understand why males are more expensive: Being larger, they nurse more?

Male kangaroos, depending on the species, can be twice as large as females. Dominance hierarchies seem to exist, and to depend almost en-tirely on size, but it is not clear how important they are or how much serious fighting goes on. Most challenges are declined, as one of the an-imals simply moves away. There is also a submissive cough given by eastern grey kangaroos. When battles take place, they look like human boxing matches, with the kangaroo stretching himself up to his fullest height, even standing on tiptoe, balancing on the tip of his tail, forearms extended. The males may scratch their chests, as if pointing to themselves, and David Croft has suggested it might have the message: *Here I am, look how big I am!*

Not all species engage in boxing matches. And even among those who do box, sometimes the large males look bored and simply ignore the challenge from a smaller opponent, as if they could not be bothered to respond to such a silly suggestion. Status refers to the usual: mating rights, food, and, in the hot desert outback, the prime place in the shade. It might be hard to study dominance in the wild, but studies conducted in captivity lend themselves to a serious criticism: To what extent are we seeing the results of a contrived situation? Kangaroos in the wild could also simply walk away from confrontation. In general, kangaroos are a tolerant species.

In speaking of the plight of Australia's kangaroos, Peter Singer recently said: "We need a *Mabo* decision for Australia's wild animals, a legal recognition of their special status as original residents of Australia, alongside its original inhabitants. The only ethical approach is one that gives their interests equal consideration alongside similar human interests." He is referring to the 1992 High Court of Australia landmark *Mabo* decision, which said that under Australian law, indigenous people have rights to land—rights that existed before colonization and still exist—throwing out forever the legal fiction that when Australia was "discovered" by Captain Cook in 1788 it was *terra nullius*, empty land. It would indeed be wonderful if Australian indigenous animals had the same rights as Australian indigenous people.

KIWIS

Apteryx spp.

THE WORD KIWI comes from the Polynesian word *kivi*—the name of a different bird. Because this bird can be found only in New Zealand, the term has been adapted to describe any human New Zealander. This is the most mammal-like of birds. It cannot fly. And its feathers resemble hair: They have what look like whiskers. Unlike most birds, kiwis have a good sense of smell, using real nostrils to sniff for worms. They also have a distinction: Relative to body size, the females lay the largest egg of all birds, a single egg that weighs about a quarter of the female's body weight. Perhaps this is why the males generally do the incubating, allowing the mother to recover and, four weeks later, offer a second egg for the clutch. They are long-lived birds: A captive female on the North Island is approaching her fortieth birthday.

Like several New Zealand birds, the kiwi probably developed flightlessness because there was little to fear. New Zealand was a pretty benign place way back when, just as it has remained for humans today; were it not for introduced predators, it would be safe for birds as well.

Before humans arrived a thousand years ago, there were up to twelve million kiwis on New Zealand's two main islands. Today there are just twenty to fifty thousand, and the kiwi is endangered. They have been killed off mostly by introduced animals, especially dogs, attracted to their strong odor. The tragedy is that hunters often release wild pigs, themselves a great menace to kiwis, then hunt them later with a pack of dogs, who sometimes then go missing. These pig dogs, as they are called in New Zealand, are superb hunters. The poor kiwi, who evolved without such enemies, doesn't stand a chance. On the other hand, cats do not seem to bother adult kiwis at all, respecting their strong kicks. They do, however, pose a menace to kiwi chicks, who forage and roost independently from an early age. The chicks are highly precocial, and can run within hours of being born. Rats seem stumped by kiwis and their eggs, and rarely pose a threat.

Perhaps the greatest threat today is that humans still want more land and clear native forest for farming. Since an individual kiwi may require as much as a hundred acres, even a relatively large privately owned forest can support only ten to fifteen pairs. A population needs two hundred to five hundred pairs to avoid genetic deterioration and infertility. This is something we have only come to realize fairly recently.

Since the kiwi has no tail, no wings, and no obvious color patches, and is a nocturnal bird, one wonders how the male attracts the attention of the female. Evidently the males lie on their backs and kick their feet in the air, then proceed to roll down a bank. Along with human children, and this writer, female kiwis find it irresistible.

I have yet to meet anybody in New Zealand who has seen a kiwi in the wild, but there are many places where they can be seen in a cage designed to reproduce nocturnal conditions. They become quite friendly in captivity, behaving like puppies, sniffing legs and feet. They can also be fussy: Some have been known to refuse their food unless it is prepared by the keeper they know.

The Maori brought kuri dogs from Polynesia, and used them for hunting kiwis by the thousands. Then came the European bushmen, prospectors, adventurers, and professional hunters. They wanted to eat kiwis or send their feathers to London for the fashion industry and museum collections. Sometimes they killed them for the sheer fun of it. The dogs they brought with them were avid hunters. Today there is a new breed of kiwi-hunting dogs: golden retrievers working with forest rangers. Their job is only to sniff kiwi presence in an underground burrow, wag their tail, and wait for praise from their human companion. As Neville Peat puts it, this is "the kindest dog a kiwi will ever encounter." The purpose of finding them is to radio-tag them to be able to track them. The straps, similar to those put on newborn babies, are specifically designed to fall off after twelve to twenty weeks. A benign bird has at last met benign dogs and benign humans. Maybe we can all start again!

KOALA

Phascolarctos cinereus

THE KOALA IS AN AUSTRALIAN MARSUPIAL (the term means "having a pouch"), much loved in its native country. It is also *not* a bear. But Winnie-the-Pooh, "a bear of very little brain," seems to be a reference to the koala, for in fact the koala is an animal of very little brain. Neuroanatomist John Haight from the University of Tasmania and John Nelson from Melbourne's Monash University recently made a comparative study of the brains of thirty-three marsupial species, only to confirm that the koala brain was small and smooth with hardly any folds.

Why would an animal evolve to have such a small brain? Because for twenty out of the twenty-four hours in the day, koalas are asleep. Storing no fat, they need to conserve energy! Koalas also do not need to drink. They eat only leaves, mostly eucalyptus leaves on the tree upon which they sleep and rest. They hardly interact with any other animal, even other koalas. They are basically a solitary species. So why invest in an expensive brain that requires nourishment? And hunting down a leaf requires little gray matter. The lifestyle of the koala is simple and has remained relatively unchanged for some twenty-five million years. It works. Who are we to knock it? And of course we don't, certainly not the children of the world, for whom this animal remains the ultimate icon of cuddliness.

Probably no other animal looks as cute as a koala. Humans evolved to love something this adorable. But I suspect, having held one, that their helplessness makes a difference, too. They are always falling asleep. How can you harm an animal who is asleep? How can you not protect a sleeping animal? I suspect that it is hardwired into our brains as well: *Do not harm sleeping babies.* They wake up, they look at you with a still-dreamy gaze, they briefly ponder where they are, and then they fall back into deep slumber. For twenty hours of every day! There is something primordial, something deeply satisfying about this. How can the problems of the world matter when you are only there very briefly, and the rest of the time you are asleep?

I found myself holding an eight-month-old female koala at the Tauranga Zoo in Sydney, thanks to the kindness of Darrylene, one of the keepers. She was holding on to a teddy bear, for the keepers find it is easiest to move them that way. I can confirm that they have sharp and powerful claws. Along with the two thumbs on each front paw, they need them for climbing the smooth bark of gum trees. It would not feel good to have these claws get a firm grip on your flesh. This little girl looked up at me, and I began to stroke her soft furry head. She closed her eyes, asleep in seconds. I did not hear any sound from her at all.

Koalas do make a sound, though. It has been described as a bellow. Hearing it in the forest can badly frighten a person. Its only purpose seems to be to maintain distance, since koalas call when changing trees, or to announce to a female that they are available for mating. One name given by the Upper Yarra tribe to the koala is *koob-boor*, which is clearly an onomatopoeic rendition of the call. William Govatt said in 1836 that "when disturbed they make a melancholy cry exciting pity."

Scientists who study koalas kindly pronounce their personalities to be "uncomplicated"—so much so that the males are not even sure when female koalas are in estrus, and will attempt to mate with them anytime they are present.

Like the young of all marsupials, the baby koala is born more or less undeveloped. The single baby (twins are rare) is about the size of a thumbnail—five hundred milligrams—or a small bee. (She will eventually weigh twenty-five thousand times her birth weight!) As soon as she is born, she climbs her way into the mother's pouch (pouches face the rear, and come equipped with a drawstring), latches on to a teat, and stays there for almost a year. One reason the babies are so slow to develop is that the eucalyptus diet of the mother is so low in nutrition; no mammal has a lower milk energy production. The babies only begin to feed on leaves at six months of age. There is not much competition, since most other mammals find the chemical cocktail of the leaves without taste, or even toxic.

Female koalas are among the best mothers in the animal world. It is common to have a 100 percent survival rate after weaning, unusual in any animal. The maternal bond is only broken when the female becomes pregnant the following year, although normally the young continue living in close proximity to their mother for another year, often feeding in the same tree. Nobody is certain, but the females then probably mate with their own fathers (not all animals avoid incest). Koalas live from thirteen to eighteen years.

One consequence of their lack of motion and their small brains is that koalas often fall out of trees. A sudden gust of wind might sway a branch, and a sleeping koala can be dislodged and fall to the ground. Hardy animals, they look around in amazement to see where they are, then slowly climb back up the tree and resume their sleep. They are not used to predation, for basically, except for the occasional owl or eagle, humans are their only predators.

Right now, and probably for some time in the past as well, koalas are prone to chlamydia infections. Nobody is certain where this comes from, but it is probably not endemic and was transferred from domestic animals. They have no immunity and are highly susceptible.

It may well be that this special iconic animal will one day disappear.

I say this even though it is still not listed as "vulnerable" simply because there was a time, before any humans lived in Australia, when koalas were to be found in the many millions, perhaps as many as one hundred million. Today, while no official figures are known, a good guess is that there are fewer than one hundred thousand. Attempts are ongoing to find special habitats for koalas on islands (Kangaroo, French, and other islands off the coast of Australia) and in national parks such as Lone Pine Koala Sanctuary in Queensland. But often the population in these sanctuaries falls as low as just a few individuals.

Now for the great question to which there is no satisfactory answer, and may never be: What do koalas do when they are asleep? I am certain they dream, but as far as I know there has been no scientific study of koala sleep, though it would not be difficult to hook them up to a sleep machine and test for REM sleep. But since all mammals tested *do* dream, there is no reason to believe that koalas are the exception. Perhaps they sleep so much because they dream so much. And if only we knew what they dream *about*, we would have solved the world's problems!

KOOKABURRA

Dacelo novaeguineae

L IKE THE KOALA AND THE KANGAROO, the kookaburra, the largest
bird of the kingfishers, has always been dear to the heart of Australians. Since a number of them were brought to New Zealand,
I have also seen and heard the kookaburra here. They can sometimes be
spotted sitting in a tree, laughing their heads off, which Professor
Gisela Kaplan informs me, means there may be serious territorial con-
flict or a dangerous predator about. Their name is derived from an Australian Aboriginal language and is meant to be onomatopoeic.

The laughing kookaburra has been described as the "clown of the
bush," mainly because of the distinctive sound she makes every morning and every evening (rarely in between). It sounds like human laughter—not just any laughter, but mocking laughter. It's a low chuckle of
repetitive *ooo* sounds. They rise in intensity to a loud laugh of repetitive
kakaka sounds, then lower to a chuckle. Because this call occurs early in

the morning, it has been taken to be territorial, but some observers have heard the same sound when a fledgling falls to the ground. Nobody actually knows its purpose. However, since kookaburras make many different vocalizations, there could well be subtle variations human ears do not perceive and some could well be cries for help.

Because this bird is easygoing around people, there have been many occasions when a human falls or in some other way makes a fool of himself, and the kookaburra laughs. Understandably, the humiliated person may feel the bird is laughing *at him.* It's what the Aboriginals thought, as did Australia's early settlers. However, laughter does not seem to be an option anywhere in the animal nonprimate world. It may be that some animals, such as dogs, smile, and certainly some have a sense of humor, but no nonprimate, I believe, actually doubles over with mirth. The kookaburra is simply singing a song, not commenting on the human condition.

Another piece of human projection lies in the opposite direction: Many settlers in Australia loved this bird because they mistakenly thought the kookaburra was benevolently protecting them against poisonous snakes. It is not uncommon to see a kookaburra attempting, mostly successfully, to kill and swallow highly poisonous snakes. But these snakes are simply part of the birds' diet; they are not actively protecting anybody but themselves. Kookaburras are among the large birds known as "generalist hunters": They will eat anything small enough to swallow. They do not have talons. Instead they are equipped with powerful beaks, from whose viselike grip no animal escapes.

Wild kookaburras will, over time, become relatively tame, even taking food from a person's hand. Strangely enough, their close relative the blue-winged kookaburra is extremely shy. Humans tend to appreciate any species that has the good sense to befriend us.

The reason ornithologists are so taken with these birds has nothing to do with their laughter or their diet, but because kookaburras are cooperative breeders—a term referring to birds who have helpers caring for young who are not theirs. Relatively rare in birds, this is practically unknown in mammals other than humans. However, in Australia at least eighty species of birds engage in this practice, including magpies, fairy-wrens, apostle birds, some thornbills, and all species of babblers.

In a group of kookaburras, one breeding pair is dominant. These two remain faithful for life, which can be as long as twenty years. The helpers are close relatives who hatched in previous years, but always in the same group, never from a different group (except for kidnapping— we'll come to that). What's in it for these caretakers? Well, they increase their genetic fitness, by proxy as it were; they are learning how to successfully rear their own young for when that time comes, at least so goes the sociobiological argument. When one of the pair dies, neighbors quickly pick up this information about the "widowed" group (either from the many surreptitious reconnaissance trips around distant territories, or from the fact that only a single bird is singing). Then another bird arrives to continue the tradition. This bird is from outside the group, avoiding the problems of inbreeding. For an evolutionary biologist, what's interesting is that over the next year most of the helpers disperse, because in helping the new stepparents, to whom they are less related, they receive less genetic advantage. The theory is that the genetic fitness advantage is greater when you help full siblings than when you help half brothers and half sisters, but it remains simply a theory.

It is not that the male forces monogamy onto the female. Most of the time she *chooses* to be faithful, for kookaburras are reverse size dimorphic—that is, whereas normally male birds are bigger than females, in the case of kookaburras the females are heavier and stronger than the males by about 15 percent. So perhaps the female bird decides to be faithful because in that way she can be sure her partner will be a good father. Indeed, male kookaburras are good dads. During the day, they spend more time on the clutch of eggs than females do, and most of the food brought to the nestlings is brought by the male. Sometimes he makes fifty trips a day.

The helpers are also ready to assist the mother and father. When one of these younger birds wants to try out parenting, he perches near the nest entrance (often in a tree hollow or even a giant termite nest—the birds and the termites seem to tolerate each other without animosity) and makes a soft contact call, indicating that an offer is on the table. If the bird inside does not come out right away, the helper may softly enter and try persuasion. Usually, this is successful.

David Curl, in his work on blue-winged kookaburras, has found that almost routinely these birds kidnap neighboring fledglings who are enticed to remain with their adoptive family. What's in it for the kidnapped? Not much that I can see, but the benefit for the kidnapper is obvious. And, of course, there are genetic benefits to this intermingling of different groups.

Another intriguing piece of behavior observed in kookaburras has to do with what is often called extra pair couplings. Even monogamous birds often manage to sneak in a little affair to make certain their children have the best possible genetic endowment. The surprise is this: While a female kookaburra is often seen mating with a male other than her partner, she does so only when she is not fertile and there is little chance of her becoming pregnant. Moreover, these encounters often take place in conspicuous places, such as on treetops, with all members of the group looking on. Even more surprising, sometimes these sexual encounters are between two males or two females. This has led researchers to seek an explanation that bears no relation to sexuality or to propagation. Possibly there is some social signaling involved, or maybe it is a way for the group to cohere more tightly, as we see in bonobos. Our interpretation of their actions actually may have little to do with what's really going on.

LEMURS

Aye-aye, babakoto, sifaka,
and ring-tailed lemur

THESE PRIMATES' HAUNTING, otherworldly calls led to the Roman word *lemur*, spirit of the dead. They are found only in the Comoros and on the island of Madagascar, the world's fourth-largest island (about the size of Texas or France). Just a few thousand years ago there were fifty species, some larger than gorillas, but at least fifteen died out because of hunting and habitat destruction. Today at least one species, the lesser bamboo lemur, is critically endangered, with only a few hundred individuals barely surviving. Unlike most other primates, lemurs sometimes live in monogamous pairs, though fathers do not appear to be involved in raising infants.

AYE-AYE

Daubentonia madagascariensis

THE FAMILY DAUBENTONIIDAE consists of a single extant species, the strange-looking aye-aye, a lemur that has always fascinated people. It was not until the middle of the nineteenth century that scientists realized these animals were primates, not rodents. They have a dexterous, slender middle finger that can rotate 360 degrees, perfect for scooping out coconut flesh (a fruit they are fond of, along with other cultivated crops such as mangoes and lychees—which makes them unpopular with farmers). They often feed on insect larvae, which they find by tapping with their middle digit on tree trunks. The females are in estrus for only a few days in the year.

Nocturnal and shy, they were thought extinct in the 1930s. In 1957 researchers "rediscovered" aye-ayes in the Ambato Mahambo forest on Madagascar's east coast, and a reserve was created to protect what were thought to be the last aye-ayes in the world. Now, however, it is recognized that they have a relatively wide geographic distribution; because they are nocturnal and secretive, they are simply hard to find. In 1989 the large Man and the Biosphere Reserve was established in Mananura on the east coast by presidential decree for the aye-aye. Nobody knows for certain how many there are in the wild, but the numbers are probably declining. The species is listed as endangered. Unlike other lemurs, the reason for this decline has less to do with habitat destruction than with the realm of superstition.

The strangest thing about these animals is the way they affect humans, especially the Malagasy. This is where the real threat to the existence of the aye-aye comes from. There are local taboos about the aye-aye, called *fady*. But these differ radically from village to village, even within the same geographic region. According to the taboo in some villages, if an aye-aye were so much as seen, it had to be killed, the entire village had to be burned down, and everybody had to move. In other villages the aye-aye is considered an ancestral spirit and is worshipped. Of course the latter view is a bit closer to my own appreciation of these mysterious creatures.

BABAKOTO

Indri indri

ANOTHER FAMOUS LEMUR is *Indri indri*, a large black-and-white lemur with enormous eyes that is strictly diurnal. This is the only lemur without a long tail. Most visitors to Madagascar are familiar with the creature's characteristic eerie wailing song (similar to that of the white-handed gibbon from Southeast Asia). Part of the song, at least the introduction, is communal. Songs are probably sung for group spacing or to demarcate territory.

Babakotos move through the canopy with spectacular bounds of up to thirty feet between trees. They are strictly monogamous, and seek out a new partner only after the death of a mate. They do not reach sexual maturity until nearly nine, and then give birth only every second or third year, so their survival is severely threatened. But this threat derives entirely from habitat destruction, since unlike the case of the aye-aye, no Malagasy would ever kill one: They, too, are *fady*, but in this case, the taboo is strictly against killing them. They are given the local name of *babakoto*, which means "ancestor of man."

SIFAKA

THE SIFAKA IS THE LARGEST LEMUR and is widely considered the most beautiful. Sifakas have long silky fur; the head is white with a black crown; the long arms and legs are a rich orange to yellow-gold, and both the feet and hands are jet black. They give one sound, *tzisk-tzisk-tzisk*, for a ground predator, and a completely different call, *honk-honk-honk*, for an aerial predator. The Malagasy word *sifaka* refers to all three members of this species and to the explosive sound they make when alarmed. (The third species was only discovered in 1974, with an estimated population of only a few hundred individuals.) I have heard that when separated from their group, sifakas make a long, ghostly wailing sound, the meaning of which is clear even to another species: *Come get me!* They also communicate with posture, facial expressions, and territorial scent marking. They make long soaring leaps from tree to tree, and when on the ground, they bounce like kangaroos.

Hunting has taken a toll of these exquisite animals, but so have other factors: Predation by other animals probably accounts for the fact that nearly half of all infants die before they are a year old. Infanticide has also been observed, though rarely (five times in fifteen years, so it is impossible to say how often it occurs or how important it is). In fact, promiscuous matings on the part of females probably evolved to confuse males as to paternity in order to defend against infanticide. Females displace males at feeding sites and on other occasions; the males cower when challenged, and make a strange, appeasing chattering sound.

RING-TAILED LEMUR

Lemur catta

THESE ARE MADAGASCAR'S TRADEMARK. With their long black-and-white-ringed tails and racoonlike face masks, ring-tailed lemurs can never be mistaken for any other. They can be seen walking single file along a forest path, their tails like giant question marks. They live on and depend upon tamarind and other trees, eating the fruit and leaves throughout the year. They are not vegetarians, however, and happily eat locusts, cicadas, even chameleons. They have at least three different alarm calls: one for snakes (a click), another for ground predators (a yap), and a third for hawks and other predators from the air (a scream).

The females are in estrus for only four hours the whole year! The males compete for them during the mating season, and the fights leave almost all males wounded by the end of the season, but mortal combat is rare. Some of the fighting among males is less vicious, and is called stink fighting—they wave their tails, rich in scents from glands in their wrists and scrotum. The odd thing is that, almost uniquely among mammals, female dominance is generally true of all lemurs, and especially the ring-tailed lemur. Females also vie for status, but wounds are unusual, and mortal fights unheard-of. Mothers, daughters, and sisters frequently form what is called a lemur lump, huddling together against the cold. Like other "true" lemurs, they are cathemeral—that is, active by day or night.

The lemur genealogy goes back at least forty million years, perhaps even a hundred million. Unlike us, though, they live entirely in the present. While watching a group of ring-tailed lemur babies playing games while their parents took a siesta, Alison Jolly noted that they "do not look to past or future, only to the warm afternoon, their play-mates, and their mothers' milk, in the enchanted forest."

LION

Panthera leo

STRANGE TO REALIZE that there was once a North American lion (*Panthera atrox*), now extinct. Also, during the Pleistocene epoch, lions lived in England. I know from my reading of ancient Sanskrit texts that lions were common in India. Today they are gone, except for a small population of three hundred Asiatic lions in the Gir Forest in northwestern India.

Female lions are considerably smaller than males, and males have manes. Why manes? They're protective, of course, but in addition, since biologists are able to identify a given lion by his mane, it is almost certain that other lions can do the same. So they may be signature manes, the equivalent of signature whistles in dolphins or whales.

Males and females are also distinguished by what they do. Females do all the hunting, while the males mostly rest—up to twenty hours a day! But when a male lion can be induced to run, it is at a speed of thirty-five miles per hour, much faster than any human. The job of the oldest, strongest male is to be head of the pride, generally a group of two to eighteen adult females, their cubs, and one to seven males. The females are related. The lionesses and their offspring may occupy the same area for generations.

There's no other way to put it: The males are lazy. Studies in the Serengeti and Ngorongoro Crater show that some individual pride members, generally males, consistently lag behind. They don't take part in the hunt and don't help expel intruders. According to natural-ist George Schaller, out of more than a thousand stalks he recorded, only 3 percent were made by males! How come these completely selfish pride members are tolerated? Perhaps lion culture is more complex than we think, and these slackers have some other function we have simply not yet discovered.

The female lion knows that any strange male approaching the pride is a danger to her children. Females with cubs attempt to herd their chil-dren out of danger. If they must confront a male, the females often join together and threaten the invading males. With enough of them, they can be successful. But if a lone female tries to protect her cubs, she pays with her life—odd, considering that the whole point of killing the cubs is to bring the mother into estrus, something she cannot do if dead. In reproductive logic, it is to the male lion's advantage to kill the cubs of a different male, thereby forcing the mother into bearing *his* cubs and propagating *his* genes. As a rule, males do not manage to remain in a pride for much more than a year before they are in their turn ousted by another male. A female will not be ready to mate again until her cub is at least eighteen months old. So if a male arrives in a new pride where there are young, he might wait in vain for the female to come back into estrus before he is ousted, and his time will have been wasted. On aver-age, a lion can only expect to remain at the head of the pride for at most two years. Because lion cubs are vulnerable to adult males for about two years, if a male wants to be around to protect his own cubs, he must mate quickly with the female or his turn will be up before his cubs are old enough to defend themselves. Surely there are some cases where a male takes over a pride and does *not* engage in infanticide. However, we simply don't know enough to have accurate statistics on such matters.

I am hardly the first to suggest that lions do not seem fully adjusted to communal life. Of course lions are not a solitary species—but neither are they a social species in the way wolves are. It is as if they have not had much practice in living together; as if their present social system evolved only relatively recently.

During the four years of Schaller's study of the Seronera and Masai lion prides, of the seventy-nine cubs born, fifty-three, almost 70 percent, died of starvation, predators, other lions, or unknown causes. In other parts of the Serengeti and in other parks in Africa, the survival rate is 50 percent or less. One cause of death that seems particularly repulsive to humans is maternal abandonment: If there's not enough food, a mother may simply walk away from her litter, or if there is only one cub left, she may abandon him, perhaps because it takes too much energy to raise a single cub. Schaller put it well: "The response of a lioness to her cubs is so finely balanced between care and neglect, between her own desires and the needs of her offspring, that the survival of the young ones is threatened whenever conditions are not the optimum."

The males, who do practically nothing, and certainly rarely participate in the hunt, are nonetheless the first to benefit from the spoils. They roughly shove everyone else aside, generally eating more than everyone else when there's a kill. I am beginning to think that the problem with lions is that they are equipped by nature with such lethal tools for one purpose that it is almost impossible not to use them for others. It is like giving a human a machine gun. It goes to their head.

When I visited a big-cat sanctuary in Northern California, there were some rescued lions in a large enclosure. We sauntered past, and the lions barely registered us. Then my son Ilan, two years old at the time, came running up. Two lions suddenly perked up. Jumping to their feet, they came to the bars and fixed Ilan with an unwavering stare whose message was all too clear. As we continued walking, they followed us in a low crouch. There is no doubt in my mind that had they been free, they would have taken Ilan for lunch. And I don't mean to McDonald's.

And then, just when one is about to despair, the Internet brings us salvation: Like many people on June 22, 2005, I woke to find on BBC News: KIDNAPPED GIRL "RESCUED" BY LIONS. It was the story of a twelve-year-old Ethiopian girl who had been taken by four men on her way home from school early in June. Evidently, the four men were trying to force her to accept a marriage to an older man. They held her captive for seven days, repeatedly beating her. One morning a pride of three—most probably female—lions came across the group. They chased the men away, then returned to the terrified girl and stood guard over her until the police arrived. Stuart Williams, a wildlife expert with the Rural Development Ministry, said it was likely the young girl was saved because she was crying from the trauma of her attack. "A young girl whimpering could be mistaken for the mewing sound from a lion cub, which in turn could explain why the lions didn't eat her."

It seems to me highly unlikely that the lions mistook the girl for a lion cub. However, her moaning may well have mobilized protective instincts honed over millennia of trying to protect their cubs from infanticidal males. Most people, me included, would have cheered the lionesses had they actually caught the men.

I F YOU TYPE "LOBSTER" INTO GOOGLE, you'll get a listing for 24,800,000 sites, the vast majority about eating lobsters, lobsters on the menu, ordering lobsters, and killing lobsters. This is not surprising, considering that the United States produces around eighty million pounds of lobster per year. There are far fewer sites about lobsters as living, breathing crustaceans. Despite this, it is clear that people are becoming increasingly more interested in what lobsters are like and not just in how they taste.

The females carry up to one hundred thousand eggs internally for nine to twelve months, and then for the same amount of time they are externally attached to the swimmerets under her tail. These eggs hatch, a process that can take several weeks. (The female stands on the tips of her walking legs with her claws outstretched and creates a current of water that carries the young up to the surface of the sea.) Then, the larvae (about a third of an inch long) float near the surface for four to six weeks. When only an inch long, they already bear a striking resemblance to an adult, and they still swim on the surface of the sea. Eventually, the few who survive settle to the bottom and develop as baby lobsters. The odds aren't good. From every fifty thousand eggs, two lobsters are expected to survive to adult size. From then on, their entire life is spent on the sea bottom.

If allowed, they can live for nearly a century. However, they rarely do, simply because man is such a persistent and efficient enemy. They can also grow quite large: In 1956, a lobster weighing more than forty-four pounds was hauled from deep water off the eastern end of Long Island. (They can live at depths of more than 2,400 feet.)

They have ritualized fights in which there is little actual damage inflicted. One ritual involves a kind of arm wrestling that scientists call claw lock—a handshake contest in which the animals attempt to pull each other sharply over an invisible line, until "eventually one animal attempts to withdraw and the other releases his grip."

Lobsters are cannibalistic when they are held in artificially high densities (a tank)—something that does not normally happen in their ocean life. Moreover, field studies show that they frequently interact, even amicably, if they inhabit individual nests (shelters). A pair often bonds after intercourse (the male has a double penis), spending quiet time together for several weeks. The female chooses the male lobster she wants to mate with. The male sometimes protects her during pregnancy. Sexual maturity depends on the temperature of the water in which the lobster is living: the warmer the water, the more quickly the female reaches adulthood. She can be ready for motherhood when she weighs less than a pound, but in colder waters she must wait until she is two pounds, which could put her in her teens.

Many people have felt revulsion at the thought of plunging a live fellow creature into a pot of boiling water. What other animal, after all, do we kill in the kitchen before eating it? The ethics of the practice call for examination. For most to do this requires a belief that lobsters feel no pain. Whether this is true depends upon whom you ask. In 2003 there was a great deal of interest around the world in an article related to this issue written by Lynne Sneddon, Victoria Braithwaite, and Michael

Gentle of the Roslin Institute at the University of Edinburgh. In "Do Fishes Have Nociceptors? Evidence for the Evolution of a Vertebrate Sensory System," an experiment was described wherein bee venom was injected into the lips of rainbow trout. Their heart rate increased, and they tried to rub their lips against the gravel on the bottom of their tanks. Clearly, then, they have nociception, and their behavior "suggests discomfort" (to use the careful words of the scientists involved). Mechanical thresholds were lower than those found in, for example, human skin. Fish thus have a *lower* threshold for pain than we do, meaning it takes less to hurt them. They are *more* sensitive than humans, not less. I wrote to the senior author, Lynne Sneddon, probably the world's leading authority on pain in fish, of the University of Liverpool, about lobster pain, and this is what she told me:

> Essentially you must have the relevant brain areas to process painful information, which means you have to have a brain, and lobsters don't. They have two ganglion, which is similar to the area of our spinal cord where reflexes are produced, so really lobsters would react to the hot water but they would not be able to process the information so would not suffer pain. They are capable of nociception, which is the simple perception and reflex withdrawal—nearly all animals are capable of this—it's like when you touch a hot iron you feel a painful sensation and instantly withdraw your hand, then there is a lag period followed by the burnt skin throbbing, you alter your behaviour and it feels sore—this is pain. It is highly unlikely invertebrates feel pain as they do not have a brain—only vertebrate animals do. The question is not that they can perceive and react, but do they know they are in pain and do they suffer?

I am not sure I can follow her logic. Whether creatures *know* they are in pain seems to me irrelevant. If they *have* the pain, surely that is what matters.

Let me offer a different opinion from another scientist, Dr. Jaren G.

Horsley: "As an invertebrate zoologist who has studied crustaceans for a number of years, I can tell you the lobster has a rather sophisticated nervous system that, among other things, allows it to sense actions that will cause it harm . . . [Lobsters] can, I am sure, sense pain."

At present, there is great scientific interest in lobster behavior, much of the research focused on male aggression. The problem is that these studies are usually conducted in laboratories and rarely in the wild. The circumstances are unnatural, so whether what we see is natural behavior or an artifact is impossible to say. It would be like attempting to understand male aggression based on experiments conducted in San Quentin. In a cage, a lobster has no option of wandering away, thus ending a potentially lethal encounter. I don't believe anyone has yet succeeded in joining a lobster community in the wild. Until that day, our knowledge will be only partial and necessarily biased.

I often notice that in aquariums people stand in front of exhibits that contain lobsters and are surprised to see their color. We tend to think of lobsters as red. In fact, in the wild they come in many different colors, mottled olive green or dark blue-green above, or dusky orange with green-black spots, or rich indigo blue with bright clear blue on the sides of the body. There are even "calico" or "leopard" lobsters—light yellow with purple-blue marbling for spots. They can be as beautiful as any tropical reef fish, and an increasing number of enlightened tourists would rather see them in their natural habitat during the day than on their plates that night, drained of color and life.

MANATEES AND DUGONGS

ALTHOUGH THESE TWO MARINE ANIMALS can grow to be ten feet long and can weigh more than thirty-five hundred pounds, they are completely inoffensive to humans and are correctly perceived to be gentle and harmless. Because of this, for the entire history of human interaction with them, they have been killed. Native peoples hunted and ate them, as did explorers. Hunters kill dugongs in Australia and Papua New Guinea; Amazonian manatees are captured and eaten in the Amazon River basin; and the West Indian manatee is killed and eaten by Central and South Americans and even by Floridians. Until recently, human concern with these animals has been exclusively in order to exploit them. They have been traditionally seen only as a resource. Fortunately, that is changing. You can see the immense amount of research and interest by visiting http://www .sirenian.org/sirenians.htm.

Manatees and dugongs are very similar, except for the shape of the skull and tail. They become sexually mature when they are between ten and fifteen years old. During mating season, several males gather around a female and affectionately nuzzle her, hoping to gain her interest. She usually mates with several at a time, giving birth a full year later to a single calf, who nurses at her side for nearly two years, possibly even spending her entire adolescence in her mother's presence. She may not give birth for another six years, hence the low fecundity. But this is normal for a long-lived mammal with few natural enemies. However, this slow reproduction can prove disastrous when humans hunt the animal for meat. The dugong is now rare over much of its range in the Indian Ocean, but is found in Australian waters. It is considered vulnerable under the IUCN Redlist classification scheme for species threatened with extinction. There are perhaps 70,000 off the coast of Australia. As for manatees, they are one of the most endangered aquatic animals on earth. Approximately 2,600 Florida manatees remain in the wild. While they are protected by law in the United States, they are slow-moving, and often collide with the propellers of outboard motor boats, leading to extensive injury if not death.

Manatees are often called sea cows, not because they bear any genetic relationship to cows (as they do to elephants—note the long, flexible nose—and aardvarks), but because they are vegetarians who eat only sea grasses. This fact distinguishes them from all other aquatic animals.

Like whales, sirenians, as they are called, have lost their hindlimbs. The forelimbs of the manatee are flippers, but they can be turned inward and the tips used for walking on the sea- or riverbed in shallow waters.

There is only one genus of extant dugong, but it was not long ago that there was another member of the Dugongidae family—the Steller's sea cow, a large sirenian who lived in coastal waters around the Aleutian Islands. It was only discovered by shipwrecked Russian hunters in 1741. At that time there were probably just two thousand Steller's sea cows in the world. Twenty-seven years later, the species became extinct. The best statement on this comes from distinguished marine scientist Victor Scheffer:

Only twenty-seven years after the discovery of Alaska the last [Steller's] sea cow was clubbed to death by a hunter in the shallows of the Bering Sea. It weighed perhaps four or five tons and it was the only mammal outside of the tropics that lived on seaweed. We shall never know the secrets of its life: how it survived the freezing winters, how it dealt with the hazard of salty food, what defenses it raised against its enemies, and all the other factors of its body structure and habits. Men will never get insight into the processes of their own lives through study of those of the sea cow.

Upon first seeing a manatee, many people find her ugly, but perhaps like the French *jolie laide*, a woman who is attractive although not conventionally pretty, a manatee's look grows on you. And we seem to grow on them. As they become used to seeing divers in coastal waters, they have been known to approach for a scratch. They also come up close to boats and even play with swimmers in the water. Perhaps, observing us swim, they think we are in trouble and need help. Captive manatees have been observed assisting others in trouble. Two poolmates helped a manatee who was having trouble reaching the surface to breathe, by supporting him on either side until their weak friend could make it to the surface.

ENTOMOLOGISTS KNOW MANTISES AS MANTIDS, members of the orthopteroid insects, the group that includes grasshoppers, crickets, and cockroaches. There are an astonishing nineteen hundred species of mantids, in four hundred genera, most in Africa, Asia, and the Americas. The European mantid (*Mantis religiosa*) was introduced to the eastern United States but is now found in many other places, especially California. California also has two native species that are common and yet almost never seen, since they live mostly in the foothills of the Sierra Nevada.

As a teenager in Hawaii, I opened our door one morning and found a praying mantis standing in the doorway, her legs in boxing or praying position, looking up at me with something resembling expectation. I picked her up, something to which she had no apparent objection, and over the rest of the day she and I became friends (as it were). I took her with me to school the next day. I was a vegetarian; she was a carnivore.

Our biology teacher told me Virginia would like to nibble on my finger. We all laughed, but it was true. She daintily ate small amounts of my finger that first day. At night I put her on a tropical plant, and in the morning she seemed to be waiting for me. I took her to school the next day and for the rest of that week. By Friday my finger was sore, and the teacher, feeling bad for me, said Virginia would also eat my hair (how did he know that?). I gave her a single hair, which she contentedly munched on for hours. We all noticed her stomach growing day by day.

She had been pregnant when I found her. Sure enough one morning, on the plant where she lived at night, there was a one-inch oval-shaped cocoon. (It is called an ootheca—the female inserts two rows of eggs into a foam she produces from her abdomen.) My teacher told me to stay alert for the big event. One night while our family was having dinner, I noticed some strange activity on the plant. The caps at the tops of what looked like little chambers were being forced up. We rushed over to see what looked like a single tiny string emerging. Then a second, a third, a fourth, two hundred! They had fine filaments attaching their thin bodies to the ootheca, and these lifelines allowed the newly molted nymphs to abseil down to the floor. Within seconds they were no longer little strings, but hatchlings, perfectly formed miniature praying mantises, their tiny legs already in boxing position and with small wings that allowed them to fly around the room. (Some viable eggs, I later learned, can hatch a whole year later.) I was enchanted. (I would have been less so if I had realized that the reason they flew away so quickly was because the nymphs have no compunction about eating one another.) Virginia didn't live much longer, as if her life's work had been accomplished.

Did I have a friendship? Well, from my point of view, I did. Consider how ignorance forces us to make anthropomorphic comparisons that could be way off-base. When I first met Virginia, she flashed her colors at me. I took this as an insect *hello*—wrong. Since the majority of mantids are cryptic when at rest, when they are disturbed or threatened in any way or need to shock an opponent or a predator, they react with a startle display and/or flash coloration. Sometimes their eyespots are indeed disconcerting to see for the first time. Am I being watched? For example, *Polyspilota aeruginosa* is a mantid common in parts of Africa and in Madagascar. When an aggressor approaches, the mantid reveals red wings, red and black marks on the abdomen, and the bright red of the jaw. *Get lost!* is the clear message, not *Let's be friends!*

Perhaps insects are simply too unlike us in their appearance, physiology, and behavior to encourage any kind of anthropomorphism. We do not project human qualities onto insects easily or readily or even, generally, at all. But simply because we are reluctant to ascribe feelings to insects does not mean they don't have them. We may have been looking in the wrong place, or in the wrong way, or with the wrong vocabulary.

Take "my" praying mantis. She may not have felt friendship for me. But she did not feel fear, either. Whatever the reason (habituation, for example, or perhaps something we don't yet know anything about), Virginia did not respond to me the way other praying mantises would. I have, in the years since my friendship with Virginia, encountered many praying mantises. As a species, they do not rush away from humans with anything resembling terror. Virginia had numerous opportunities to fly away, to walk away, to disappear on me, both in school and out, and especially at night. The large French doors were always wide open to the garden. Nothing prevented her from leaving. So, I claim, she *chose* to stay.

The praying mantis is most famous among the general public for one thing: the female grazes on the male's head while he is in the act of inseminating her. This was explained as an act of extraordinary generosity on the part of the male; that he was offering his life as a nuptial gift and for the benefit of his unborn heirs. But why would any male do this unless he was assured that he was the last partner the female would ever have? In fact, the early accounts were all based on captive species, and captivity almost invariably introduces variables that would not occur in the wild. Our knowledge of "cannibalism" in mantids came from a single paper written in 1886, which was based on experiments with a single species, and with only two members of that species. It did, however, capture the imagination of the general public, and this "fun fact" is referred to in films, literature, and art as if it were scientifically unassailable. Joanne Elizabeth Lauck claims that "for all our lack of knowledge about insects, this is one fact that, once heard, is never forgotten because it reinforces our misgivings about insects." One of the world's leading authorities, Ken Preston-Mafham, spent five years looking in the tropics, and only found six pairs of mating mantids. What he saw surprised him: In five of these cases the conjugal relations were peaceful. The female, it turned out, "called" (with pheromones) the male. (Researchers from the University of California–Santa Cruz recorded dozens of copulations and discovered an elaborate courtship ritual.) The problem, among mantids as among humans, is that the males don't always understand the meaning of no. Some have a tendency to drop in unannounced and uninvited. Since they are so much smaller than the female, the jerk in question will never make that mistake again. His error proves fatal. I would love to know his last thoughts. The explanation by experts is that the pheromones released are not sufficiently species-specific, and the males often drop in on the wrong species altogether. She then uses her long front legs to make short work of the confused guest. Those legs, by the way—which we think of as praying— are actually raptorial and are used for impaling prey. One early observer noted that the term Linnaeus used to name an Old World species, *Mantis religiosa*, is poorly chosen: "The only thing mantids would seem to pray for is a square meal." They are diurnal hunters, completely carnivorous.

So if "my" mantid seemed friendly to me, maybe she had simply made a category mistake, or maybe she simply had no reference for somebody like me, or maybe she felt *nothing*. And yet, as many people point out, when a praying mantis looks at you, you feel looked at. They have two large eyes set far apart at the sides of their highly mobile triangular heads. (They can turn more than 180 degrees.) You can actually look into these translucent eyes and see a speck of brown right at the bottom. There is definitely somebody home. I believe mantids may be the only insects in the world who will turn their heads to look at you.

Mine was always swaying, in what I saw as an attempt to hypnotize me. She was merely furthering her extraordinary powers of mimicry. Bright green, she was almost invisible when on a green leaf. When the branches swayed in the breeze, so did she, enhancing her invisibility. Moreover, what I thought of as her good table manners—she carefully wiped her mouth with her forelegs—were really her attempts to get rid of small bits of debris that could damage her waterproof exoskeleton. She did this with small pads of soft flattened bristles, known as femoral brushes, on the insides of her forelegs. She also gently wiped her eyes with these pads, to keep her vision crisp and sharp. So it appears that she was not greeting me when she lifted herself up and raised her forelegs. She was trying to scare me, or at least confuse me with what looked like eyes (indigo, grading to lighter blues and turquoise at the edges) on her thorax, giving her time to escape.

MEERKATS ARE A SPECIES OF MONGOOSE. They are small, agile animals with slender bodies and short limbs. Somewhat resembling weasels, they weigh only about two pounds. According to Indian archaeologists, remains of the mongoose can be found in ruins dating from 4000 to 3000 BCE, which indicates that the mongoose may have been domesticated in these early times in the Indus Valley. Certainly many people in India keep them as pets, and the habit goes back a long way. I was told, when I lived in India for two years, that when a mongoose is bitten by a cobra, he retires to the jungle to look for a plant known as mungo root, which he will eat as an antidote to the poison.

In a Kashmiri Sanskrit text called *The Ocean of Story*, written in 1070 CE, is a touching tale:

A Brahmin by the name of Devasharman lived in a certain village. He had a wife of equally high birth, named Yajnadatta. She became pregnant, and in time gave birth to a son. The Brahmin, though poor, felt he had obtained a great gem. After she had given birth to the child, the Brahmin's wife went to the river to bathe. Devasharman remained in the house, taking care of his infant son. Meanwhile a maid came from the women's apartments of the palace to summon the Brahmin, who lived on presents received by performing religious ceremonies ... To guard the child, he left a mongoose, which he had raised in his house since it was born. As soon as the Brahmin left, a snake suddenly slithered toward the child. The mongoose, seeing it, killed it out of love for his master. In the distance, the mongoose saw Devasharman returning. Happy to see him, he ran towards him, stained with the blood of the snake. But when Devasharman saw the blood, he thought: "Surely he has killed my little boy," and in his delusion he killed the mongoose with a stone. When he went into the house he saw the snake killed by the mongoose and his boy alive and safe. He felt a deep inner sorrow. When his wife returned and learned what had happened, she reproached him, saying, "Why did you not think before killing this mongoose which had been your friend?"

Readers will recognize the familiar Llewellyn and Gellert story. Is it only, as some have claimed, an "urban legend"? I would not be so certain. Mongooses are often kept as pets in India, and mongooses do in fact prey upon snakes, including cobras and other highly venomous species. There is a well-known article by Berkeley's great Sanskrit scholar Murray Emeneau in which he concludes that the modern report "is one of factual events." I asked Professor Emeneau about this, and he told me that he has changed his mind several times over the years as to whether it did or did not happen. Legend or fact, the story resonated with many cultures. There are versions of the tale in many languages: Mongolian, Arabic, Syriac, German, medieval English, and others.

Those who study mongooses never fail to remark upon their altruism. The animals even seem to show gratitude. In the Kenyan bush one evening, Tatu, a young dwarf mongoose, became separated from her family after an antelope, frightened by a dust devil, hurtled through the group. At dusk mongooses retire into a termite mound, but Tatu was on a mound fifty yards from her family, afraid to cross the intervening ground. She uttered *Where are you?* calls and trotted back and forth on her mound. Her family called back repeatedly with louder and louder *Here I am* calls, but she dared not cross. By the time it was dark, Tatu was hoarse, and huddled on top of the mound. Her parents and another mongoose (probably her sister) finally set off toward her, keeping under cover as much as possible, while the rest of the band watched, scanning the earth and sky for predators. When the three arrived, Tatu flung herself upon them, licking and grooming them. When she had groomed all three, they went back to the group.

This same mongoose once injured her forepaw badly in a fight with another group of mongooses. (Altruism does not preclude aggression.) She could no longer catch prey by pouncing with both paws. As she favored the paw and its nails grew long, making it even more unusable, she traveled slowly and lost weight. The other mongooses spent more time with Tatu, grooming her when she stopped grooming herself. They never brought her food but according to observer Anne Rasa, they began foraging next to Tatu at an increased rate. When they caught something, she would ask for it and they would relinquish their food to her. As a higher-ranking mongoose, it wasn't surprising that they gave up food to her, only that they chose to forage near her so that this happened. At first, Rasa thought it was coincidence, but she was soon convinced it was a deliberate choice on the part of the other mongooses. Although Tatu was getting almost half her food in this way, it did not prevent her eventual death. When she died, in a termite mound, the group stopped traveling, and only moved on when her body began to decompose.

These are not unique occurrences. Oxford animal behaviorist David Macdonald tells of a group of banded mongooses climbing a tree to rescue one of their companions from the talons of a martial eagle, a dangerous, even heroic act.

Not all mongooses are social, but eight of the thirty-six species are—none more so than the meerkat. They are, as Macdonald puts it, "close to the pinnacle of carnivore sociality." The details of their social lives were unknown even as recently as the 1980s, and as more information comes out of the Kalahari Gemsbok National Park, where much research is ongoing, we are having to reevaluate theories about the origins of cooperation, kindness, friendship, and altruism among all mammals, humans included.

Is there then nothing to complain about in this idyllic society? According to Macdonald, the dark secret of the meerkat is female infanticide, where a dominant pregnant female kills the litter of a subordinate, to make certain that all food brought by the helpers to the den is available for her own kittens. But here is the puzzle: "There is little evidence that the offspring of dominant females actually do better as a result of her murderous actions."

In zoos, meerkats seem to thrive. (The crucial word here is *seem*—how would we ever know without a control study and direct questioning of the research subjects?) It's a familiar sight to see a single meerkat raising himself to his full height to get a good look at his surroundings and standing sentinel duty. All eventually take their turn, except for the kittens. The sentinel emits regular peeping sounds, a "watchman's song" that lets everyone else know that all is well. Meerkats have a full set of calls to represent degrees of threat, ranging from a soft peep to a shrill growl that means imminent danger.

They have a close partnership with hornbill birds, for they flush out prey the birds could not get on their own. The birds, in turn, warn the meerkats of any raptor in the sky, even if they themselves are not in any danger. The hornbills wait outside the dens of the meerkats early in the morning, not wishing to begin their daily foraging without their partners.

Meerkats treat their kittens with great solicitude, providing babysitting—even if it means that an animal who normally eats every few minutes must fast for a whole day. The females also act as wet nurses, even if they are not themselves pregnant, something rare in mammals. When the kittens emerge from the den, they are adopted after a few weeks by an adult tutor, not necessarily genetically related, as an apprentice.

Meerkats are one of the few species to hug a companion when anx-
ious or when they are so relaxed they cannot help themselves. What
human doesn't appreciate a good hug? One would hope this animal lesson in compassion would teach humans to respect and protect this engaging creature.

MULBERRY SILKWORM

Bombyx mori

THERE'S A SAYING IN CHINA: "Patience and the mulberry leaf become a silk gown." Pretty, but is something missing? Yes, some*body* is: the silkworm. Not many people think much about where silk comes from. I used to love the raw silk shirts that I bought in India. It never occurred to me back then that silk was a hardened glandular fluid, or that hundreds of thousands of animals died to give me my shirt. Now I know better: Silk is not a "natural" fiber, it is an animal fiber.

The Silk Road refers to the fact that in 139 BCE the world's longest trade route stretched from eastern China, where silk was "invented," to the Mediterranean Sea. How silk was produced was jealously guarded information. Monk silk-spies would attempt to hide moth silkworms in hollow canes during pilgrimages to other countries. The secret did not reach India and Japan until 300 CE, and Europe and America until much later. It is remarkable that Aristotle discovered that fabric could be made from the cocoons of certain caterpillars, some eight hundred years before the true silkworm came to Greece.

Once I began investigating this matter, I ran up against the usual denial when it comes to products involving exploitation of another species. I was told the silkworm farmer treats his worms as royalty. (They are really caterpillars. I think we call them worms to denigrate them and make what we do to them seem trivial.) Needless to say, this careful treatment is not because the farmer feels any affection for the silkworms, but because they are a valuable commodity. In China and Japan he might even turn his house over to them. He covers his floors with mulberry (*Morus alba*) leaves, and sleeps outside on the roof. He must be very quiet, and it is important to keep everything spotless.

Silkworm moths lay three to four hundred pin-sized black eggs. The eggs are put in cold storage for six weeks and then bathed in warm water, dried in air, and placed in incubators until they hatch, about thirty days later. A tiny quarter-inch white worm hatches from each egg. The delicate worm is put on a bamboo tray on which the best mulberry leaves are laid. Each worm eats fifty thousand times its initial weight in plant material. They molt four times. At the end of about thirty days, they stop eating, attaching themselves to a stalk of straw to begin creating a silk cocoon. Silkworms possess a pair of salivary glands called silk glands, or sericteries, which are used for the production of silk cocoons. These glands secrete a clear, viscous, proteinous fluid that is forced through openings called spinnerets on the mouthpart of the larva. As the fluid comes into contact with the air, it hardens. The worm slowly pupates—that is, it covers itself with silk filaments over the next three to eight days. (Before the invention of nylon, surgeons used silkworm gut: Immediately before the cocoon stage, pupae were killed by immersion in an acid bath. Their bodies were opened and the thread that was intended to build the cocoon was removed from their silk glands.)

Pupation consists of producing a fine thread by making a figure-eight movement some three hundred thousand times, constructing a white cocoon in which pupae intend to spend the chrysalis stage, when they are in a state of sleep. Then the pupae begin the sixteen days that would normally result in the miracle of transformation to a winged being: the beautiful creamy white moth who emerges at the end of this drama.

In order to emerge from the cocoon, the pupae (or chrysalides) secrete an alkali to eat their way through the cocoon. From many humans' perspective, this alkaline substance spoils the silk. From the moth's perspective, this breaking of the single silk filament into ever-smaller pieces is part of the birth process, necessary to his very being. He is doing what nature has programmed him to do. But a silk manufacturer doesn't care about nature. He suffocates the chrysalides while still inside the cocoon, sometimes using boiling water, other times putting the chrysalides in a hot oven or even electrocuting them. (In a mean-spirited symmetry, he then feeds the dead pupae to the mulberry trees as fertilizer.) Now a long thin fiber can be reeled from the intact cocoon. A single cocoon can yield a single silk thread up to a mile and a half long! But it would take at least ten thousand cocoons to make my silk shirt. There are alternatives that involve no cruelty to a living creature: Fibers from the pineapple, for example, can be made into fabrics as silky as any silk.

An opponent to my position patiently explains: "Look, the moth is only going to live a short time: Three days after they hatch, they mate, lay eggs, and die. What's wrong with interfering with this cycle? What good are moths anyway?" Moths are good because they are moths. They lay eggs and the worms spin cocoons and it has been that way for hundreds of millions of years. It should stay that way. You can buy a rayon shirt, and the moth will live out its destiny. Think about it: If we discovered some animal who lived a thousand years, would we consider it justified for that animal to squash us to death on the grounds that we lived for such a short time? I also find it sad that while we have domesticated the silkworm, in the wild it is now extinct. Presumably it has been so pampered that it is no longer able to withstand natural events such as rain and wind. It has become an artificial animal—unlike the hardy magical insect it had been before enslaved by humans.

Equally awesome is the fact that pheromones were only discovered in 1959 by scientists at the Max Planck Institute in Munich working with female silk moths. She disperses just a billionth of a gram of her pheromone, and yet the male's elaborate, highly sophisticated, comblike olfactory sensors (antennae) trawl the air and pick up the scent from a calling female several miles away! Not surprising, really, when you consider that each antenna has about seventeen thousand sensilla (hairs), and each sensillum has about three thousand olfactory pores. Each moth has a total of 102 million pores to work with. My dog is nose-dead in comparison.

I don't buy silk any longer. Far better the silk-cotton tree filaments! In India the company Designer Weaves is making silk from the cocoons of caterpillars who are allowed to become moths and fly away. Now, that's progress!

NAKED MOLE RAT

Heterocephalus glaber

NAKED MOLE RATS MAY RESEMBLE a mole and a rat, but are neither—they are related to guinea pigs and chinchillas. Some think these rodents beautiful, while others find them the epitome of ugly. They have wrinkled, saggy, pink, hairless cylindrical bodies. Their ears are tiny, and they have four buckteeth. They have long skinny tails and only a few hairs between the toes; a few whiskers on the lips; and a few scattered hairs on their bodies and tails. Definitely not about to win a beauty contest.

Nearly blind, they see only light and dark. They live their entire life underground, in total darkness, in a humid, hot burrow system that can wind for two miles. They spend most of their time in communal slumber chambers, eating only the giant tubers whose roots go directly into their tunnels. Moreover, they are the only mammal that is eusocial—that is, like insects, they live in colonies of from ten to three hundred individuals (average: eighty). But the naked mole rat is a mammal, and nurses her young. The colony is similar to an ant colony in that there is only one female who gives birth, one queen. Most others are the queen's close relatives, children from previous litters who have stayed at home to help their mom raise little brothers and sisters rather than striking out on their own. They are all servants digging tunnels, finding food, and fighting enemies—almost exclusively snakes, since these are the only animals who enter their tunnels. One reason there are so many fans of this animal may have to do with the fact that whereas many mammals are born nude, only humans and naked mole rats remain nude (furless, hairless) as juveniles and adults.

There's something intriguing about naked mole rat burrows. (Think of Badger's underground burrow in *Wind in the Willows*—a venue that has fascinated many children.) The fact that their food grows on the ceiling and is always renewed, that the temperature remains the same and is never cold (around eighty degrees, with 80 percent humidity), that they have virtually no enemies and never encounter anyone except their own relatives . . . it's like living in some sort of dream world. Still, a nagging doubt remains: If we lived like this, would we be bored to death and start fighting? It is true that naked mole rats are mildly aggressive on a continuous basis, perhaps out of simple boredom. However, Paul Sherman, the world's expert on these animals, tells me "as an evolutionary biologist, I don't think boredom is a viable explanation. They are mildly aggressive because different individuals have different reproductive interests. Every female would like to breed, so the breeding female must constantly maintain and reinforce her physical dominance. Also, the breeding female wants everybody to cooperate fully to raise her pups, whereas older, larger, less-related nonbreeders tend to be lazy, saving themselves to capitalize on a possible breeding opportunity, should the current breeder die."

The workers are constantly improving the tunnels. In one year a single colony can move more than two thousand pounds of soil. In a single hour they move thirty pounds. I cannot improve on Paul Sherman's words: "Naked mole-rats form digging chains, in which the first individual gnaws at the blind end of a tunnel and a series of colony members sweep loosened dirt back along the burrow to a large individual who kicks it onto the surface," creating volcano-shaped mounds with a central hole. They quickly plug this to prevent driver ants and predatory snakes from entering. The ants bite and can even prey on small pups, so they definitely don't want them there. There are sleeping chambers and toilets; among the eighteen different sounds that naked mole rats make (many for alarm purposes) there is a special toilet-assembly call (used for pups, I presume).

While there is aggression in the burrow, it almost never involves serious injury unless it concerns mating privileges—like us, a big deal for them. Mostly these fights are about food or access to the toilet or the bedroom. They shove and make loud chirps, but that's pretty much it except when the breeding female dies.

The more I learn about the lives of naked mole rats, the more complicated things become. Science has a way of deflating our fantasies. For example, I thought they cuddled with one another because they *liked* one another, but it turns out that they have to regulate their temperature from without. Huddling keeps them warm.

It is definitely not an egalitarian society: The queen is a tyrant. She is always shoving everyone she meets to get them to work harder for her. And when she meets another in the tunnel, already engaged in working for her, instead of passing the lesser mole rat on the side, she walks on top of her, demonstrating her status. Moving or sharing would be perceived as lèse-majesté. The workers weakly retaliate by working less in her absence.

Naked mole rats are found only in the dry regions of Kenya, Ethiopia, and Somalia. It is so dry and there are so few rain showers that when they do occur, the naked mole rats have to engage in rapid, cooperative digging to find food within the burrow that will be able to carry them through the long droughts. That food consists of tubers, bulbs, and geophytes with enlarged underground storage organs. The naked mole rats treat these tenderly, packing them with soil after eating to ensure their continued grow and health. They also appear to be the only rodent to use a tool: They keep a chip of wood behind their teeth to make sure that when they are digging soft dirt, none of the particles gets into their lungs.

Only the queen breeds. She chooses one to three males as her mates, usually brothers. Once they are chosen, their only job for the rest of their lives is to breed and help care for the pups. Seasons play no role, and she has four to five litters a year, each containing between ten and fifteen pups, up to as many as thirty. She and her consorts do no other work. Housekeepers feed her and build a nest for her, while soldiers defend her young. Her main job after breeding is to see to it that all the other colony members are hard at work. She spends most of the day wandering around the burrow, shoving housekeepers and soldiers around to keep them focused on their appointed tasks. She is the one who decides what needs to be done and who will do it. She makes certain none of the other females reproduce by mercilessly bullying them. This appears to be the only reason the other females do not become sexually mature: They are too frightened. If there is any other example of this in an animal species, I am unaware of it.

When the queen dies or becomes weak, an often bloody and fatal battle royal takes place to succeed her. It may last weeks or even months. Although the new queen is an adult, once she takes control of the colony she undergoes a metamorphosis: Her length increases more than 30 percent. No other known mammal does this. She needs to be long to accommodate large litters of pups, sometimes for up to thirteen years, without getting so wide that she would not be able to navigate the burrows.

And here's yet one more fascinating naked mole rat fact: They are among the only mammals to be able to run backward as fast as forward.

These animals have led scientists to study the evolution of sociality. Cooperative breeding seems almost utopian. But alas, they are not altruistic because they have perceived the wisdom of it, but because rainfall is so erratic that they have no choice but to cooperate if they want to eat. Scientists say they are "frustrated dispersers" rather than "content families." But that also makes them interesting to us, for as Tolstoy recognized, "happy families are all alike; every unhappy family is unhappy in its own way."

NARWHAL

Monodon monoceros

CLOSELY RELATED TO THE BELUGA WHALE, these whales are most famous for their spiraled tusk—an elongated tooth that in males can reach up to ten feet long. There might be no more than three hundred narwhals in the Northeast Atlantic area. There are many more in West Greenland and even more in Baffin Bay, between Greenland and Canada, but the total world population is estimated at only 25,000. So far, no narwhal has been kept successfully in captivity.

I was once traveling in Chile, and happened to visit the home of the great Chilean poet and Nobel Prize winner Pablo Neruda. His house had been maintained exactly as he left it when he died just after Pinochet took power in 1973. Pride of place was given to a perfectly formed long narwhal tusk. Neruda loved it, the little placard said. I doubt he knew the suffering involved in the history of that tusk.

Like the horn of the legendary unicorn, the narwhal's horn is alleged to have healing abilities, and supposedly this wild, shy animal could only be captured using a virgin as bait. (See Odel Shepard's marvelous book *The Lore of the Unicorn*.) Inuit hunters in Greenland and Canada have long hunted them for these valuable tusks. There are times, too, when large numbers of narwhals, up to a thousand, may get entrapped in ice and lead to what the Inuit hunters call a *sassat*, which I suppose means "massacre." Alas, even today private collectors and museums pay monetary rewards for long intact narwhal tusks.

Speculation as to the function of the tusk is rife: Is it a tool to pick up sea grass? Could it be an icebreaker? Is it a prop to allow the animal to sleep on the surface while his tooth rests on an ice floe? Or perhaps it's a cooling mechanism? It might be used for vocalizations (for narwhals emit sonar pulses). All we know for certain is that it has a pulp cavity rich in nerves and blood vessels. The tusk was known long before the animal was. In fact, scientists have only been observing narwhals for less than a generation, whereas the tusk was traded many centuries ago. We now know that tusks are found almost exclusively on males, appearing when they are a year old. They start off smaller than a pencil and slowly grow the first few years. With the arrival of sexual maturity at eight or nine, there is a sudden growth spurt in the tusk. It eventually reaches more than six feet in length and ten inches in circumference.

Big males often cross tusks in a leisurely fashion, seeming to belie the view that they are used for aggressive contests (unless they are just practicing). Even without tusks, males manage quite well. So if it is true, as some scientists hypothesize, that they act like the tail of the peacock, as a male advertisement of genetic vigor to females, one wonders why nature bothers. It's strange to think that there may well be no more tusks to take by the time scientists discover the function of this magic tooth.

A more fascinating mystery to me is the intense socialization among narwhals. They often come together in the hundreds, and the number of clicks, squeaks, and whistles is truly bewildering. It is astonishing to learn that they are making sounds in streams of a thousand individual

clicks per second! What are they talking about? Us? Their chief predator, the killer whale? The meaning of life? Will we ever know? If we
allow them to survive (they are still legally hunted by Inuit), perhaps
one day they will tell us.

When it comes to whaling in general, I agree with Greg Gatenby,
who writes in *Whale Sound*: "God knows we have harmed enough
things on this planet, but to remove the largest animals God ever made
seems to declare an arrogance and shortsightedness that speak volumes
more about the intelligence of *homo sapiens* than any great mathemati-
cal equation or work of art." Henry David Thoreau already saw it all in
1864: "Can he who has discovered only some of the values of whale-
bone and whale oil be said to have discovered the true use of the
whale? Can he who slays the elephant for his ivory be said to have
'seen the elephant'?"

NEW ZEALAND LONGFIN EEL

Anguilla dieffenbachia

I FIND EELS FASCINATING TO LOOK AT and fascinating to touch. Most of all, I find them fascinating to think about. But the public, at least until recently, disagreed strongly: "There is a very real public fear of and revulsion against eels," says the authoritative *New Zealand Freshwater Fishes: Guide and Natural History.* A scientist at the National Institute of Water & Atmospheric Research (NIWA) offers his explanation: "This is mostly because of their sliminess, their great and enduring activity out of the water, and their tenacity of life."

Let me get this straight: Elvers, what little eels are called, migrate up the faces of dams and across damp fields to reach ponds and water holes . . . and this makes them offensive or obnoxious? Or is it that if you try to kill them, they tenaciously cling to life, not wanting to die? True, you hear stories of people thinking they have killed an eel, only to discover a day later that she is still alive, desperate to live. Is this horrible or wonderful?

The Maori had at least 180 names for eels, an indication of how important the animals were to them. When you consider how mysterious they are, it is unsurprising that the Maori regarded them as the progeny of supernatural beings. Alas, this did not prevent them from killing them in large numbers. At one point, with an endangered eel population, the Maori used a *rahui*, a ban, on the killing of any eel except at specific times of the year. The point of the *rahui* was to ensure the survival of the eel as a food source. It was not done out of respect for the animal, but at least the Maori protected the environment upon which the eels are so dependent.

Even though they spawn in the millions, few actually make it to adulthood. Moreover, their wetlands have been reduced by 90 percent since the arrival of Europeans in New Zealand. Nor did they, during their evolution, ever have to contend with dams that block the upstream passage of elvers. Hydroturbines kill most downstream-migrating large female long-finned eels. During the 1940s fishermen were urged to "make war on eels" because they were eating the trout they wanted to catch: "Every angler should KILL EELS every day he is on the water." The long-finned eel lives only in New Zealand, but for how much longer? Isn't it time that we put into effect a permanent *rahui* that would ban taking the life of any long-finned eel forever?

The world is changing. The children I meet these days are not repulsed by eels. Like me, they are enchanted. And one particular reason for my curiosity is the eel's mysterious life. They breed somewhere in the tropical or subtropical Pacific Ocean somewhere east of Australia. As they age, they continue to grow. And while some are huge—they can be longer than six feet and weigh up to 110 pounds—nobody is sure how long eels live. It's not unusual to find females more than fifty years old, and some even live to be a hundred.

How do you determine the age of an eel? Although eels have poor hearing, the inner ear contains a small bone called the otolith in a small capsule on each side of the brain. Into this otolith annual growth rings are laid. When polished, they can be seen in a microscope and counted, revealing the exact age of the eel. (Sadly, the eel must be dead for this method to work.) It's awe inspiring to consider all the experience eels must accumulate over a hundred years.

While the female breeds only once in her life, it is an extraordinary experience. As she matures sexually (perhaps not until she is sixty years old), her eyes become larger (to take in more light in the deep ocean) and a blue eye ring forms. One dark evening the freshwater eel feels compelled to make her way to the ocean. She travels at night, starting in late April to May. If she has to, she crosses land. And when she reaches the sea, she swims perhaps thirty-six hundred miles to the place in the Pacific Ocean where she was originally hatched. Nobody is certain exactly where this is, but large female eels are just now being fitted with tags that will allow them to be tracked by satellite to solve this mystery.

Once she reaches her destination (alone?—nobody yet knows), she lays up to twenty million eggs. A mature male who has also made the same trip externally fertilizes the eggs. She dies. He dies. Do they die because their purpose in life has been fulfilled, in that they have reproduced? Or is it because they have been fasting from the moment they got into the ocean? Do they die because they fast, or do they fast in order to die? It's an odd, fascinating life.

About January, the eggs hatch as tiny larvae, barely visible. When they are a bit bigger they metamorphose into what are called leptocephali. For nearly a year they are swept along by ocean currents in the direction of New Zealand. As they approach the islands, they metamorphose again into glass eels (so called because they are transparent). From this point on they are able to swim on their own toward the land of New Zealand. They enter the brackish waters of river and stream estuaries where fresh water meets salty. They are searching for the home of their mothers. They grow, develop coloration, and become what are called elvers. They pack closely together and begin the climb to the upper rivers, streams, ponds, and lakes that they will inhabit the rest of their long lives. Good climbers, they even scramble over steep dam walls nearly a hundred feet tall. It can take them up to seven years to migrate upstream, hibernating in the mud during winter. Then at last they find the exact right spot, the place where their mother lived. I may be a little sentimental here, for it is not absolutely clear that this is their goal, but they often do manage to come right back to where their mother lived.

Some evidence suggests that if a young elver grows up in fresh, running water it becomes a female; in brackish or salt water, a male. Scientists argue about this.

I love that we know so little about these creatures. One of the world's foremost experts on them, New Zealand fisheries scientist Don Jellyman, writes, "While it is possible to spawn eels in the laboratory by giving them injections of different hormones, nobody has yet succeeded in rearing the delicate larvae through to the glass eel stage."

And here is what I find completely charming: Eels tame easily. When I was living in the Coromandel Peninsula, in a stream right next to my house was a large female eel. When called, she emerged from under a rock cave and allowed herself to be handled and carried, as long as you fed her an egg. Kids named her Ellie the Eel. I have been back to see her again this winter, but she didn't come when I called. I suspect Ellie is hibernating over the cold winter months.

NORTH AMERICAN BEAVER
Castor canadensis

THE LARGEST OF THE NORTH AMERICAN RODENTS, the beaver lives up to fifteen years. Because of their remarkable water-proof fur, beavers have been hunted since Europeans first came to North America. Part of the reason that the interior of North America was explored was the great European demand for their dense, luxuriant pelts.

And it's not just their fur that has made them valuable to hunters: Beavers have castor sacs in their stomachs that contain castoreum. This complex substance consists of hundreds of compounds and was considered by Hippocrates and other early physicians to have healing properties, especially for gynecological illnesses. Modern research has shown that it contains salicylic acid, the active ingredient in the synthetic drug aspirin. Castoreum is also used as a base for perfume. Its exact function in beavers is unknown.

Engineers have long admired beavers' large lodges, sited on a bank or in the middle of a pond. Cone-shaped, with a hole in the center to allow air in, made of logs and branches, they can be very elaborate and can withstand the strongest storms. (All the more remarkable, then, that they can be built in only two nights!) The living chamber is above water, its winter temperature warmer than what it is outside, and so the beavers often remain indoors the entire season. They store their food, mostly wood, and have enough to last the whole family for the cold season.

Clumsy on land, they are remarkable swimmers, and so are never far from water. They are safest there, often building dams to create large ponds, with many canals leading to their home from their feeding areas. A single family can have several such homes and waterways in several different ponds. For years it was thought that beavers damaged the territories in which they lived; we now realize that the opposite is the truth. As the *New Oxford Encyclopedia of Mammals* notes, "The dams boost sediment deposition—a natural filtration system that removes potentially harmful impurities from the water," and with the decrease in erosion, reeds, sedges, trees, and many animals are benefited. Even when abandoned, these ponds become rich new ecosystems. And contrary to popular belief, gnawing trees is not harmful. The trees that beavers prefer, such as cottonwoods and willows, grow quickly, and what beavers do could be considered more like pruning. True gardeners of the wetlands, they deserve our respect. And their dams are remarkable feats of engineering: They can be as long as 350 feet and 10 feet high.

Beavers are difficult to observe in their moments of intimacy, and so we do not have a full portrait of beaver family life, although we know that, remarkably for a mammal, the fathers are very involved in child rearing. (The late professor Donald Griffin showed me a video recording of the inside of a lodge that he managed to take via a spy camera he had inserted—it was marvelous!) Part of the reason must be that they have a distinct inhibition of aggressive tendencies. Their teeth are so large and powerful (they can cut through a tree almost as fast as an electric saw) that they have had to devise reliable means of curbing any aggressive use of these deadly weapons. (Uniquely among mammals, beavers create large scent mounds, which probably also help avoid aggressive encounters with other beavers. Their extremely sensitive noses can smell whether another beaver is a relative or not.) It is extraordinary that colony members almost never use their teeth as weapons. Beavers

live in harmony with one another and with muskrats, whom they appear to welcome into their homes, much as badgers have been known to
receive, and make friends with, coyotes and foxes. Also, in northern climates they are forced to live under ice the whole winter, sometimes two
or three generations of parents along with their yearlings and two-year-
olds, together in close proximity, with a limited supply of food in a
small space (sometimes just three or four feet in diameter). Pure vegetarians, they do not need to hunt cooperatively like wolves, but they do
need to cooperate in building their remarkable dams and lodges.

When I wrote *When Elephants Weep*, I was unaware that, according
to some scientists, when caught in a trap, beavers cry real tears. Writer
Hope Ryden notes that in a report before the World Symposium on
Beavers, scientist L. S. Lavrov verified that the North American beaver
produces a "copious emission of tears" when under duress, and is likely
to do so when "manually restrained." Hunters say that while awaiting
the blow of a club about to be lowered on their skulls, beavers cover
their heads with their forepaws.

The beaver is one of the few mammals who is not just monogamous,
but mates for life unless one of the pair dies. As Hope Ryden points out,
beavers form their lifetime alliances months before mating season casts
its heady spell on both sexes. "Beaver pairing is based on an attraction
that is as mysterious as it is compelling, one that is unrelated to any immediate urge to copulate," she says. This is unusual in the animal kingdom. In Professor Dietland Muller-Schwarze's wonderful book *The
Beaver: Natural History of a Wetlands Engineer*, he notes that three
things seem to go together: reduced sexual dimorphism (where males and
females are more or less the same size), monogamy, and the male's partic-
ipation in rearing the young. How do humans stack up in comparison
with beavers? I am afraid beaver males have the edge over human males.

Baby beavers (kits) are well developed at birth, though they weigh
less than a pound. With bodies covered in waterproof fur, eyes open,
their sharp little incisor teeth fully erupted, they can swim within
hours of birth. They nurse for up to two months, an unusually long
time for such a well-developed infant. The kits usually stay with their

family for a year, even two. Hope Ryden points out that two-year-olds have been known to remain at their birth pond for an extra year, sometimes longer. Moving out seems to depend entirely on the offspring's inclination. The reason for their long childhood is similar to ours: The baby beaver has a great deal to learn, and learns it by observing older siblings and parents.

People who have seen beavers cavorting about their ponds in spring gain the definite impression that they are rejoicing in their ability to once again play in the water. Housebound for winter, they become delirious with the onset of spring. A father beaver porpoises over the body of his young kits and then all swiftly swim back and forth across the pond as if delighted to be in the same world with the willow trees in leaf. You can observe a father beaver floating on his back during this time while his kits plunge and surface over and over. They experience pure animal pleasure in their release. The whole family can be seen rolling, porpoising, and somersaulting. It is possible to spot a father beaver swimming with great speed across a lake with one of his kits hanging on, then turning around and swimming back, sometimes out of sheer exuberance.

I have just touched on the issue of the beavers' huge impact on the history of North America. For that, you must read *The Beaver*, where it is noted that "no other wild animal has shaped history as much as the beaver." With complete authority, Professor Muller-Schwarze also says we must stop calling any beaver a "nuisance." Any damage done to golf courses or campgrounds is because *we* have encroached on *their* habitat—not the other way around. They were here long before us, and as far as destroying habitat, they are busy doing quite the contrary. The Forest Service has even parachuted beavers into remote forest meadows to build dams for reservoirs for fighting forest fires! The beaver is, as Professor Muller-Schwarze so felicitously puts it, our "greatest original wetland conservationist."

OCTOPUSES

Octopus spp.

ACQUES COUSTEAU was perhaps the most popular of the many marine biologists (starting with Aristotle) to take a scientific interest in octopuses. (*Octopi* and *octopuses* are both used for the plural.) However, back in 1875 English naturalist Henry Lee had already written a popular book about these ever-fascinating sea animals.

Both authors were determined to prove wrong the calumnies of the French literary stars—Victor Hugo and Jules Verne—who saw them as man-devouring "monsters of the deep." In Hugo's *Toilers of the Sea*, there is a chapter about a giant octopus that has these resounding lines: "the poulp is almost endowed with the passions of man; it has its hatreds. In fact, in the Absolute, to be hideous is to hate." Jules Verne has Captain Nemo, in 20,000 *Leagues Under the Sea*, nearly lose his boat, the *Nautilus*, when a "terrible monster" attacks it. This was repeated in Peter Benchley's novel *Beast*, which the publishers falsely claimed was cutting-edge science—at least *Jaws* had plausibility. (There is no recorded attack by an octopus or squid on a human.)

The only way to counter these prejudices (based on perfect ignorance) was to meet these animals on their own ground. Cousteau first encountered them when he invented the Aqua-Lung, the first scuba-diving gear, in the 1950s. What fascinated him was the octopus's ability to change colors as a means of indicating emotional state. Their normal coloration is brown, and many scientists now believe they turn white with fear and red with anger. (Their blood, by the way, is green-blue.)

In Seattle on his way to look for the giant octopus, Cousteau was warned that these vicious beasts often mauled divers. Of course, the reality turned out to be quite different: With octopuses as shy and wary of humans as most animals, the problem was not getting away from the giant animals but getting *to* them. At the same time, Cousteau and his American divers discovered that these timid creatures are insatiably curious about humans. Cousteau's spellbound divers were being observed by their giant yellow eyes with black pupils, directed with intense interest. They felt a strange, almost alien intelligence sizing them up, no doubt to see if their intentions were friendly or hostile. Octopuses have excellent vision, similar to that of humans (although they are completely deaf). The first diver to attempt to befriend an octopus discovered, to everyone's amazement, that it took but a few minutes for the octopus to realize that no harm was meant, and then to play with the diver like a frisky kitten.

Cousteau succeeded in capturing a giant octopus off the coast of Seattle, but was so spooked by what he called a look of *knowing* that he and his crew watched her escape without interfering: "I think each of us, in our hearts, was happy to see the octopus slide over *Calypso*'s side and drop into the sea." Elsewhere Cousteau speaks of "a sensation of lucidity" in the enormous eyes of an octopus.

Intelligence in an octopus—cousin of the lowly oyster and clam? The power to reason? In the 1970s Cousteau was reluctant to go against scientific convention and say more than that these animals "learn quickly." However, his book with Philippe Diole, *Octopus and Squid: The Soft Intelligence*, is a superb classic that cannot be outdated. Toward its end, he writes of the octopus: "So far as their intelligence goes, we have only begun to suspect its breadth." Today most scientists would agree. Why did we underestimate them for so long? Cousteau has the obviously correct answer: Man, he says, "habitually underestimates other species as a prelude to slaughtering them."

I tell the story, in my book *When Elephants Weep*, of Charles, a small octopus who was the subject of an experiment to see whether invertebrates could learn conditioned tasks as vertebrates do. With two others, Albert and Bertram, each housed in a small tank, Charles was to be trained to pull a switch so that a light went on, and then swim over to the light to be rewarded with a minute piece of fish. Albert and Bertram learned to perform this task, and Charles seemed at first to be doing the same. But then Charles rebelled. He began anchoring himself to the side of the tank and yanking on the lever so fiercely that he eventually broke it. Instead of waiting under the light to receive his smidgen of fish, Charles reached out of the water, grabbed the light, and dragged it into the tank. Finally, he took to floating at the top of the tank with his eyes above the surface, accurately squirting water at the experimenters. Is this a cephalopod's sense of humor?

American biologist and diver Joanne Duffy reported that octopuses are so sensitive that if they are roughly handled, even without being physically hurt, they can "go into a state of emotional shock and sometimes die." Why they *never* defend themselves against humans is puzzling: After all, the giant octopuses have enormous beaks that could cause great damage, and yet there are no reports of anyone being killed by the bite of a giant octopus. (I am leaving out of this account Australia's tiny, beautiful, but deadly blue ring octopus.)

At fourteen, walking along a Hawaiian beach early one morning, I found an unusual-looking seashell. When I turned it over, a tiny octopus—no more than a few inches long—shyly emerged. I suspect this was a dwarf octopus. Fascinated with her eight tiny legs, I wanted to keep her. I filled my bathtub with seawater and swam with the little gal for a day. But then I was persuaded that she would not live and returned her to the ocean. I went to the library to find out more, and discovered that nothing about my friend was known. Had I kept her, I might have been among the first to learn about these extraordinary creatures, but I am glad I returned her to her ocean home, even if she would live no longer than a few years.

There are about two hundred species of octopuses. Females of the most common species, *Octopus vulgaris*, lay between two and four hundred thousand eggs. They live only for fifteen to eighteen months. The giant octopus lives for three years. Almost all octopuses lay eggs, brood them, then die. Dr. James Wood tells me that the record brooding time is more than four hundred days for the deep-sea octopus *Bathyplopyus arcticus*, about whom he wrote his PhD thesis. The females waste away and break down their own bodies to provide energy to care for the eggs. Champion moms!

The largest octopus, the North Pacific, can weigh in at 250 pounds, with a body thirty feet long. By the way, the one I found on the beach was by no means the smallest of all octopuses: That honor is reserved for the California octopus (*O. micropyrsus*), which is less than an inch. My Hawaiian friend could have grown to all of four inches.

Found in its throat, the octopus's brain is more complex than any other invertebrate's. (She also has three hearts!) The octopus has excellent long- and short-term memory, and functions at about the same level of learning as a dog. She can recognize individual people, even unscrew glass jars to get food. There are reports of octopuses escaping from aquaria, raiding nearby fish tanks for food, and then returning to their own tank.

OKAPI
Okapia johnstoni

THE OKAPI IS THE ONLY KNOWN RELATIVE of the giraffe. Still, though closely related, they are very dissimilar. The okapi looks like a zebra or a horse, and unlike the gregarious giraffe, the okapi is solitary. They both have long tongues. The giraffe uses hers to eat from the crowns of trees nineteen feet up, whereas the okapi is the only animal who cleans her own ears with her tongue. Male and female giraffes have horns, whereas only male okapi have them.

They are to be found only in the Ituri Forest in the northeastern corner of Congo-Zaire. Jane Goodall says that "the mysterious okapi of the Ituri Forest" is close to extinction. There are perhaps only thirty thousand left in the world.

The history of the attempts to bring this little-known animal to European and American zoos makes for depressing reading. In 1935 London received its first okapi, a gift from Prince Leopold of Belgium to the

Duke of Windsor. He died within four months. The first European birth occurred at the Antwerp Zoo in 1954. The calf did not survive. Three subsequent offspring also died. The zoo claimed (a frequent excuse in the years to come) that it was due to maternal aggression. Here is what the leading book has to say about a female at the Brookfield Zoo who attacked several of her offspring: "It is speculated that these mothers had an inherent tendency toward aggression." Here is the kicker: "Or that this behavior resulted from the stressful and foreign state of captivity." It does not take much imagination to guess which is more likely. Although almost nothing at all is known about okapi behavior in the wild, I'd be surprised if mothers in their natural habitat routinely kill their own babies. How could such behavior evolve or thrive? The laws of evolution demand that it would be selected against, for such behavior would fly in the face of the preservation of the species.

The first okapi born in England, at the Bristol Zoo in 1963, died from a fungal infection caught from the barn hay. Four sets of twins have been born in captivity; none survived. In 1979 cesarean deliveries were performed in Bristol. Neither the calves nor the mothers survived. Recent attempts at the London Zoo to perform a cesarean also failed. What a dismal record. Yet zoos claim that they are necessary for the preservation of okapi. Surely it makes more sense to put our efforts into protecting them in their own environment rather than forcing them into ours, where they clearly cannot and do not thrive.

The key to this animal's survival in captivity seems to lie in its diet. When you realize that okapi in the wild spend most of their time foraging from more than two hundred species of plants, it is not surprising that they often refuse to eat what they are given in captivity. Consider that the okapi is a most attentive mother and will nurse on demand up to five times an hour (like a good human mother). Like all mammals, she has milk especially evolved to be the perfect food for her calf. Some zoos boast of successfully hand-rearing calves on a mixture of canned evaporated milk, powered cow's milk replacer, and water. In fact, it probably would have been better to seek another female: Okapi often allow nursing from calves other than their own, and may even adopt motherless calves.

A trait unique to okapi calves is that they do not produce any feces at all for a prolonged period, often well over one month. Not knowing this, veterinarians in zoos attempted to relieve constipation, which led to early infections and often death. Okapi have only one enemy in their natural habitat, the leopard. So delayed defecation may have evolved as a means of keeping the calf completely hidden without ever having to leave the nest at all for the first month and risk being sighted.

One recent discovery is that okapi communicate with one another at frequencies too low for the human ear to hear. This was suspected in 1990, when researchers noted that okapi often coordinated their movement without any apparent vocalization. Also, calves seemed to somehow call their mothers for nursing without any obvious signal. In 1992 researchers in San Diego and Florida were finally able to make recordings revealing that okapi produce low-frequency sounds in the nine- to seventy-hertz range. Humans cannot hear below twenty. We now know that elephants, four species of rhinoceroses, various birds, reptiles, and insects all communicate with infrasound. Two adult male okapi housed at the Dallas Zoo emitted periodic, repetitive, and distinctive infrasonic calls (at fifteen hertz) during evenings while pacing.

Although the okapi has had protected status since 1933, hunting of these shy animals (primarily for bush meat) is still a major problem. How it can be stopped is a problem that reaches beyond okapi, since the bush-meat trade threatens almost all large forest mammals.

I cannot bear to see these animals in zoos, knowing what the trip will have cost them. This is a personal matter, I realize, but zoos rarely tell us about their own past failures. In fairness, I should cite the e-mail from my friend Bradley Trevor Greive, the author of the best-selling *Blue Day Book*:

I firmly believe that the best zoos have a vital role to play in salvaging our natural heritage. I'm sad that the fate of our living planet has come to this but come to this it has. Zoos are, perhaps in some ways, a necessary evil . . . Most of the people who are behind zoos are wonderful, passionate fully committed animal lovers who would do anything to see the wildlife in their charge return to a healthy and safe natural environment. Furthermore, however misguided some of their efforts may have been, I have never met a cruel zookeeper in the several hundred zoos and parks I have visited.

It is perhaps true that my tone about zoos here and elsewhere is too negative and may be influenced by my own reluctance to visit zoos, even better ones. I am sure that the research in zoos is excellent, and that most of what we know about animals who are difficult to study in the wild comes from zoos. Nonetheless, to find the best way to move forward we must ask ourselves the hard, truly compassionate questions about how we share this planet, and so must zoos. Surely recognizing the horrors of the past when it comes to the treatment of okapi is a necessary first step. When it comes to studying animals such as the okapi, we want to encourage young scientists to meet them on their territory. We need a Jane Goodall of the okapi more than we need a zoo program, at least when it comes to understanding natural behavior.

ORANGUTAN

Pongo pygmaeus

T HE NAME ORANGUTAN is a Westernized form of the Malay *orang hutan*, which translates as "man of the forest." These primates are, along with chimpanzees, bonobos, and gorillas—the great apes—our closest animal relative. We share at least 97 percent of our DNA with orangutans. The only great apes of Asia, orangutans are now found exclusively in northern Sumatra and the tropical rain forests of Borneo.

Orangutans are supposed to be almost entirely solitary. Males, at least, spend 98 percent of their time alone. And yet, once exposed to humans, they have been known to do, in the words of one of the leading researchers, Anne Russon, "a multitude of prodigiously intelligent things. They took canoes for rides down the river, for instance. Humans heading upriver might spot one of them cruising down; if humans were surprised, the orangutan just nonchalantly floated on by. Orangutans also siphoned fuel, made fires, washed laundry, unlocked doors with keys, weeded paths, untied the most complex knots humans could make, hung hammocks up and rode in them, cooked pancakes and brushed their teeth." Here is an example of an animal who clearly closely observes humans and learns from them.

Orangutans, inspired by the presence of humans, improve their cognitive abilities, but their sociability remains that of solitary animals. This in contrast to cats, who started out as solitary animals but, exposed to us, have learned to be sociable, improving their social life but not their intelligence. Orangutans, who as adults generally ignore humans, seem go in the opposite direction: Exposure to humans leads to cognitive growth.

As an example of just how little we know about these animals, Oxford's authoritative *Encyclopedia of Mammals* states that orangutans live "up to about 35 years in the wild, up to 60 in captivity," yet soon thereafter it says that "in the wild, females live for about 45 years." We should be skeptical, though, about the age in the wild—the University of Zurich's Carel van Schaik, for example, claims some wild orangutans can live at least to 58.

There are two subspecies of orangutans, those from Sumatra and those from Borneo, who are different in looks and in behavior. For example, in Borneo some 90 percent of matings are forced, whereas more than half of the Sumatran matings are cooperative. The Sumatran animals are smaller, lighter, and more graceful than their cousins from Borneo.

It has long been known that orangutans make an elaborate nest for sleeping every single night in a different spot—an excellent way to avoid parasites. What was not known until van Schaik reported it is that the animals make what appears to be a leaf-doll that they take to bed with them! They also decorate their nests with a row of neatly arranged twigs. These examples suggest that orangutans have perhaps more in common with humans than any other animal. For one thing, and perhaps most important, orangutans are slow to mature. It can take up to a quarter of a century for what are known as "subadult" males to grow into fully adult males.

A fully adult male is flanged. He has the large cheek flaps and throat sac that allow him to make a deep booming sound that can be heard from more than a kilometer away. If you are standing close, it is like sitting in the front row of a very loud rock concert. Dr. Biruté Galdikas, president of Orangutan Foundation International, says this "long call"—so named because it can last for up to four minutes—is the loudest and most intimidating sound in the Bornean rain forest, surpassing a lion's roar in volume and intensity. Males are only fully flanged at about thirty-five or older. No other animal takes that long to reach full maturity, with the exception of the human male, who in most cases is only fully mature just before death, and even then not in all cases.

In ideal conditions, the relation between a female orangutan and her infants is among the most intense in the natural world. The average interval between births is eight years, and children will often stay with their mother even after a sibling is born. A female orangutan breastfeeds her infant for a long time. They are not weaned until age seven, as is true of only a few enlightened La Leche moms today. (In a personal conversation in 1987, the late Ashley Montagu convinced me that this was the ideal age for humans to wean a child since at this age the immune system is first fully functional.)

Primarily vegetarians, orangutans eat only food that humans could also eat. A rule of thumb in the Sumatran and Bornean forests is that humans can always eat whatever an orangutan has eaten—not true for any other animal species. Orangutans have been known to eat more than four hundred different food types—for which they must know obscure facts of botany, including details about trees that bear fruit only once in eight years.

Although nobody has ever directly witnessed it, it appears that male orangutans, much like lions, engage in infanticide (to force a female to bear his children as opposed to those of a rival). At least this is the opinion of van Schaik. Biruté Galdikas believes that "wild orangutan males do not kill infants."

Is the orangutans' solitary nature perhaps due to the fact that they were hunted from the very beginning of human habitation in Borneo and Sumatra, about forty thousand years ago? Nobody knows, of course, how many orangutans were alive then (several hundred thousand, at least). The estimate of today's wild population, as given by Anne Russon, is seven to twelve thousand in Sumatra and ten to fifteen thousand in Borneo.

In the last twenty years their habitat has decreased by at least 80 percent. They are still hunted and eaten. The pet industry, as well as zoos, circuses, and laboratories, still demand baby orangutans, who can only be separated from their mothers by killing the mothers (though my understanding is that no orangutans are at present being experimented upon, and certainly the Convention on International Trading in Endangered Species forbids any traffic in them). The World Wildlife Fund recently estimated that the 1997–98 drought and fires destroyed 40 percent of the orangutan habitat that remains. Of that, Russon tells us, "millions of hectares are still slated to be cleared for plantations."

Along with humans, male orangutans may well be the only animals who have forced sex with a member of another species. It has been claimed by no less an authority than Biruté Galdikas that her cook at Camp Leakey was raped by a male orangutan.

While I am somewhat skeptical of the rape claim, I am, for temperamental reasons, less skeptical of her claim that she has witnessed orangutans awakening in terror from what she assumes are nightmares. Like the best human mothers, a mother orangutan *never* hits, bites, or chastises her infant. They are the essence of perfect mothers: indulgent, patient, and compassionate. However, once the kids are gone, the mothers lose interest in them.

Orangutans are unlike us in interesting ways. Canopy dwellers, they rarely descend from the trees. It is safer up there; it is also possible that, in their evolution in swampy forests and peat swamps, there was never much dry land for them to walk on had they wanted to. Also unlike many male humans, male orangutans participate not at all in infant care.

ORCA (Killer Whale)

Orcinus orca

THE ORCA IS THE LARGEST of the dolphins (family Delphinidae) and inspires both fascination and awe in most humans. In the ocean they are easily spotted. Colored jet black and white, the males (called bulls) have high, usually vertical fins. These magnificent animals are also huge. Males can reach thirty feet and can weigh as much as 20,000 pounds.

They are the top predator of the ocean: There is no creature in the sea they fear or who would ever dare to attack an adult killer whale. They feed in packs and will eat just about anything that moves: sharks, seals, sea lions, and dolphins—even other large whales, such as the enormous blue whale, which can weigh as much as three hundred thousand pounds! Fast and immensely powerful, they are also highly intelligent.

It's extremely rare—almost unheard-of—that a killer whale in the wild would attack a human being. Naomi Rose informed me of a recent incident, however, though it wasn't serious. The boy involved was only "bumped" hard. This was almost certainly an aborted attack—he was behaving very much like a seal. The difference between this attack and a shark attack was that the orca was smart enough to realize in time that he was mistaken and didn't have to actually taste the kid to realize he wasn't prey.

Scientists have been interested in every aspect of killer whales' behavior, biology, and ecology, yet the fact that they do not attack humans has never been the subject of a single serious article. It *must* throw light on the mind and psychology of the killer whale, so why has it not been subjected to study? I think the answer is that it humanizes the killer whale too much. Killer whales somehow *know* that we are like them, and that if we are attacked we will attack back. They must make conscious—let me stress that word, *conscious*—decisions regarding us. That's spooky for a scientist. It means that there is another animal on our planet with a consciousness similar to ours. An animal who calculates the future much the way we do. And this animal lives in the ocean.

But while this aspect of their similarity to us has been neglected, other similarities are proving equally intriguing to scientists and laypeople alike: They live in highly organized social groups, centering on the oldest female. She teaches the others hunting skills. Each group has a vocal dialect specific to that group, much as human groups speak different languages.

It was only in the 1970s that a method was found to differentiate individuals, based on differences in the dorsal fin and the saddle patch just behind the dorsal fin. High-quality photography easily shows who an individual is, and given their size and the fact that males are so much larger than females we are now able to conclusively identify all members of a killer whale pod in different parts of the world, including British Columbia, Washington, and Alaska. In the 1980s more detailed studies of vocal traditions and social structure became possible. While this research has been sophisticated and elaborate, there are inherent limitations. For one, there are no studies of killer whales at night (except for their sounds); it is simply too difficult to see them.

True cosmopolitans, killer whales can be found in every ocean of the world. They do not appear to migrate as so many whales do. (After all, killer whales are not whales, but dolphins.) Recently there were sightings of killer whales deep in Antarctic sea ice in winter. In the British Columbia and Washington study areas, some pods are found year-round. But salmon, a key ingredient in their diet, are often absent or at least found in lesser numbers in winter. The whales seem to have found a way of compensating, perhaps using temporal segregation for some pods.

Killer whale groups vary in size from single animals (only in transients) to as many as several hundred individuals. The most typical pod is matrilineal, consisting of a single female and her offspring, male and female, of the past one to four generations. There is also what is called a subpod—two or more matrilineal groups (sisters, say) who are genetically related. Two or three of these subpods can travel together over a period of years, and then this is called a pod even though they may spend only half their time together. The astonishing thing is that there is no evidence that any individual from the original group ever leaves! Nor—and this is even more astonishing—is there evidence of intra-subpod aggression. There are dispersals, or a further division, over a period of decades, and this almost certainly occurs after the death of the oldest female in the group (usually in her fifties, but possibly in her eighties or even nineties). It would be as if human children only left home when their parents died.

In one population, seen only in southern residents, when different pods have been separated for more than a day, they have a greeting ceremony when they meet: They line up abreast on the surface facing the other pod, approach to about thirty feet, then remain motionless for about thirty seconds. Then they submerge and begin to swim together in tight formation. This is when there is increased sexual behavior between the pods. It is assumed that copulation does *not* take place within pods but only between them, minimizing the chances of inbreeding. There are almost no documented sightings of copulation between an adult male and an adult female in the wild. Killer whales are only territorial temporally, rather than spatially, perhaps because of the enor-

mous size of their home ranges. The largest documented range for a resident pod is about fifty-four thousand square miles!

Nobody knows when they wean their young, somewhere between
eighteen months and four years. A curious thing is that there is a high
mortality rate for calves between birth and six months of age—almost
50 percent. It is not predation and not aggression on the part of any
other killer whale. (There are no documented cases of infanticide among
killer whales, but this does not mean it never happens; it took decades
before infanticide was first observed among bottlenose dolphins.) But
once past six months in age, their mortality rates dramatically decline.
Males can live up to sixty years; females, ninety years. The females generally don't give birth to a calf until late in adolescence, between
twelve and sixteen. They stop reproducing around forty, though one female had a calf at fifty. It is unusual for any mammal except a human to
live so long after reproductive senescence.

Only two whale births in the wild have been documented. In both
cases the birth took place among a large group of related individuals,
and many of them lifted the baby into the air (a birth ceremony, perhaps, or more likely simply assisting the baby to take its first breath).
This cohesiveness is demonstrated most obviously in the fact that resident killer whales are the only mammalian population in which no dispersal of either sex has been recorded.

The brain of an adult orca weighs more than thirteen pounds, and
the convolutions in its well-developed cerebral cortex indicate a superior intelligence. This structural complexity has fascinated scientists.
Given that this brain originated tens of millions of years before the ho-
minid brain, even speculating just what this massive brain is used for
leaves one in awe. Ingrid Visser, a New Zealand orca scientist (www.
orcaresearch.org), has documented occasions when the orcas she studied approached her with a gentle playfulness that indicated a powerful
curiosity about us. They seemed particularly curious about her manual
dexterity. She speculates that, using their sonar, they could see we had
the same number of bones in our hands as they do in their pectoral flippers. Could they be wondering about our brains and what we use them

for, just as we wonder about theirs? Long ago, in a celebrated essay called "The Long Loneliness," writer Loren Eiseley lamented, "It is difficult for us to visualize another kind of lonely, almost disembodied intelligence floating in the wavering green fairyland of the sea—an intelligence possibly comparable to our own." It is humbling to think there's a powerful mind in the ocean waters that has used its powers in ways that differ significantly from ours.

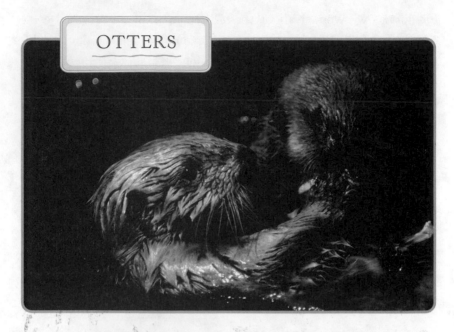

OTTERS

I was taken out in a little boat . . . and there were the California sea lions sitting on the breakwater honking at us, then after about five minutes we came to the kelp beds, those extraordinary seaweed beds that are so long, glossy and thick, and there in these kelp beds were all the sea otters carefully wrapped up as though they were in bed, all lying on their backs in the water with their heads sticking up and their paws together. They looked like a convention of bishops in mud baths in Baden-Baden or somewhere like that.

—GERALD DURRELL

THERE ARE THIRTEEN SPECIES of otters, the only member of the weasel family to be truly amphibious. River otters are as comfortable on land as they are on sea, traveling miles to reach a stream or lake. However, the true sea otter (*Enhydra lutris*), as well as the South American marine otter (*Lontra felina*), are only at home in the ocean and rarely venture onto land. Smallest of the marine mammals, the sea otter is also the only mammal who does not need to come to shore to give birth. The main difference with the North American river otters is that sea otters are two or three times as large. River otters also swim belly-down, where sea otters like to swim on their backs. The hind feet of sea otters resemble large flippers and are webbed to the tips of their toes, compared with the much smaller and less flipperlike feet of the river otter. The sea otter is also the only marine mammal to have eyelashes!

These animals are considered easy to tame, though only one member of the family, the ferret, has been domesticated. In Southeast Asia fishermen have trained captive short-clawed otters (*Amblonyx cinereus*), who live in streams and rice paddies, to catch fish. Could the ease with which they are tamed have to do with their intelligence?

Sea otters are the only mammals apart from primates to use tools while foraging, and they do so with spectacular efficiency. When they dive for abalone, for example, they carry a large stone between their forepaws, which they use to dislodge the abalone from the rock on which it has suctioned itself. It may take three or four dives to complete the operation. Otters usually dive for less than a minute (like us), although they easily go down a hundred feet.

This highly professional operation is necessary to satisfy the sea otters' massive food requirements. They have almost no fat, relying for insulation on an efficient pelage system. But despite their amazing fur (the tightly packed fur fibers contain around eight hundred million hairs), they still lose body warmth to the cold oceans in which they swim. Also, they have an extremely high metabolism, which means they must constantly replenish lost energy with food. Sea otters eat a quarter to a third of their weight *every day* merely to survive. So a fifty-pound otter has to eat about fifteen pounds every twenty-four hours. In one year an adult otter consumes five to six thousand pounds of food.

The otters surface with a clam or abalone in their paws and a stone in a special flap of skin under the armpit. They eat on the surface, usually anchored in a bed of kelp. They roll onto their backs, and then place a large stone onto their chests to act as an anvil. They smash the shell as many as twenty-two times on the flat rock until it opens to reveal the meat inside, all the while rolling over to rid their body of debris.

Humans cannot get enough of seeing otters slowly propel themselves through the water on their backs, moving seemingly without effort. Their webbed back feet are especially designed like fins to create movement with minimal force. (When they need to move fast, they turn onto their stomachs to swim.) And often enough the viewer is rewarded with a precious sight: a female with a pup on her stomach. Hardly any animal mother is as devoted as the female otter. She never stops grooming her single pup's fur and does such a good job that the fur becomes completely buoyant. The pups cannot dive until they are older.

Pups are nursed on demand, and even when the pup is nearly the same size as the mother he insists on a free ride on Mother's tummy as well as a quick suck. They remain in constant intimate contact with their mother for a whole year. A good 75 percent of a pup's life is spent out of the water resting on his mother's chest. So devoted are these mothers that males routinely grab pups while a mother is underwater and only relinquish them if the mother hands over the food she has just foraged. The mothers invariably give in to this blackmail. Here's a wonderful description of the otter mother at work, written by the late Margaret Owings, founder and president of Friends of the Sea Otter:

> In the confines of a rich pattern of kelp, a mother otter emerges through the strands and moves directly to her screaming pup. She rolls her body to lie on her back, lifting this eager clinging baby to her chest where she grooms and blows her breath under the surface of its wet fur, causing it to stand up like thistledown. Then, reversing the position of the tiny body, she places her baby's head on her nipples. In the gentle rocking cradle of the sea, the mother stretches her neck and head in contentment, her forepaws held high.

After a horrific history of slaughter to procure their fur, these days fishermen insist that the small number of California sea otters (no more than twenty-two hundred) are taking abalone and oysters "meant" for humans. This is anthropocentric in the extreme. It's also shortsighted: We now know that sea otters eat the sea urchins that would otherwise completely devastate the giant kelp forests of Northern California. Kelp is the main source of algin, the harvesting of which is a huge industry in itself. The California kelp industry reaps about fifty million dollars'

worth of kelp each year, vastly more than is netted by abalone fishermen. Moreover, kelp forests are essential to an entire ecosystem that
permits myriad fish to exist. Even more important, as marine mammolo-
gist Marianne Riedman points out, every year thousands of tourists
flock to California coasts to see sea otters. They spend enormous
amounts of money doing so—far more than could be had from the
abalone the fishermen believe is their due.

Even if all direct human cruelty were to cease, there would still be
the problem of what we do to the ocean. Victor Scheffer put it well:
"More than three billion gallons of industrial and domestic wastes pour
in California's marine water *daily*." When we think of these heavy met-
als, pesticides, mercury, and PCBs, we can wonder how any sea creature can long withstand the assault, something they never had to deal
with in their evolutionary history.

One person who made friends with a wild otter described how he
would dive with him and would "snuggle his face under my chin and let
me scratch him. He would grab my arm and pull himself up to sniff my
mouth. Once we swam side by side for a good half-mile. I often tried to
coax him onto the beach, but he wouldn't leave the water." The same
person noted how odd it is that otters don't like to be touched unless
they are in the water. Does this not suggest that they want our friendship on their terms?

PARROTS
Order Psittaciformes

P ARROTS IN GENERAL ARE SO FASCINATING that I had to devote an essay to more than just one species. There are 350 parrot species, and each is remarkable. How could I choose?

Books about *wild* parrots are few and far between. We have extraordinary accounts of chimpanzees, or gorillas, or orangutans; why not parrots? Because in each of those examples there has been a dedicated person (Jane Goodall, Dian Fossey, and Biruté Galdikas) who has lived among these animals. The animals became accustomed to her presence and allowed her to observe them undisturbed. In theory there's no reason parrots would behave any differently; in fact, there is good reason to believe that it should be even easier to join a parrot flock. From the point of view of the parrots, we are not a great threat. (If they had a larger perspective, they might alter that optimistic stance.) But we suffer from a serious drawback when it comes to studying wild parrots: We are earthbound. How could any researcher follow a flock of wild parrots and enter their complex society?

The parrots themselves have solved the problem. A whole flock came to a homeless man in San Francisco by the name of Mark Bittner. He has produced an absolutely charming book telling the whole astonishing tale: *The Wild Parrots of Telegraph Hill.* Moreover, the book is paired (the exact right word, as you will discover when you see the film) by an even more wonderful (if that is possible) film of the same name that everyone who loves parrots—no, anyone who loves *birds*—must see. The birds in the flock of which Mark became an honorary member are red-masked parakeets, *Aratinga erythrogenys.* (*Parakeet* is simply a word for any small parrot.) Bittner calls them cherry-headed conures, what they are usually called by people who sell them in pet stores. If you believe that the parrots came to Mark only to be fed, read his book and become enlightened. If love passed from Mark to them, it would be hard to claim that the traffic was one way only. These parrots had a choice. Most parrots with whom humans bond—and the bond is incredibly strong in both directions—do not. They are either caught in the wild or they are bred in captivity. Either way, the life they live with a human bears little resemblance to the life they would lead in the wild.

In her marvelous *The Parrot Who Owns Me: The Story of a Relationship,* Rutgers University professor and leading American ornithologist Joanna Burger tells a captivating love story. She fell hard, but then so did her red-lored Amazon parrot named Tiko . . . once he was convinced the relationship was real and for life. That took five years, but then he believed he had found true love, and showed it the way only parrots can. (For me the epiphany occurred when Professor Burger really understood "deep down, that his life was as important as mine, his desires and inclinations equally valid.")

These books are important because there is tremendous hunger on the part of the public to understand the United States' third most popular "pet" (after dogs and cats). I understand the urge to live with a parrot, but unless the parrot is rescued, it is not something I would recommend. If you have read anything about how parrots are captured in the wild, you will know why. (Majestic one-hundred-year old trees are burned down to get to the nests; parents are slaughtered, and traumatized baby parrots are taken, most of whom will die en route.) Millions and millions of parrots are killed every year by smugglers and dealers who are attempting to satisfy the public's apparently insatiable craving for pet parrots. (Since the 1992 Wild Bird Conservation Act, it is illegal to import any species of parrot into the United States.)

Moreover, living with a parrot is not living with a dog or cat. It can be a full-time activity, and you can be certain that the bird is not living the life he or she would choose. While it may not be illegal to own the majestic and beautiful rain-forest macaw, beware: your life will never be the same. I recommend you go to any number of good websites (e.g., http://www.blackpineanimalpark.com/pets/index.htm#macaw) to find out why.

But while the smuggling of baby parrots is a heinous and murderous activity, it is not the main culprit in the swift and horrifying disappearance of wild parrots from around the world, especially from South American rain forests. That honor goes to an equally insatiable craving on the part of Americans for hamburgers. As we all know by now (*Fast Food Nation*, *The Omnivore's Dilemma*, and especially *The Way We Eat*), to satisfy this unhealthy food choice, rain forests are cut down and turned into grass meadows that cows can graze on only to be slaughtered for American burgers. When we consider that the number of species of birds in one square mile of Amazon rain forest is more than exists in all of North America, we realize the real cost of each fast-food hamburger is the death of dozens of birds, not to mention other mammals, reptiles, and insects.

We know so little about basic parrot physiology that it has never been determined whether they see into the ultraviolet range. We know that they show empathy for humans, and I would be astonished, therefore, if they did not show it to one another, but no studies in the wild have ever been undertaken along these lines. The remarkable ability parrots have to mimic is something that has remained a mystery: evidently they do not mimic other animals in the wild. (Two researchers, in a celebrated study, looked for mimicry in the Nariva Swamp in Trinidad, but found that neither the orange-winged Amazon nor the red-bellied macaw, imitated other birds.) So why are they so eager to mimic the human voice? Is it purely a means of communication?

And why, I wonder, do parrots suddenly leave a tree with one great upward movement and then go racing across the sky shrieking an almost deafening roar? What is the purpose of that intimidating but also enchanting noise? Do parrots ever pluck their feathers in the wild as they do in captivity? This has been a major problem for many people who live with parrots, but I believe it is entirely confined to parrots in captivity and has not been documented in the wild. If that is the case, it's yet another strong reason not to keep parrots as domestic pets. Some feather plucking is caused by incorrect trimming of the flight feathers of the pet bird. Yes, flight feathers of almost all pet parrots are trimmed (to be more accurate, they are cut). Otherwise, they would simply fly away. The trauma this causes can only be imagined. Every parrot has a strong instinct to take flight, especially when frightened. The frustration caused by the inability to do so is constant and of immense consequence. I see no other way around it: as a boldly worded sign in the bird house at the Bronx Zoo puts it: "Never buy a parrot or macaw. They are declining everywhere."

I am writing this entry on Norfolk Island, a small island that is part of Australian territory. Walking on this lovely island, I spotted a beautiful parrot, a crimson rosella (*Platycercus elegans*). How enchanting, I thought. And then, later, walking in the national park, I saw a different parrot, a much quieter and smaller one, almost all green, with just a bit of bright red on the crown and behind the eye, and a blue outer edge on the wing. How lovely, I thought, two kinds of parrots living next to one another in peace. I happened to meet the park administrator and told him my thoughts. He took strong exception to what I said, and explained how wrong I was. The red parrot was introduced. It came from Australia. It does not belong on Norfolk Island. "Can't we all just get along?" I pleaded. Absolutely not, he explained.

The red parrot is stronger and harasses the smaller, shier indigenous Norfolk Island green parrot or, to give the parrot its scientific name, *Cyanoramphus novaezelandieae cookii*. This bird is found *only* on this one island, in the whole world. And here comes the bad news: There are only about 160 of them left, with fourteen known breeding pairs. Its Australian competitor exists in the millions. The green parrot evolved in a particular forest, and it likes that forest, the fruit that grows there, and the hollow holes it can find in the island's old ironwood trees (*Nestegis apetala*). The problem is that these hardwood trees make great fence posts, and there are few left. To make matters even worse, these birds did not evolve in the company of any other predator, so they have never learned to defend themselves. *Rattus rattus* came to the island fairly late, only in the 1940s, but these are ferocious predators, taking eggs, nestlings, and even the female parrot herself. Even worse than the rats are the feral cats who have been on the island since the late 1700s.

Norfolk Island green parrots were once on the island in the hundreds of thousands. They belonged here. They did no harm. Now they are reduced to just a few birds hanging precariously on to existence. The park rangers are doing everything they can to make certain they do not pass into oblivion. I can only salute their efforts. What a horrible thought it would be to return to the island in a few years and discover that there is not a single parrot left. What a great emptiness of spirit that would be.

I believe I would live in Australia just for the parrots alone, all fifty-two species of them (more than any other country except Brazil). I have seen galahs and Australian ringnecks in every park in Perth, and rainbow lorikeets in every garden in Sydney, and red-tailed black cockatoos in Alice Springs. Parrots, parrots, wherever you go in Australia, they are there! What an *embarras de richesses*—like waking up inside a rainbow. Who could possibly resist?

PAUA

Haliotis spp.

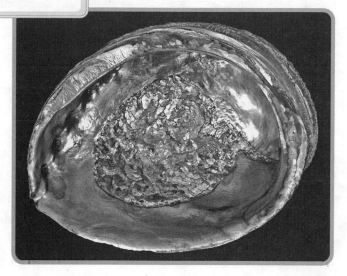

MY DESK IS LITTERED with beautiful, iridescent paua shells. *Paua*, the Maori word for a type of abalone that grows in the waters off New Zealand, has been used for hundreds of years to make jewelry and fishhooks, to decorate buildings, as inlay in wooden boxes, and for thousands of other uses. We have it in the cement mix that is the floor to our house. That was my idea, and everyone compliments me on it.

My son Ilan and I were walking along a remote cove, Whale Bay, near the top of the North Island when we found several diminutive paua shells. We were especially intrigued by the six symmetrical holes on their hard, barnacled outer surface. Turning them over, Ilan and I were enchanted to discover that the shells were pink and blue and green—like a small rainbow.

This beautiful material is nacre, also called mother-of-pearl. But what is it doing inside a shell? Hard as it is, it must serve a purpose in the life of the shell. (I have heard that materials scientists at the University of California–San Diego are studying abalone's strong calcium carbonate–tiled structure for insight into a new wave of bulletproof body armor.) Hmm, I wondered, could the nacre act as a defense against parasitic organisms, something like a pearl? Then it dawned on me: The abalone was not a shell; the shell was merely the home of the animal inside, just as the oyster lives inside an oyster shell. (The pearl is formed by a process called encystations, wherein an offending foreign object is entombed in layers of nacre—that is, pearls.) This was the home of a living animal, and the mother-of-pearl was a secretion that the mollusk was depositing to protect itself.

What was I doing with its home, then? How did I come to possess, or for that matter how does *anyone* come to possess, an animal's shell? Only by evicting and killing the original and legitimate inhabitant! After all, an abalone doesn't just walk away from its shell, does it? True, those tiny ones that washed up on the shore of the bay were already empty. No doubt the abalone inside had long ago died, and I bore no responsibility. But was that the case for the large shells, the ones so prized by artists, jewelry makers, and collectors? That seemed unlikely. I have never seen a large paua shell washed up on any beach I have ever been on in New Zealand. The shells are, I learned as soon as I became curious enough to make a few phone calls, the *by-product* of an industry that is devoted to killing abalone as a source of meat.

So what about the animal who lives inside the abalone shell? (It is hard to identify a shellfish as either *he* or *she*, so I am being an intellectual coward by describing this animal as *it*.) *It* is an herbivorous mollusk, belonging to the family Gastropoda (from the Greek for "stomach" and "foot," since its foot is in its stomach area). It behaves much like an underwater snail, and feeds, inoffensively, primarily on red algae. Abalone belong to the genus *Haliotis*, "sea ear," referring to their appearance, and there are seventy different species. They may spend most of their time securely attached to a rock, yet they are not immobile. They can move about, even run away from predators such as crabs, lobsters, octopuses, and starfish. (They have little defense, however, against the California sea otter or the bat rays who eat them in enormous quantities by breaking open their shells with a rock.) Moreover,

they munch on seaweed by sitting up—almost like a rabbit eating a car-
rot, says one observer.

The small holes Ilan and I admired are respiratory pores, which they
use to eject semen or eggs into the water. From time to time as the shell
grows and the abalone ages, a new hole is formed while an older one
closes over. These disused holes remain evident, forming a spiral pattern
around the shell's exterior. Abalone are highly fertile, more so as they
grow in size, producing from ten thousand to eleven million eggs at a
time. This is because few of the eggs, which hatch in about a week, ever
hatch into floating larvae, since they are mostly eaten by fish. Those
who survive feed on plankton until, in about a week, they grow their
own shell. After that, they are called veligers and sink to the bottom. It
takes a long time to become fully grown, from ten to fifteen years. (It
takes an abalone seven years to reach seven inches, the size at which
they can first be legally "taken," and they become sexually mature
around age three.) Some species, such as the white abalone, can live for
as long as forty years, or perhaps even longer. The abalone has a muscular foot with strong suction power (more than four thousand times its
own body weight), which it uses to clamp onto rocks under the surface
of the sea so tightly that divers must use a heavy iron bar to wrench it
away.

And what is wrong with that, precisely? As a strict vegetarian I
have my objections, but I know they are not likely to carry much
weight with most people reading this book. I can hardly appeal to the
Lewis Carroll sentiment ("It seems a shame," the Walrus said, "To play
them such a trick"). So I appeal to something else. These animals are disappearing. Chinese gourmets cannot get enough of them, and in Japan
and Korea they are considered (wrongly, of course) aphrodisiacs. So a
kilo (2.2 pounds) of abalone, including the shell, sells for one hundred
euros. Abalone is now in greater demand even than the red tuna so
prized in sushi. (A single large fish can sell for nearly half a million dollars on the Japanese market.) There will always be people willing to
break the law and take more than their quota. Already the western
seaboard of the United States is empty of them. And the five species

that lived along the central and southern Pacific coast of California have been depleted.

Australia and New Zealand supply 70 percent of the world's abalone, but much of that is illegally cut—by some estimates, more than half. For example, the recreational limit in New Zealand is ten paua per diver, and each shell must be a minimum length. But poaching is big business, and is further complicated by the fact that the right to harvest paua can be legally granted under Maori customary rights. In West Africa the situation is even worse, and it is expected that abalone will soon be extinct there. Aquaculture is being attempted, but there are many problems, not the least of which is the diseases being introduced, including withering foot syndrome. Will the day ever come when we simply observe these intriguing animals as things of beauty without wishing to exploit them? I hope so.

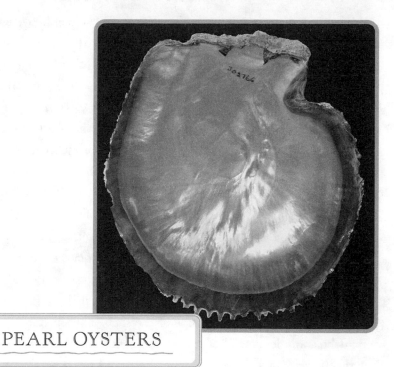

PEARL OYSTERS

EARLS COME FROM MOLLUSKS and have always done so—that is, for the last 530 million years. Fossil pearls have been found embedded in rocks from more than thirty species of mollusks, including oysters, mussels, and scallops. They were common when dinosaurs were on the earth. Some fossil pearls found in Eocene rocks in England have retained their exquisite luster for fifty million years. A pearl oyster lives in the wild for about eight years. What happens to the pearl after that is not clear, but it is likely that somebody in ancient times found one on the ocean floor quite by accident. It's hard to imagine such an event causing no interest. Nobody knows, though, when or how humans first found pearls.

A natural pearl (or, as it is also called, a fine pearl) is found wild in oceans and in river systems. Cultured (or cultivated) pearls are also "real" pearls, except that they come from mollusks who have been implanted with an irritant, causing the creatures to secrete nacre to protect their soft tissues. The pearl is the product of a living animal.

Many oysters are pearl oysters, but generally the edible oysters (also called true oysters) are only remotely related to pearl oysters. They, too, can produce pearls, although they do so rarely; theirs are more like white marbles. Of historical significance (but not of commercial importance today) are the Atlantic pearl oyster of the Caribbean (*Pinctada imbricata*), which Columbus was searching for, and the Ceylon pearl oyster of the Indian Ocean (*P. radiata*), which produced most of the world's natural pearls in the past (from the Red Sea, the Persian Gulf, the Indian Ocean, and even the eastern Mediterranean).

What makes a pearl? Not the proverbial grain of sand. But, yes, some irritant. Usually it is a small crab, a parasitic worm, or a small particle of organic tissue. The pearl oyster then secretes from the epithelial cells of the mantle the aragonotic material known as nacre, or mother-of-pearl. The same tissue coats the inside of its own shell, so naturally the pearl is the same color as the inside of the shell. The substance, mostly conchiolin and calcium carbonate, is iridescent (found, as well, in coral), but this is seen much more starkly in the pearl since a pearl consists of thousands of almost microscopically thin concentric sheets of nacre (the same as on the inside of the shell—the pearl shows it more starkly because of its round shape). The pearl develops within what has been called a pearl sac—a hollow in the soft tissue next to the hard shell. It is usually close to the gonad, or sexual organ, of the animal.

A cultivated pearl's formation generally takes three years; how long it takes in the wild is unknown. A perfect pearl is produced only rarely. It is wise to remember that this concept is entirely human; nature has no concept of perfection. For the animals themselves, there is no aesthetic appreciation of what is for them pure nuisance. It is only by chance that we as a species find pearls beautiful, and in nature only one or two out of a thousand pearls are round. Refraction, too, holds appeal for humans. Light rays that penetrate below the surface reflect off the deeper inner layers, giving pearls a sheen, a depth, and a brilliance that is peculiarly attractive to us but is presumably meaningless to all other animals.

Oysters generally don't move, but attach themselves to a rock or a reef with a strong set of organic threads called a byssus. They filter planktonic food through their gills, and release sperm and eggs into the water. Some of them, including the *Pinctada maxima* pearl oyster, harbor a tiny pea crab that lives in the mantle cavity, sharing scraps of its filtered food supply and performing certain essential cleaning services. In the wild these oysters live for twenty years. Their cousins, the *P. margaritifera*, live more than thirty years.

Freshwater pearl mussels have even more complicated lives than those of pearl oysters. The females release larvae called glochidia. But before a larva can metamorphose, it attaches to the gills or fins of a fish, dropping to the bottom when mature, weeks or months later. Sometimes only one particular fish will do as the host (who is not harmed). Some freshwater mussels live astonishingly long lives: The European pearl mussel (*Margaritifera margaritifera*) can live eighty to one hundred years. It produces a pearl that takes twenty years or more to grow.

Before the artificial cultivation of pearls, barely a hundred years ago, the only way to get pearls was for somebody to dive for them. This was dangerous, poorly rewarded work. In 1835 Robert Browning wrote in *Paracelsus:* "Are there not, dear Michal, two points in the adventure of the diver: One—when, a beggar, he prepares to plunge? One—when, a prince, he rises with his pearl?" Browning's literary skill was greater than his knowledge; a diver rarely became rich. In Australia, for example, Aborigines who had never even seen the ocean were often kidnapped from their desert communities and forced to dive, in shark-infested waters, to depths of nearly ninety feet. They were often stung by the deadly box jellyfish, whose toxin drives people nearly insane with pain when it does not kill them outright.

In the Red Sea enslaved boys were often used as pearl divers, as the following account details: "The lofty Bedouins refuse to dive themselves but train their young slave-boys to the art. The slave while training, will be shown a shell at the bottom, and told to fetch it. If he fails to bring it up, he is bound to be flogged, and his very life is jeopardized; and even when he brings up the most valuable shells, scanty food is his own reward." The misery and oppression, the dangers, and the actual deaths made pearl diving one of the most dangerous of professions. Still, I wonder if a single diver ever compared his own misery with that of the animal he was killing, perhaps wondering why any of it was necessary. Perhaps this is a luxury of twenty-first-century thinking. I mention this because my own father was a pearl merchant who was absolutely fascinated by pearls and perliculture, but he never once told me anything about this other side to the profession, from the point of view of either the exploited diver or the exploited animal. With his open mind, were he alive today, I suspect he would be sympathetic to my position: Pearls belong on the bottom of the sea. Wearing them is only slightly less reprehensible than wearing fur that belonged to an animal murdered for her coat.

The first Western person to understand how a pearl was produced was probably the Swedish naturalist Carl von Linné (1717–1778), also called Carolus Linnaeus and best known for developing the system of nomenclature all biologists and zoologists use today. He produced the first spherical cultured pearls in any mollusk, although the Chinese in the fifth century had already succeeded in producing blister pearls in freshwater mussels. His secret went undiscovered until the beginning of the twentieth century, when his manuscript was found in the Linnean Society of London by W. A. Herdman, 144 years after von Linné took the secret to his grave.

The first successful implantation techniques and commercialization of cultured pearls were invented and introduced to the West by the Japanese pearl merchant Kokichi Mikimoto in the 1930s. When he introduced them to the United States, it has been reported that the value of natural pearls plummeted by 85 percent in a single day, for people realized they could not tell the difference between a natural pearl and a cultivated pearl. (It is still impossible to do so without the aid of special machines.) People thought the cultivated Japanese pearls were fake, which they were not. The only difference between a natural pearl and a cultured pearl is that in the former the irritant occurs accidentally in nature and in the latter it is deliberately introduced by humans (a process called grafting or nucleation). Unlike most forms of aquaculture

(about which I have great qualms), the impact on the environment of artificial pearl farms appears to be minimal. Still, in Japanese *akoyas* half
the oysters die when they are artificially nucleated (when the irritant is
inserted). Moreover, once the pearl is extracted, the oyster is, as the industry delicately puts it "culled." Call it what you like, the truth is an
animal is killed. Paula Mikkelsen informs me that most pearl oysters
used today in periculture are reared in the lab. This is 100 percent true
for Japan and for the majority of French Polynesia. Only Australia
dives for adult shells anymore.

Before grafting can take place, the oyster must relax, for the first response of any bivalve when handled or removed from water is to close
tightly. The animal is given a mild anesthetic so that he eventually
gapes. The men who perform this work are almost all Japanese special-
ists, paid high sums for their work, much like medical surgeons. And it
is literally a surgical operation: A small incision is made in the gonad to
make a pocket, the pearl sac. Using specialized tools, a bead nucleus is
inserted along with a piece of tissue called the graft. The graft is a tiny
square of nacre-producing epithelium. This was the secret that was not
discovered for many years. This graft immediately begins to coat the nucleus. The nucleus itself has a long and complicated history, which I
will not repeat, but suffice it to say that it comes from a single source:
pearl mussel shells from the Tennessee River in Tennessee and Al-
abama. In 1993 the United States exported seven thousand tons of these
shells to Asia to be used as nuclei in cultured pearl cultivation.

Both surgeon and patient experience stress. For the surgeon, there is
a long wait to find out whether the oysters will survive the operation,
whether the nacre will be evenly deposited, and whether they can be
properly cared for over the next three years. And it has been discovered
that stress on the part of the oyster makes for poor-quality pearls. So in
recent years they have come to be handled gently, kept out of water for
as little time as possible. Stress management in oyster pearls is now a
hot field of scientific inquiry. How primitive could a pearl oyster be if
it can be stressed? Obviously nucleation itself is stressful to the animal.
Imagine if our body discovered a foreign object for which our immune

system had to mount a major defense. A pearl could be defined as a response to an insult. Humans artificially create the insult, and then the work is done by the animal. The fact that in so doing more than half of all oysters die is not a record to be proud of. Losing half your workforce is hardly inspiring. In a horrible ironic twist, I suspect this is close to the figure for divers who eventually die from the stress of finding the oysters in the first place. But the only reason the cultured pearl industry does not laugh at the notion of stress in oysters is that it has seen profits rise when attention is paid to what otherwise might be seen as a loopy idea of some fanatic animal rights activist. That would be me.

PIGS

Family Suidae

THE DOMESTIC PIG, the wild pig, and the eastern Asiatic wild pig are all in the family Suidae, which also includes the bearded pig, warthog, pygmy hog, and babirusa. By human standards, many of these animals are considered ugly, which may be where we derive some of our anti-pig prejudices.

Pigs and hippopotamuses belong to a mammalian order, the even-toed ungulates. Eurasian wild pigs, or boars as they are called, are the antecedents of the overwhelming majority of domesticated and feral pig populations. They have one of the widest geographic distributions of all land-based mammals; they're found on all continents except Antarctica, and on many oceanic islands. Due to hunting, they are now extinct in the British Isles, Scandinavia, and most of the former USSR. The pig has been domesticated many times in many different places. A number of authors have noted that pigs are among those animals psychologically preadapted to domestication, predisposed as they are to cooperate with humans. Why this is so is far from clear.

In ancient Egypt pigs were used for threshing. Bundled grain was spread in a contained area and trampled on by the sharp hooves of pigs. They were considered extremely valuable. In an illustration on the granite sarcophagus of Taho (about 600 BCE) in the Louvre Museum, we see a boat with a domesticated pig onboard guarded by two monkeys standing upright and holding what look like whips. Evidently they are protecting their precious charge. In some cultures pigs were used for planting grain, since the holes their hooves created in soft earth were the ideal depth for seeds. Indeed, there were (and are) pigs who can do many of the tasks normally assigned to dogs. Thus domestication expert F. E. Zeuner reports an 1807 story of Slut, a hunting pig who would "find, point, and retrieve game as well as the best pointer dog."

An old English adage claims, "Dogs look up at you, cats look down on you, but pigs are equal." Pigs are more or less the same size as human beings and resemble us in many ways. The organs of pigs are so similar to our own that surgeons have resorted to pig heart valves for replacing patients' aortic and mitral valves.

It is undeniable that we humans have a great deal in common with pigs, though people have been reluctant to acknowledge this. Like us, pigs dream and can see colors. And they are sociable. The females form stable families led by a matriarch with her children and female relatives. Piglets are fond of play, as human children are, and chase one another, play-fight, play-love, tumble down hills, and generally engage in a wide variety of enjoyable activities. As Karl Schwenke points out in his classic 1985 *In a Pig's Eye*, "Pigs are gregarious animals. Like children, they thrive on affection, enjoy toys, have a short attention span, and are easily bored." He reports that when pigs were put into a small pen, as they are on most farms, "the tedium of their existence soon became apparent: They were lethargic, exhibited ragged ears, had droopy tails, and rapidly acquired that dull-eyed glaze that swineherds associate with six- or seven-year-old breeding hogs." Piglets do not develop in a normal way when they are deprived of the opportunity to engage in play.

Though they are often fed garbage and eat it, their food choices—if allowed them—would not be dissimilar to our own. They get easily bored with the same food. They love melons, bananas, and apples, but if they are fed them for several days on end, they will set them aside and eat whatever other food is new first. We don't often think of pigs and cleanliness in the same breath, but if permitted, pigs are more fastidious in eating and in general behavior than dogs. When offered anything unusual to eat, a pig sniffs it and gently nibbles. About 90 percent of their diet in the wild is plant-based, consisting of fruit, seeds, roots, and tubers. In fact, a study of what fruits pigs routinely eat, conducted on one of the Indonesian islands, found that they would eat more than fifty varieties of fruit. Perhaps this is why of all animals their flesh most resembles human flesh, which is somewhat disconcerting when you consider that more than 40 percent of all meat raised in the world is pork.

Like people, pigs avoid extreme temperatures. Since they have sweat glands only on their noses, it is important that they do not overheat. Water is not effective in cooling them because it evaporates quickly, whereas mud provides evaporative cooling over a much longer period of time. This is why pigs, like elephants, need to roll in mud. Mud protects their sensitive skin from sunburn, dangerous to a pig, and also from flies and other parasites. It is not, then, that pigs are dirty; quite the contrary. Never will a pig defecate near its sleeping or eating quarters. In fact, fastidiousness is one of the pig's most salient characteristics.

There are cultures in the world that revere their pigs. In Papua, New Guinea, villagers have a special relationship with pigs. The Enga men of the western highlands say "pigs are our hearts." Highlanders in the Nondugl area in the Middle Waghi on the same island insist that pigs are so central to their social and religious life that no amount of money could persuade them to sell one. The piglets among the Siuai of Bougainville's Great Buin Plain, on the same island, share their owners' food, are baptized, and are each given a ritual name. When ill, they receive magical medications, and the women chew tubers for them to eat. While the men "own" the pigs, it is the women who care for them, allowing them to share their sleeping quarters, even nursing orphaned piglets.

The capacity, even talent, for cross-species friendships that pigs possess is not confined to the domesticated pig. Wild boars also clearly possess this quality. In his remarkable 1986 book *Mein Leben unter Wildschweinen* (My Life with Wild Pigs), Heinz Meynhardt writes of his acceptance into a herd of wild boars. Were Meynhardt to have seen these boars only as quarry to be hunted, his detailed knowledge about their social relations, their child rearing, and other intimate aspects of their lives could never have been compiled. Extraordinarily sensitive to danger as boars must be to have survived centuries of active hunting, why they would allow a member of the enemy into their ranks is mysterious. That they were willing to forgive and trust a human is humbling.

It is gratifying to see that in the last few years more people are discovering the joy of living close to a pig. One example is *The Good Good Pig* by Sy Montgomery, which tells in charming detail about her life with Christopher Hogwood, a pig with an extraordinary capacity for friendship, joy, and trust (although this is undoubtedly normal for the species). Another is the fine book by Lyall Watson, *The Whole Hog*, which ends with this ringing endorsement: "Pigs process thoughts. They understand 'if, then' situations, they apply previous experience to novel circumstances, and they interact with their environments, and with each other, as though they are conscious of the consequences. What more do you want? Pigs with wings?"

PINNIPEDS

Pinnipedia

W HEN MOST PEOPLE THINK of seals, they think of sea lions. Perhaps because these exuberant creatures seem intermediate between an animal who lives on land and one who lives in the ocean, seals have always fascinated humans.

Seals, sea lions, and walruses are collectively called the pinnipeds (from Latin words meaning "having feet as fins"). They are mammals, so they give birth to live young and suckle them just as we do. But unlike us, they can dive deep underwater. (Unlike us, they are able to drink ocean water and excrete the excess salt in highly concentrated urine, thanks to their powerful kidneys.) Elephant seal adult females are able to dive as deep as forty-one hundred feet and can stay under for more than an hour. And they do it over and over, almost without resting. They are so well adapted to water that fur seals, who remain for months at a time at sea without coming to land at all, sleep in open water. Not only that, but some seals sleep underwater. Northern elephant seals, for example, possibly sleep underwater at depths of a thousand feet!

What I find most fascinating is that seals who sleep underwater show no REM (rapid eye movement) activity, which means they probably do

not dream when sleeping underwater. But when they sleep at the surface, they show REM activity: They dream. I imagine this lack of
dreaming underwater is to protect them: Since they must surface to
breathe, should the dream become too engrossing, they might fail to do
so and drown. This is, of course, only my own hypothesis.

One puzzle: Many pinnipeds ingest large stones called gastroliths,
some of which can be as large as a small orange. In one well-documented
case, a large southern elephant seal was carrying almost eighty pounds
of pebbles in his stomach. Most scientists believe they probably serve
as ballast, much like a diver's weight belt.

Harp seals (so called because they have what looks like a harp on their
back), with their large black eyes and round faces, are pretty much universally recognized as among the most appealing baby animals on the
planet. Call me a sentimentalist, but I find myself appalled at the way
these animals can be called *cull*. Even so sensitive a writer as Victor
Scheffer refers to the "take" of baby harp seals (which in 1940 was half
a million a year). *Crop* is yet another false word, as if we were talking
about a vegetable. Murder most foul is more like it. I am completely on
Paul Watson's side, when he writes (as an editorial on Monday, January
23, 2006, in the *National Post of Canada*):

> During the last three years, the Canadian Department of Fisheries
> and Oceans has permitted the destruction of over one million
> young seals in a heavily subsidized program that has sullied the
> reputation of this great nation with the stain of cruelty. As long as
> seals are clubbed and shot, their bodies skinned alive, and the ice
> nurseries of the harp and hood seals stained with blood, my crew
> and I will continue to oppose the policy of the Canadian Depart-
> ment of Fisheries and Oceans. If opposing this slaughter is a crime,
> then we are proud to be compassionate criminals defending life
> from the profits of destruction.

(See his website: www.seashepherd.org).

Sea lions are especially popular because they seem to habituate easily
to the presence of humans. They are easily recognized because the males

have a sagittal crest, unique to *Zalophus*. That is what brings so many tourists to Pier 39 in San Francisco. Moreover, their faces resemble dogs, albeit very large dogs. (The males are seven feet long and can weigh as much as a thousand pounds, though they are what scientists call highly sexually dimorphic; the females are a third the weight of the males and less than half as long.) They are extremely gregarious, and can sometimes be seen floating all together on the ocean's surface in "rafts."

There are three species of sea lions, the California, Galápagos, and Japanese. Hunting has left a mere fifty to sixty of the Japanese sea lion. They are, effectively, extinct.

Sometimes, as I read what I anticipate will be a dry scientific account, I am brought up short by a passage that must be read and reread, so wonderful is it. Here is an example, from page 184 of the *Encyclopedia of Marine Mammals:*

California sea lion females are very particular about male behavior. Boisterous, overly attentive, or aggressive males are typically abandoned and left to sit alone on their territories. Any interference with female movements is simply not tolerated. Should a male attempt to block a female's path, she needs only to extend her neck out and up, and sway it side to side as she walks. This long-neck display signals males that she requires free passage; the rare male that does not respond to this will likely be subjected to a display of jerky hopping and flipper slapping, which will dissuade him from interfering further. Males seem to have little option but to acquiesce if they are to be successful at breeding.

Anybody who has visited a sea-life park is familiar with California sea lions, since they are, along with killer whales and dolphins, star attractions. In 1986 Schusterman and Krieger found that sea lions are capable of thinking in images, including the concept of size, so that if a trainer gives one a complex command with hand signals—say, *Find the larger of two black balls and push it to the smaller one*—she can do it. When she is told to look for a black ball, she scans the pool for all black objects, then for all balls. It is phenomenal to watch. But I would much rather know exactly what this ability is used for (one can imagine, of course) in the open ocean. I would also like to know exactly why sea lions do this. It is not just for the fish. One of the trainers I talked with told me they do it for positive reinforcement—that is, they like to be praised. But why do they like to be praised? A clue comes from a report by Riedman of the work of Hanggi and Schusterman in 1987: The bonds of a familial relationship between a mother and her pups can last an entire lifetime. These social animals *like* to be with somebody they know. ("Duh, Dad!" said my son Ilan when I told him this.) So, in captivity, deprived of their normal familial relationships, like parrots, they accept the next best thing: us. A little bit sad, when you think about it.

POLAR BEAR

Ursus maritimus

SOME YEARS AGO, while living in England, I had the sad experience of watching a polar bear pacing back and forth in the London Zoo. In an article published in *Nature*, Georgia Mason and Ross Clubb from Oxford University pointed out that in a zoo a polar bear is confined to a single one-millionth her natural range's size. *Of course* such a bear suffers. This explains the strange behavior of Gus, a polar bear living in the Central Park Zoo in 1994, who incessantly swam in figure eights in his pool. With typical English modesty, Mason and Clubb understate their conclusion: "Our results show, to our knowledge for the first time, that a particular lifestyle in the wild confers vulnerability to welfare problems in captivity."

This formidable animal inhabits an area of our unconscious that easily resorts to myths. Even if they have never seen it themselves, Inuit hunters believe that a hunting bear covers her giveaway black nose while lying in wait for a seal, so that the seal will not notice her (but I'm not sure they really do this). No scientist has observed this, and it appears to be a myth. Inuit people also believe that a dead polar bear properly treated would spread the news, and the rest would then be eager to be killed!

Scientists estimate that there are between twenty and twenty-five thousand polar bears throughout the circumpolar north—Alaska, Norway, Russia, Denmark, and Canada—where more than half of all polar bears live. (They do not live in the Southern Hemisphere.) Males can be more than eight feet tall and weigh as much as seventeen hundred pounds. But when they are born, the cubs are only a foot long and weigh about a pound. Mortality in the first year is high, mostly due to starvation. Since they have no natural enemies, however, except for themselves, and humans, once the polar bears make it to adulthood they are more or less immortal—living into their midtwenties or more in the wild, and even longer in captivity. Ian Stirling has written that "death by gunshot is probably the greatest single cause of mortality in wild polar bears." This is true at least for North America and Greenland, though not for Norway and Russia.

For some periods, there is little to eat in the Arctic, and polar bears must be consummate hunters of their staple food: ringed seals. They stalk them much as cats stalk their prey. (When threatened or angry, polar bears chuff and pop their jaws—it can sound like a steam engine.) Freezing when they first notice a seal on ice, they crouch and slowly move forward until, with a burst of amazing speed, they charge the unsuspecting prey. The other, more frequent if less spectacular, method is waiting in absolute silence by a breathing hole until a seal surfaces to breathe, then pouncing with great force. In winter, when the ice is completely frozen, all signs of the breathing holes have been effaced. Polar bears, who see more or less as much as humans, then call into play their amazing sense of smell. With this, they locate a ringed seal breathing hole beneath the snow or a birth lair with pups in it from several miles away. When they find a lair, they crash down with their front paws in an attempt to break through the roof of the snow cave the mother seal has fashioned for birthing.

Like many charismatic megafauna, the salvation and the future for polar bears seems to be in preserving them for a different kind of consumption: human curiosity. Humans pay enormous amounts of money to see polar bears under natural conditions. The fortunes of the declin-ing Manitoba town of Churchill were magically reversed when they in-vented a Tundra Buggy to allow tourists to go for long rides (up to a week being in a moving hotel) to see pristine country and polar bears.

Yet the Tundra Buggy cannot save the polar bears from global warm-ing and decimation of habitat. It is possible, scientists believe, that polar bears will entirely disappear within a century. I agree with what Richard Davids says to end his fine book:

> How empty the Arctic would be without its lordly bears. For me, every encounter with one is brushed with magic; I have the dis-tinct feeling that I have had an audience with royalty. Here is a creature that doesn't shrink from the sight or sound of humans but accepts them as interesting fellow animals. A big female was buffeting my plastic container of water. I couldn't keep from shouting, "Get away from here." She left it and came up close, fix-ing her black eyes on mine. "Why?" she seemed to be saying. "What gives you authority over this land?"

I have never heard of a wild polar bear befriending a human being. However, they are immensely playful with one another, engaging in wrestling and boxing matches that look like real aggression but are merely pretend, at least in the case of males. No doubt it is this fond-ness for play that explains the following observation, which is, I be-lieve, unique: In 1994 a playful relationship developed between a Siberian husky and a polar bear near the town of Churchill, Manitoba. On first meeting, the dog performed a play-bow, which the bear ap-peared to recognize, and the two played for several minutes, embracing and parting when the bear grew overheated. The relationship, docu-mented by professional wildlife photographers and appearing as a cover story in *National Geographic*, lasted a week. Then the winter ice formed and the bear left for his winter feeding grounds. This is per-haps a unique case; it is not unusual for polar bears to attack and kill sled dogs. In fact, Andrew Derocher seems to remember that this sled dog was killed by another polar bear a year later. He pointed out to me that far more astonishing is the fact that a pregnant female polar bear can go eight months without eating, and then go from 220 to 880 pounds in a single year.

D ARWIN WAS INTRIGUED when he learned that certain ants kept slaves. Of course we tend to think that we are the only species that does certain things, even if those things are negative, such as slavery. So when I learned that there was a type of jumping spider found in Africa, Asia, and Australia that was in many ways a hunter as sophisticated as human hunters, it caught my attention, as well as Robert Jackson's. A professor of zoology at the University of Canterbury in New Zealand, he has been studying the *Portia fimbriata* spider for more than twenty years. His article in *National Geographic* introduced this amazing hunter to many more people. Suddenly it was no longer a joke to attempt to answer an ancient question: "Who can fathom the mind of a spider?"

The portia is odd for many reasons. For one, most spiders either build webs to capture prey, or hunt away from the webs in which they live. Portias do both. They also don't look much like a spider. As a means of camouflage, they look more like a piece of detritus blown by the wind into another spider's web. They don't scurry the way other spiders do, but move more like a robot. And they love to eat other spiders.

The portia has eight legs like any other spider, but she also has two leglike palps. When a portia arrives at the web of a spider she wishes to deceive into thinking a prey has been caught, she employs an astonishingly sophisticated plan of attack: She plucks the web silk strand, or slaps it, or pulls on it, or flutters it, with one or two or three or any other number up to ten of her legs, not to mention the twitching of her abdomen up and down, and is therefore able to make literally hundreds of thousands of different combinations. Sometimes she tries just about everything without success. Suddenly, one combination gets the attention of the resident spider. She thinks an insect she is used to eating is struggling in her web and approaches. But she can become suspicious and stop. Portia goes through her repertoire again, and the spider is wary, until, bingo, the exact right combination comes up and she slowly moves forward. Portia now "knows" what works, and plays the same combination over and over to lure her victim ever closer, until she comes to within striking distance. Then the rightful but unwary owner of the web is history.

Portia has wonderful eyes, which include color vision (though what, exactly, color means for jumping spiders—salticids, as they are called— is something of a puzzle). A jumping spider has two eyes right where they should be, on the center of her head, but also three pairs of secondary eyes used for detecting motion. Portia therefore has fairly acute vision. Maybe not as good as ours (we have 130 million photocells in our retinas, and portia only a few thousand), but unusually useful for such a small animal. She hunts with her eyes, much as we do. Visual hunters rarely let their prey out of sight, though portia does. Once she realizes (I relish the use of this word here!) that she has been sighted, she takes a long detour, losing visual contact with the web. She has not forgotten what she is after. Rather, she has a plan. She climbs a nearby tree, moving slowly along a vine growing over the spider's web, which she still cannot see. All of this maneuvering can take up to an hour. Then portia drops on her own silk line alongside the web and begins swinging until she is able to grab her unwitting victim (sometimes even another portia—she has no innate distaste for cannibalism). If we bear in mind that

portia has no visual contact—already unusual behavior for a spider—
we seem forced to acknowledge that she has memory. As Jackson has so
well put it: "It is difficult to escape the conclusion that *Portia* solves detour problems in its head, makes plans and then acts on these plans."

What is extraordinary here is to see a spider, often thought of as a
pure automaton, using trial and error (unknown in any other spider).
There seems no escaping the thought that in portia we have a "thinking" spider; a flexible spider; a spider with a good memory. True, spider
brains are only about the size of a pinhead. Yet in their hunting techniques, spiders are nearly as sophisticated as humans. The detours a portia takes, scientists now recognize, must be or at least appear to be
planned ahead of time. Moreover, she uses deception unrelated to her
natural camouflage. For example, when stalking other jumping spiders,
she hides her palpa outlines. When entering a delicate spiderweb, it is
as if she knows that it is impossible for her to remain silent and go unde-
tected. So she sets out to deliberately broadcast deceitful signals. As
Professor Jackson puts it: "A spider like *Portia* is supposed to follow
rigid, simple behavior patterns. There's not much room for thinking.
But from its deadly skill at mimicry to its elaborate attack strategies,
Portia is one of the most behaviorally complex predators in the animal
kingdom."

Jackson doesn't go further than that. But I, not being a scientist, can:
Could it be that brain size, even with respect to body size, is a human
prejudice, or even a myth, since it supplies us with the comforting and
narcissistically satisfying information that we come out on top of the entire animal kingdom? That in fact some spiders, or at least portia, come
close to equaling human hunting techniques?

PRONGHORN

Antilocapra americana

J OHN BYERS IS PROFESSOR OF ZOOLOGY at the University of Idaho
and the world's leading authority on the pronghorn, a North
American hoofed animal that resembles an African gazelle. Byers
began to study pronghorn in 1981, in the Flathead Valley in the National Bison Range in western Montana; he has been back every year
since, to observe, test hypotheses, and do research.

In 2003 he published a popular summary of his work, *Built for Speed:
A Year in the Life of Pronghorn*. It is rare that a book by a scientist is so
compelling that it makes converts to the cause of the author. This was
such a book. Reading it was like having an epiphany; rarely has science
been written with such a combination of authority, humor, and
warmth. Everything I know about pronghorn I learned from this wonderful book.

The one thing that anybody who has ever heard of pronghorn knows
is that they are the fastest mammals in North America. From an explosive start, in about six seconds they reach speeds up to sixty miles per

hour, faster than any other land animal that has ever existed on earth except for the African cheetah. Obviously, they can outrun any animal in their environment. With hardly any effort they cruise for many miles at forty-five miles per hour. Talk about precocial: When a fawn is two weeks old, she can outrun a thoroughbred horse!

Pronghorn constantly fight one another. Male fawns are so sexually aggressive to their own mothers that they are weaned two to three weeks earlier than the female fawns. Jockeying for power never seems to cease, even when there is no discernible advantage. Dominance and subordination seem to be categories that exist for their own sake in pronghorn society, without conferring any tangible benefits. Dominance does not improve nutritional status, nor does it impact reproduction. Indeed, it seems that subordinate females live longer and produce more offspring than the bullies. Hollow victories seem the stuff of everyday life for them.

Finally, you might ask why pronghorn bother to form herds, since the bullying is constant and there is no apparent benefit. Usually if an animal joins a group it is because doing so lessens the chance of being singled out for attack by a predator. But coyotes, the main predator of fawns, have absolutely no chance of ever taking a healthy adult pronghorn.

Byers discovered the single explanatory event that illuminated both behaviors: They are relicts, evolutionary carryovers, or afterthoughts. The speed, it turns out, is a relict (similar to the human male nipple, something left over from our evolutionary past that has never been selected against, as Gould argued). For millions of years, until a mere twelve thousand years ago, America was filled with long-legged and fast-running bears, North American lions, and especially *Miracinonyx trumani*, the American cheetah, larger and possibly faster than the African cheetah of today. They were locked in an evolutionary arms race with the pronghorn. As predators grew faster, prey had to evolve in the same direction or fall victim quickly and decisively. As for the pronghorn's nasty behavior, to be subordinate in those days meant to be relegated to the outer edge of the group, where the chance of being selected as prey was far greater than for the dominant animal occupying the circle's center. As for groupings, well, it made sense to be part of such a group when your world was filled with dangerous hyenas, as it was just ten thousand years ago. The urge stayed, its point lost. As Byers puts it with his usual succinct, felicitous phrasing: "They are survivors from another world, sculpted by natural selection in that world into running machines that in today's environment blow the competition away."

But Byers's discoveries by no means exhaust the fascinating parts of his entrancing book. Think of the fact that a mother stares for only about two seconds at the place where her fawn disappears into hiding, and then wanders several miles away, but is able to immediately find the exact spot if danger prematurely forces her to return. Her ability to take things in with so little effort strikes us as almost miraculous. This ability is fed by her love for her fawn, a word that Byers, unlike other animal scientists, is unafraid to use. Here is the puzzle: Since pronghorn can outrun any animal in their environment, and such bursts of speed are very expensive in terms of energy, why bother?

Okay, don't get grossed out, but I find it bizarrely fascinating that fawns urinate and defecate into the mouths of their mothers. There's a perfectly logical reason they do so. As my pediatrician wife reminded me when I told her about it: "If the fawn has an intestinal or urinary tract infection, the microbes that cause it will be present in the feces or urine. In the mother's intestine, specialized areas detect and bind to the microbes, and make antibodies to them. The antibodies then are transferred to the mammary glands and so into milk. The mother can, in effect, custom-design the antibodies that her fawn needs."

Pronghorn are renowned for their curiosity. David Macdonald's *New Encyclopedia of Mammals* claims that they will approach and inspect moving objects, even predators, from long distances. Now, I can easily understand that this curiosity, common to just about all prey, serves an obvious function: Know thine enemy. It is hardly idle curiosity, but lifesaving research these animals undertake. The more we understand of a potential predator, the safer we are. Is this true of pronghorn as well, or is there some less obvious benefit? Perhaps curiosity, too, is a relict of predator inspection behavior.

Pronghorn were nearly extinct by 1930. Two of the four subspecies are still listed as critically endangered and endangered, respectively. I am relieved to learn that the current population is more than a million—nothing like their former glory, but enough to give me hope that unless we are very stupid, our grandchildren will still be able to see them in their natural home.

PUMA (Cougar, Mountain Lion)

Felis (or Puma) concolor

THESE CATS ARE GENERALLY CALLED mountain lions in California—a term used by Christopher Columbus. Concolor means "one color," though this animal's coat varies from grizzled gray to dark brown. In the Old World, the word *panther* means a leopard, while in the Americas, it generally refers to a puma. All told, there are forty different names for the same animal, though many people mistakenly believe they are different animals. *Cougar* is preferred by the general public, at least in the East, whereas scientists prefer *puma*, the name given the animal by Indians and the word commonly used in South America.

Though now they have their own genus, cougars are sometimes classified among the smaller cat family because they do not roar and—unlike the lion, tiger, and all other large cats—they groom themselves by licking their fur. Also, they purr! Still, despite the designation, they are huge, and some cougars are heavier than many jaguars or leopards. So how can they be so elusive? Because that's what they do for a living: They remain concealed, as park ranger Jordan Fisher-Smith puts it.

They live in a remote habitat, or what *was* remote until humans invaded it. They are not called *Puma concolor* ("cat of one color" in Latin) for nothing—their tawny gold blends in with the boulders and dry summer grasses and bushes. And as all scientists who study them agree, they are cryptic and elusive, or is it possible they are shy?

What does shyness mean in an animal so high up on the food chain? Well, they are social (daughters often live close to mothers), but not sociable (they almost never meet one another unless it is to mate or fight—up to half of cougar deaths can be attributed to attacks by other cougars). Ken Logan, one of America's leading puma field biologists, however, did not see any evidence of fighting between females. All of the aggression was from the side of the males, killing one another over territory, breeding females, or food caches. Sometimes, for reasons I cannot imagine, males killed females and cannibalized their young. They travel alone, almost never in pairs and certainly never in packs. Their nutritional needs are too high—it has been estimated that a male cougar needs a home range of between thirty-six and four hundred square miles. Moreover, to hunt successfully, they rely on stealth. Descriptions of their hunting behavior are identical to what we see when we watch our house cats track prey. They slither forward on their bellies, their tails twitching, and then they pounce. The only difference is that a mountain lion, with hind legs longer than front, can leap vertically fifteen feet in the air, and horizontally forty-five!

Also, they have been hunted. Ken Logan says that trophy hunting is by far the single greatest mortality factor for lions throughout the West. (They no longer live anywhere else in America, with one exception: There are a very few in Florida, perhaps as few as one hundred.) In 1990 the Animal Damage Control program spent more than forty million dollars attempting to destroy animal and bird pests, including forty-one pumas. The amount of damage the pumas actually did was estimated at less than a million and a half dollars, considerably less than was spent trying to get rid of them. For most of American history, cougars were considered "varmints."

If it seems we are encountering pumas more often today, it's not necessarily because they are becoming acclimatized to us. It is rather that we are invading *their* natural habitat. There are four to six thousand lions in California, according to the Department of Fish and Game; in the same space are thirty-two million people. So if they are killing more dogs and cats, this is surely because there are more of them available for these consummate hunters to kill. Why wouldn't they kill them for food? Evolved to eat deer, they also subsist on much smaller animals, such as hares.

Not long ago I took my wife, Leila, and our children (Manu and Ilan) on a trip to Northern California. As we set out for a three-hour hike, we saw a trailhead ranger sign warning us that mountain lions lived in the hills and canyons beside the trail, and advising us how to behave in the (unlikely) event of an encounter. Ilan read the sign aloud, and as you might well imagine there was hardly any room over the next three hours for any conversation not directly related to human–mountain lion encounters. If you do encounter a mountain lion, stand up straight and try to appear as big as possible, all the while speaking in a calm, soothing voice. Never try to run away.

Between 1890 and 1989, in the United States and Canada, records show a total of thirty-six attacks, eleven of which resulted in human deaths. We need to keep perspective, but not lose our compassion. Of the fifteen cats who were later killed, a full 80 percent were sick or underweight.

Back to my kids. They wouldn't leave the subject alone. I resisted until I realized that this is exactly the reaction of *anyone* who first learns about this top predator, namely "Could I be next?" Well, Rick Hopkins, a cougar biologist who has studied the cats in the Diablo Mountains of Northern California, says the risk of a lion attack is one in twenty-five million. So, although my rational mind knew that I would not even so much as *see* a cougar, somewhere lurking in my unconscious was the primal fear that I just might. And then what would I do? Gary Snyder has written, "The wild is perhaps the very possibility of being eaten by a mountain lion."

There is something atavistically exciting about learning that we are sharing our hike with an animal who could finish us off in no time. It colored the entire excursion and gave it a kind of magic that it would not otherwise have had. After the talk about danger had been exhausted, there was something equally exciting: All that my kids could think about was the possibility of just glimpsing, for a second, this fabled beast. They badly wanted to see that gold fur racing off.

In truth, had we had the great good fortune to spot one, that is undoubtedly what would have happened. Mountain lions usually want to get away from us far more urgently than we want to get away from them. Consider that the single most elaborate study ever done of pumas is by Kenneth Logan and his wife, Linda Sweanor. They spent ten years studying pumas in the desert of New Mexico. They marked 241 individual cats and fixed nearly fourteen thousand radio locations. They closely observed eighty-two individuals in 256 observations—the most that wild pumas have ever been viewed by anyone doing a study. In all that time pumas threatened them sixteen times. And in each case it was a female trying to protect her three- to twelve-week-old cubs. "Usually we observed families that were unaware of our presence or were apparently indifferent to it." In the authoritative book on wildcats by Mel and Fiona Sunquist, they write, "like cheetahs pumas are gentle, retiring cats, more eager to flee than fight, and both species rarely confront humans."

All researchers agree that the single best thing we can do for cougars is to preserve their habitat. Why is it that almost everybody, everywhere, feels awe when in the presence of beautiful, unspoiled wild places? And why is that awe heightened when we are fortunate enough to see a large predator such as a mountain lion in that very wild place? Ken Logan ends his superb scientific treatise by suggesting that as a species we have evolved to feel this sense of wonder precisely because it encourages us to nurture our natural environment rather than destroy it. When we are outside in the presence of other animals in their own place, we feel a kind of pleasure that we often think is uniquely human but I would suggest is probably shared by every other animal. We are where we belong.

PYTHONS

Family Pythonidae

IZARDS AND SNAKES are in the same order, Squamata, within the class Reptilia. It is not always easy to tell them apart. Most lizards, though, have external eardrums, while snakes do not. Until fairly recently it was widely believed that snakes were deaf, and it is true that they depend on vibrations far more than on hearing. Most lizards have movable eyelids, and snakes have a fixed transparent scale over each eye. Unfortunately, this unblinking stare has given rise to the fantasy that they have evil on their minds.

When I was six, I had a card printed that read: JEFF MASSON, SNAKE EXPERT. What I really meant was "snake lover," for I actually knew little about them. When I was twelve at summer camp, I grabbed a small, brightly colored snake (black with red or orange and bright, thin, yellow stripes) climbing up a tree, and was bitten. It didn't hurt. The camp counselor was not a whole lot older than I, but he seemed to know a great deal about snakes. What he said was not reassuring: "Red on yellow, kill a fellow." Thanks a lot. "Looks a lot like a deadly coral snake to me." What! "Of course, it could have been the scarlet king snake, which is totally harmless," he explained. He mused about snakes that are aposematic (warningly colored), and then warmed to his subject by sub-jecting me to a mini-lecture on Batesian mimicry, where a nonpoisonous snake takes on the color pattern of a poisonous one, benefiting from the respect other animals pay the dangerous snake. Was it a dry bite? he wondered. A bite without injecting venom? Half of all coral snakebites are dry. The puncture wound was tiny, but how could I tell if the snake had envenomed me? He didn't know. The bite was not painful. There was no swelling. There was no discoloration. He meditated. "Hmmm, it can take several hours, even a whole day for symptoms to show up." You vomit. You salivate. You become euphoric. You have difficulty breathing. And then you have to get to a hospital, and quick. He was right. It's possible to die of respiratory failure. However, in this case, all's well that ends well. The bite must have been nonpoisonous, for I'm still here!

Is it a relief or a regret that I live in a country, New Zealand, where there are no snakes? Am I happier or more wary when I cross over to Australia, a country with the dubious distinction of having more ven-omous snakes than any other in the world, and nine of the ten most ven-omous snakes in the world? Out of nearly 170 species in Australia, 120 of them are venomous.

Snakes have the most space dedicated to them in *The Guinness Book of Animal Records*. Is this because of how much we fear them? Some bi-ologists argue that humans have an inborn fear of snakes because we de-scend from animals who lived in trees, and these trees are easily invaded by poisonous snakes. Of the world's twenty-six hundred species of snakes, 80 percent are harmless. But that still leaves 20 percent who aren't. It would be a wonder if we did not fear them. In any given year from three hundred thousand to a million (depending on whom you be-lieve) people are bitten by snakes worldwide, and according to the World Health Organization thirty to forty thousand of them die from the bite.

Freud, in 1917, claimed, "Most of us have a sense of repulsion if we meet with a snake." Snake phobia, we might say, is a universal human characteristic. Darwin also claimed we have an "instinctive fear and hatred of snakes." But I wonder . . . I vividly remember when my daughter Simone was three and we were walking in the woods outside Toronto. A snake emerged from the forest and Simone bent down and gently picked him up, then carried him about. Neither the snake nor my daughter seemed the least bit nonplussed. If humans have evolved to have an instinctive fear of snakes, why didn't Simone display it?

All snakes are cold-blooded. Terrible word, for it immediately conjures up someone who intentionally harms you without the slightest remorse. All it means scientifically, though, is that the animals cannot regulate their own body temperature but are dependent on the environment. This is why we see snakes and lizards sunning themselves on warm rocks in the desert.

Perhaps humans also find it unnerving that some snakes need to eat infrequently, as seldom as a couple of times a year, which is why they are rapidly becoming the preferred pet-lite in the United States. However, when they do eat, they do so with a vengeance, which can offend our sensibilities. I saw a picture of an African rock python (which can grow to thirty feet long) distending its mouth to swallow an impala!

How dangerous are snakes, really? Mostly, not at all (unless you happen to meet one swimming in the ocean: all fifty of the world's sea snakes are venomous). As the herpetologist C. H. Pope once said, "snakes are first cowards, next bluffers, and last of all warriors." That is, they will run away, pretend to strike, and only when forced into a battle actually become aggressive. Snakes are entirely defensive. No snake has ever chased a human without cause.

Despite our fascination with snakes in general and pythons in particular, little is known of their behavior in the wild. (They are primarily nocturnal.) Not surprisingly, there is no Jane Goodall of the serpents. Well, maybe it is surprising that snakes have not yet found a field biologist willing to live among them, because, in fact, there seems no good reason why snakes would *not* accept a human in their territory and become habituated, or even tame. I say this because when we were visiting the National Botanical Garden in Vanuatu, there was a ten-foot reticulated python who took a shine to our son Ilan, then eight years old. The feeling was mutual. And for the two hours that we wandered through the garden, this large snake hung around Ilan's neck, examining flowers and trees by stretching his neck parallel to Ilan's head. It turned Ilan into a great aficionado of pythons, and it was he who demanded I write this entry about his favorite snake.

When we think of pythons, we tend to think big. Actually, the thirty-two species of pythons in eight genera come in all sizes. Some weigh just a few ounces, and are only a foot long, whereas others can weigh up to 320 pounds and reach thirty-three feet in length. There are none in the Western Hemisphere, but they are plentiful in Africa, southern Asia, Southeast Asia, Indonesia, the Philippines, and Australia. The three biggest species—reticulated pythons, African pythons, and Indian pythons—have been known to grab and constrict humans. This is extremely rare, but it has happened. In rural Indonesia pythons are greatly feared as human predators, but as far as I know there is no documented case of any actual death there in the last fifty years. That said, twice in the last decade eight- or ten-foot pet pythons, supposedly harmless, have gotten into cribs and suffocated infants.

In America, the world's largest snakes, constrictors, have become popular as pets in the last twenty years, especially among macho teenage boys, who like to walk around the Village in New York City with a large snake draped around their neck like a scarf. Not all snakes tame easily, but both the emerald tree boa and the boa constrictor tame when handled frequently by humans. The largest of all the New World snakes are the magnificent golden brown anacondas (*Eunectes murinus*), who range through Amazonia. They can reach thirty feet and can weigh up to three hundred pounds. They are not great swimmers, but need to live in water to support their great weight. They avoid humans, but will eat crocodiles.

Freud once said: "No one lives in the real world." When it comes to snakes, we live in a world of false beliefs, and have, generally, not knowledge but anti-knowledge, a tissue of lies, fabrications, fantasies, and fears.

RABBITS AND HARES

WHAT'S THE DIFFERENCE between a rabbit and a hare? For most people, there's none, and you hear the word *rabbit* used indiscriminately, whether a true rabbit is being described or a hare. Both rabbits and hares are lagomorphs (gnawing herbivorous mammals having two pairs of incisors in the upper jaw); the only other member of this order is the rodentlike pika. Of course, when the word *rabbit* is used, what most people have in mind is actually the domestic rabbit we keep as pets (or raise for food).

It can get confusing: Both the popular black-tailed jackrabbit (known scientifically as *Lepus californicus*), and the snowshoe rabbit (the only nonvegetarian hare, known scientifically as *L. americanus*) are not rabbits, but hares. The primitive hispid hare from the Indian subcontinent (known scientifically as the *Caprolagus hispidus*), on the other hand, is a rabbit! The domestic rabbit is actually the European rabbit: *Oryctolagus cuniculus*. The wild rabbits of Europe, also called Old World rabbits, are not wild at all; they're feral. Not native to Europe outside the Iberian Peninsula, they were introduced across the rest of Europe by the Romans. They escaped and led lives free from human interference—like feral cats, only more successfully.

Speaking of which, we should bear in mind precisely *why* rabbits deserve their reputation as prodigious breeders. After all, they can have eight litters a year with up to eight in each litter. They are sexually mature as early as three months old, and a rabbit's postpartum estrus allows her to conceive almost at the same instant as she gives birth. For female hares, there is the amazing feat called superfetation—conceiving a second litter *before* the first is born. These animals breed so much to cope with extraordinarily high mortality rates. In other words, if there weren't so many, there wouldn't be any. Despite this adaptational plasticity, twelve species are listed as threatened (critically endangered, endangered, or vulnerable) and six as near threatened, including the tiny pygmy rabbit of the United States and the extremely rare riverine rabbit from South Africa. Even in ideal circumstances, only a minority of hares survive their first year. Studies on the snowshoe hare of North America show they bear twice as many young when numbers are low.

Hares are the perfect example of an animal evolved to avoid predation: They have very long ears, much longer than rabbit ears; their hearts are bigger; their eyes are larger, the better to detect predators; and their legs are longer, the better to outrun predators. They also have extremely sensitive noses. Few animals in the world can outrun a jackrabbit in an open field, who races along at fifty miles an hour with single bounds of twenty feet, the fastest small mammal on the planet, almost twice as fast as a rabbit and almost three times as fast as a fox! For a wonderful depiction of one, see Albrecht Dürer's 1502 work *The Hare*, one of the first realistic paintings of an animal in the wild.

Unlike rabbits, hares are not gregarious, they don't build warrens, and—most important of all—they are extremely precocial: When leverets are born, in an open field, they have fur, their eyes are open, and they are more or less ready to flee from a predator. Rabbit kittens, on the other hand, are altricial, like humans. Born with no fur, their eyes closed, barely able to move, they are hidden underground. Does nurse them with a highly nutritious milk for just one brief period (less than five minutes) once every twenty-four hours (or even less) for the next twenty-three days. I presume that this arrangement is done to minimize the chances of the highly vulnerable nestlings being found by a predator.

If they are in nursery nests in tunnels, the doe carefully seals the entrance after each nursing visit. Each leveret, on the other hand, goes to a separate hiding place three days after birth. They regroup at sunset in the spot where they were born, and await their mother. She arrives about forty-five minutes later, when she determines that it is safe, and nurses them briefly. After four or five weeks, she ceases to return and they begin eating vegetation. Males, as far as I know, have almost no function in raising the young, except that, oddly enough, bucks have been known to intervene when a doe is too harsh to her young. The bucks, however, often accompany the does before they give birth, almost certainly to guard against other males mating with her. Hares are a far wilder animal, which is why there are no domesticated hares. They will not breed in captivity, whereas of course rabbits do so readily, much to their own detriment.

Wild rabbits were first controlled in what are called leporaria, rabbit gardens. French monks about a thousand years ago believed, falsely of course, that newborn baby rabbits were aquatic, and so could be eaten during Lent when eating meat was not allowed! The monks might have learned this from the Romans, who also greatly enjoyed eating newborn rabbits. The Romans were just as happy to eat hares, also kept by them in leporaria (along with captive snails and dormice), but the two species never warmed up to each other, to the benefit of the hare. Rabbits were not introduced into England until the thirteenth century.

I believe one of the reasons it has been easy to domesticate wild rabbits is that they are such sociable animals in the wild. Hundreds can live together in enormous warrens, with up to sixty different entrances. We can only guess at how profoundly lonely they must feel confined to a cage when they are raised for research. It is almost as if they are appreciative when let out to live with a family, for they often make wonderfully attractive "pets."

Stories Rabbits Tell: A Natural and Cultural History, the best book about rabbits, points out that they even have a sense of humor. They like to get away with something they know is forbidden, and as they skip away "their actions look much like a full-body laugh." They can also be feisty, and are sometimes in a bad mood for no known reason. In such cases rabbits tend to thump their hind feet, something that in the wild would have alerted nestlings underground that there was trouble aboveground. I never heard rabbits I lived with make any sound other than this, although wild rabbits have alarm calls, and anyone who has had the misfortune to be present at the slaughter of a rabbit knows that they make a dreadful, horrifying, and unforgettable scream. White cottontail rabbits have an unusual means of communicating to other cottontails: When running from a predator, the white tail-flag serves as a signal that trouble is abroad.

I love what the House Rabbit Society has to say about the importance of introducing a friend to your solitary rabbit, so I thought I should reproduce it here: "The solitude of an empty apartment would be unnatural even for the wild animals whom we label as solitary. As she goes about her daily business, even a solitary animal like an orangutan is surrounded by other living creatures." Rabbits were never meant to live in solitude. This sentence is a good and important point for anyone who wants to leave *any* animal alone all day.

RATITE BIRDS

A MONG THE MALE BIRDS who take most responsibility for sitting on nests (brooding) are ostriches, rheas, cassowaries, and emus—the ratite birds found in South America, Australia, and Africa. Many people think of ostriches as being from Australia, but they are an introduced bird there, raised only on farms. The wild ostrich, *Struthio camelus*, is now found only in Africa.

These are huge, flightless, two-toed terrestrial birds with long necks and powerful legs. They are the largest living birds as well as the heaviest. At six feet tall, they can weigh up to 285 pounds. Each foot is armed with a formidable, sturdy, four-inch-long flattened claw on the thick inner toe, making the birds strong enough to kill a lion. Given their stride of eight feet, it is unsurprising that they are an extraordinarily fast runner. Both male and female ostriches sprint up to forty-five miles per hour. Their huge eyes (the better to see enemies) are the largest of any terrestrial vertebrate.

Ostriches can live for forty or more years in the wild. When cor-
nered, or when incubating, the ostrich tries to escape detection by remaining immobile, with his body, neck, and head flattened out on the
ground. No doubt this gave rise to the popular (but mistaken) notion
that an alarmed ostrich buries his head in the sand. At night they roost
in communal sites. Eyes closed, they sleep with their necks raised most
of the night. For the deeper kind of sleep, done only for short intervals,
they rest their heads and necks stretched out on the ground in front of
them. The male ostrich is one of three birds to have a penis. (Ducks and
geese are the other two.) Ostriches are so well suited to their arid environment that they do not even require drinking water.

Their giant eggs, more than three pounds each, are laid in a communal nest by several females, including what is known as a major hen and
several secondary females, or minor hens. (Sometimes they alternate,
though the designation has nothing to do with dominance.) The major
hen and the dominant male share the task of incubation and care of the
young. The minor hens mate with several males and lay their eggs in different nests, but do not usually incubate. Before hatching, ostrich chicks
make a melodious contact call, which is answered by both parents. The
reasons for communal guarding and communal nesting are not well understood. If ostriches are simply unselfish parents, less concerned with
enhancing their own reproductive success than with taking care of children, how can this be reconciled with Darwinian theory?

South America's rheas, *Rhea americana*, are closely related to the ostrich. The male leads the female to a nest that he has previously prepared. He does this with several females. One after another, they lay
their eggs in the hollow, returning every two or three days to deposit
more eggs. The male alone incubates and rears the chicks. The chicks
hatch synchronously, in a period of twenty-four to twenty-eight hours.
After a few days the male leads them away and then stays with them,
constantly calling them with plaintive contact whistles. In danger,
when it is too hot, or at night, the chicks hide under his wing. Lost
chicks are liable to be adopted by another male. This can lead to a dis-
parity in ages among the members of a crèche. The father cares for them

for six months, but the chicks stay together until they attain sexual maturity at two to three years of age. They are easily tamed. In the south of Chile I saw great bands of them and was able to approach them and stroke their long, elegant necks.

In the same family are the cassowaries, closely related to the emu, found in New Guinea and Irian Jaya. They have a curious structure on top of their heads: a casque, a tough, elastic, foamlike substance. Wattles hanging from the birds' necks, unfeathered and brightly colored in different shades of gaudy colors—red, blue, purple, yellow, and white—are thought to act as a social sign of emotion in the dark rain forest. The bare parts of the neck change colors with the birds' moods, according to whether they are joyful or angry. Displaying a trait unusual among birds, the females are more brightly colored than the males. Only the male guards and incubates the eggs, but unlike the rhea and the emu, the male mates with a single female, who lays three to five eggs in a clutch. Because these birds are extremely difficult to observe, little is known about them. They eat the fruit of at least seventy-five different varieties of fruit trees. The male prepares the nest, which is so well disguised that only a few have ever been found. So hard are these birds to breed in captivity that huge sums have been offered for a clutch. The chicks walk and feed by themselves just a few hours after hatching. The father stays with them for nine months, protecting them primarily from their greatest enemy: feral pigs. To the Kalam tribe of New Guinea's Upper Karonk Valley, cassowaries are reincarnations of their female ancestors. It is forbidden to hunt or trade them or to keep them in captivity.

The emu, *Dromaius novaehollandiae*, is restricted to mainland Australia. It is a huge, inquisitive bird who will follow humans merely to see what they are up to. The emu is the only bird, I believe, who purrs during copulation. The male builds the nest, but as with the cassowary, it is so well camouflaged that only rarely has anyone observed an incubating bird. The male and female stay together for at least five months before incubation begins. The male guards and incubates the eggs. Incubation lasts eight weeks; during that time the male does not eat, drink, or defecate, only getting up several times each day to turn the eggs and tidy the nest. After forty-six days the chicks are born, a maximum of four days apart. The chicks are able to walk after five to twenty-four hours. In a week they are competent swimmers and runners. Despite this fast maturation, the father stays with the chicks at least five months longer. The fully grown adult emu has no enemies other than humans, but dingoes, foxes, and birds of prey take the chicks. A male allows chicks from other broods to join his group as long as they are smaller than his own offspring. Although the bond loosens, a male may stay with the chicks for up to eighteen months.

In 1932 the Australian government, under pressure from farmers, sent an army artillery unit to western Australia to exterminate twenty thousand emus who were causing extensive crop damage. Soldiers drove the birds along fences until they were within the range of machine guns and grenades. As soon as they were shot at, the emus rapidly dispersed into small groups. After months of fruitless pursuit, the Royal Australian Artillery had killed only twelve emus and had to withdraw in humiliation.

Unbeknownst to the soldiers, male emus sometimes co-parent: Two males may attend one nest at the same time, incubating all the eggs together. The two fathers then cooperate in raising their chicks together, calling to them with purr-growls and jointly defending them from predators. According to Bruce Bagemihl, emu co-parenting probably occurs in about 3 percent of all nests. Would not those soldiers have been better off studying the parenting habits of these interesting animals instead of trying to exterminate them?

A S A YOUNG FULBRIGHT SCHOLAR studying Sanskrit in India, I lived in Calcutta. My friends tended to be rather orthodox Hindu religious types, who were fascinated by my interest in spoken Sanskrit. One of the first places they took me was Curzon Park, in the heart of this enormous metropolis, where to my astonishment we saw a large enclosure with a small fence no taller than a foot high. Inside, thousands of wild rats ran free in tunnels and mazes they had built for themselves in the earth. They could easily escape, but did not seem interested. I was with a young painter from New York, who was horrified. "Rats!" she screamed, as if warning us away. But many there had come deliberately to feed the rodents. It was the thing to do on a Sunday: "Let's go to the rat park and watch the rats." I was intrigued. Westerners may be said to have an "instinctive" horror of rats. Hindus do not. So do Hindus and Westerners have different instincts, or have we been taught different things?

Since I was a Sanskritist, I knew that the "vehicle" (the mount) of the great elephant-headed lord Ganesha (also called Ganapati), the symbol of prosperity and the god Hindus turn to when they want an obstacle removed, was none other than a rat called Mooshika (the hoarder). As a result of this strange symbiosis between an elephant and a rat, Hindus all over India loved rats.

The rat is considered enormously wise, because of a lovely story: Ganesha, the son of Lord Shiva, was in a race to circle the globe. He won easily because Mooshika advised him to simply walk around his father and mother, and that way he circumnavigated the entire world, for they were the world to him! There is a temple, Deshnok, where rats are revered and even worshipped. If you Google this temple on the Internet, you will be led to a sophisticated website with amazing photos and a fine text about it and its rats—including the fact that they are a super-colony of some twenty thousand animals who manage never to fight among themselves (though they will not permit other rats from outside to join the colony). I also recommend www.ratshaverights.org, especially for a fine article by Françoise Cooperman called "The Sacred Rat of India."

In Bombay I rented a room and complained one day to the landlord that there was a strange noise under the bed. "No problem, it's only the rat. Look under, you will see him in his nest." Sure enough, there was a giant rat, the size of a small dog, settled into a comfortable-looking nest. My landlord considered his having chosen to live there a sign of good luck and expected me to feel the same. Actually, I did. We never became friends, though. I never quite got used to his scurrying over my body in the middle of the night, and he probably didn't appreciate my snoring.

Contrast this with England during the 1800s, where a common Sunday sport was to amble over to the local park to watch the "ratting," where dogs were put into pits filled with rats to see how many of the terrified rodents they could kill in a short time. The abusive terms for rats are endless—starting with "he's a rat," which we might hear once every day, but also "to smell a rat," "to rat on somebody," "a dirty rat," and to "look like a drowned rat." When we fail miserably we simply say, like Charlie Brown, "Rats!"

You couldn't read about rats at any time in history, except the present, without encountering the universal adjective *odious* appended to them. The reason could be the notion that rats carried the plague in the

Middle Ages. Beginning in the fourteenth century, the Black Death killed some twenty-five million people in Europe, a fourth of the population. The population of course blamed the Jews, who were tortured and killed, not suspecting the flea but wondering about the rat. Only at the end of the nineteenth century did a Japanese scientist solve the mystery of how the Oriental rat flea carried the deadly *Pasteurella pestis*. The rats were immune to the bacillus, but when humans, suspecting the rat might be the cause of the deadly illness, began killing them in large numbers, the voracious fleas sought out humans instead.

I had rats as pets as a child, and had no fear of them. They learned their name and came to it. They were affectionate, clean, friendly, and curious animals. I loved hearing them grind their teeth because I learned that this is how they expressed contentment. I didn't realize then they make the same sound when frustrated, and that is exactly how they may have felt confined to a six-year-old's tight fist. I knew they were intelligent, in fact, considered the most intelligent of all the seventeen hundred species of rodents (with the possible exception of the squirrel).

On the other hand, if we are to believe Konrad Lorenz (and few do not) in his book *On Aggression*, rats are the only other mammal (besides humans, naturally) who kill members of their own species. He painted a terrifying picture of pure aggression, talking about the "satanic cry" they use against strange rats, how they "slowly tear it to pieces," and the "constant warfare" in neighboring families of rats. For Lorenz, rats were one of the few animals capable of pure group hate. One must always be alert for political bias, even in the work of a Nobel laureate like Lorenz, for more recent research has shown that rats placed for the second time in a strange colony will instantly emit an ultrasonic sign of submission, which is then honored by the resident rats. Moreover, what is valid for rats in crowded, artificial conditions is usually atypical. Lorenz's observations were made in laboratories, not under natural conditions, where such aggression is rare. Other research in laboratories showed that rats are notoriously altruistic, willing to press a lever to stop the torture of another rat rather than the lever that would provide them with food.

Jerzy Kosiński was undoubtedly under the influence of Lorenz when he wrote in *The Painted Bird* of how rats devour humans with relish, re-peating a tenth-century German legend of how Bishop Hatto was locked in the Mouse Tower in Bingen and eaten by hungry rats. Orwell, too, in 1984, repeats these negative fantasies. Fortunately, the English have the enchanting *Wind in the Willows* with Water Rat and Sea Rat to make amends.

I admire mothers who raise their babies communally, and this is what female rats do with their pups, even nursing the pups of other mothers. Food is readily shared among all members of the colony, and pups can remove food from a hungry adult without fear of retaliation. Moreover, rats are remarkably tolerant of any relation. Fathers are gentle with pups, and grandparents are tolerated, even fed when they can no longer look after themselves. In short, rats seem to be the ideal society! I like, too, the fact that rats somehow convey to other rats that certain foods are to be shunned, as they are harmful to the health of rats in general. How this is done remains to be discovered. This information can be transmitted from generation to generation. But since this "fact" comes from Lorenz, perhaps I should be as skeptical of what pleases me as I am of what displeases me!

RAVEN

Corvus corax

All the actions of this somber bird, all the circumstances of its flight, and all the different intonations of its discordant voice, of which no less than sixty-four were remarked, had each of them an appropriate significance; and there were never wanting imposters to procure this pretended intelligence, nor people simple enough to credit it.
— AMERICAN ORNITHOLOGIST THOMAS NUTTALL, 1903

THERE ARE FORTY-TWO SPECIES in the crow family (Corvidae), which includes ravens, jays, magpies, and rooks, found in all parts of the world from the Arctic (where they withstand temperatures of minus eighty degrees Fahrenheit) to the tropics, except, for unknown reasons, South America and New Zealand. The raven is the largest of the songbirds, and the largest all-black bird in the world.

Often a person's attitudes toward animals reveal more about the person than they do about the animal. This is especially true when we decide that an animal is bad luck or represents some feared part of the world or of mythology. Consider the "grim, ungainly, ghastly, gaunt, and ominous" raven in Edgar Allan Poe's poem of that name. The bird is presumed to have come from hell, and in many cultures the raven is regarded as "the messenger of death." In Europe it's even worse: They are birds of ill omen, ominous birds, and the devil's henchmen. Indeed, because of their coloration ravens and crows are often associated with black ideas. In England, were the ravens in the Tower of London to leave it would portend bad luck for the entire kingdom, and so even today their wings are clipped to prevent any test of the belief.

But, remarkably, our views about ravens have undergone a transformation. If you mention ravens today, you are more likely to hear something like "Aren't they the geniuses of the bird world?" than a superstition. Credit for this might be given to Bernd Heinrich, professor of biology at the University of Vermont. He has written passionately and with great empathy about many animals, notably two popular books about ravens, animals with whom he has lived in great intimacy.

Heinrich believes ravens might in fact be "wolf-birds"—that is, that they evolved with wolves in a kind of mutualism that is millions of years old. This would explain why they seek out their company and seem to be uncomfortable during certain times when wolves are not around (to afford them protection from predators that would be afraid of the wolves?). Heinrich takes this "mutualism" a step further, and wonders if it is also possible that ravens have a similar relationship to humans, or at least did in the past when we were primarily hunter-gatherers. The ravens he raised "know" him; he is their wolf. Of course, this human–raven relationship could have arisen as a more certain means of the bird scavenging food from a superior hunter. But over time it evolved into something slightly different, at least for the birds. They would seek us out, or would seek wolves out, when they were no longer hungry, simply for the pleasure of our company. It could also be, suggests biologist Lawrence Kilham, that "one of the most difficult of all things to endure for a crow, a raven, a wolf, or a human is to feel alone and separated from one's own kind." Could it be that, faute de mieux, humans stand in for other ravens?

This is somewhat different from wild birds who accompany humans in expectation of food. Seagulls are a notorious example of a bird who hangs out seeking a handout. And while pigeons can become tame in their search for food, they do not display this tameness *in the absence of food.*

The ability of ravens to imitate is so advanced that they can imitate the sound of the wind. Why they would do so is unexplained. For some ravens, an imitated sound acts as a designation of that particular bird— the individual's name, in fact. Heinrich gives the example of a bird who loses a mate, and then calls her using her specific call, which might turn out to be a particular dog bark. He speculates that the ability of ravens to mimic human words could be related to calling the name of somebody the raven is attached to. Derek Goodwin noticed that his captive Eurasian jays often barked when a dog ran through the garden and me-owed at the sight of a cat, the way human children do. Do they ever talk to themselves? The American ornithologist Arthur Cleveland Bent thought so: "More than any other bird I know, the raven will converse with himself for hours at a time, a curious gargling, strongly inflected talk." Ravens seem to have more sounds than any other animal except humans. We have not even begun to decipher them or understand their function.

In her lovely book *Crows: Encounters with the Wise Guys*, Candace Savage notes that crows are seemingly capable of acts of kindness to-ward sick or injured birds. One female was deformed and partially blind. A bird who was *not* her mate regularly brought her food while also feeding hungry chicks in his nest. According to Heinrich, ravens do something that no other animal does: When they spot a feast, juveniles (but not paired mates) call other unrelated but unpaired juveniles to share the spoils. In a world where feeding is survival, what are they thinking? Heinrich thinks they are showing off to potential mates and letting them know that they would be a good choice for a partner to rear young. Ingenious.

I will allow the last word to Candace Savage, the last words of her book as well:

We live in a world of wonders. In a universe that is so prodigal in its invention, why should we restrict ourselves to a few dried-out old ideas that clearly cannot do justice to our experience? The possibilities of nature, and of understanding, are not limited by the conventions of positivistic science. By their example, crows, ravens, magpies and jays call us to open our minds to the full possibilities of intelligence—our own as well as theirs.

RED FOX

Vulpes vulpes

PART OF THE PROBLEM WITH FOXES for many humans stems from what's known as surplus killing. Typically, a fox gets into a henhouse and kills *all* the chickens, more than he can possibly eat. Or a fox jumps a fence and kills a flock of geese, making off with just one. Such surplus killings are cited by humans as examples of cruelty, evil, and wastefulness in animals. This is used to justify killing foxes—that is, humans killing animals they have no intention of eating.

Foxes cache food. They may surplus kill even when unable to store the excess, or even when they do not expect their pups to feast on the excess. Why they do so remains a puzzle, but it is anthropomorphism gone amok to claim that this little-understood practice is evidence of *evil*. Apart from the survival value of surplus killing (which may be greater than we recognize), on the emotional side the question is whether some creatures *enjoy* the surplus killing. David Macdonald, author of *Running with the Fox*, says: "I have watched foxes surplus killing. Certainly their postures and expressions were neither aggressive nor frantic. If anything they looked playful, or perhaps merely purposeful." More recently, Macdonald has suggested that surplus killing is widespread among carnivores: "This is somewhat akin to the modern man's tendency to take too much sugar! Whether or not a fox takes pleasure in killing is, of course, unanswerable."

If we are not certain whether foxes enjoy killing, we are less in doubt about humans who kill foxes. Foxhunting, "the unspeakable in full pursuit of the uneatable" as Oscar Wilde so unforgettably put it, entertains about fifty thousand Britons a year. (This is the number who have signed a declaration that they will disobey any ban on foxhunting.) Translate this into the death of at least thirteen thousand foxes and six thousand abandoned cubs who slowly die of starvation each year. What about the fabled English love of animals? Someone once quipped that the English don't really like animals, they just dislike children. (There are also 169 organized mounted foxhunting clubs in North America and about fifty-four thousand registered foxhounds.)

Most relations between foxes and humans have centered on the human coveting the animal's beautiful fur. (I always loved the chant of PETA: "We need our coat, you don't.") Macdonald believes that the trade in furs in general, and foxes in particular, largely determined the European settlement of Canada and Alaska. I had believed this odd love affair with the skin of another animal had been relegated to the moral middle ages of humans, but recently, thanks to an extremely expensive campaign on the part of fur companies, it is undergoing a revival of sorts. I can only hope this is the death rattle before the total demise.

Not only is the wearing of fur entirely unnecessary, not only are foxes killed in extraordinarily high numbers to satisfy a passing fashion whim, but the methods used to kill the fox are remarkably cruel: The first principle is not to damage the fur. Commonly, "two workers hold the animal down, and one clips an electric plate to its lip while the other inserts a probe into the fox's anus. The animal is then electrocuted by a current passed through its body." There can be no excuse for such cruelty to an animal who has captured our imagination for thousands of years.

A fox den can be a thing of beauty: Often a marmot burrow is taken over and modified. Its tunnels can be up to thirty feet long, and lead to a chamber ten feet below the surface, with as many as a hundred entrances! The better to make a wily escape, I suppose. The oldest and largest dens may have been in use for centuries.

Leonard Lee Rue, who observed red foxes in Alaska in 1966, said he witnessed several meetings between male and female foxes that could be described with only one word: *ecstasy*. As the male approached the den with food he was bringing for the pups, the female flopped down on her belly, raised her tail up over her back, and waved it furiously. Then she sprang up and kissed the male all over with her tongue. He'd experience the same wonderful greeting from his pups when he brought them their dinner. Macdonald describes a new father wriggling with eagerness to care for his children: He warbled at the entrance to the den, and if the mother did not respond, he used his nose like a billiard cue to poke the lumps of food through the entrance and into the den. His favorite occupation was to play with the cubs.

Macdonald called this diligent and playful father Smudge. He notes that as the kits grew older, Smudge's ambition was to play with them, something the mother and her sisters did not always allow: "Smudge would skulk in the vegetation, waiting for Big Ears [their maternal aunt] to fall asleep, whereupon he would quietly warble to the cubs who would sneak off to gambol with him. Soon their exuberance led to squeals and snirks that awoke Big Ears who would vigorously reprimand Smudge."

For not entirely clear reasons, we project onto the fox possibly more than any other single animal. Are foxes considered "sexy" merely because they are beautiful, or is there a more sinister motif at work here? In ancient Japanese and Chinese literature a beautiful stranger arrives, seduces a man, marries him, and then slowly consumes his body to prolong her own life. She is not human, but a fox with the ability to shift shape. The Chinese believed that the foxes could survive in this manner for a thousand years.

For some of these anthropomorphic comments, we have observations that seem reliable. For example, when it comes to being mischievous, consider how foxes tease less nimble hyenas by coming close, circling, then sprinting away until the hyena can no longer ignore the foxes and lunges for them. Several cases of hyenas actually catching and killing such a fox have been reported. Why would the fox take the risk? Maybe she is gaining crucial information about the hyena's powers, or lack of them, useful when she later snatches bites from the hyena's kills. Or maybe the fox is accustoming the hyena to her presence, also useful when pillaging kills. But the fox seems to enjoy teasing the hyena.

Foxes live just about everywhere—in fact, on every continent with the exception of Antarctica. They often live quite close to humans, and it is not entirely clear why, though I suppose it is because where humans are there is always surplus food. Some people are enchanted; others want them swiftly eradicated, on the grounds that the foxes pose a danger to their pets. However, no fox ever attacks a dog, and most do not kill cats, either. They will, of course, eat chickens, ducks, and geese. People also do not realize that in summer foxes are primarily vegan, eating blackberries, strawberries, juniper berries, raspberries, plums, grapes, apples, and the hips of the shrub called dog rose. As many as twelve foxes once lived surrounded on three sides by a residential development in the University of Wisconsin Arboretum at Madison. As an official campus guide put it, "It was obvious that these foxes were well-acquainted with pedestrian and vehicular traffic patterns and showed no alarm unless a deviation from the usual routine occurred. These animals regularly used a pedestrian underpass beneath a four-lane highway."

Biologist David Macdonald has said that the first commandment of the red fox is "Thou shalt not share thy food." Nevertheless, he has seen foxes bringing food to other injured adult foxes. One fox, Wide Eyes, was injured by a mowing machine. The next day her sister Big Ears brought food to the spot where Wide Eyes had been injured, uttered the whimper that summons cubs to eat (though Big Ears had no cubs), and left the food on the bloody spot where her sister had lain. Another time a male fox got a thorn in his paw that became infected. The dominant vixen in his group brought him food, and he recovered.

RHINOCEROSES

Diceros bicornis (black rhinoceros)
and *Ceratotherium simum* (white rhinoceros)

A FTER THE TWO SPECIES OF ELEPHANTS, rhinoceroses are the largest mammals on earth. (The plural of *rhinoceros* is *rhinoceroses* or *rhinoceri*, the first being preferred.) Richard Despard Estes says this is "possibly the largest pure grazer that ever lived." And even though brain size has never been demonstrated to bear a one-to-one relationship with intelligence, the fact that the brains of these large mammals are relatively small has led many people to speak of their low intelligence.

How an animal as little studied as the rhinoceros can be evaluated for intelligence remains unexplained. For example, there's been only one published observation of a wild birth. How much, then, do we know about this elusive animal? Even expert biologists fail to agree on something as simple as whether rhinos are by nature more than usually aggressive. *The New Encyclopedia of Mammals* says that "black rhinos have the highest incidence among mammals of fatal intraspecies fight-ing: almost 50 percent of males and 33 percent of females die from wounds." But can we be certain that this is an actual observation, and not an extrapolation from an unusual set of events?

Consider what Jonathan Kingdon explains in his *East African Mam-mals*, about how an intruding black rhino bull displaces a resident male, who then moves into a neighbor's range. The status quo is upset, often because of human interference. Just such "a chain of displacements might have been a factor in the situation reported by the warden of East Tsavo shortly before the 1960–61 drought, when all the rhinos seen in that area were covered in fresh wounds and a number died as a result of fighting." Estes points out that "fights are likeliest to occur in the presence of an es-trous female, *but seem rarely to result in serious injury* ⟦my emphasis⟧."

Moreover, why not point out that direct observation has shown that black rhinos can demonstrate unselfish behavior? Three female rhino cows were seen helping a very pregnant companion walk, actually rub-bing her flanks in affection. Kingdon rightly remarks: "Perhaps preg-nancy elicited maternal or protective responses in the other females but, unusual though it is, this observation serves to show that apparently al-truistic social behaviour is not unknown in black rhinos."

It is generally acknowledged that the white rhino is a remarkably easygoing animal. Estes, for example, says that for the white rhinoceros, "aggression is rare and mild except on the part of territorial males," and that even an aggressive dominant male will respond to another male loudly suing for peace—or, as he puts it, "screaming for mercy." In one three-year study, only two serious fights were observed. And in each case, the defeated bull remained on the property, simply changing to the status of satellite male.

From comments made in 1927 by a naturalist who visited Uganda, it would seem that humans could walk right up to rhinos, who showed ab-solutely no aggression, only curiosity. Of course, hunters then took ad-vantage of this docility to slaughter the trusting animals in huge numbers.

The curse for all rhinos is having horns worth their weight in gold (made of keratin, the major protein in nails and hair). In Yemen on the southwestern tip of the Arabian Peninsula, rich nobles give their adolescent boys a traditional ceremonial dagger known as the jambiya. It is a mark of status for the handles of these daggers to be made of rhino horn, which becomes almost translucent and very beautiful as it ages. They were fairly rare prior to the 1960s, but as oil wealth increased in the 1960s and 1970s, the demand for rhino horn increased in proportion. Since 1970 horn from as many as 22,350 rhinos may have been imported into Yemen. They've been illegally smuggled since 1982, when they were banned—which meant that the price simply increased. I think it is wonderful that the Grand Mufti in Yemen issued a fatwa stating that the killing of rhinoceroses to make dagger handles was against the will of Islam, though it is not clear how effective this has been.

Few researchers have had any up-close-and-personal direct experience with rhinos. Anna Merz, while no scientist, did. Her evidence is not cited by scientists, but should be. As Desmond Morris says in his foreword to her book: "Nobody in the world knows these amazing animals as she does." In 1985 a calf she called Samia was abandoned for unknown reasons by her mother, and Anna took on the task of raising her in her house—even in her bed, since for the first weeks she was constantly cold! Her book *Rhino* recounts the remarkable experience of looking after a young rhino until she became an adult. Her remarks deserve serious consideration, for they are more or less unique in giving us a detailed account of the daily life of a young rhino.

It is especially important to pay attention when she goes against conventional "rhino wisdom": "The longer I live with these rhinos, the more I realize that aggression and bad temper are not normal aspects of their behaviour, and that being nervous and highly strung are." Merz is particularly good at attempting to understand the many sounds rhinos make, and in particular the intricacies of "breathing communication." "When she breathes heavily she is not out of breath but is telling me something." When she met an older rhino, "she pranced up and down the fence and told me a very long story." There is a remarkable photo of

Merz planting a kiss on the mouth of a happy-looking young rhino, which alone is worth the price of the whole book. It is captioned: "Samia's gentleness and affection belie rhinos' reputation for ferocity." I can't see anyone looking at this photo and begging to differ. As with Elsa, the lioness raised and returned to the wild, Samia went back into the ten thousand acres of the sanctuary, but returned periodically to see her human friend. Merz concludes: "Her intelligence, her ability to work out problems that have nothing whatsoever to do with instinctive behaviour, her sense of fun which goes beyond mere playfulness, and her extreme sensitivity to my moods, have all combined to make me deeply aware of what a remarkable animal the rhino is and how horribly maligned it has been by humans."

SEA HORSES

Hippocampus spp.

They are the only fishes I know that hold your hand.
—A. C. J. VINCENT

W E KNOW SO LITTLE ABOUT SEA HORSES—teleosts or "bony" fish—that even the total number of sea horse species is uncertain. Nonetheless, their appearance appeals to just about everyone, and always has. Their heads look like those of a horse; their tails are like monkeys. They have a pouch like a kangaroo, and their eyes move independently like those of a chameleon. And like that animal, sea horses change colors in a matter of minutes to better camouflage themselves against seaweed. They also have small fins that emerge from slits in their bony armor. The ancient Greeks thought of them as *hippocampi*, horselike sea monsters, hence the name of the single genus to which all sea horses belong: *Hippocampus*.

There are thirty-four kinds of sea horses presently known (more on the way), ranging from the pygmy sea horse, the size of your baby finger-nail, which lives in the oceans near Indonesia and the Philippines, to the fourteen-inch giants of the eastern Pacific. When it comes to being a good father, no animal rivals the sea horse dad, for it is the male who becomes pregnant. Sea horse expert Amanda Vincent was able to show that male and female sea horses of an Australian species (*Hippocampus whitei*) are sexually faithful to each other in ways unexpected for a fish. In the morn-ing they greet each other with an elaborate dance. Both the male and the female sea horse change colors, from dull to bright orange, as they dance, often clinging with their tails to the stalks of waving sea grass that serve as their dens. One possible explanation for this behavior is that it may help the female determine when the male is ready to become pregnant.

The male sea horse has a small pouch on his tail. When the female de-cides that her eggs are ready and she likes the look of her partner (a healthy, normal male sea horse), she presses her belly against her part-ner, inserts what looks like a penis, an ovipositor, into the brood pouch on his abdomen, and off-loads her eggs into it. Here is Amanda Vin-cent's description:

> As they ascend, the seahorses face each other with their tails bent back, and the female inserts her ovipositor into the open pouch of the male and releases her eggs in a long, sticky string. To transfer the whole clutch—which depending on the size of the species, ranges from tens to many hundreds of eggs—takes only about six seconds, and then the pouch opening is sealed shut. The pair breaks apart, and the male gently sways to settle the eggs in his pouch. Both then settle down on the bottom with their tails wrapped around holdfasts. Each time I watch, I am newly aston-ished at the beauty and uniqueness of this graceful courtship and mating.

The female leaves, and the father sea horse takes over. Over the next few weeks he carefully controls conditions in it, providing oxygen and nutrients as needed (though this may be something he accomplishes au-

tomatically). He even secretes prolactin, the same hormone that stimulates milk production in human women. He is definitely pregnant by
any definition of that term.

The sea horse gives birth to a few dozen to a few hundred young, although one hero, James from the Caribbean, gave birth in his pouch—
only half a tablespoon in volume—to 1,572 babies! After several weeks,
they emerged one after another—in little explosive charges from the
male tail—as fully formed, independent tiny sea foals. Once they're out
of the pouch, the male has done his work, for he is already pregnant the
same day, and now concerned with the next batch. He has been a good
enough father, and in any event his children are already in the plankton,
drifting miles away. As for the mother, her duties ended when she
handed over her eggs.

About twenty million sea horses are traded every year. They are
used in traditional medicine, often for sexual disorders, such as impo-
tence. In her attempt to be fair to traditional medicine, Amanda Vincent, the world's authority on this animal, writes that sea horses "are
used by Asian communities to treat a range of ailments, some of them
potentially life-threatening." I'm skeptical. I know of no medical evidence that sea horses cure such conditions. But Vincent writes me that,
although "thus far we lack the studies to test these claims, traditional
Chinese medicine is trusted by one quarter of the world's population
and has been documented for two thousand years." For her, the challenge is "to make sure that such use is not harming wild populations of
seahorses." And traditional Chinese medicine communities are proving
to be her allies.

Vincent and I do not entirely agree on the question of "using" and
"sacrificing" sea horses for human purposes. She has asked me to read
the statement on her website (www.projectseahorse.org) on these matters, and I urge readers to do likewise. As a sample, here is the position
on traditional medicine from the site:

Project Seahorse accepts the sustainable use of marine species in
traditional medicine but urges caution where there is conservation

concern. We recognize that some syngnathids (seahorses, pipe-fishes, and pipehorses) are an important component of health treat-ments in numerous countries and that their trade provides income for many fishers, traders and merchants. We also understand that the World Health Organization considers traditional medicine to be a valid form of health care. Project Seahorse therefore concen-trates its efforts on ensuring the sustainability of marine resource use, for traditional medicine as for other forms of consumption. At present, the designation of many seahorse species and some pipe-fish species as Endangered or Vulnerable on the IUCN Red List argues that consumption should be adjusted to reduce pressure on wild populations.

Several hundred thousand sea horses are exported to North America (usually from Indonesia and the Philippines) each year for home and public aquaria. They make poor pets for most people, needing live food and being prone to many diseases. As far as I know, few captive-born young survive to adulthood, and even fewer reproduce. Even for public aquaria that engage in research into sea horse biology, there is the larger question of how they acquire their animals. How many die en route? How can even the most vigilant aquarium be certain that the animals they buy have been "ethically" harvested—or indeed, if there can even be such a thing? Another several hundred thousand a year are killed as souvenirs, key rings, or earrings. I see no justification for this use.

As Vincent has pointed out, sea horses are vulnerable for many rea-sons: Because of the lengthy parental care involved, they cannot give birth to as many young as most fish can. And when a wild sea horse is caught, the male brings with him his babies, all of whom die. When the male is caught, the female often refuses to mate with another sea horse for some time, and the population can become seriously depleted. At present, sea horse fishing is fully legal and unregulated. The main preda-tors of sea horses are humans; when fish who can live up to five years are taken from their natural home, replacement can be difficult or even nonexistent.

What is it that makes some creatures appear to us adorable and others leave us cold? Who would not succumb to the first sight of a sea horse, with her little coronet on the top of her head (nearly as distinctive as a human thumbprint)? Their appearance fascinates and enchants us, resembling as they do creatures of our fantasy, rather than the fish in the ocean that they are. And when we learn of the heroic feats of the male, well, we are hopelessly hooked.

SHEEP

W HEN WE THINK ABOUT SHEEP, the adjectives that come to
mind have to do with a certain placidity and lack of agility.
In fact, *wild* sheep are "possessed of tremendous speed and
leaping ability, [and unlike goats] they don't have to rely on scaling
rock walls to escape a predator; they can outrun it in elegant bounds."
Domestic sheep may have lost the ability to run that fast, but some ancestral memory survives: Sheep always run uphill if they sense danger.
This is doubtless because in their past incarnation as wild animals, that
was their only way to escape a predator. Atavistic memories linger:
While lambs may occasionally be born during the day, most are born
during the night, even in modern domestic breeds. This allows them to
gain strength before daylight, which would have been of survival value
in the wild.

A common misperception is that sheep lack intelligence. Fortunately,
the pointless human activity of constantly measuring other people's or
other animals' intelligence is beginning to give way to the more sensible
view that every animal is as intelligent as it needs to be to survive in its
world. Keith Kendrick from England's Babraham Institute has shown

that sheep process facial images similarly to humans, and that, contrary
to earlier scientific understanding, "they are capable of some level of
consciousness."

As the most populous, widely distributed domestic ruminants, sheep
are one of the most heavily exploited of all domestic animals. They extend from the Arctic Circle to the southernmost tip of South America.
Sheep and goats were first domesticated in western Asia during the
eighth and seventh millennia BCE. From the beginning, they were and
are mercilessly exploited. In Russia and in some Eastern European and
Middle Eastern countries, sheep produce milk as well as wool, and are
slaughtered for their skins and for meat. In Tibet and other parts of the
Himalaya Mountains, sheep produce all these commodities and also
serve as pack animals. Additionally, their dung is used for fuel, their
guts as sewing thread, and their horns as needles and as trumpets.

A young lamb will imprint on a human if he encounters one within
hours of being born. A woman coming across an abandoned young lamb
in ancient times might well have nursed or otherwise cared for the helpless small animal. Sheep are said to be animals "predestined" for domestication. All mountain breeds tend to stay in one place, for example, a
trait called hefting. This instinct acts a bit like imprinting, except that
instead of being imprinted on a person, a sheep becomes attached to the
place of birth. Mountain sheep graze within a few hundred yards of
their birthplace all their lives. This is the reason mountain farms are
sold with their native flock. It also allows the shepherd to find where
any particular sheep is likely to be grazing. The ease with which sheep
can be handled and their obvious vulnerability has not produced compassion on the part of humans, but disdain and an eagerness to exploit
them.

Sheep have always been more responsive to other animals than to humans, sheepherding dogs being the most obvious example. The dogs
achieve their results through fear. The sheep respond to the dog, either
to his barking or to his eye, because they look upon dogs as their natural
predators (which they are). A good dog, of course, never hurts the
sheep; his aggression is under control, but it is nonetheless real. Sheep-

guarding dogs, on the other hand, go about their work because they love sheep, or at least have affection for them. Whether the dogs think they are sheep (which is what those who train them believe, since they raise them as puppies in the presence of sheep), or whether they only behave this way out of a desire to please their human companions cannot be definitively answered. I suspect the latter.

Sheep also respond to other sheep who have been especially trained by the shepherd to lead the flock. There is a practice in contemporary slaughterhouses of using a tame sheep to entice the others to come in. In a rare instance of human candor, this animal is called the Judas lamb in recognition of the treachery that she engages in, though it is unlikely that she is aware of her true function. A seventeenth-century medallion by Julius Wilhelm Zincgreff shows a flock of sheep leaping from a bridge to cross a river, led by a tame ram with a bell around his neck. Italian sheepherders in the Abruzzi in central Italy used what they called a *guidarello*, a castrated ram, to herd the sheep. He responded to commands of the shepherd from the time he was small. The shepherd would use his body as his pillow, thereby increasing their bond.

Domestication has led to many physical changes in sheep. Compared with their wild forebears, domesticated sheep have smaller hearts and smaller eye sockets, and their brains are 20 to 25 percent smaller, too. The bodies and horns of domesticated sheep are smaller. The tendency to molt has disappeared, and most are now white. Wild sheep are white only on their bellies, and a dull brown everywhere else. There is much that we don't understand about sheep, such as the strange—and still unexplained—fact that white sheep, like white pigs, suffer from or even die from eating buckwheat, whereas black or dark-wooled individuals are not in the least affected, a fact that intrigued Charles Darwin. It's possible they have lost some of their immunity to lungworms, tapeworms, and intestinal parasites—the bane of sheep farmers today. The major diseases tormenting sheep today have been introduced by domestication. In the wild, sheep would be at least partly immune and therefore lead healthier lives *without* drugs or other medical intervention.

Sheep have facial expressions that we find hard to read and seem to

ALTRUISTIC ARMADILLOS, ZENLIKE ZEBRAS

bear pain with so much fortitude that we think they are not like us. Somewhere, of course, we must understand how deeply vulnerable they are, or we would not have the expression *Agnus Dei*, the Lamb of God, to describe Jesus Christ. Surely one of the reasons we use this expression is that we recognize the innocence of the animal, how a lamb poses no threat to anyone. Yet is killed.

We think of lambs as innocent, but we think of sheep as passive and ignorant. How stupid can a sheep be, though, when "sheep and goats can distinguish between different strains of the same plant species so similar that a botanist might find the same task difficult"? Some scientists believe that sheep show what has been called "nutritional wisdom." Given a free choice of foods deficient in certain minerals, the sheep select and balance their diet, correcting for any deficiency.

It will come as a surprise to my readers, as it did to me, that leadership in a flock of sheep does not go automatically to the strong, large male, but on the contrary, belongs to an older, smaller, even frail female. This was a point made long ago by the great animal behaviorist J. P. Scott: "Leadership of the flock went to an elderly ewe, inferior in strength and fighting ability to almost any ram, and often inferior to the young ewes. The position was achieved mainly by the care and feeding of her descendants without, as far as the observer can tell, any instance of violence toward her offspring." Not a bad model for humans as well as sheep!

STICK INSECTS

Family Phasmatidae

THE STICK AND LEAF INSECTS are probably the most successful of all camouflaging insects. I would have preferred to give this entry its correct title, phasmids, the lovely word for "ghosts," a name given to these animals because they are so well adapted to their environment that they cannot be seen at all. (In America, they are called walking sticks.)

There are twenty-one species of stick insects in New Zealand, and twenty-five hundred worldwide. I see them every day because my son Manu brings them to me. He loves them. I can see why. They don't run away from him. Completely lacking in aggression, they don't threaten him in any way. Wonderful to look at, they resemble a stick, not an insect. A short while ago Manu brought me two: one riding the other's back. They were mating. The little trip they took with my son did them no harm: The male can stay with the female for up to two weeks—probably to ensure sexual fidelity—both eating between bouts of intercourse. Phasmids usually do not live longer than a year, and I have seen it claimed that some males ride a female their entire life to prevent rivals from getting to her.

A male and female mating was a fairly rare sighting because most stick insects are parthenogenetic—they reproduce without males. The females who lay eggs in this way give birth to only female insects. There are some species of stick insects where no males have ever been found and may not even exist, although some biologists believe that sooner or later the all-female progeny become gradually smaller and smaller and weaker and weaker. But this is so far only a (male) theory. There's a whole field of scientific research devoted to phasmids. Writes one of its leaders, J. T. Salmon: "In all my collecting through the country over many years, I have never found a male specimen of *Acanthoxyla*. I have concluded, therefore, that males do not exist in this genus of Phasmids, and that they must breed continuously by parthenogenesis."

The eggs the female produces fascinate me: Up close, some look like miniature sculptures, like small Egyptian scarabs. The ones I saw were just a bit larger than a grain of rice. They were beautiful, with a little cap on the top. The seed-shaped eggs have a hard shell. These tiny eggs will be dropped by the female onto the ground and can lie there for a year or more until they eventually hatch, although normally live babies emerge in about six months' time. Certain species of ants carry the eggs into their nests and eat off the cap (known as the operculum), but leave the larvae inside alone. The nymphs develop, and when they emerge, little perfect miniature adults, they find their way unharmed out of the ant nest. It appears to be a form of evolved mutualism, where one animal helps another in exchange for certain benefits.

The stick insects I have seen in New Zealand are apterous (they lack wings) and either bright green, blending in with the green foliage on our property, or brown, blending in with the tree trunks I find them on. Most of the time they just walk onto my finger when I hold it out. They seem to have no fear of humans. Does it have anything to do with autotomy, their ability to grow back a severed limb? Stick insects have been around for at least two hundred million years. Could it be that because they evolved so long ago, their behavior cues did not include humans? Humans are not natural predators of stick insects. (The only people who "take" stick insects in the wild are people who want to keep them as pets.) My favorite explanation is that phasmids are as curious about us as we are about them.

But sometimes they do not just walk onto my finger, they go completely cataleptic, falling to the ground and lying there as if dead. I pick them up, but they make no movement; nothing stirs. It really looks as if they are dead. They are not, of course, but the ruse has worked even with me, who should know better. Or they sometimes begin a strange dance: They keep their backside still, and weave their heads and trunk back and forth as if trying to hypnotize me. If there are several stick insects present, they all do it at the same time. Are they "talking" to one another, trying to distract me, or telling me something? I cannot tell, and as far as I know no entomologist has deciphered this odd behavior. Evidently they engage in this dance just before sunset. Researchers who study phasmids have observed this behavior all over the world. It appears to be some sort of alarm reaction. It is also possible that they are simply moving up one notch in their attempt to present the perfect camouflage: Since they keep their forelegs stretched in front of their heads, close together, and their other two pairs of legs close along the body, they appear even more twiglike, and the movement suggests a light breeze moving thin branches of a tree.

They can look like twigs, or bark, or lichen, or moss, or even leaves, going so far in their artistry as to contain veins and mildew spots just like the leaf they are imitating. It is a myth, though, that stick insects can change colors like chameleons, but scientist Richard Sharell discovered that phasmids, when sitting on manuka (tea trees) infected by blight, look as if they, too, had been stricken with the disease; that is, they turned dark gray with black spots. Have they contracted the fungus, or are they able, after generations, to take on the protective coloration of the sick tree? It is true that the insects become darker at night, as part of the diurnal rhythm.

The stick insects I have seen in New Zealand are about the size of a pencil, generally. But the largest stick insect in Australia, the *Clemacantha regale*, is nine inches long and colored green and pale yellow. The bases of its wings are bright red, as are their undersurfaces.

The membranes have a bluish tint that is almost transparent. They look like insect parrots! I have also seen spiny or tuberculated (knobbly) stick insects here. This genus in New Zealand is called *Acanthoxyla* and has eight species, but a male has been found for only one of these, confined to an island off the coast of Northland on the North Island. According to *The Guinness Book of Animal Records*, the longest insect in the world happens to be a stick insect, *Pharmacia kirbyi*, from the rain forests of Borneo. The same source claims that the largest egg laid by any insect belongs to the six-inch Malaysian stick insect *Heteropteryx dilitata*. It measures an immense half an inch in length. Finally, while most stick insects lay a few hundred eggs, females of *Acrophylla titan* lay more than two thousand relatively large eggs!

STURGEONS
Family Acipenseridae

THERE ARE TWENTY-SEVEN VARIETIES of sturgeons, the fish that produce caviar. *Caviar* is simply a name for the roe (fish eggs) produced in the ovaries of the female sturgeon. Three species living in the Caspian Sea produce the most highly prized caviar: beluga, osetra, and sevruga.

Beluga sturgeons (*Huso huso*) can grow to twice as long as a pickup truck, and routinely weigh as much as two thousand pounds. They're the largest freshwater fish on earth. The record holder is a beluga weighing 4,570 pounds and reaching twenty-eight feet. Even the Pacific white sturgeon in California, Washington, and British Columbia waters can weigh up to sixteen hundred pounds. The longer sturgeons live, the heavier they become. Some live as long as 150 years. Like salmon, the sturgeon always returns to the same place to spawn. Most are anadromous—that is, they live in the ocean, but give birth in rivers. It is not unusual for a female to carry ten million eggs, though perhaps only one or at most two will make it to adulthood.

Moreover, the beluga sturgeon is at least 250 million years old. It has existed without any appreciable change since the time of the dinosaurs. (I would prefer to say *he*, but realize how strange that sounds for a fish, at least for now.) It has always been slow moving, passive, and completely nonaggressive—not even fighting to preserve its life when caught.

Once again, human greed has driven an ancient and noble animal to the brink of nonexistence. Consider that caviar sells for as much as two hundred dollars an ounce, or thirty-two hundred dollars a pound, making it a candidate for the most expensive food in the world. "It is more important now than ever for consumers to realize that it is in bad taste to eat the eggs of an endangered species . . . ," says Vikki Spruill, executive director of SeaWeb, one of three U.S.-based groups that form the Caviar Emptor campaign.

In January 2006 the ten countries that dominate wild-caviar production (Azerbaijan, Bulgaria, China, Iran, Kazakhstan, Romania, Russia, Serbia-Montenegro, Turkmenistan, and Ukraine) were slapped with an international ban on exports until they prove their sturgeon fishing is sustainable. It is not. As for aquaculture, I believe that while it may eventually prove "sustainable," from an ethical point of view it's even worse than taking free-living sturgeon from the wild. The quality of a farmed sturgeon's life is miserable, no better than that of cattle raised for slaughter. When they are three years old, a blood test distinguishes males from females. Since they produce no eggs, males are slaughtered, as are females not "good-looking" enough to guarantee good-looking eggs. The point of aquaculture, after all, is purely commercial, and so only economic values are taken into account. "Is this fish happy?" has no place in the thinking of the men in charge of these fish farms. Moreover, a fish that easily lives for a hundred years is killed before ten.

Why are animal rights groups opposed to eating caviar? For the simple reason that the female sturgeon is killed for her eggs. Her belly is slit open, often while she is still alive (the trick is to get the eggs as fresh as possible), and the eggs extracted. As writer Inga Saffron puts it, "processing" caviar requires a "certain cold-blooded resolve: The fish should still be gasping for breath when the knife rips down her leathery belly."

Paul McCartney, the former Beatle, put the matter succinctly when asked how he became a vegetarian:

I was fishing and I caught one. I realized I was killing it as I reeled it in, and I thought, "I'm taking his life—I don't want to do that." So we threw him back. That was the end of fish. We still ate caviar for a while because we thought nobody got hurt; we thought someone "milked" the fish for her eggs. Then we found out that the mother sturgeon gets slit from top to bottom and the eggs fall out.

I cannot agree with Inga Saffron when she ends her excellent book on the history of caviar by praising the "sensation of eggs bursting like fireworks in the mouth" and then lamenting that "if we lose this experience, and the fish that is responsible for it, we are destined to lose a part of ourselves." Perhaps the hardest thing for us to do as a species is to realize that other life-forms do not exist for what they can give us in gustatory sensations or even in aesthetic appreciation, but exist in their own right, and are valuable simply because they exist. They need not provide us with anything to deserve to live, and the time will eventually come when we realize the best we can do is to leave other species alone.

That said, I'm grateful to Saffron for pointing out that young sturgeons have "a frisky cuteness," that they resemble young otters as they splash joyfully in the water, and have some of that enchanting animal's playfulness. All they lack is a human champion.

Belugas (and kalugas) reach sexual maturity between twenty-four and twenty-six years of age. Females spawn only every five years. To do so, they often cover long distances, meeting up with other females at favored spawning grounds. A large female can carry up to four hundred pounds of eggs—caviar to the greedy. After spawning, the various females again go their separate ways. Why they came together in the first place remains a mystery. Henry David Thoreau said that he had never yet met a philosopher who could tell him the difference between a fish and a man. Here's one: fish mind their own business.

TWO SPECIES OF TAPIRS live in South America: *Tapirus terrestris*, who lives in the forests east of the Andes, and the mountain tapir (*T. pinchaque*), who lives high in the Andes. The Central American tapir is *T. bairdi*. There is also an Asian tapir, found in Malaysia, Indonesia, and Myanmar, known as the Malayan tapir (*T. indicus*).

Tapirs are often referred to as "living fossils" because they have retained so many prehistoric features. (It was a tapir bone hurled into the air at the beginning of Stanley Kubrick's *2001: A Space Odyssey*.) They have hardly changed in the last twenty million years. Unfortunately, despite the size of these animals, they are not considered charismatic megafauna, the way elephants or giraffes are, and there is little literature about them. Scientists find them fascinating, and the general public loves to stand in front of their cages in zoos and speculate what kind of animal is inside, but probably less is known about tapirs than just about any other wild animal.

Pronounced *TAY-puhr*, these animals are related to the horse and rhinoceros, though they look more like pigs. They have short, heavy bodies and thick necks. Their noses are drawn out to form movable, short trunks. They live in the depths of the forests and near water, in which they love to swim. They are preyed upon by jaguars, but can escape by submerging with the jaguar on their back, forcing the predator to swim away. They can walk on the bottom of ponds or rivers. Their chief predators, however, are humans.

Tapirs feed on the twigs and foliage of trees and shrubs, and on fruit and other vegetable food. In zoos, their favorite food is bananas. Baird's tapirs consume up to seventy-five pounds of forage in a single night. Large-seeded fruiting trees such as avocado and palm species depend on the feces of tapirs, where their seeds germinate. They are the major seed disperser for many of the plants they consume. Humans hunting with dogs disturb this mutually beneficial relationship, which is bad for the tapirs, for the seeds, and for the rain forest in general.

Habitat destruction to make way for pastureland for livestock and agricultural crops is equally destructive of the forest and the tapirs, who are then subjected to diseases, stress, persecution, and the inbreeding that comes from a shortage of suitable partners. There are imaginative plans to encourage Andean peoples to become less dependent on livestock by planting their traditional quinoa grain. This food, which sustained the ancient Incas, offers more iron than other grains, and contains high levels of potassium and riboflavin, as well as other B vitamins: B_6, niacin, and thiamin. It is also a good source of magnesium, zinc, copper, and manganese, and has some folate (folic acid). When you consider that it takes at least sixteen pounds of soy and grain, not to mention nearly four hundred gallons of water, to make one pound of beef, and that fifty-five square feet of rain forest are destroyed for that single pound of animal flesh, beef consumption makes no sense—and destroys one of the oldest living things on our planet. All tapirs are endangered. We could help tapirs and other jungle animals if we switched to more efficient crops and by decreasing our dependence on livestock.

An adult tapir can weigh as much as eight hundred pounds, and moves like a tank through the thick rain forest, making his own tunnels in the undergrowth. Scientists and zookeepers who work with them call little tapirs "watermelons with legs" because of their shape and the patterns on their skin. They weigh about fifteen pounds at birth, and gain a pound a day over their first year. They make surprisingly birdlike sounds: chirps and other high-pitched squeals that have not yet been adequately studied. There is little doubt, of course, that they have a communicatory function. Perhaps because tapirs eat so many different fruits and need to know when one is spoiled, they have a highly developed sense of smell. They can move their nose in many different directions to pick up faint odors. Until fairly recently, it was thought that they were solitary, but new research indicates that this seems to be an individual choice; many tapirs spend more time with other individuals than was previously thought. Not much is known about their mating habits, although gestation is even longer than among humans, about thirteen months. Some scientists believe monogomy is prevalent.

Known to raid crops at night, tapirs are sometimes seen as being agricultural pests. Yet some farmers have learned to tolerate this and live in harmony with the local tapirs. There is even a tapir in Brazil who was raised by a local family and then returned to the wild. At nightfall he returns, and in exchange for being hand-fed by the family, he allows the kids to ride on his back. Another tapir in Brazil, however, in self-defense, killed a man who had attacked him with a knife.

I have heard that tapirs tame quite easily, and it would be interesting to read an account by somebody who lived with a tapir on terms of intimacy, the way Joy Adamson did with lions. I am sure that sooner or later such a project will come about, and I very much look forward to learning a great deal more about this mysterious and sometimes gentle animal. Tapirs deserve to be better known, and they especially deserve to live! I hope that a young person right at this moment is reading this and deciding to be the first person to live among tapirs the way Dian Fossey lived among the gorillas.

. . .

I wish to thank Gilia Angell from the Tapir Specialist Group for help with this entry.

The IUCN Tapir Specialist Group is a scientific organization founded in 1980. It has nearly one hundred members from around the world who are passion-ately committed to learning more about the mysteries of the tapir, and making sure that tapirs have a secure place in the future of our planet. Visit their website at *tapirspecialistgroup.org/about-tsg/index-about.html.*

TASMANIAN DEVIL

Sarcophilus harrisii

THE TASMANIAN DEVIL is the largest carnivorous marsupial in Australia. It is an icon species, much like the panda, the Asian tiger, and the American bald eagle. Once abundant throughout the mainland of Australia, it's now confined to the island of Tasmania, an island state some three hundred miles over the Bass Strait from mainland Australia, where there could be as many as 150,000 Tasmanian devils.

The name *devil* is of course a European importation. The Aboriginals in Tasmania called it by various names, including *tardiba*, which has nothing to do with the devil. They are black-and-white animals, about the size of a large cat, with red ears, pink mouths, and big wide teeth. Males are much larger than females, but rarely weigh more than twenty-five pounds. They have extremely powerful jaws (four times the strength of a dog's jaw) and, although they are solitary, these nocturnal animals come together to feed, for example, at carrion. To prevent any serious fighting, they make a series of ritualized sounds (eleven have been recorded) that settlers found frightening—hence the name. It was an unfortunate choice since it immediately set up a negative association.

Until recently, Tasmanian farmers blamed every loss of livestock on this animal (and some still do), much the way American ranchers unjustly blamed the coyote. They set about systematically slaughtering as many as they could find: "They are very savage, and have frequent fights among themselves, while they slay other creatures for the mere wanton lust of slaughter," said a 1917 text. But eighty years of bounty records show that the true causes were poor management decisions and practices, and large packs of feral dogs. Settlers were also convinced that should they be lost in the bush and wounded or incapacitated, they would be attacked. This was almost a universal fear, although no such attack has ever been recorded. Bounty hunting gave way to strychnine poisoning in the middle decades of the twentieth century.

Unlike dingoes, Aboriginals never kept Tasmanian devils as pets—once weaned, they become asocial. However, in 1914 a woman kept several in an enclosure and spoke about how they would struggle "to get their little black faces close to mine with evident delight."

The Tasmanian devil seems to have survived on mainland Australia until about five hundred years ago. It could well be that the introduction of the dingo some six thousand years ago marked the beginning of the end for the less-social Tasmanian devil. The invention of the boomerang and spear by Aboriginal people some ten thousand years ago probably had nothing to do with it, since these same tribes exist on the island of Tasmania and have never come close to decimating the population. For some reason hunter-gatherers prefer the flesh of herbivorous animals to carnivorous ones. Is this a superstition, perhaps related to the recognition that humans are (or were) a hunting species as well?

The Tasmanian devil is related to the Dasyuridae family: the quolls and the small marsupials resembling mice. They have wonderful Australian names like dibblers, antechinuses, kowaris, mulgatas, kalutas, phascogales, planigales, ningauis, dunnarts, and kultarrs! You could spend a day with Google just looking them all up, as I just did. I do not bring up these mouselike marsupials just for the fun of naming them. At least some of them—for example, the tiny dusky antechinus, which weighs in at about two ounces—are semelparous. That is, the males die soon after they have sex. In fact, the two animals are closely related, and recently, in the face of a mysterious new disease affecting devils, young male devils have also begun dying shortly after mating. This is an extraordinary adaptation that cries out for closer study. Is it at all possible that there is a psychology at work here, preposterous as that may sound?

The greatest tragedy to have happened to the Tasmanian devil occurred only a few years ago: Devil facial tumor disease causes horrible, cancerous tumors on the faces of these animals, terrible disfigurement that prevents feeding and causes death within six months. Nobody knows the source of this retrovirus: It could be poison or pesticide or toxic spills. Tasmanian devils could be the Australian canaries in the Australian mines, a warning and a dire prediction of what awaits the rest of us unless we act before it is too late. It would be a tragedy to lose the Tasmanian devil. Greater tragedies await us if we don't wake up in time.

Their sexual life is complicated. The male does everything possible to keep "his" female from mating with any other male. He keeps her prisoner in a copulation den and copulates with her pretty much continuously for five days. He will not even let her out to eat or drink, and one thirsty male was even observed dragging a female with him from a den to a water source and back to the den! At all other times it would appear that despite the size differential, females are pretty much dominant over males, especially so at feeding, where the rule seems to be that the most food goes to him or her who is the hungriest, or who needs it most (usually a female with a litter to feed). The female generally gives birth (after a mere eighteen days) to as many as twenty young. Marsupials, they are born as tiny embryos, no bigger than a grain of rice, and slowly make their way from the womb into their mother's backward-opening pouch. Only four of them are able to attach themselves firmly to her teats, which swell in their mouths. By the time they are mature, they will be fifteen thousand times heavier. (Kitten to cat, in comparison, is only a twentyfold increase.)

No other solitary carnivore feeds communally. When we consider that Tasmanian devils will routinely eat up to 40 percent of their body weight at a single feeding in less than half an hour, we have to marvel at how they manage to avoid serious aggression. The most devoted observer of Tasmanian devils, David Pemberton, recorded only a single instance of physical injury in 119 interactions during feeding. Contrary to popular opinion, they are hardly a brawling mob. But it took careful observation by Pemberton to establish this. This is precisely the kind of research that could never be carried out in captive conditions.

TUATARA

Sphenodon punctatum

THE MAORI WORD *TUATARA* means "spiny back" or "peaklike back." The relatives of this reptile died out about sixty million years ago, which is why the tuatara is sometimes called a "living fossil." The Maori regarded these animals as living treasures. Tuatara were in Europe, Africa, and North America *before* the dinosaurs. They have a fossil record of about 225 million years, even before the Jurassic age. When they became extinct everywhere else, long after the dying out of the dinosaurs about sixty million years ago, they survived in a single landmass that separated from the southern continent of Gondwana. That landmass is New Zealand.

Tuatara still live in New Zealand, though only on thirty-two outlying islands free of introduced predators. (Six islands have never been visited.) The Polynesian rat known as the kiore (*Rattus exulans*) and the introduced cat were sure to kill the last of these ancient animals unless they could be protected from them. The only way to do so was to make sure that they were eradicated from the islands where tuatara still lived. Miraculously, this has been achieved on all but four of the islands. For many years now, no tuatara have been removed from the island they inhabit for any reason whatever, and there are strict regulations in place for showing them in zoos. The New Zealand Department of Conservation puts their importance this way:

> They are the only extant members of the Order Sphenodontia, which was well represented by many species during the age of the dinosaurs, some 200 million years ago. All species apart from the tuatara declined and eventually became extinct about 60 million years ago. Tuatara are therefore of huge international interest to biologists and are also recognized internationally and within New Zealand as species in need of active conservation management.

When women talk about a male reptile brain, they may well be thinking of this animal. When two males come together, they line up next to each other, one facing one direction, the other the opposite. They inflate their lungs and throats, open their mouths, then snap them shut. Their skin darkens: *I'm as tough as they get!* One backs down, or they lunge and bite each other. When the victor swaggers off to a female, he can't remember any other way to behave except to use the same aggressive stance he just took with his male enemy: He engages in a clumsy dance known as the *stolzer Gang* (a German term meaning "proud gait"). The tuatara, like birds but unlike most reptiles, lack a penis. The male slowly and stiffly circles the female, his crest erect and his throat inflated. *What a guy* is his message; *how can you possibly resist?* If she cannot, they stay together for an hour, then go their separate ways. Even though mating can take place once a year, a female is in estrus and lays eggs only every four years, and only about nine months after mating. The sex of the hatchlings depends on the temperature in a complex variation only now being deciphered. Basically, the colder the temperature, the more likely that a female will be born. Females become sexually mature at about twenty years of age. They continue to grow until they are fifty or sixty, and can live up to a hundred years.

Four to fifteen eggs are laid in a shallow depression and covered with loose soil. The male is no longer in evidence (remember his brain); the female, too, abandons the nest for good. The eggs take twelve to fifteen months to hatch, the longest of any egg-laying animal. They are already capable of swift movements from birth. They have to be: Neither parent is around to help them find food. In fact, *they* will become their own parent's food should they happen to meet. That's why the baby tuatara is diurnal whereas the adults are nocturnal. The babies don't want to get eaten.

Tuatara make poor houseguests: Often sharing the burrow of seabirds, if hungry, they may eat the egg, or the chick, or the adult petrel. However, thanks to a very slow metabolism, tuatara eat less often than any other reptile, once or twice a month.

There has always been a certain amount of excitement over the fact that the tuatara have a "third eye," much like Tibetan masters. Except in the case of the Tibetans it is merely a fantasy, while tuatara definitely have a complex organ situated on the top of the head with a lens, retina, and nerve connection to the brain. It is open in very young tuatara, then gradually covered in opaque scales. Evidently it soaks up UV rays rich in vitamin D in the first few months of life, then shuts down. What function, if any, it has in later life is still a mystery. Now, if that isn't a spiritual metaphor, I don't know what is!

TURKEY

Meleagris gallopavo

I ONCE VISITED A SANCTUARY for farm animals in Northern California, and had the privilege of holding a large male turkey in my arms. He seemed to like being stroked, and I was delighted to see up close the deep purple, magenta, and blue colors of his neck. The woman taking care of them told me that the colors changed according to their moods, and that other turkeys could tell at a glance what one bird was feeling. This particular bird had been rescued from a slaughterhouse, and seemed to gravitate to humans and enjoy their company. It was almost as if he'd been aware of his fate, and was grateful for having been saved. He was a large, majestic, gentle bird, and I found his company intriguing. It reminded me of how often our perceptions of domesticated animals are skewed, false, or downright mean.

Turkeys are far from stupid. In fact, they are capable of alarming feats of ratiocination, including deception, as the following startling case history demonstrates. In his book *The Wild Turkey*, A. W. Schorger tells of turkeys who pretended to be tame to avoid detection, noting that:

I have known them to remain quietly perched upon a fence while a team passed by; and on one occasion knew a couple of hunters to be so confused by the actions of a flock of five, which deliberately walked in front of them, mounted a fence, and disappeared leisurely over a low hill before they were able to decide them to be wild. No sooner were they out of sight than they took to their legs and then to their wings, soon placing a wide valley between them and their now amazed and mortified pursuers.

Consider that it is now recognized that turkeys in a flock can recognize and remember hundreds of individual flock members. We have certainly attempted to breed out of the domesticated turkey everything that makes a turkey a turkey, but I don't believe we have succeeded as well as we think. In many parts of the world turkeys go feral, and they increasingly resemble their wild cousins, especially in behavior. Even the tamest and most docile domestic turkey takes pleasure in the company of wild turkeys; they, too, seem drawn to their less-fortunate cousins.

In a remarkable book, *Illumination in the Flatwoods*, Joe Hutto uses his experience with wild turkeys to give us a most persuasive description of imprinting. Nearly two dozen eggs were hatched in his presence, and he became the leader of a flock of extraordinary birds. He lived their life for one year in the forests of Florida and learned more about these birds than anyone else has ever recorded. Hutto discovered that they are extremely intelligent (more so than crows, for example, which he also raised). He tells us that "I have never kept better company or known more fulfilling companionship." Hutto is driven, despite his scientist self, to recognize that "in the most fundamental sense our similarities are greater than our differences." He considers himself privileged to be in their presence, feeling less desolate, less isolated, as he is "bathed in the warm glow of these extraordinary creatures." For a naturalist who has hunted wild turkeys all his life, he goes about as far as anyone can in his affirmation of their uniqueness: "As we leave the confines of my language and culture, these graceful creatures become in every way my superiors. More alert, sensitive, and aware, they are vastly more conscious than I. They are in many ways, in fact, simply more intelligent. Theirs is an intricate aptitude, a clear distillation of purpose and design that is beyond my ability to comprehend." What draws him to them, beyond their unusual intelligence, is "observing the absolute joy that these birds experience in their lives . . . they are in love with being alive." We see this concretely when he describes his friendship with one particular bird, Turkey Boy: "Each time I joined him, he greeted me with his happy dance, a brief joyful display of ducking and dodging, with wings outstretched and a frisky shake of the head like a dog with water in his ears. Occasionally, he would jump at me and touch me lightly with his feet. His anticipation and enthusiasm made it difficult for me to disappoint him."

Of course, turkeys do not drown in rain, as a silly legend has it. On the contrary, the position they take—head up, neck raised, body erect, and tail down—keeps them relatively dry by exposing as little as possible to the rain. I asked Karen Davis, who knows more about turkeys than anyone, where this drowning-turkey myth may have originated, and she thought it may have come from the fact that baby chicks, separated from their mothers and without the protection of her wings in a storm, may well look up, inquiringly or beseechingly, accidentally fill their beaks with water, and drown. Like so much of what we consider to be stupidity, however, this is a human artifact, an example of our own need to rationalize our next turkey dinner.

Is it even remotely possible that turkeys have a concept of death? I think it might be. Schorger in his book speaks of what he calls "the great wake." This defies, he claims, "logical explanation"—which simply means that he does not understand it. He is referring to the fact that he has observed, as have others, that when a turkey hen is shot, there are times when instead of flying off in a panic, the flock "stopped beside the dying bird." One hunter wounded a hen, who began to call piteously, and at least thirty toms answered her calls and advanced toward where she lay dying even though the hunter began killing them off systematically and, one might add, heartlessly. On factory farms a bird who dies of a heart attack is often surrounded by other birds who seem to die in sympathy. How ironic that the bird most often associated with insensibility and comatose stupidity may well turn out to have a complex and deep understanding of death.

TURTLES

M Y DEAR FRIEND MARILYN GOODE lives in the Valley of the Moon in Northern California. Years ago I was introduced to her many African spurred tortoises (*Geochelone sulcata*), who originally come from the Sahal Desert in sub-Saharan Africa. She inherited them from her son Eric, who had 150 of his own tortoises. When Marilyn first got them, little did she realize these majestic creatures would come to dominate much of her life. Large animals, full-grown sulcatas can weigh more than 220 pounds and easily move a piano. Marilyn's garden became their enclosure, and it needed a fence that would prevent them digging their way out. (Then again, they are perfectly capable of walking through the wall of your house.) Another fact of life with these animals: Females can produce as many as ninety eggs a year. Oh my.

The oldest living animal on earth today is Harriet, a giant Galápagos land tortoise, who turned 175 in 2005. She lives in northern Australia, and is reputed to have been collected as a baby by Charles Darwin in 1835, though some dispute this. Slow moving, deliberate in everything they do, these animals *look* wise, and when animals live as long as these do, well, surely they accumulate something other than merely years.

How anyone could want to harm these animals is beyond me, but any book about them will show you horrifying photos of men who turned them on their backs to render them helpless, leaving them weeks or longer on sea voyages to use as a source of fresh meat. One shudders to think of what went through their minds as they lay there in perpetual agony. Paul Chambers ends his book *A Sheltered Life* with these prophetic words:

> Humanity is often incapable of learning from its past mistakes and it is more through luck than judgment that the magnificent and inspirational animals that we call giant tortoises are still available for us to visit and study in the wild. If, in a hundred years' time, somebody should pick up a battered and faded copy of this book, it is my hope that they too will be able to travel to the Galapagos or Indian Ocean islands and there find the world's giant tortoises, safe and unmolested in their natural environment.

Turtles first appeared on the earth about two hundred million years ago, the oldest living land reptiles (reptiles being the first creatures to emerge from water and breed on land). Able to withdraw all their critical body parts beneath a hard shell, they were extremely successful in avoiding sharp-toothed predators. But for some reason, about a hundred million years later, some land turtles returned to the sea. They lost their ability to pull in their limbs, and turned their legs into paddles. (Some might even call them wings, considering how efficient they are at creating speed.) Now they could escape most enemies with short bursts of speed, not to mention the ability of the green turtle to hold her breath underwater for a full five hours (though they will normally surface to breathe once an hour). Freshwater turtles fall somewhere between the other two species: They tend to have webbed feet rather than flippers.

I have been fascinated by these animals from the first time I was on a Costa Rican beach and watched a green turtle drop her ping-pong-ball-sized pure white eggs into a deep nest she had just hollowed out. (Costa Rica's Tortuguero National Park is visited by more nesting green sea turtles than any other beach in the Western Hemisphere.) This turtle looked sad, and seemed aware of something I didn't know about. I asked my companion what would happen to the tiny hatchlings who emerged two months later. "They wait until dark, then race to the sea. Most don't make it. But those who do will one day return, to lay their eggs on this very beach." It sounded like magic. How could they possibly return to the same beach years later? It turns out they have a little magnetite crystal in their brain (as homing pigeons do), and they use this to sense the earth's magnetic field.

My friend thought they might imprint on the unique magnetic field of their homes. Actually, despite the magnetite, nobody is certain exactly how they find their way home. It could be smell, sight, currents, the chemical fingerprint of the taste of the water where they first hatched, navigating by stars, or the sun, temperature, or the patterns of ocean waves. Still, return they do, often only twenty years later at or very near the beach where they were born. That fact alone is enough to make them one of the most intriguing animals on our planet. It's also heroic: Only one in one thousand makes it back.

Many sea turtles are keystone species—that is, the ecological niche in which they flourish depends upon them. Their absence affects every other form of life in the vicinity. The thought that *all* species of sea turtles are in danger of extinction is unbearable. As Anders Rhodin from the Chelonia Research Foundation put it:

> Survivors of countless millennia, turtles on the brink of our new millennium face imminent demise at the hands of humans. We are facing a turtle survival crisis unprecedented in its severity and risk. Without intervention, countless species will be lost over the next few decades.

James R. Spotila points out that when humans first came on the scene there were more than 600 million green turtles, 5 million hawksbills, 500 million olive ridleys, half a million Kemp's ridleys; tens of millions of loggerheads and another million and a half leatherbacks; in short, "a billion or so sea turtles helped make the ocean an aquatic Garden of Eden."

Anybody who sees a hatchling the size of a silver dollar peck its way out of its egg much like a baby chick and begin scampering at breakneck speed to the ocean will be hooked for life. To know that they return years later raises the question of where they go in the meantime. Scientists call this period "the lost years," but of course they're not lost to the turtles, only to us, and scientists are now learning the answers.

I asked Marilyn if she had ever seen evidence that her tortoises felt affection for her. She answered in the negative, but seeing my disappointment she brightly added that the males showed more than affection for the females. They were champion lovers, she told me, often copulating for hours at a time. But some tortoises definitely solicit attention from humans: At the Philadelphia Zoo one elderly Aldabran tortoise, from the Aldabran Atoll in the Indian Ocean, plods over to his longtime attendant and rises up on all four legs to solicit neck scratching. Only this one attendant is sought out for attention, regardless of his clothing. Other Aldabrans there also solicit neck scratches, and one even nips at the attendant's leg if his solicitations are ignored. Herpetologists use the term *titillation* to describe the way a male turtle vibrates his long foreclaws (feet turned outward) against a female's face during courtship. You might not think that touch would play a central role in the lives of some tortoises, but it certainly does.

WALLACE'S FLYING TREE FROG

Rhacophorus nigropalmatus

ONE OF THE MOST FAMOUS of all natural history books was written by Alfred Russel Wallace, the co-discoverer, with Charles Darwin, of the theory of natural selection. That book is called *The Malay Archipelago: The Land of the Orang-Utan and the Bird of Paradise (A Narrative of Travel with Studies of Man and Nature)* and was published in London in 1869; it has never been out of print. It makes for distressing reading because of how easily Wallace describes killing every animal he encounters. He was in the Malay Archipelago for eight years, and when he headed for home in 1862 he had collected 125,660 total "specimens," including many orangutans that he shot out of trees—even when he saw their babies clinging to the mothers—without the slightest compunction.

At the beginning of the book, just before he begins his long account of the many orangutans he happily slaughtered, he reported sighting one animal that I had never previously heard of:

One of the most curious and interesting reptiles which I met with in Borneo was a large tree-frog, which was brought me by one of the Chinese workmen. He assured me that he had seen it come down, in a slanting direction, from a high tree, as if it flew. On examining it, I found the toes very long and fully webbed to their very extremity, so that when expanded they offered a surface much larger than that of the body. The forelegs were also bordered by a membrane, and the body was capable of considerable inflation. The back and limbs were of a very deep shining green colour, the under surface and the inner toes yellow, while the webs were black, rayed with yellow. The body was about four inches long, while the webs of each hind foot when fully expanded, covered a surface of four square inches, and the webs of all the feet together about twelve square inches. As the extremities of the toes have dilated discs for adhesion, showing the creature not to be a true tree-frog, it is difficult to imagine that this immense membrane of the toes can be for the purpose of swimming only, and the account of the Chinaman, that it flew down from the tree, becomes more credible. This is, I believe, the first instance known of a "flying frog," and it is very interesting to Darwinians as showing, that the variability of the toes which have been already modified for purposes of swimming and adhesive climbing, have been taken advantage of to enable an allied species to pass through the air like the flying lizard. It would appear to be a new species of the genus *Rhacophorus*, which consists of several frogs of a size much smaller than this and having the webs of the toes less developed.

In fact, not much more than this is known about this flying frog. The toe pads are not unique to this species, but the gliding ability is. Frogs have webbed feet for swimming (like fins), but the fully webbed hands and feet, and the skin along the side of the body, allow this frog to achieve remarkable feats. With her powerful hind limb, she can launch herself from a high tree, where she customarily spends her time, and glide like a tiny sail for fifty feet, coming down slowly to land gently on a tree near the forest floor, using her suction-cup-padded feet to latch on a safe distance from any surprised predator.

There are many colored photos on the Web where you can see the deep apple-green and banana-yellow colors of these amazing amphibians. You can see that even the sheetlike webbing between their fingers and toes, which serves as their parachute, is brightly colored: yellow and black.

If nothing more about them is known since Wallace's days, it is not surprising. After all, they live high up in the rain forest canopy. They come down only at the beginning of the rainy season: to mate, nest, and spawn.

I can think of few animals I would rather see than a green and black and yellow frog hurling herself out of a tropical rain forest tree and sailing through the air with a translucent parachute over her tiny airborne body.

WANDERING ALBATROSS
Diomedea exulans exulans

THE WORD ALBATROSS evidently comes from the Arabic word for "pelican," *al-qadous*, which Spanish and Portuguese sailors corrupted to *alcatraz*. It was Englishman George Shelvocke who, on an ocean voyage around the world between 1719 and 1722, was impressed by "the largest sort of sea-fowls . . . extending their wings 12 or 13 foot." He called them "Albitroses." His journal described a storm near Cape Horn during which one of his officers shot a black albatross who had been accompanying the ship for several days. Wordsworth, who read Shelvocke's account in 1797, took a long walk with Samuel Taylor Coleridge, and told him the story. The rest is literary history.

If, like me, you first heard about the albatross by reading Coleridge's *Rime of the Ancient Mariner*, you probably believe, as I did, that sailors considered the albatross a sign of good luck. When Coleridge's mariner shot the albatross, his ship was becalmed. Without water, all its sailors except the mariner died. And then one day while watching sea snakes swimming along the ship in the moonlight, the mariner experiences an epiphany—he sees their beauty, and by extension, the beauty of every living thing: "A spring of love gushed from my heart, and I blessed them unaware." But Coleridge had never seen an albatross, and in fact sailors did not hold them in high regard. Most were superstitious and considered a sighting of the bird to be a bad omen. Those who were "realists" killed them in unprecedented numbers because their feathers and down were in high demand.

Robert Cushman Murphy, the great American ornithologist, took his first trip to the South Atlantic in 1912 and exclaimed: "I now belong to a higher cult of mortals, for I have seen the albatross!" And in his extraordinary two-volume book he noted, "The flight of the Wandering Albatross as observed over the ocean, has been a subject for rhapsodizing since ships first penetrated into the southern hemisphere."

No other animal has such a low cost of flight. Albatross appear not to fly, but merely to glide with no evident movement. The French scientist P. Idrac described it in the 1920s as "dynamic soaring." They glide for hours at a time, and people who study this ability believe it reaches perfection with this majestic bird. They don't really hold their wings out; the wings lock into place. Darwin, in 1833 during a terrible storm on the *Beagle*, wrote, "Whilst we were heavily laboring, it was curious to see how the Albatross . . . glided right up the wind." Storms don't affect them. Nor are they slow: in a strong wind, they can reach speeds of a hundred miles per hour.

They have the longest wings in nature—more than eleven feet tip-to-tip. They are not light, either. Wandering albatross weigh up to twenty-six pounds. Longer than any other bird, they can (and do) remain at sea for years, never once setting foot on land, even sleeping while they glide, foraging in the darkness. It has been calculated that a fifty-year-old albatross has flown close to four million miles in her lifetime. Murphy long ago recognized that "Wandering Albatrosses actually may circumnavigate the world in the west-wind zone." The Wandering Albatross is indeed, as Murphy acknowledged, "king of the air in our modern world."

They are remarkably like humans in many ways. They may not mature until they are teenagers. Courtship can take two full years. But unlike humans, females can reproduce their entire life. An albatross in New Zealand gave birth to a chick when she was more than sixty years old! Nobody is certain how long they can live. That bird holds the *known* record, but it's possible others may live an entire century.

Consider, too, the extraordinary parental feats of the male and female wandering albatross. They breed on sub-Antarctic islands in the Southern Ocean. To find their chicks food, they travel tremendous distances. A bird fitted with a radiotelemetry device tracked by a satellite showed that on each single foraging trip an albatross might travel 2,237 to 9,320 miles. Michael Bright, who reported this amazing feat, said that this particular bird flew at speeds of 50 miles per hour and covered 560 miles a day, flying day and night with few stops for two to three days. When they fledge, albatross chicks spend from four to fourteen years circling the earth before returning home to breed. Flying at such heights over such vast distances for such long periods probably ensures that these large birds meet few enemies. The chicks often have to fast for long periods (up to a month) in the nest while Mother or Father is out getting food to bring back. These trips defy the imagination: One wandering albatross with a chick in her nest flew a mind-boggling nine thousand miles, round trip, between feedings!

The birds are monogamous and engage in the most intricate courtship of any nonhuman being. It can last months, even years—unsurprising since they sometimes stay together longer than two decades. Strangely enough, they almost always breed on the same island where they hatched. They haven't all that many chances to produce offspring. After mating, they fly off. Whether the pair stays together at sea, nobody knows, but they often return to the island where the egg will be laid and incubated within just a few hours of each other. So either they *were* together, or in sight, or they have an internal clock that beeps when it's time to return home. Within a day of returning, the female lays her egg. I feel privileged to live where I do, for ten species of albatross breed only on New Zealand islands.

In the Southern Ocean, that area around Antarctica ten times the size of the United States, they take advantage of the circumpolar winds collectively known as the west-wind drift. These allow them to range widely over this vast area.

Albatross require fresh water, yet drink seawater. They distill their own. Their nostrils filter seawater. The secretion that emerges from the other end has been mistaken for tears. The ancient Maori said they were weeping for their distant home, unaware that they *were* home.

On Captain James Cook's second circumnavigation, in 1772, naturalist George Forster and his father noted of the birds: "We found them to be extremely curious . . . but they paid with their lives for this curiosity." Ha ha. Worse, much worse, was still to come. Japanese fowlers, responding to worldwide demand for feathers, killed millions of albatross on the remotest islands in the Pacific, dipping live chicks into boiling water and stripping them of their thick down. Conservationist Carl Safina rightly comments: "If you were born a seabird, it was a holocaust."

Many of them have probably lived their entire life without encountering people. When they do, they seem as curious about us as we are about them. One author, writing in 1865, noted: "Never have I seen anything to equal the ease and grace of this bird as he sweeps past, often within a few yards, every part of his body perfectly motionless except the head and eye, which turns slowly, and seem to take notice of everything." The famous ornithologist John Gould, also in 1865, noted that it is "the only species that passes directly over the ship, which it frequently does in blowing weather, often poising itself over the masthead, as if inquisitively viewing the scene below."

WHOOPING CRANE

Grus americana

If any single bird species symbolizes the North American conservation move-
ment of this century, and the closest many wildlife species came to extinction,
it is the whooping crane.

—PAUL A. JOHNSGARD

ONE OF THE LAST KNOWN WHOOPING CRANE nests in the
United States was found early in the twentieth century in
Iowa by ornithologist and egg collector J. W. Preston. He
wrote, "When I approached the nest, the bird, which had walked some
distance away, came running back . . . wings and tail spread drooping,
with head and shoulders brought level with the water; then it began
picking up bunches of moss and sticks which it threw down in a defiant
way; then, with pitiable mien, it spread itself upon the water, and
begged me to leave its treasure, which, in a heartless manner, I did not
do." This might have been either a male or female crane, since both sit
on the eggs.

In Canada the birds lasted just a bit longer in the wild. As late as 1922, a nesting pair was discovered at Muddy Lake, Saskatchewan. They had a lone chick in their nest. He was "collected" for a Canadian museum. That was the last known nesting site of the species in North America.

Before it was realized how important it was that the cranes *not* imprint, there was a now-famous incident. When Tex, a female whooping crane hand-reared by humans, was ready to mate, she rejected male cranes. Instead she was attracted to "Caucasian men of average height with dark hair." With whooping cranes so close to extinction, it was considered vital to bring Tex into breeding condition so that she could be artificially inseminated. To do this, International Crane Foundation director George Archibald, a dark-haired Caucasian man, spent many weeks courting Tex. "My duties involved endless hours of 'just being there,' several minutes of dancing early in the morning and again in the evening, long walks in quest of earthworms, nest building, and defending our territory against humans . . ." Archibald's efforts were successful and eventually resulted in a crane chick. The baby was called Gee Whizz, and he later fathered seven chicks himself.

The International Crane Foundation hatched a different survival strategy. So that baby cranes did not become imprinted on humans, lose their fear, and be killed by unscrupulous members of our species, their human friends created a whooping crane costume. Wearing it in their presence, people behaved like cranes. Later, the cranes would be released into the wild. But they still needed help: An airplane had to guide them along their migratory route!

If the whooping crane dance and nest building are fixed action patterns (as Konrad Lorenz would call them), the lovingness seems to be a more diffuse impulse. The crane has made an error through no fault of her own. If Tex had been raised by cranes, she would have fallen in love with one, as most cranes do. And if George Archibald had been raised by cranes, he may well have fallen in love with a bird.

Whooping cranes can rely on their formidable appearance to discourage most predators. After all, they are five feet tall. However, there is a well-known report of two males who approached each other at the edges of their territory. (These breeding territories can be huge—averaging nineteen hundred acres.) These two birds stood a mere yard apart—a showdown. Each dropped his black primary wing feathers and raised his ornamental wing plumes. Then they pointed their bills to the sky and uttered loud trumpeting calls. They were soon joined by their respective spouses. The males walked around each other, heads low to the ground. They made short bowing movements, finally putting their bills so low they were between their legs, the males' crimson crowns nearly touching. That was it. End of display. End of aggression. They separated. In this case, the cranes' human observer didn't know who had "won" the confrontation, but the cranes had evidently made their point, whatever that was. It was like a ballet or a Noh drama. (Indeed, Yeats believed the stylized Noh dramas were derived from observations of cranes, whom the early Japanese believed to live for a thousand years.)

What a lovely way to end an argument—with a dance! It is worth noting that this dance is a version of the courtship dance. So which comes first: aggression or pair bonding? Almost all geese and swans engage in "triumph ceremonies" when bonding, and most ornithologists believe these are derived from redirected aggressive displays.

Cranes, like swans and most geese, mate for life, and their lives are long, at least thirty-five years. Dancing is more important than copulation, for they will often choose a mate on their wintering grounds, but nobody has ever observed them mating there. The nests the pair eventually builds together are huge, up to five feet in diameter and a foot above the water. The female usually incubates at night, and the male helps during the day when the female is off feeding. There are usually two eggs in a nest, and they take about a month to hatch. The chicks can run, swim, and keep up with their parents within twenty-four hours of hatching, and by six weeks they are sixteen times their hatching weight (about five ounces).

There are at least twenty-seven different calls between whooper chick and parent. Most no doubt describe different dangers the parents perceive and probably provide the solution as well. *(Eagle! Get down!)* Colts, as they are called, fledge when they are seventy days old. Until then, they are in danger from wolves. They continue to be fed by their parents, especially their mother, even after they have fledged. Colts are often called upon to perform an amazing feat: In their annual winter migration from northern Alberta southward to warmer climates, fledglings and parents often make a single-day flight of nearly five hundred miles in about eleven hours, averaging almost fifty miles an hour. They return in spring with their parents, but after that they are pretty much on their own. They must seek out a mate by the time they are two or three. This delicate, drawn-out process can last as long as two years.

It seems only appropriate to end this entry with a quotation from one of the world's greatest nature writers, Peter Matthiessen, who at the end of his book about cranes describes how a pen-raised whooping crane, without the assistance of ultralight aircraft or surrogate parents, chose a route leading him back to his ancestral breeding grounds: "Who can say what primordial instinct turned his beak north like a compass needle and led this pioneer and his steadfast mate on their long journey home across the heavens? And who is not uplifted by the mystery of life implicit in a question that we cannot answer?"

WILD PIGEON

Columba livia

THERE IS NO REAL DISTINCTION between a pigeon and a dove. When we think of pigeon we generally think of the birds we call street pigeons or city pigeons, all of which are names for the feral pigeon, that is, a wild pigeon who is descended from an erstwhile domesticated bird.

In the pigeon family, 825 species have been described. The domestic pigeon, of which there are 140 species, derives from the rock dove, or wild rock pigeon. These birds live in relatively remote places, such as the Outer Hebrides, northwestern Sardinia, the Negev Desert, or Himalayan foothill regions such as Kashmir, where it is difficult to conduct studies of free-flying birds. The rock dove is an extraordinary flier. Members of a subspecies living in the Ennedi Mountains of Africa are able to evade falcons by plunging vertically along cliff walls at speeds of more than 120 miles an hour and, with barely any deceleration, flying into crevices in the cliff. The beautiful snow pigeon (*Columba leuconota*), a close relative of the rock dove, lives in the high mountains of Asia. These birds feed at lower altitudes, but as evening approaches they form great flocks and fly up the valley cliffs to their sleeping nests at fifteen thousand feet. As soon as the sun comes out, they reverse direction, thousands of them descending from the high valleys, always using the identical flyway.

Darwin was fascinated by domestication and its ability to create such different creatures. It was when he became a pigeon expert that the truth dawned on him. Stephen Jay Gould explains this fascination as the key to the entire text of Darwin's *Origin of Species*:

> If human breeding, in a few thousand years at most, could produce differences apparently as great as those separating genera, then why deny to a vastly more potent nature, working over millions of years, the power to construct the entire history of life by evolution? Why acknowledge the plain fact of evolution among pigeons, and then insist that all natural species, many no more different one from the other than pigeon breeds, were created by God in their permanent form?

Pigeons were used by Egyptians during the coronation of Ramses III (reigned 1198–1166 BCE) to carry the news to people in far-off lands. In the First World War, carrier pigeons also played an important role. First bred 150 years ago in Belgium, they could cover six hundred miles in a single day. In fact, it has even been suggested (seriously) that pigeons were responsible for the French Revolution: Aristocrats kept enormous columbaria, with hundreds of thousands of feral pigeons in them. These birds ate whatever was available, including the ripening grain of farmers and peasants who were forbidden to kill them since the birds were considered property of the upper classes. Rebellion against such privileges played no small role in the 1789 revolution. The domesticated pigeons kept in dovecotes by aristocrats were released by peasants, and these escaped birds were probably the first large numbers of feral pigeons, though of course many had been escaping for centuries prior to this.

Pigeons are second only to rats in their role in the history of experimental psychology. In the second volume of his autobiography, B. F. Skinner explains how in 1940 he first became interested in pigeons:

> I bought some pigeons from a poultry store that sold them to Chinese restaurants and began to see how they could operate a mechanical device . . . I found that I could conveniently package a pigeon in a man's sock with its head and neck protruding through a hole in the toe and its wings and legs drawn together at the back and lightly tied with a shoestring. The jacketed bird could be strapped to a block of wood and put into an apparatus.

Such were the humble beginnings of experimental work with pigeons. But of pigeons as *living, breathing, feeling* creatures, there is not a word in the three volumes of Skinner's autobiography, despite the fact that his entire reputation was built on the backs of these birds. In later work, his students recognized that pigeons had the ability to use symbolic reasoning and were capable of self-awareness. The pigeons were trained to peck at spots on their own plumage that they could see only in a mirror. They appear to realize that they are looking at images of themselves, something that a chicken cannot recognize. Human children recognize themselves in mirrors at about ten months of age.

People erroneously believe pigeons are dumb. This supposed defect does not preclude pigeons from an astounding ability to perform mental rotation problems. The pigeons are tested with the comparison shapes rotated at various angles relative to a sample shape. Humans tested on exactly the same task make more errors and need longer to react. The scientist who performed these experiments said that pigeons were geniuses in comparison with humans. Flying and looking down at objects give pigeons proficiency in something in which humans are deficient. The late Alexander Skutch, dean of American ornithologists, pointed out that pigeons could make generalizations we usually attribute only to humans: They knew that a drop of water, a puddle, a pool, and an ocean all belong to the same category. They can do the same with trees. And humans. You could argue that all these categories involve objects important to the lives of pigeons in their natural habitats. What was not remotely expected was that they could apply this same ability to objects with no special importance to them, such as fish. They learned to distinguish (always for a reward, of course; these were hungry pigeons) pictures with fish from the same picture without fish. In other words, they are capable of symbolic abstraction.

Personally I find it unbearably sad that I will never see a passenger pigeon. Many Americans in the twentieth century had this privilege, but they abused it. The cliché is always that they "blackened" the sky as they flew past in vast flocks. The classic passage is from John James Audubon: "I spotted a flock of passenger pigeons, and I realized that the number of pigeons in the flock was greater than I had ever seen before, and I decided to count them. I got off my horse, sat down and began to pencil a dot on a piece of paper for each bird that I saw." Soon he realized he could not possibly continue as legion after legion of passenger pigeons flew by. He estimated the number at 1,115,000,000. There were indeed between three and five billion passenger pigeons at the time America was "discovered." At one time this pigeon formed 25 to 40 percent of the total bird population of the United States. The last wild passenger pigeon was killed just before the turn of the twentieth century. The last captive bird died in September 1914 in the Cincinnati Zoo.

On a bluff in Wyalusing State Park, at the junction of the Mississippi and Wisconsin rivers, stands a monument to the passenger pigeon. It was dedicated on May 11, 1947. The legend on the bronze tablet reads:

DEDICATED
TO THE LAST WISCONSIN
PASSENGER PIGEON
SHOT AT BABCOCK, SEPT. 1899

THIS SPECIES BECAME EXTINCT
THROUGH THE AVARICE AND
THOUGHTLESSNESS OF MAN

ERECTED BY
THE WISCONSIN SOCIETY FOR ORNITHOLOGY

I often wonder what pigeons think of us. They are so often right in front of us, yet we rarely succeed in touching them. While not terrified of people, feral pigeons are clearly jealous of their personal space, and rarely allow us to invade it, unless we are in the process of feeding them. Feral pigeons are clearly not nearly as shy as wild birds when it comes to humans. Is that because their ancestors were once domesti-cated, or is it just that they have become habituated to us over time?

WOLVES

Canis lupus

SOMEWHERE BETWEEN TEN and a hundred thousand years ago, humans domesticated dogs from wolves. This may give us the false sense, however, that if we understand dogs, we understand wolves. It doesn't work. Although they were once a single species, they are no longer. Domestication makes changes that some will exult in and others may lament (Konrad Lorenz, for example), but what it ultimately means is that you end up with two very different animals.

The late John Paul Scott, a great dog expert, claimed, "There is strong evidence that every basic behavior pattern found in dogs is also found in wolves," and he may well have been right, but it does not seem to work the other way around: There are many things wolves do that dogs do not. This is probably because we have selected against those characteristics during the long process of domestication. We don't like single-mindedness (a form of independence) in our dogs. Wolves have a sense of purpose that dogs don't. When wolves set out to do something, they seem to have a picture in their minds of what they want to accomplish. They do not get distracted. Some dogs are like that (and of course we can train dogs, as we do guide dogs for the blind). Most are not: Everything on a walk can and will distract dogs. It's part of their charm. We envy this freedom. The wolf has a living to earn; we free the dog from such distractions. A dog's purpose is to serve us, either with work or with pleasure.

It may well be that we somewhat exaggerate monogamy among wolves, but it is certain that they do not display the sexual promiscuity of almost all dogs. Could this have anything to do with the fact that their brains are 30 percent larger than those of dogs? Wolf expert Harry Frank, a professor of psychology at Michigan State University, raised both wolves and dogs as companion animals (not to be recommended). By watching humans open a door, wolves quickly learned how to turn the knob. His dogs never did.

According to legend, the founders of Rome, Romulus and Remus, were raised by wolves. In the 1940s the American public was startled to read about the one case of a wolf child reported in the literature that was assumed to be entirely authentic, and the only firsthand account by one of the major players in the story. No less an authority on child development than Arnold Gesell, professor of pediatrics at Yale, vouched for the authenticity of the case. Ashley Montagu told me he was emotionally in favor of the story, but as a scientist he could not accept it. What I find interesting is not whether it is a biological possibility, but that *humans* have long believed a female wolf would suckle a human child, and that a male wolf would permit this and protect the child from harm.

The alpha wolf, head of the pack, displays physiological characteristics that separate him from lower-ranking wolves. He has a higher heart rate, presumably because of the responsibility that accompanies his role as leader and the concomitant stress. A wolf pack usually consists of eight animals or fewer, most of whom are related to one another. The breeding pair is the most important element in the pack. The male and the female have chosen each other, and the bond they form often lasts many years, sometimes an entire lifetime. Producing a litter of young, which the pair frequently raises together, only strengthens this bond. In the first weeks of their lives, the pups are intensely interactive with one another, and clearly it is this closeness early in life that acts as the glue that keeps a wolf pack, consisting mostly of brothers and sisters, together in later years. When pups are about three weeks old, they start interacting with other adult pack members. The emotional bonds are carried over into young adulthood, and give remarkable cohesion to pack life. David Mech has shown that there is far more lethal aggression among wolves than was previously known, but it seems to be only lethal *between* packs, never within a pack.

It is in the den, or near the den, that we find the male wolf behaving as a father. The male wolf hunts for his young; he often licks them, cleaning them thoroughly; he guards the den and protects the cubs inside; and once they are able to follow him, he teaches them to be wolves. Wolves go through a socialization process, much as humans do. They need to learn rules; they need to learn about hierarchy within the pack, and discover where they fit into it. Father and Mother together facilitate this learning. There is no indication that wolf fathers ignore their young or leave their raising to the female. Even hunting must be learned.

Perhaps we believe we know more about wolves than we really do because we perceive a similarity between wolves and humans. We are social animals, even pack animals; we reflexively, alas, seek out hierarchal order; we are also at the top of the food chain. Wolves have no natural enemies other than humans, and we once hunted much the way wolves do. We both use sounds and postures to communicate with one another; we care for our young; and at times we are aggressive toward our own kind. Even a wolf's facial expressions are similar to ours and not difficult to read: the alert and happy face, the friendly grin, and the closed eyes as signs of pure pleasure. The submissive face and the submissive grin (with the ears back), first identified by Rudolf Schenkel, an early expert on wolves, are likewise easy to read. Like us, wolves have lived just about everywhere on the planet—from Saudi Arabia and central India to the Arctic Ocean, from Japan to Greenland, Europe, North America, and Mexico. They can be found wherever there is food and water.

Such similarities should not be exaggerated, however, because in truth we know little about the behavior of wild wolves. They are elusive, and observing them up close has proven difficult. Just seeing a wolf in the wild is a rare event. As a result it is not entirely clear how a wolf pack is formed in the wild. Usually, a pack consists of littermates, but sometimes a stranger is accepted, and to date nobody knows the basis of such acceptance.

Wolf howls have been studied in some depth. The wolf's howl advertises and maintains territorial boundaries, acting as a spacing mechanism to keep wolf packs from intruding on one another. Wolves need a lot of space to survive. It is amazing how far the howl carries. On quiet nights a single howl can announce a pack's presence over an area of from 50 to 140 square miles. Lone wolves howl to call other wolves. Wolves can also howl to let the den pups know they are returning from a hunt, or for the sheer joy of being together.

Many people have been tempted to keep wolves or wolf hybrids by reading the extraordinary book by Lois Crisler, *Arctic Wild*, which is probably the most eloquent account of wolves living with humans. It is a romantic book, but it should be read in conjunction with her second book: *Captive Wild*. Crisler took her wolves and wolf hybrids to Colorado, with tragic results. All the wolves and hybrids died untimely deaths—some were run over, others were shot, and some had to be euthanized. You receive an almost palpable sense of the chaos they brought to Crisler's life and the destruction she brought to theirs, even though she was trying to keep them from the certain death they'd have suffered if she'd simply released them in the Arctic, for they were no longer purely wild animals and would not have survived.

There appears to be no documented case of a healthy, nonrabid North American wolf in the wild fatally attacking a human being, though at least nine children in the United States from 1986 to 1994 were killed by pet wolves and wolf-dog hybrids. A review of wolf attacks in Europe and Central Asia showed that nearly all of them involved wolf-dog hybrids or rabid wolves.

The early image of a savage creature bent only on wanton destruction and the more recent myth of pure benevolence are both false. Yes, wolves prey from time to time on domestic animals. But the Yellowstone and Idaho wolf reintroductions, which cost between a thousand and thirty thousand dollars in livestock losses per year, had a yearly gain of twenty-three million dollars per year in increased tourist spending! Moreover, since 1980 wolves have occupied the North Fork of the Flathead River in northwestern Montana, where residents raise cattle and horses, but wolves have killed none to date. And in Wisconsin, wolf researcher R. P. Thiel watched a pack walking single-file through a herd of cattle, with no apparent reaction by either predator or prey.

WOMBATS

Family Vombatidae

THERE ARE THREE SPECIES OF WOMBATS. One is a large herbivorous Australian marsupial that looks like a cross between a beaver and a badger. (Early settlers called them badgers because of their burrowing behavior.) Some people thought these animals resembled giant rats, but that would have to be some giant: Wombats can be four feet long and weigh up to a hundred pounds, larger than most golden retrievers. They are more closely related to koalas than to any other marsupial (as suggested by molecular studies and the fact that both have rudimentary tails, and pouches that open to the rear). But the relationship is strictly formal, for the koala lives in trees and the wombat burrows in the ground.

With their immensely strong front feet and powerful bearlike claws, they dig elaborate burrows six feet under the earth and up to ninety feet long. These tunnels contain more than one bedroom, and it appears that while wombats are not exactly social, neither do they seem to take exception to sharing their burrows. Each night a wombat visits several burrows. Wombats object to other wombats entering their feeding territories (they shriek!) but not their sleeping quarters.

Because of their size, they have few predators. If they must, because of their strong legs they can race away at speeds of up to twenty-five miles an hour. I love to picture the herds of giant wombats (*Diprotodon* spp.) the size of a rhinoceros roaming the plains of southern Australia during the Pleistocene era. They appear to have little fear of humans, though man has been their greatest enemy, sometimes inadvertently. For example, to destroy rabbits, seen as "pests," farmers often followed them into burrows that actually belonged to wombats, and then poured in kerosene and set fire to them. Dingoes also take wombats, but if they follow them into the warren, they find themselves crushed to death against the roof by the powerful backs of the wombats.

A baby wombat (only a singlet) is the size of a pea, and spends a whole year inside his mother's pouch. When he emerges, he spends much of the next year inside the burrow or near his mother.

There are perhaps only 113 of the northern hairy-nosed wombat, also called the yaminon, left alive in the Epping Forest National Park in central Queensland—making it the rarest large mammal in the world, and among the most seriously endangered animals on the planet.

The expression you hear in Australia is "as muddled-headed as a wombat." They have the reputation for little intelligence. Finding their favorite foods (wallaby grass and kangaroo grass—they drink almost no water) requires few skills, and they have almost no social relations, so this would make sense. They sleep all day and forage for eight hours at night. With their slow metabolism, it takes them fourteen days to digest their food. Their metabolic rate at rest is at least 30 percent lower than that of other marsupials. However, the cerebral hemispheres of the wombat are proportionately larger than in any other marsupial. The mystery is: What's that brain power used for? In captivity, they are easily housebroken (probably because their burrows contain separate bathroom facilities). They will come when called by name.

YETI

THE WHAT! THE YETI?

I can already hear the reader exclaiming: "Wasn't this supposed to be an encyclopedia of animals, not an encyclopedia of
mythology?" Is the Yeti a known animal or a beast of the imagination?
To Tibetan Sherpas, the Yeti is real. They say he's either somewhat
taller or somewhat smaller than a human. Furthermore, he walks upright and possesses enough strength to kill a yak without a weapon.
The Yeti is usually described as being a combination of ape and human.
Reports from explorers in the Himalayas started coming to the attention
of the West in the early 1900s. But it was not until Eric Shipton took
photographs of mysterious footprints during his failed expedition to
climb Mount Everest in 1951 that interest dramatically increased.

Recently I visited Sir Edmund Hillary in Auckland, and asked him
about the Yeti footprints he and zoologist Marlin Perkins photographed
in 1960. He told me that he'd never resolved the issue to his own satis-

faction. However, now the man Hillary and many others call "the world's greatest mountaineer," Reinhold Messner, claims to have solved the riddle. The Yeti—also known as the *chemo*, the *migio*, the *chemong*, and the *dremuo*—is a bear!

In Messner's book, if he doesn't definitively solve the mystery, he does take a strong stance. It's a bear, no question about it, he says. He has the authority of somebody who has made numberless trips to Tibet and the entire region, and has climbed almost all of the tallest mountains in the world to be found there. I think he's right, though I was persuaded mainly by the absence of any good evidence that a creature other than a bear accounts for the many descriptions of the Yeti. And yet an important question is never really addressed, let alone answered, by Messner: What kind of bear?

At one point he says the brown bear (*Ursus arctos*). (This family contains the grizzly bear and the world's largest bear, the Kodiak bear.) At another, he says the Yeti is a *chemo* (the Tibetan word for the Yeti)— that a *chemo* is, in fact, nothing but a "rare species of bear." But there's nothing rare about the brown bear. According to Messner, *Yeti* translates as "snow bear." He also thinks it might be a cave bear of Central Asia, of which little is known. He is convinced the Yeti is a rare bear species: "The creature's habitat was mountain valleys lying at altitudes between twelve thousand and eighteen thousand feet. The Sherpas, the sowers of the original Yeti myth, had migrated from this very region. The Yeti, in other words, was a *chemo* blown up to mythic proportions." Is there an Asiatic bear that lives between twelve and eighteen thousand feet in the Himalayas?

The bear in question may be the Asian black bear (*Ursus thibetanus*), also known as the moon bear and the white-breasted bear. His coat is black, with a white V on the chest and a ruff around the neck, all of which pretty much corresponds to what people who think they see a Yeti say. Also, this bear is nocturnal (which the Yeti is supposed to be as well) and often stands on two feet. Moreover, he fights using his front paws much like a punch. All these are details given by people who say they have seen a Yeti.

I once studied the Tibetan language and I remember that *yeh-teh* referred to a small, humanlike animal. I am not sure where the idea of a giant came in, but people who describe the Yeti always talk of how he is between five and eight feet tall. I suppose a bear standing up could be or appear that tall.

The main "myth" about the Yeti is that the male likes to capture maidens and take them to a cave to keep them as mistresses. The female Yeti supposedly does the same, taking men. Where did this fantasy come from? It is unrelated to bears, yet almost everything else about the Yeti corresponds to some piece of recognized behavior in bears. Have the Sherpas simply grafted on to one account a completely different set of tales?

In any event, I believe the Yeti is a bear, and that the only mystery, as is often the case, involves the human propensity for searching for mystery where none exists. When that propensity is linked to our natural fascination with all things animal, we create a myth that can live hundreds of years. Messner's book is unlikely to be the last word.

ZEBRAS

Equus spp.

T HERE ARE THREE SPECIES of zebras. There is the plains, or common, zebra (*Equus burchellii*), found in the grasslands and sa-
vanna of East Africa, a subspecies of which Grant's zebra is
the only zebra that remains common. Then there's the endangered
mountain zebra (*E. zebra*), from the southwest African grasslands. Also
rare is Grevy's or imperial zebra (*E. grevyi*). Formerly found in southern
Ethiopia, Somalia, and northern Kenya, this animal can weigh nearly a
thousand pounds. Despite the fact that these zebras all have stripes,
they are no more closely related than horses to asses, and have never in-
terbred in the wild.

Zebras are part of the horse family (Equidae). This raises the obvious
question: Why were humans able to tame wild horses whereas nobody
has ever succeeded in domesticating any zebra? We must remember the

distinction between "tame" and "domesticated." Tamed zebras have been found from time to time—that is, a zebra captured in the wild is raised by a human and the animal adjusts, more or less, to human society. Nineteenth-century Londoners were able to see them, occasionally, drive an elegant carriage. Carl Hagenbeck had two plains zebras in his Hamburg menagerie and would hitch them along with two oxen, two elands, and two mules, but this was entirely for the pointless and thoughtless amusement of visitors.

That zebras have successfully resisted domestication has fascinated scientists. Their lack of stamina led to their being hunted down by men on horses and may also have discouraged settlers from even attempting to domesticate them. But they are also completely intractable.

Even keeping zebras in zoos is problematic. Stallions, especially, will attack a keeper with little provocation, and even when they are kept in a zoo habitat as large as seventy acres, they are prone to attack and kill impalas and other antelope sharing the space. In the wild, plains zebras commonly form mixed herds with various antelope and share space with giraffes. I have never heard that the zebras attack these species, so I assume increased aggressiveness is an artifact of being kept in captivity.

Zebras are capable of altruistic rescue behavior, which make them formidable foes. The late Dutch photographer Hugo van Lawick (who was married to Jane Goodall) witnessed a mare and her two foals surrounded by a pack of wild dogs, and fighting for their lives. (Foals, when attacked, scream like a human child, which brings them to the attention of distant stallions.) Suddenly the rest of the herd galloped to the rescue. They bunched around the mare and her two children, wheeled, then galloped off in tight formation, foiling the murderous attempt of the wild dogs. Mares have been seen to distract lions intent upon killing their foals, at considerable danger to their own safety. For zebras, there is no greater bond than that between mother and child.

Certain of their strength, stallions allow hyenas to come within a few yards during daylight without paying them much attention. Even lions avoid attacking a healthy, alert zebra. Stallions have been known to break a lion's jaw with their hooves. The easiest hunting success is when the lion surprises a young foal. Noted zoologist George Schaller watched as one male lion, ambling across the plains, spotted a zebra foal "so deeply asleep on the grass that it even failed to hear the alarm snorts of its family. The lion wakened it briefly."

Newborn young are extremely precocial: They can be up and about within an hour of birth, though they are not weaned for more than a year. Relatively independent at seven months, nevertheless, foals remain with their mother in an intense bond for up to three years. The mothers avoid large groups, and tend to look for and join other mares with young foals. They are reluctant to part even from a herd of giraffes they accompany. Whether the giraffes afford company or protection is unknown, but I have not read of a single aggressive encounter in the wild.

Is the zebra a light-colored animal with dark stripes, or a dark one with light stripes? The answer (the former) came in the 1950s when it was discovered that the dark parts of zebras fade while the light parts remain unchanged. But the function of these stripes remains a matter of controversy. It's possible that under certain light conditions—for example, in the reeds by a water hole—they provide camouflage. But since zebras never attempt to hide, this seems unlikely. Another idea is that the black stripes (under which there are special layers of protective fat) get hot and the rising air forces cool air down around the white areas of the body, thus keeping the zebra cool. The problem here is that zebras never seem to seek out shade, and thus don't appear to need cooling down. Perhaps, some have argued, the patterns make it harder for a predator to single out an individual against the backdrop of a whole herd. But lions do so in the case of foals, and Schaller found, to his surprise, that the vast majority of zebra kills by lions involve old and weak members of the herd, obviously deliberately targeted.

So all of these conjectures fail to hold up, and the most likely explanation is that the stripes play a social role, helping individuals recognize one another, since no two animals have identical stripes. Jonathan Kingdon has shown that stripes facilitate socialization, having to do with sensitivity to stripe frequency and spacing. He is also convinced that horses evolved from a narrow-striped zebra. Aberrant patterns are extremely rare, suggesting that "The function of stripes must be of central importance in the biology of zebras." George Schaller says that the striping serves a function similar to our unique fingerprint. Naturally, to us, all zebras look alike. But in groups that can be as large as five thousand, families (stallion, mare, and foals) are distinctive and consider themselves a group apart from the larger herd. The foal, after only a few days, is able to recognize his own mother by her stripe pattern (as well as voice and scent).

Alas, their stripes have also served a purpose they were never evolved to do: They satisfy human desire for hide. One species of zebra, namely the quagga (*Equus quagga*) of the Cape, was hunted to extinction by white settlers in the 1870s. Grevy's zebras are in grave danger, since their beautiful coats fetch high prices. Their numbers have drastically fallen in recent years. Even on the Serengeti, during the 1990s plains zebras suffered a 40 percent loss, more than they did in the entire preceding century. Kingdon points out that pastoralists are generally tolerant of zebras, and in fact the Karamojong consider them the epitome of beauty, while in Singida, where zebras no longer survive, the Wanyaturu look upon them as the supreme symbol of fruitfulness. Not so the farmer or rancher. Livestock ranching is likely to prove the most intractable of all enemies. Kingdon believes, sadly, that the decline will only continue. Ironically, people would pay far more to see zebra herds in these places than could possibly be made from killing livestock for food. It is only a failure of imagination that makes this difficult, putting the existence of all zebras into question. Kingdon, a former professor of fine art who has done so much for African animals, writes: "It will be a sad and condemning reflexion on the values of our civilization if one of the most beautiful and interesting of all mammals becomes another victim of the current indiscriminate rush to exploit East Africa's natural resources."

Sound, too, plays an important role in the social lives of zebras, as it does in horses. The squeals of dominant and subordinate differ considerably. The dominant animal is able to instantly hit a high-frequency note, whereas the subordinate cannot. Thus braying can avert a fight: One zebra immediately recognizes who is superior and therefore stronger and more likely to prevail in a battle. Stallions nevertheless do fight one another, though nobody knows how often this happens or how serious the consequences. Why they bray at night is not clear, but some humans are thankful they do. Schaller evocatively wrote that "there are some feelings inaccessible to reason, and a zebra's braying always made the perfection of a Serengeti night complete."

ACKNOWLEDGMENTS

THE FOLLOWING EXPERTS (in some cases the world's authority for their animal) were kind enough to read individual entries and make corrections and suggestions. They are not, obviously, responsible for the errors that despite my best efforts still remain:

Australian magpie: Gisela Kaplan*; beetles: Arthur Evans; bilby: Rebecca Gotch; bison: Valerius Geist; black-tailed prairie dog: Con Slobodchikoff*; bottlenose dolphin: Naomi Rose; bowerbirds: Gerald Borgia; cheetah: Patricia Tricorache; cows: Valerius Geist; coyote: Mark Bekoff; gannet: Bryan Nelson*; gecko: Eric Pianka and Aaron Bauer; glowworm: David Merritt; gorilla: Liz Williamson and Hope Walker; hippopotamus: Bill Barklow*; koala: Deborah Tabart; lemur: Eleanor Sterling and Ian Tattersall; lion: Andrew Loveridge; naked mole rat: Paul Sherman; New Zealand longfin eel: Don Jellyman; North American beaver: Dietland Muller-Schwarze; octopus: James Wood; orca: Naomi Rose; orangutan: Anne Russon; pearl oysters: Paula Mikkelsen*; polar bear: Andrew Derocher; portia: Robert Jackson*; pronghorn: John Byers; puma: Harley Shaw, David Baron, and Ken Logan; sea horses: Amanda Vincent; sea turtles: Manjula Tiwari, David Godfrey, and Gale Bishop; stick insects: Thomas Buckley; tapirs: Gilia Angell*; Tasmanian devil: Androo Kelly; tuatara: Nicola Nelson*; whooping crane: George Archibald*; wolves: David Mech.

I especially want to thank BTG, Bradley Trevor Greive, the Tasmanian Polar Bear, author of *The Blue Day Book*, who, out of pure kindness (and a love of animals), went far out of his way to find me experts to vet each entry.

* These experts generously supplied photos as well.

I have long admired the work of Frans Lanting, and am delighted that I was able to use some of his photos for this book. I visited Pavel German, who has won many awards for his amazing animal photographs in Sydney, while I was doing research for this book, and am happy to be able to include here many of the wonderful pictures I admired at the time. Indeed, I wish to express my gratitude to all the photographers whose stunning photos appear in this book, with special thanks to: Whitney Cranshaw for the cochineal; the Waitomo Museum of Caves for the glowworms; Steve Jury for the lobster photo by Win Watson; Mark Maguire for the pigs; Paddy Ryan for the rhacophorus nigropalmatus; and Rachel Rosenthal for the photo of her wonderful companion rat known as Rattie.

For other help, I want to thank the following people: Oskar Conle, David Croft, Nina Fascione, Samantha Fenton, Jeff Flocken, Margaret Gee, Bradley Trevor Greive, Carl Safina, Rick Shine, Terese Storey, Jo Thompson, Lyall Watson, and Richard Wrangham. At Ballantine Books Random House, Mark Maguire in production was very helpful. As usual my friend Nancy Miller has proved to be the treasure every author who has published with her knows her to be. I am so happy that Nancy Miller's assistant, Lea Beresford, is back to help me, with competence and her unfailing cheerfulness so necessary to grumpy authors. I cannot adequately express my thanks to Dana Isaacson, who handles a literary scalpel with the skill of a surgeon and helped the thin book struggling to emerge from my obese manuscript into the light of day.

BIBLIOGRAPHY

For reasons of space, I have only been able to give a maximum of three books for each animal. They are in descending chronological order, with the most recent book first. A longer, annotated bibliography can be found on my website: www.jeffrey masson.com. If you have suggestions for supplementing this bibliography, please send me a comment via my website.

PREFACE

R. M. May, J. H. Lawton, and N. E. Stork: "Assessing Extinction Rates." In Lawton and May, eds. *Extinction Rates*. Oxford: Oxford University Press, 1995.

ARMADILLOS

Larry L. Smith and Robin W. Doughty: *The Amazing Armadillo: Geography of a Folk Critter*. Austin: University of Texas Press, 1984.

Roy Bedichek: *Adventures with a Texas Naturalist*. Austin: University of Texas Press, 1961.

AUSTRALIAN MAGPIE

Gisela Kaplan: *Australian Magpie: Biology and Behaviour of an Unusual Song-bird*. Australian Natural History Series. Collingwood, Victoria, Australia: CSIRO Publishing/University of New South Wales Press, 2004.

BADGERS

Ernest Neal: *The Natural History of Badgers*. New York: Facts on File, 1986.

BALD EAGLE

Brenda Cox: *Conversations with an Eagle: The Story of a Remarkable Relation-ship*. Vancouver: Greystone Books, 2002.

David Jones: *Eagles*. Vancouver: Whitecap Books, 1996.

Jon M. Gerrard and Gary R. Bortolotti: *The Bald Eagle: Haunts and Habits of a Wilderness Monarch*. Washington: Smithsonian Institution Press, 1988.

BATS

John D. Altringham: *Bats: Biology and Behaviour*. Oxford: Oxford University Press, 1999.

M. Brock Fenton: *The Bat: Wings in the Night Sky*. Buffalo: Firefly Books, 1998.

Don E. Wilson: *Bats in Question: The Smithsonian Answer Book*. Photographs by Merlin D. Tuttle. Washington: Smithsonian Institution Press, 1997.

BEETLES

Paul Beckmann: *Living Jewels: The Natural Design of Beetles*. Introduction by Ruth Kaspin. New York: Prestel, 2004.

Thomas Eisner: *For Love of Insects*. Foreword by Edward O. Wilson. Cambridge, MA: Harvard University Press, 2003.

Arthur V. Evans and Charles L. Bellamy (with photographs by Lisa Charles Watson): *An Inordinate Fondness for Beetles*. Berkeley: University of California Press, 2000 (first published in 1996).

BENGAL TIGER

Ruth Padel: *Tigers in Red Weather*. London: Little, Brown, 2005.

Richard Ives: *Of Tigers and Men: Entering the Age of Extinction*. New York: Doubleday, 1996.

Arjan Singh: *Tiger! Tiger!* London: Jonathan Cape, 1984.

BILBY

Raymond Hoser: *Endangered Animals of Australia*. Sydney: Pearson, 1991.

Tim Flannery, Paula Kendall, and Karen Wynn-Moylan: *Australia's Vanishing Mammals: Endangered and Extinct Species*. Sydney: RD Press, 1990.

Ronald Strahan: *The Australian Museum Complete Book of Australian Mammals: The National Photographic Index of Australian Wildlife*. Sydney: HarperCollins, 1991.

BISON

Dale F. Lott: *American Bison: A Natural History*. Foreword by Harry W. Greene. Berkeley: University of California Press, 2002.

Andrew C. Isenberg: *The Destruction of the Bison.* Cambridge: Cambridge University Press, 2000.

Valerius Geist: *Buffalo Nation: History and Legend of the North American Bison.* Stillwater, MN: Voyageur Press, 1996.

BLACK-TAILED PRAIRIE DOG

David Alderton (photographs by Bruce Tanner): *Rodents of the World.* London: Blandford, 1996.

John L. Hoogland: *The Black-Tailed Prairie Dog: Social Life of a Burrowing Mammal.* Chicago: University of Chicago Press, 1995.

John A. King: "Social Behavior, Social Organization, and Population Dynamics in a Black-Tailed Prairie Dog Town in the Black Hills of South Dakota." *Contributions from the Laboratory of Vertebrate Biology,* University of Michigan, 67 (April 1955): 1–120.

BONOBO

Frans de Waal and Frans Lanting. *Bonobo: The Forgotten Ape.* Berkeley: University of California Press, 1997.

Takayoshi Kano: *The Last Ape.* Palo Alto, CA: Stanford University Press, 1992.

Randall Susman, ed.: *The Pygmy Chimpanzee: Evolutionary Biology and Behavior.* New York: Plenum Press, 1984.

BOTTLENOSE DOLPHIN

Toni Frohoff and Brenda Peterson, eds.: *Between Species: Celebrating the Dolphin-Human Bond.* San Francisco: Sierra Club Books, 2003.

Rachel Smolker: *To Touch a Wild Dolphin: A Journey of Discovery with the Sea's Most Intelligent Creatures.* New York: Doubleday, 2001.

Janet Mann, Richard C. Connor, Peter L. Tyack, and Hal Whitehead: *Cetacean Societies: Field Studies of Dolphins and Whales.* Chicago: University of Chicago Press, 2000.

BOWERBIRDS

Paul A. Johnsgard: *Arena Birds: Sexual Selection and Behavior.* Washington: Smithsonian Institution Press, 1994.

E. Thomas Gilliard: *Birds of Paradise and Bower Birds.* Garden City, NY: Natural History Press, 1969.

A. J. Marshall: *Bower-Birds: Their Displays and Breeding Cycles.* Oxford: Oxford University Press, 1954.

Butterflies

Phil Schappert: *A World for Butterflies: Their Lives, Behavior and Future.* Buffalo: Firefly Books, 2005.

B. Cassie, J. Sandved, R. M. Pyle: *A World of Butterflies.* New York: Bulfinch Press, 2004.

Valerio Sbordoni and Saverio Forestiero: *Butterflies of the World.* Buffalo: Firefly Books, 1998.

Camels

Hilde Gauthier-Pilters and Anne Innis Dagg: *The Camel: Its Evolution, Ecology, Behavior, and Relationship to Man.* Chicago: University of Chicago Press, 1981.

H. M. Barker: *Camels and the Outback.* Rigby: Seal Books, 1972 (first published in 1964).

G. Cauvet: *Le Chameau.* 2 vols. Paris: Bailliere, 1925–26.

Cheetah

Mel Sunquist and Fiona Sunquist: *Wild Cats of the World.* Chicago: University of Chicago Press, 2002.

T. M. Caro: *Cheetahs of the Serengeti Plains: Group Living in an Asocial Species.* Chicago: University of Chicago Press, 1994.

Jonathan Kingdon: *East African Mammals.* Vol. IIIA: *Carnivores.* Chicago: University of Chicago Press, 1989 (first published in 1977).

Chicken

William Grimes: *My Fine Feathered Friend.* New York: North Point Press, 2002.

Page Smith and Charles Daniel: *The Chicken Book.* San Francisco: North Point Press, 1982.

J. P. Kruijt: *Ontogeny of Social Behaviour in Burmese Red Junglefowl* (Gallus gallus spadiceus). Leiden: E. J. Brill, 1964.

Cochineal

Amy Butler Greenfield: *A Perfect Red: Empire, Espionage, and the Quest for the Color of Desire.* New York: HarperCollins, 2005.

Coconut Crab

Rod Preston-Mafham and Ken Preston-Mafham: *The Encyclopaedia of Land Invertebrate Behaviour*. London: Blandford Press, 1993.

I. W. Brown and D. R. Fielder, eds.: *The Coconut Crab: Aspects of Birgus latro Biology and Ecology in Vanuatu*. Canberra: Australian Centre for International Agricultural Research, 1991.

Cow

Laurie Winn Carlson: *Cattle: An Informal Social History*. Chicago: Ivan R. Dee, 2001.

Sara Rath: *The Complete Cow*. New York: Barnes & Noble, 1998.

John Webster: *Understanding the Dairy Cow*. Oxford: Blackwell Science, 1993.

Coyote

Marc Bekoff, ed.: *Coyotes: Biology, Behavior, and Management*. Caldwell, NJ: Blackwell Press, 2001 (first published in 1978).

Hope Ryden: *God's Dog: The North American Coyote*. New York: Lyons & Burford, 1979. 2nd ed., with postscript, 1989.

François Leydet: *The Coyote: Defiant Songdog of the West*. Revised and updated. Norman: University of Oklahoma Press, 1977.

Dog

Patricia B. McConnell: *For the Love of a Dog: Understanding Emotion in You and Your Best Friend*. New York: Ballantine, 2006.

Raymond Coppinger and Lorna Coppinger: *Dogs: A Startling New Understanding of Canine Origins, Behavior and Evolution*. New York: Scribner, 2001.

Vilmos Csanyi: *If Dogs Could Talk: Exploring the Canine Mind*. New York: North Point Press, 2000.

Domestic Cat

Dennis C. Turner and Patrick Bateson, eds.: *The Domestic Cat: The Biology of Its Behaviour*. Cambridge: Cambridge University Press, 1998. 2nd rev. ed., 2000, contains new chapters.

Howard Loxton: *99 Lives: Cats in History, Legend and Literature*. London: Duncan Baird, 1998.

Roger Tabor: *The Wild Life of the Domestic Cat*. London: Arrow Books, 1983.

DUCKS AND GEESE

Bernd Heinrich: *The Geese of Beaver Bog*. New York: HarperCollins, 2004.

Frank S. Todd: *Natural History of the Waterfowl*. San Diego: San Diego Natural History Museum, 1997.

Joel Carl Welty: *The Life of Birds*. New York: Alfred A. Knopf, 1968.

ECHIDNA

Peggy Rismiller: *The Echidna: Australia's Enigma*. Sydney: Hugh Lauter Levin Associates, 1999.

ELEPHANTS

Shana Alexander: *The Astonishing Elephant*. New York: Random House, 2000.

Katy Payne: *Silent Thunder: In the Presence of Elephants*. New York: Simon & Schuster, 1998.

Cynthia Moss: *Elephant Memories: Thirteen Years in the Life of an Elephant Family*. New York: William Morrow, 1988.

EMPEROR PENGUIN

Tony D. Williams: *The Penguins Speniscidae*. Oxford: Oxford University Press, 1995.

Dietland Muller-Schwarze: *The Behavior of Penguins Adapted to Ice and Tropics*. Albany: State University of New York Press, 1984.

Jean Prévoste: *Écologie du Manchot Empereur*. Paris: Hermann, 1961.

FLAMINGOS

Nigel Collar (photographs by Carolo Mari): *Pink Flamingos*. New York: Abbeville Press, 2000.

A. Landsborough Thomson, ed.: *A New Dictionary of Birds*. New York: McGraw-Hill, 1964.

L. H. Brown: *The Mystery of the Flamingos*. London: Collins, 1957.

FROGS

William Souder: *A Plague of Frogs: The Horrifying True Story*. New York: Hyperion, 2000.

David Badger and John Netherton: *Frogs*. Vancouver: Voyageur Press, 1995.

William E. Duellman and Linda Trueb: *Biology of Amphibians*. New York: McGraw-Hill, 1986.

GANNET

Bryan Nelson: *The Atlantic Gannet.* 2nd ed. Norfolk: Fenix Books, 2002.

GECKOS

Michael Hutchins, James B. Murphy, and Neil Schlager, eds.: *Grzimek's Animal Life Encyclopedia.* 2nd ed. Vol. 7: *Reptiles.* Farmington Hills, MI: Gale Group, 2003.

Jay M. Savage: *The Amphibians and Reptiles of Costa Rica: A Herpetofauna Between Two Continents, Between Two Seas.* Chicago: University of Chicago Press, 2002.

Tim Halliday and Kraig Adler, eds. *The Encyclopedia of Reptiles and Amphibians.* New York: Facts on File, 1988.

GIANT PANDA

Vicki Croke: *The Lady and the Panda: The True Adventures of the First American Explorer to Bring Back China's Most Exotic Animal.* New York: Random House, 2005.

Donald Lindburg and Karen Baragona, eds.: *Giant Pandas: Biology and Conservation.* Berkeley: University of California Press, 2004.

George Schaller: *The Last Panda.* Chicago: University of Chicago Press, 1993.

GIANT SQUID

Richard Ellis: *The Search for the Giant Squid: The Biology and Mythology of the World's Most Elusive Sea Creature.* New York: Penguin, 1999.

GIBBONS AND SIAMANGS

R. H. van Gulik: *The Gibbon in China: An Essay in Chinese Animal Lore.* Leiden: E. J. Brill, 1967.

C. R. Carpenter: *A Field Study in Siam of the Behavior and Social Relations of the Gibbon* (Hylobates lar). Baltimore: Johns Hopkins University Press, 1940.

GIRAFFE

Michael Allin: *Zarafa: A Giraffe's True Story, from Deep in Africa to the Heart of Paris.* New York: Walker, 1998.

Lynn Sherr: *Tall Blondes: A Book About Giraffes.* Kansas City: Andrew McMeel Publishing, 1997.

Richard Despard Estes: *Behavior Guide to African Mammals*. Berkeley: University of California Press, 1991.

GLOWWORM

Gerard Hutching: *The Natural World of New Zealand: An Illustrated Encyclopaedia of New Zealand's Natural Heritage*. Auckland: Viking, 1998.

V. B. Meyer-Rochow: *The New Zealand Glowworm*. Waitomo Caves, New Zealand: Waitomo Caves Museum Society, 1990.

GOATS

David Macdonald, ed.: *The New Encyclopedia of Mammals*. Oxford: Oxford University Press, 2004.

Juliet Clutton-Brock: *A Natural History of Domesticated Mammals*. 2nd ed. Cambridge: Cambridge University Press, 1999.

Ronald M. Nowak: *Walker's Mammals of the World*. 6th ed. Vol. 2. Baltimore: Johns Hopkins University Press, 1999.

GORILLA

M. Robbins, P. Sicotte, and K. J. Stewart, eds.: *Mountain Gorillas*. Cambridge: Cambridge University Press, 2001.

Bill Weber and Amy Vedder: *In the Kingdom of Gorillas: Fragile Species in a Dangerous Land*. New York: Simon & Schuster, 2001.

Dian Fossey: *Gorillas in the Mist*. Boston: Houghton Mifflin, 1983.

GREAT HORNED OWL

David Hollands: *Owls: Journeys Around the World*. Melbourne: Bloomings Books, 2004.

John A. Burton: *Owls of the World*. London: Peter Lowe Eurobook, 1992.

Elena Cenzato and Fabio Santopietro: *Owls: Art Legend History*. Boston: Bulfinch Press, 1991.

GREAT WHITE SHARK

John R. Paxton and William N. Eschmeyer, con. eds.: *Encyclopedia of Fishes*. 2nd ed. San Francisco: Fog City Press, 2003.

John A. Musick and Beverly McMillan: *The Shark Chronicles: A Scientist Tracks the Consummate Predator*. New York: Henry Holt, 2002.

Richard Ellis: *Great White Shark*. Stanford, CA: Stanford University Press, 1991.

Grizzly Bear

Timothy Treadwell and Jewel Palovak: *Among Grizzlies: Living with Wild Bears in Alaska.* New York: Ballantine, 1999.

Thomas McNamee: *The Grizzly Bear.* New York: Penguin, 1990 (first published in 1984).

Adolph Murie: *The Grizzlies of Mount McKinley.* Seattle: University of Washington Press, 1981.

Hippopotamus

S. Keith Eltringham: *The Hippos: Natural History and Conservation.* London: Academic Press, 1999.

Richard Despard Estes: *The Behavior Guide to African Mammals.* Foreword by E. O. Wilson. Berkeley: University of California Press, 1991.

Jonathan Kingdon: *East African Mammals.* Vol. 3B: *Large Mammals.* Chicago: University of Chicago Press, 1979.

Honeybees

Stephen Buchmann (with Banning Repplier): *Letters from the Hive: An Intimate History of Bees, Honey, and Humankind.* New York: Bantam, 2005.

David Grimaldi and Michael S. Engel: *Evolution of the Insects.* New York: Cambridge University Press, 2005.

Hattie Ellis: *Sweetness and Light: The Mysterious History of the Honeybee.* New York: Harmony Books, 2004.

Hummingbirds

Robert Burton: *The World of the Hummingbird.* Kingston, ON: Firefly Books, 2001.

Connie Toops: *Hummingbirds: Jewels in Flight.* Stillwater, MN: Voyageur Press, 1992.

Crawford H. Greenewalt: *Hummingbirds.* New York: Dover Publications, 1990.

Humpback Whale

William F. Perrin, Bernd Wursig, and J. G. M. Thewissen: *Encyclopedia of Marine Mammals.* San Diego: Academic Press (Elsevier), 2002.

Janet Mann, Richard C. Connor, Peter L. Tyack, and Hal Whitehead, eds.: *Cetacean Societies: Field Studies of Dolphins and Whales.* Chicago: University of Chicago Press, 2000.

Roger Payne: *Among Whales.* New York: Simon & Schuster, 1995.

Jellyfish

Graham J. Edgar: *Australian Marine Life: The Plants and Animals of Temperate Waters.* Sydney: Reed New Holland, 2005.

Edward F. Ricketts and Jack Calvin: *Between Pacific Tides: An Account of the Habits and Habitats of Some Five Hundred of the Common, Conspicuous Seashore Invertebrates of the Pacific Coast Between Sitka, Alaska, and Northern Mexico.* 3rd ed., revised by Joel W. Hedgpeth. Foreword by John Steinbeck. Stanford: Stanford University Press, 1962.

Kakapo

David Butler: *Quest for the Kakapo.* Auckland: Heinemann Read, 1989.

David Cemmick and Dick Veitch: *Kakapo Country: The Story of the World's Most Unusual Bird.* Auckland: Hodder and Stoughton, 1987.

Kangaroos

Maryland Wilson and David B. Croft, eds.: *Kangaroos: Myths and Realities.* Sydney: Australian Wildlife Protection Council, 2005.

G. Griff, J. Jarman, and I. Hume, eds.: *Kangaroos, Wallabies, and Ratkangaroos.* Chipping Norton, Australia: Surrey Beatty, 1989.

Kevin Weldon: *The Kangaroo.* Sydney: Weldons Pty. Ltd., 1985.

Kiwis

Neville Peat: *The Incredible Kiwi.* Auckland: Random House, 1990.

Koala

Roger Martin and Kathrine Handasyde: *The Koala: Natural History, Conservation and Management.* 2nd ed. Sydney: University of New South Wales Press, 1999.

Bill Phillips: *Koalas: The Little Australians We'd All Hate to Lose.* Canberra: Australian Government Publishing Service, 1990.

Leonard Cronin, ed.: *Koalas: Australia's Endearing Marsupial.* Syndey: Reed, 1987.

Kookaburra

Sarah Legge: *Kookaburra: King of the Bush.* Collingwood, Victoria, Australia: CSIRO Publishing, 2004.

P. J. Higgins, ed.: *Handbook of Australian, New Zealand, and Antarctic Birds.* Vol. 4: *Parrots to Dollarbirds.* Melbourne: Oxford University Press, 1999.

John Alcock: *The Kookaburra's Song: Exploring Animal Behavior in Australia.* Tucson: University of Arizona Press, 1988.

LEMURS

Steven M. Goodman and Jonathan P. Benstead, eds.: *The Natural History of Madagascar.* Chicago: University of Chicago Press, 2003.

Ian Tattersall: *The Primates of Madagascar.* New York: Columbia University Press, 1982.

Alison Jolly: *Lemur Behavior: A Madagascar Field Study.* Chicago: University of Chicago Press, 1966.

LION

Craig Packer: *Into Africa.* Chicago: University of Chicago Press, 1994.

Brian Bertram: *Pride of Lions.* London: J. M. Dent & Sons, 1978.

George B. Schaller: *The Serengeti Lion: A Study of Predator-Prey Relations.* Chicago: University of Chicago Press, 1972.

LOBSTER

David Foster Wallace: *Consider the Lobster and Other Essays.* Boston: Little, Brown, 2006.

Trevor Corson: *The Secret Life of Lobsters: How Fisherman and Scientists Are Unraveling the Mysteries of Our Favorite Crustacean.* New York: Harper-Collins, 2003.

J. Stanley Cobb and Bruce F. Phillips: *The Biology and Management of Lobsters.* Vol. I: *Physiology and Behavior.* New York: Academic Press, 1980.

MANATEES AND DUGONGS

John E. Reynolds III (with photographs by Karen Glaser): *Mysterious Manatees.* Gainesville: University Press of Florida, 2003.

Jeff Ripple (with photography by Doug Perrine): *Manatees and Dugongs of the World.* Stillwater, MN: Voyageur Press, 1999.

John E. Reynolds III and Daniel K. Odell: *Manatees and Dugongs.* New York: Facts on File, 1991.

Mantises

David Attenborough: *Life in the Undergrowth*. London: BBC Books, 2005.

Rod Preston-Mafham and Ken Preston-Mafham: *The Encyclopedia of Land Invertebrate Behaviour*. Cambridge, MA: MIT Press, 1993.

Richard Sharell: *New Zealand Insects and Their Story*. Auckland: Collins, 1971.

Meerkat

David Macdonald (photography by Nigel Dennis): *Meerkats*. London: New Holland Publishers, 1999.

Anne Rasa: *Mongoose Watch: A Family Observed*. Garden City, NY: Anchor Press/Doubleday, 1986.

H. E. Hinton and A. M. S. Dunn: *Mongooses: Their Natural History and Behaviour*. Berkeley: University of California Press, 1967.

Mulberry Silkworm

Sylvia A. Johnson (photographs by Isao Kishida): *Silkworms*. Minneapolis: Lerner Publications, 1982.

Naked Mole Rat

Nigel C. Bennett and Chris F. Faulkes: *African Mole-Rats: Ecology and Eusociality*. Cambridge: Cambridge University Press, 2000.

Paul W. Sherman, Jennifer U. M. Jarvis, and Richard D. Alexander: *The Biology of the Naked Mole-Rat*. Princeton, NJ: Princeton University Press, 1991.

Narwhal

Stefani Paine: *The World of the Arctic Whales: Belugas, Bowheads, and Narwhals*. San Francisco: Sierra Club Books, 1995.

Freud Bruemmer: *The Narwhal: Unicorn of the Sea*. Toronto: Key Porter Books, 1993.

New Zealand Longfin Eel

Tom Fort: *The Book of Eels*. London: HarperCollins, 2002.

Richard Schweid: *Consider the Eel: A Natural and Gastronomic History*. Chapel Hill: University of North Carolina Press, 2002.

F. W. Tesch. *The Eel: Biology and Management of Anguillid Eels*. English edition by P. H. Greenwood. London: Chapman & Hall, 1977.

NORTH AMERICAN BEAVER

Dietland Muller-Schwarze and Lixing Sun: *The Beaver: Natural History of a Wetlands Engineer*. Ithaca, NY: Cornell University Press, 2003.

P. I. V. Strong: *Beavers: Where Waters Run*. Minocqua, WI: NorthWord Press, 1997.

Hope Ryden: *Lily Pond: Four Years with a Family of Beavers*. New York: William Morrow, 1989.

OCTOPUSES

Mark Norman and Helmut Debelius: *Cephalopods: A World Guide*. Hackenheim, Germany: ConchBooks, 2000.

R. T. Harlan and J. B. Messenger: *Cephalopod Behaviour*. Cambridge: Cambridge University Press, 1996.

Jacques-Yves Cousteau and Philippe Diole: *Octopus and Squid: The Soft Intelligence*. New York: Doubleday, 1973.

OKAPI

Susan Lyndaker Lindsey, Mary Neel Green, and Cynthia L. Bennett: *The Okapi: Mysterious Animal of Congo-Zaire*. Foreword by Jane Goodall. Austin: University of Texas Press, 1999.

Richard Despard Estes: *The Behavior Guide to African Mammals Including Hoofed Mammals, Carnivores, Primates*. Berkeley: University of California Press, 1991.

ORANGUTAN

Carel van Schaik: *Among Orangutans: Red Apes and the Rise of Human Culture*. Cambridge, MA: Harvard University Press, 2004.

Anne E. Russon: *Orangutans: Wizards of the Rain Forest*. Toronto: Key Porter Books, 1999.

Biruté M. F. Galdikas: *Reflections of Eden: My Years with the Orangutans of Borneo*. Boston: Little, Brown, 1995.

ORCA (KILLER WHALE)

Ingrid N. Visser: *Swimming with Orca: My Life with New Zealand's Killer Whales*. Auckland: Penguin, 2005.

Peter Knudtson: *Orca: Visions of the Killer Whale*. Foreword by David Suzuki. San Francisco: Sierra Club, 1996.

Erich Hoyt: *The Whale Called Killer*. Camden East, ON: Camden House, 1990.

OTTERS

Douglas Botting: *The Saga of Ring of Bright Water: The Enigma of Gavin Maxwell.* London: HarperCollins, 1993.

Roy Nickerson: *Sea Otters: A Natural History and Guide.* San Francisco: Chronicle Books, 1989.

Victor B. Scheffer: *The Amazing Sea Otter.* New York: Charles Scribner's Sons, 1981.

PARROTS

Bruce Thomas Boehrer: *Parrot Culture: Our 2,500-Year-Long Fascination with the World's Most Talkative Bird.* Philadelphia: University of Pennsylvania Press, 2004.

Mark Bittner: *The Wild Parrots of Telegraph Hill.* New York: Harmony Books, 2004.

John Sparks and Tony Soper: *Parrots: A Natural History.* London: David & Charles Publishers, 1990.

PAUA

Edward F. Ricketts, Joel W. Hedgpeth, and Jack Calvin: *Between Pacific Tides.* Stanford, CA: Stanford University Press, 1987.

Robert H. Morris, et al., eds.: *Intertidal Invertebrates of California.* Stanford, CA: Stanford University Press, 1980.

PEARL OYSTERS

Neil H. Landman, Paula M. Mikkelsen, Rudiger Bieler, and Bennet Bronson: *Pearls: A Natural History.* New York: Harry N. Abrams, 2001.

George Frederick Kunz and Charles Hugh Stevenson: *The Book of the Pearl: Its History, Art, Science and Industry.* Mineola, NY: Dover, 2001 (first published in 1908).

R. A. Donkin: *Beyond Price: Pearls and Pearl-Fishing: Origins to the Age of Discoveries.* Philadelphia: American Philosophical Society, 1999.

PIGS

Lyall Watson: *The Whole Hog: Exploring the Extraordinary Potential of Pigs.* Washington: Smithsonian Books, 2004.

Karl Schwenke: *In a Pig's Eye.* Chelsea, VT: Chelsea Green Publishing Co., 1985.

William Hedgpeth: *The Hog Book.* New York: Doubleday, 1978.

PINNIPEDS

William F. Perrin, Bernd Wursig, J. G. M. Thewissen, eds.: *Encyclopedia of Marine Mammals*. San Diego: Academic Press, 2002.

W. Nigel Bonner: *The Natural History of Seals*. New York: Facts on File, 1990.

Marianne Riedman: *The Pinnipeds: Seals, Sea Lions, and Walruses*. Berkeley: University of California Press, 1990.

POLAR BEAR

Ian Stirling (with photographs by Dan Guravich): *Polar Bears*. Ann Arbor: University of Michigan Press, 1998.

Richard C. Davids (photography by Dan Guravich): *Lords of the Arctic: A Journey Among the Polar Bears*. Foreword by Ian Stirling. New York: Macmillan, 1982.

PORTIA *FIMBRIATA* SPIDER

Stimson Wilcox and Robert Jackson: "Jumping Spider Tricksters: Deceit, Predation, and Cognition." In *The Cognitive Animal*. Edited by Marc Bekoff, Colin Allen, and Gordon M. Burghardt. Cambridge: MIT Press, 2002.

R. Stimson Wilcox and Robert R. Jackson: "Cognitive Abilities in Araneophagic Jumping Spiders." In *Animal Cognition in Nature: The Convergence of Psychology and Biology in Laboratory and Field*. Edited by Russell P. Balda, Irene M. Pepperber, and A. C. Kamil. New York: Academic Press, 1998.

PRONGHORN

John Byers: *Built for Speed: A Year in the Life of Pronghorn*. Cambridge: Harvard University Press, 2003.

———: *American Pronghorn: Social Adaptations and the Ghosts of Predators Past*. Chicago: University of Chicago Press, 1997.

PUMA (COUGAR, MOUNTAIN LION)

Kenneth A. Logan and Linda L. Sweanor: *Desert Puma: Evolutionary Ecology of an Enduring Carnivore*. Foreword by Maurice G. Hornocker. Washington: Island Press, 2001.

Chris Bolgiano: *Mountain Lion: An Unnatural History of Pumas and People*. Mechanicsburg, PA: Stockpole Books, 2001.

Harley Shaw: *Soul Among Lions: The Cougar as Peaceful Adversary*. Tucson: University of Arizona Press, 2000.

PYTHONS

Michael Hutchins, et al., eds.: *Grzimek's Animal Life Encyclopedia.* 2nd ed. Vol. 7: *Reptiles.* Farmington Hills, MI: Gale Group, 2003.

Harry W. Greene: *Snakes: The Evolution of Mystery in Nature.* Berkeley: University of California Press, 1997.

Richard Shine: *Australian Snakes: A Natural History.* Ithaca, NY: Cornell University Press, 1995.

RABBITS AND HARES

Susan E. Davis and Margo Demello: *Stories Rabbits Tell: A Natural and Cultural History of a Misunderstood Creature.* New York: Lantern Books, 2003.

Juliet Clutton-Brock: *A Natural History of Domesticated Mammals.* 2nd ed. Cambridge: Cambridge University Press, 1999.

Henry Thompson: *The European Rabbit: The History and Biology of a Successful Colonizer.* New York: Oxford University Press, 1994.

RATITE BIRDS

S. J. J. F. Davies: *Ratites and Tinamous.* Oxford: Oxford University Press, 2002.

Josep del Hoyo, et al.: *Handbook of the Birds of the World.* Vol. I: *Ostrich to Ducks.* Barcelona: Lynx Edicions, 1992.

RATS

Robert Sullivan: *Rats: Observations on the History and Habitat of the City's Most Unwanted Inhabitants.* New York: Bloomsbury, 2004.

S. Anthony Barnett: *The Story of Rats: Their Impact on Us, and Our Impact on Them.* Sydney: Allen & Unwin, 2001. (Revised and updated version of the 1963 classic.)

Robert Hendrickson: *More Cunning Than Man: A Complete History of the Rat and Its Role in Human Civilization.* New York: Kensington Books, 1983.

RAVEN

Bernd Heinrich: *Mind of the Raven: Investigations and Adventures with Wolf-Birds.* New York: HarperCollins, 1999.

Catherine Feher-Elston: *Ravensong: A Natural and Fabulous History of Ravens and Crows.* Flagstaff, AZ: Northland, 1991.

Lawrence Kilham: *The American Crow and the Common Raven*. College Station: Texas A&M University Press, 1989.

RED FOX

David Macdonald: *Foxes*. Stillwater, MN: Voyageur Press, 2000.

Rebecca L. Grambo: *The Nature of Foxes: Hunters of the Shadows*. Vancouver: Greystone Books (Douglas & McIntyre), 1995.

J. David Henry: *Red Fox: The Catlike Canine*. Washington: Smithsonian Institution Press, 1986.

RHINOCEROSES

Richard Despard Estes: *The Behavior Guide to African Mammals: Including Hoofed Mammals, Carnivores, Primates*. Berkeley: University of California Press, 1991.

Anna Merz: *Rhino at the Brink of Extinction*. Foreword by Desmond Morris. London: HarperCollins, 1991.

Jonathan Kingdon: *East African Mammals: An Atlas of Evolution in Africa*. Vol. 3B: *Large Mammals*. Chicago: University of Chicago Press, 1979.

SEA HORSES

Sara A. Lourie, Amanda C. J. Vincent, and Heather J. Hall: *Seahorses: An Identification Guide to the World's Species and Their Conservation*. London: Project Seahorse, 1999.

SHEEP

Gale Monson and Lowell Sumner, eds.: *The Desert Bighorn: Its Life History, Ecology and Management*. Tucson: University of Arizona Press, 1980.

George B. Schaller: *Mountain Monarchs: Wild Sheep and Goats of the Himalaya*. Chicago: University of Chicago Press, 1975.

Valerius B. Geist: *Mountain Sheep: A Study in Behavior and Evolution*. Chicago: University of Chicago Press, 1971.

STICK INSECTS

P. D. Brock: *The Amazing World of Stick and Leaf Insects*. Edited by R. Fry. Essex: Cravitz Printing, 1999.

David Rentz: *Grasshopper Country: The Abundant Orthopteroid Insects of Australia*. Sydney: University of New South Wales Press, 1996.

Rod Preston-Mafhan and Ken Preston-Mafhan: *The Encyclopedia of Land Inver-tebrate Behaviour.* London: Blandford Press, 1993.

STURGEONS

Richard Adams Carey: *The Philosopher Fish: Sturgeon, Caviar, and The Geog-raphy of Desire.* New York: Counterpoint Press, 2005.

Greg T. O. LeBreton, F. William H. Beamish, and R. Scott McKinley. *Stur-geons and Paddlefish of North America.* New York: Springer, 2004.

Inga Saffron: *Caviar: The Strange History and Uncertain Future of the World's Most Coveted Delicacy.* New York: Broadway Books, 2002.

TAPIRS

Daniel M. Brooks, Richard E. Bodmer, and Sharon Matola, compilers: *Tapirs—Status Survey and Conservation Action Plan.* IUCN/SSC Tapir Specialist Group. (The World Conservation Union, Species Survival Commission.) Gland, Switzerland, and Cambridge, UK: IUCN, 1997.

TASMANIAN DEVIL

David Owen and David Pemberton: *Tasmanian Devil: A Unique and Threat-ened Animal.* Sydney: Allen & Unwin, 2005.

Hugh Tyndale-Biscoe: *Life of Marsupials.* Sydney: CSIRO, 2005 (fully revised edition of the classic 1973 book).

TUATARA

K. Wilson: *Flight of the Huia: Ecology and Conservation of New Zealand's Frogs, Reptiles, Birds and Mammals.* Christchurch, New Zealand: Canter-bury University Press, 2004.

A. Crowe and P. Campbell: *When the Tuatara Came: New Zealand in the Days of the Dinosaurs.* Auckland, New Zealand: Heinemann Education, 1997.

J. Jones and C. H. Daugherty: *Tuatara.* Wellington: World Wildlife Fund New Zealand, 1995.

TURKEY

Karen Davis: *More Than a Meal: The Turkey in History, Myth, Ritual, and Re-ality.* New York: Lantern Books, 2001.

Joe Hutto: *Illumination in the Flatwoods: A Season with the Wild Turkey.* New York: Lyons & Burford, 1995.

A. W. Schorger: *The Wild Turkey: Its History and Domestication*. Norman: University of Oklahoma Press, 1966.

TURTLES

James R. Spotila: *Sea Turtles: A Complete Guide to Their Biology, Behavior, and Conservation*. Baltimore: Johns Hopkins University Press, 2004.

David Gulko and Karen Eckert: *Sea Turtles: An Ecological Guide*. Honolulu: Mutual Publishing, 2004.

P. L. Lutz, J. A. Musick, and J. Wyneken, eds.: *The Biology of Sea Turtles*. Vol. II. Boca Raton, FL: CRC Press, 2003.

WALLACE'S FLYING TREE FROG

Jeet Sukumaran: "Encounter with Wallace's Flying Frog." http://frogweb.org/Articles.aspx?ArticleID=10.

WANDERING ALBATROSS

Carl Safina: *Eye of the Albatross: Visions of Hope and Survival*. New York: Henry Holt, 2002.

W. L. N. Tickell: *Albatrosses*. New Haven, CT: Yale University Press, 2000.

Robert Cushman Murphy: *Oceanic Birds of South America*. 2 vols. New York: American Museum of Natural History, 1936.

WHOOPING CRANE

Michael Forsberg: *On Ancient Wings: The Sandhill Cranes of North America*. Introduction by George Archibald and James Harris. Lincoln, NE: Michael Forsberg Photography, 2004.

Peter Matthiessen: *The Birds of Heaven: Travels with Cranes*. New York: North Point Press, 2001.

Paul A. Johnsgard: *Crane Music: A Natural History of American Cranes*. Washington: Smithsonian Institution Press, 1991.

WILD PIGEON

Alexander F. Skutch: *The Minds of Birds*. College Station: Texas A&M University Press, 1996.

Richard F. Johnston and Marian Janiga: *Feral Pigeons*. New York: Oxford University Press, 1995.

A. W. Schorger: *The Passenger Pigeon: Its Natural History and Extinction.* Norman: University of Oklahoma Press, 1973 (first published in 1955).

WOLVES •

L. David Mech and Luigi Boitani: *Wolves: Behavior, Ecology, and Conservation.* Chicago: Chicago University Press, 2003.

L. David Mech: *The Wolf: The Ecology and Behavior of an Endangered Species.* New York: Natural History Press, 1970.

WOMBATS

James Woodford: *The Secret Life of Wombats.* Sydney: Text Publishing, 2002.

Barbara Triggs: *The Wombat.* Sydney: University of New South Wales Press, 1996.

Ronald Strahan, ed.: *The Australian Museum Complete Book of Australian Mammals.* Sydney: HarperCollins, 1991.

YETI

Chris Hale: *Himmler's Crusade.* New York: Bantam Books, 2004.

Reinhold Messner: *My Quest for the Yeti: Confronting the Himalayas' Deepest Mystery.* New York: St. Martins, 2001.

ZEBRAS

David Macdonald, ed.: *The New Encyclopedia of Mammals.* Oxford: Oxford University Press, 2004.

Jonathan Kingdon: *East African Mammals: An Atlas of Evolution in Africa.* Vol. 3B: *Large Mammals.* Chicago: University of Chicago Press, 1984.

PHOTO CREDITS

ARMADILLO: *John and Karen Hollingsworth/U.S. Fish and Wildlife Service* AUS-
TRALIAN MAGPIE: *Photo provided by Professor Gisela Kaplan, University of New
England, Armidale, NSW Australia* BADGER: *Photo by Pavel German/Wildlife Im-
ages* BALD EAGLE: *Dave Menke/U.S. Fish and Wildlife Service* BAT: *Photo by Pavel
German/Wildlife Images* BEETLE: *Photo by Pavel German/Wildlife Images* BENGAL
TIGER: *Photo by Pavel German/Wildlife Images* BILBY: *Photo by Pavel German/
Wildlife Images* BISON: *Photo by Pavel German/Wildlife Images* BLACK-TAILED
PRAIRIE DOG: *Photo courtesy of Professor Con Slobodchikoff* BONOBOS: *Photo © 2006
Frans Lanting/www.lanting.com* BOTTLENOSE DOLPHINS: *Photo © 2006 Frans
Lanting/www.lanting.com* BOWERBIRD: *Photo by Pavel German/Wildlife Images*
BUTTERFLY: *Photo by Pavel German/Wildlife Images* CAMELS: *Photo © 2006 Frans
Lanting/www.lanting.com* CHEETAHS: *Photo © 2006 Frans Lanting/www.lanting
.com* CHICKEN: *Photo © 2006 Frans Lanting/www.lanting.com* COCHINEALS: *Photo
courtesy of Professor Whitney Cranshaw* COCONUT CRAB: *Photo by Pavel German/
Wildlife Images* COWS: *Photo © Steve Parish Publishing. Reproduced with permis-
sion.* COYOTE: *Photo by Pavel German/Wildlife Images* DOG: *Photo by Elizabeth
Tasker/Wildlife Images* DOMESTIC CAT: *Photo by Pavel German/Wildlife Images*
DUCK: *Photo by Pavel German/Wildlife Images* ECHIDNA: *Photo by Pavel German/
Wildlife Images* ELEPHANTS: *Photo © 2006 Frans Lanting/www.lanting.com* EM-
PEROR PENGUINS: *Photo © 2006 Frans Lanting/www.lanting.com* FLAMINGOS: *Photo
© 2006 Frans Lanting/www.lanting.com* FROG: *Photo by Pavel German/Wildlife
Images* GANNETS: *Photo © 2006 Frans Lanting/www.lanting.com* GECKO: *Photo by
Pavel German/Wildlife Images* GIANT PANDA: *Photo by Pavel German/Wildlife Im-
ages* SQUID: *Photo by Wade Doak* GIBBONS: *Photo by Pavel German/Wildlife Images*
GIRAFFES: *Photo by Pavel German/Wildlife Images* GLOWWORM: *Photo courtesy of
Waitomo Museum of Caves, New Zealand* GOATS: *Photo by Keith Harmon Snow*
GORILLAS: *Photo © 2006 Frans Lanting/www.lanting.com* GREAT HORNED OWL:
Photo by Pavel German/Wildlife Images GREAT WHITE SHARK: *Photo by Ken Hop-*

pen Photography / khphoto@iprimus.com.au GRIZZLY BEARS: *Photo © 2006 Frans Lanting/www.lanting.com* HIPPOPOTAMUSES: *Photo courtesy of Professor Bill Barklow* HONEYBEE: *Photo by Pavel German/Wildlife Images* HUMMINGBIRD: *Photo © 2006 Frans Lanting/www.lanting.com* HUMPBACK WHALES: *Photo by Ken Hoppen Photography / khphoto@iprimus.com.au* JELLYFISH: *Photo © 2006 Frans Lanting/www .lanting.com* KAKAPO: *Photo © 2006 Frans Lanting/www.lanting.com* KANGAROOS: *Photo by Pavel German/Wildlife Images* KIWI: *Photo © 2006 Frans Lanting/www .lanting.com* KOALAS: *Photo by Pavel German/Wildlife Images* KOOKABURRAS: *Photo by Pavel German/Wildlife Images* LEMURS: *Photo © 2006 Frans Lanting/www .lanting.com* LION: *Photo by Pavel German/Wildlife Images* LOBSTER: *Photo by Win Watson (University of New Hampshire) courtesy of Steve Jury (MariCal, Inc Portland, ME)* MANATEES: *Jim P. Reid/U.S. Fish and Wildlife Service* MANTIS: *Photo by Pavel German/Wildlife Images* MEERKAT: *Photo by Pavel German/Wildlife Images* MULBERRY SILKWORM: *Peter Parks/imagequestmarine.com* NAKED MOLE RATS: *Photo © 2006 Frans Lanting/www.lanting.com* NARWHAL: *K. Bruce Lane photography, www.lanephotography.com* NEW ZEALAND LONGFIN EEL: *Photo © Steve Parish Publishing. Reproduced with permission.* NORTH AMERICAN BEAVER: *Randy Lennon/ U.S. Fish and Wildlife Service* OCTOPUS: *Photo by Wade Doak* OKAPI: *Photo © 2006 Frans Lanting/www.lanting.com* ORANGUTAN: *Photo by Pavel German/Wildlife Images* ORCA: *Photo © 2006 Frans Lanting/www.lanting.com* OTTERS: *Photo © 2006 Frans Lanting/www.lanting.com* PARROTS: *Photo by Pavel German/Wildlife Images* PAUA: *Photo from the American Museum of Natural History, courtesy of Paula Mikkelsen, Curator of Malacology* PEARL OYSTER: *Photo from the American Museum of Natural History, courtesy of Paula Mikkelsen, Curator of Malacology* PIGS: *Photo by Mark Maguire* PINNIPED: *Photo © 2006 Frans Lanting/www.lanting.com* POLAR BEARS: *Photo © 2006 Frans Lanting/www.lanting.com* PORTIA FIMBRIATA Spider: *Photo courtesy of Professor Robert Jackson* PRONGHORN: *Photo by Pavel German/Wildlife Images* PUMA: *Photo by Pavel German/Wildlife Images* PYTHON: *Photo by Liz Tasker/Wildlife Images* RABBITS: *Photo © 2006 Frans Lanting/ www.lanting.com* RAT: *Photo courtesy of Rachel Rosenthal* RATITE BIRD: *Photo by Pavel German/Wildlife Images* RAVEN: *Photo © 2006 Frans Lanting/www.lanting. com* RED FOX: *Photo by Pavel German/Wildlife Images* RHINOCEROS: *Photo © 2006 Frans Lanting/www.lanting.com* SEA HORSE: *Photo by Ken Hoppen Photography / khphoto@iprimus.com.au* SHEEP: *Photo © 2006 Frans Lanting/www.lanting.com* STICK INSECTS: *Photo by Pavel German/Wildlife Images* STURGEONS: *Masa Ushioda/ imagequestmarine.com* TAPIR: *Photo by Gilia Angell, Tapir Specialist Group*

JEFFREY MOUSSAIEFF MASSON, former psychoanalyst and projects director of the Sigmund Freud Archives, is the bestselling author of two dozen books, including *Raising the Peaceable Kingdom*, *Slipping into Paradise*, *The Pig Who Sang to the Moon*, *The Nine Emotional Lives of Cats*, *Dogs Never Lie About Love*, and *When Elephants Weep*. A longtime resident of Berkeley, California, he now lives in New Zealand with his wife, his two sons, and several animal friends.

This book was set in a digitized version of Kennerley, a typeface originally designed in 1911 by the prolific American type designer Frederic Goudy. While Kennerley's overall structure more closely resembles Italian Renaissance archetypes, Goudy consciously gave his design a visual warmth more characteristic of the eighteenth-century British typeface Caslon.

Kennerley was Goudy's first commercially successful typeface, and was named for his associate and friend Mitchell Kennerley, a New York art dealer and book publisher.